ART NOUVEAU

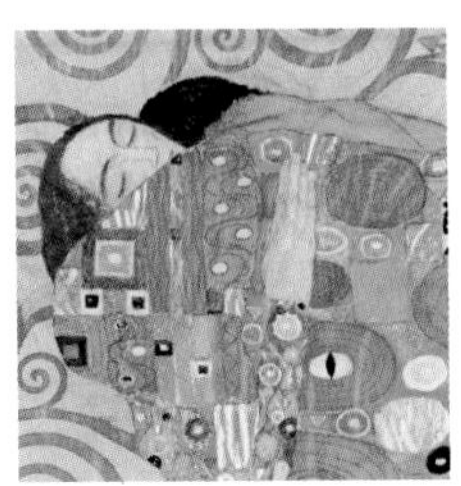

Publisher and Creative Director: Nick Wells
Development: Sara Robson
Picture Research: Sara Robson and Melinda Révész
Project Editor: Polly Willis
Editor: Sarah Goulding
Designer: Lucy Robins
Production: Chris Herbert and Claire Walker

Special thanks to: Geoffrey Meadon and Helen Tovey

FLAME TREE PUBLISHING
Crabtree Hall, Crabtree Lane
Fulham, London, SW6 6TY
United Kingdom

www.flametreepublishing.com

First published 2005

07 09 08 06

5 7 9 10 8 6 4

Flame Tree is part of the Foundry Creative Media Company Limited

A CIP record for this book is available from the British Library.

ISBN 1 84451 265 7

Printed in China

ART NOUVEAU

Author: Camilla de la Bedoyere Foreword: Alice Jurow

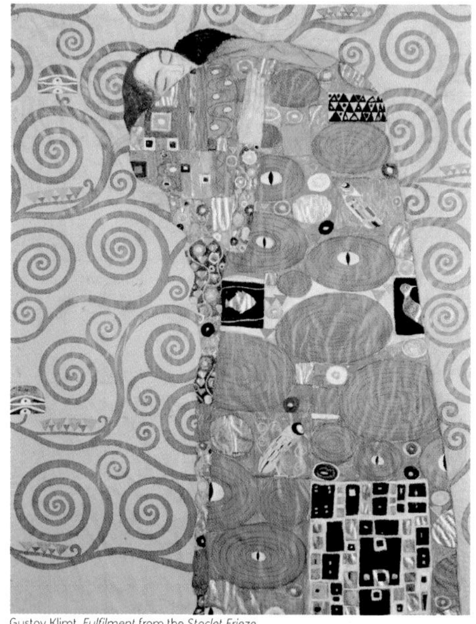

Gustav Klimt, *Fulfilment* from the *Stoclet Frieze*

FLAME TREE PUBLISHING

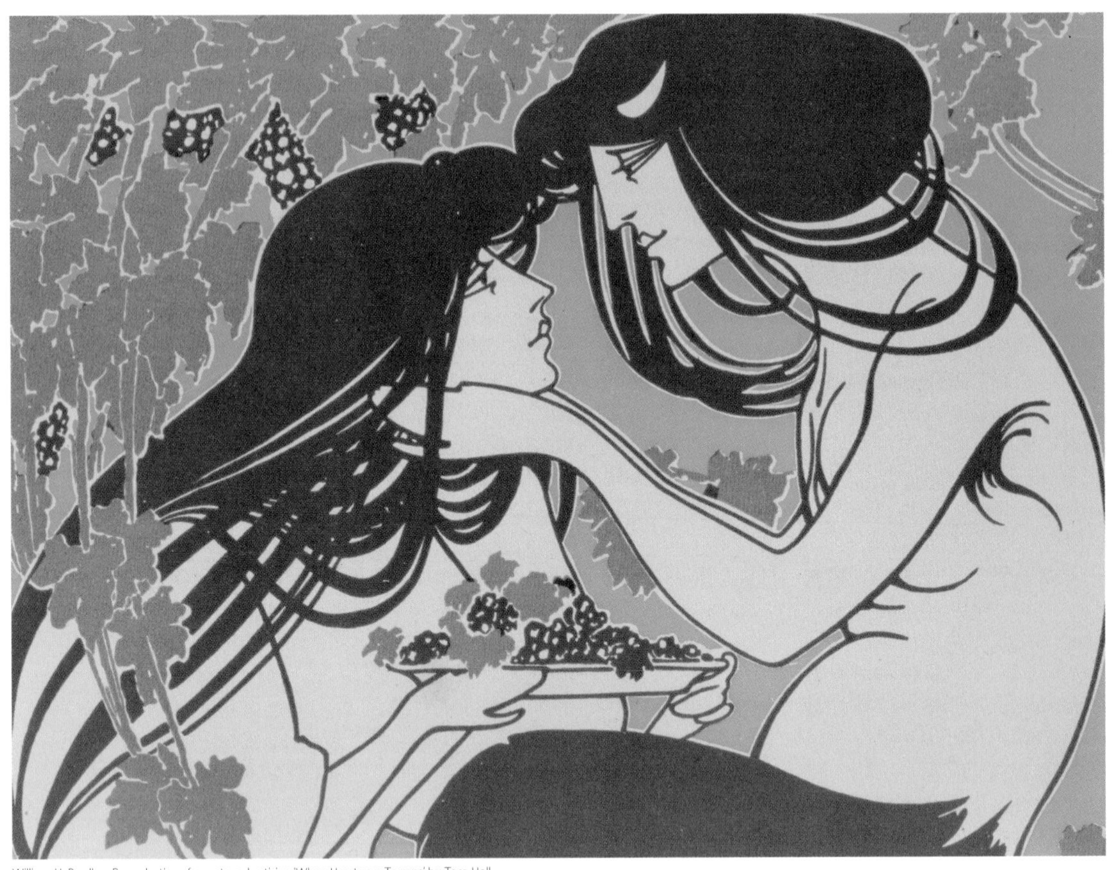

William H. Bradley, Reproduction of a poster advertising 'When Hearts are Trumps' by Tom Hall

Contents

Tiffany Studios, Peacock leaded-glass window; Johann Loetz Witwe Glasshouse, Selection of Loetz vases; Alphonse Mucha, Zodiac, Grand Bazar and Nouvelles Galeries, Tours

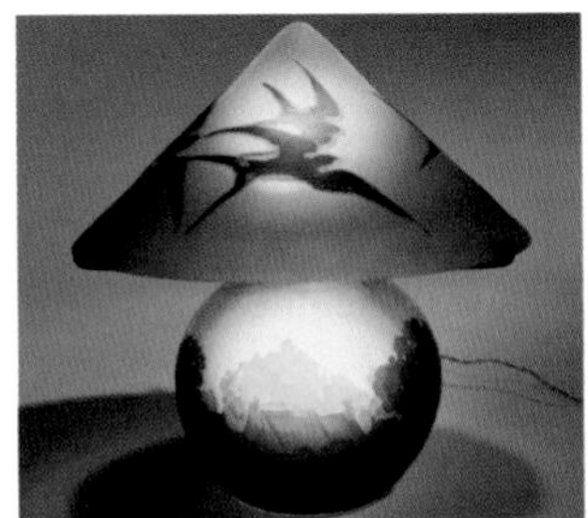

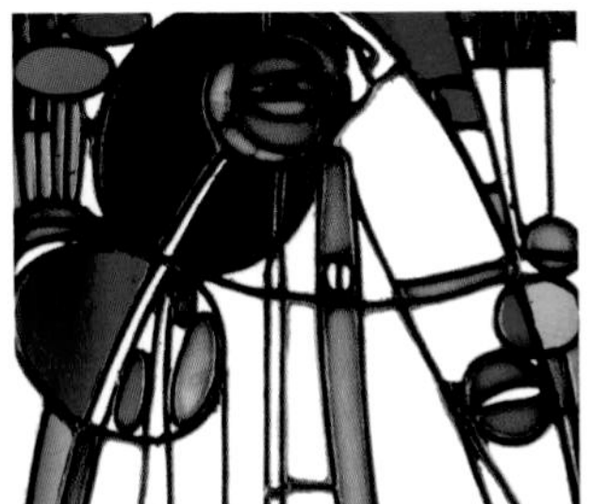

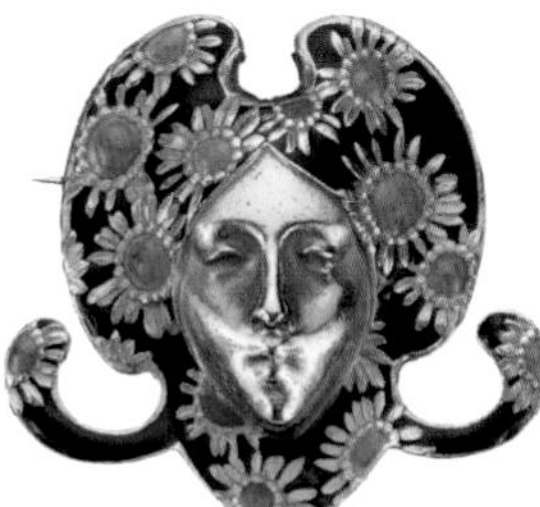

Emile Gallé, Lamp; Charles Rennie Mackintosh, Glass Panel; René Lalique, Pendant Brooch

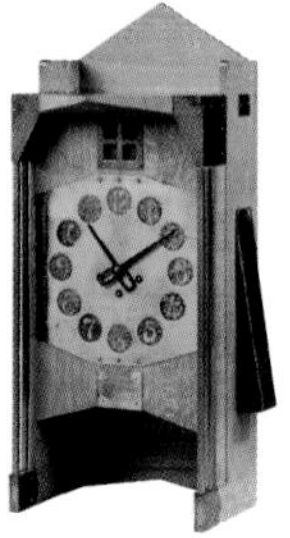

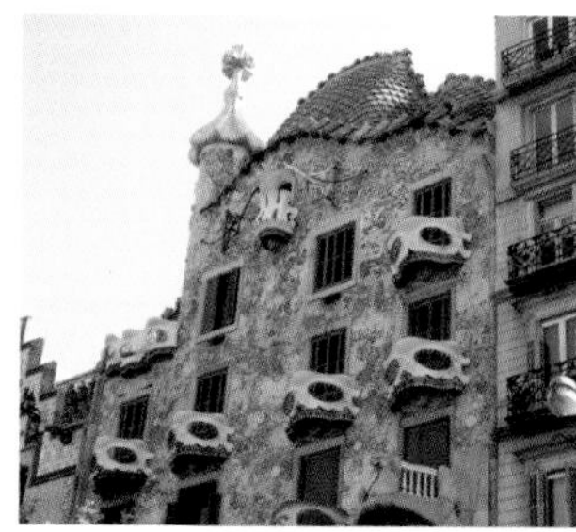

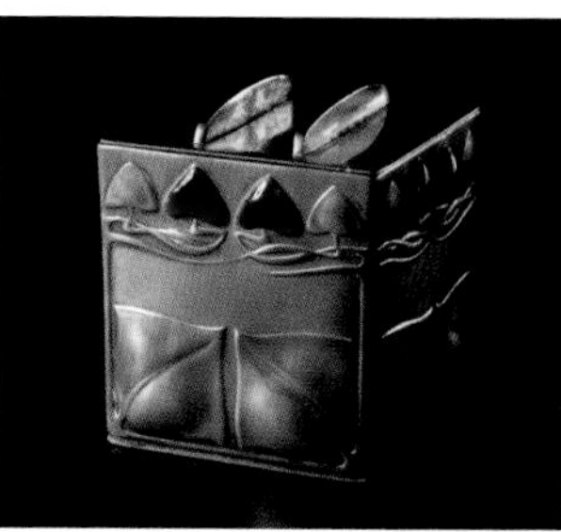

Gustave Serrurier-Bovy, Mantel wall clock; Antonio Gaudí, Exterior of the Casa Batlló; Archibald Knox, Biscuit box

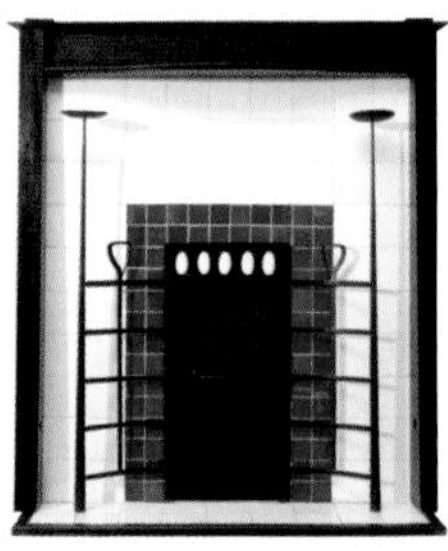

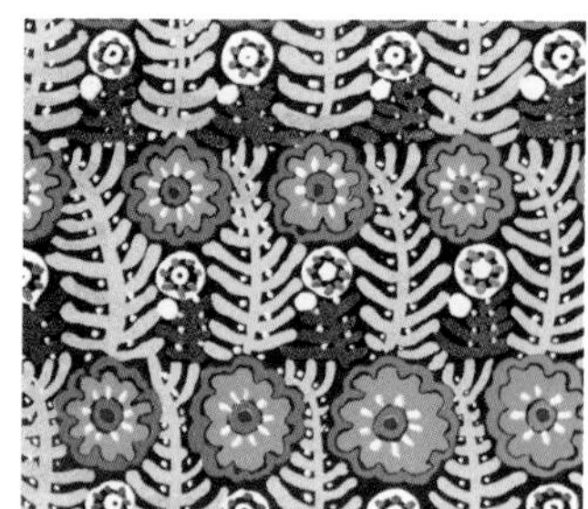

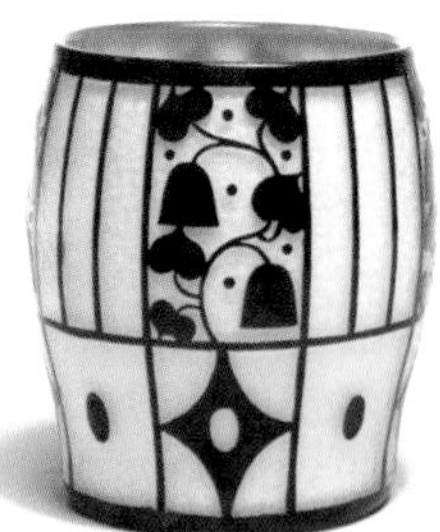

Charles Rennie Mackintosh, Fireplace for the Willow Tea Rooms; Josef Hoffmann, Christmas tree design; Josef Hoffmann, Vase

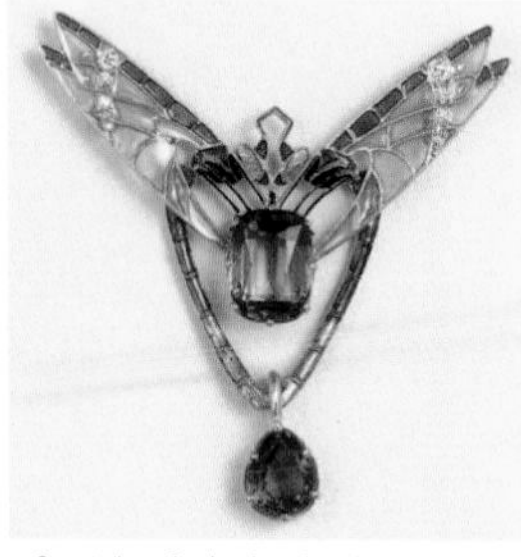

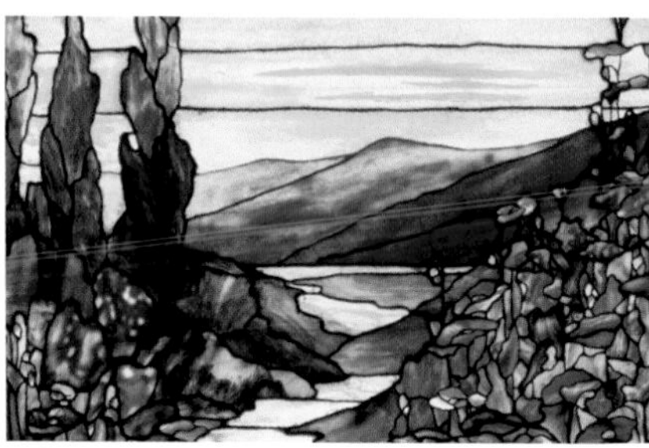

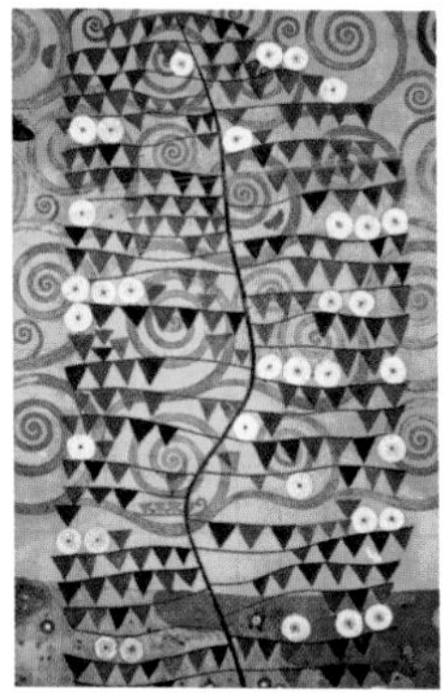

René Lalique, Pendant brooch designed as two dragonflies; Tiffany Studios, *Sunset with Mountains* leaded-glass window; Gustav Klimt, *Tree of Life* from the *Stoclet Frieze*

How To Use This Book

The reader is encouraged to use this book in a variety of ways, each of which caters for a range of interests, knowledge and uses.

- The book is organized into five sections: **Movement Overview**; **Society**; **Places**; **Influences** and **Styles & Techniques**. The text in all these sections provides the reader with a brief background to the work, and gives greater insight into how and why it was created.
- **Movement Overview** introduces the main themes that will be looked at in the rest of the book through the art and artefacts produced by the most celebrated artists of the period.
- **Society** shows how the art and artefacts reflected events and ideas of the time, and how these represent the artists' ambition to find a new design aesthetic for a new, modern age.
- **Places** looks at the various places that were significant to the movement. Art Nouveau flourished in Continental Europe, Great Britain and the United States.
- **Influences** shows the diverse range of influences that contributed to the style of Art Nouveau: Arts and Crafts, Oriental and Celtic art, Symbolism and the natural world.
- **Styles & Techniques** showcases artefacts produced using the wide range of techniques employed by Art Nouveau artists. Traditional methods and materials were given a fresh twist, and new techniques in areas such as glass-blowing were especially prominent.

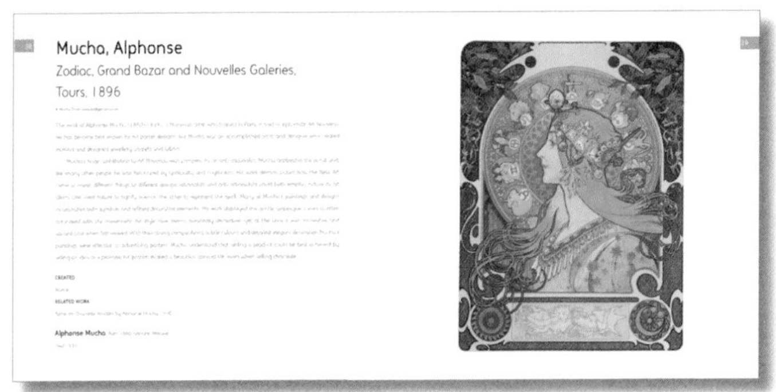

Mucha, Alphonse

Zodiac, Grand Bazar and Nouvelles Galeries, Tours, 1896

Alphonse Mucha

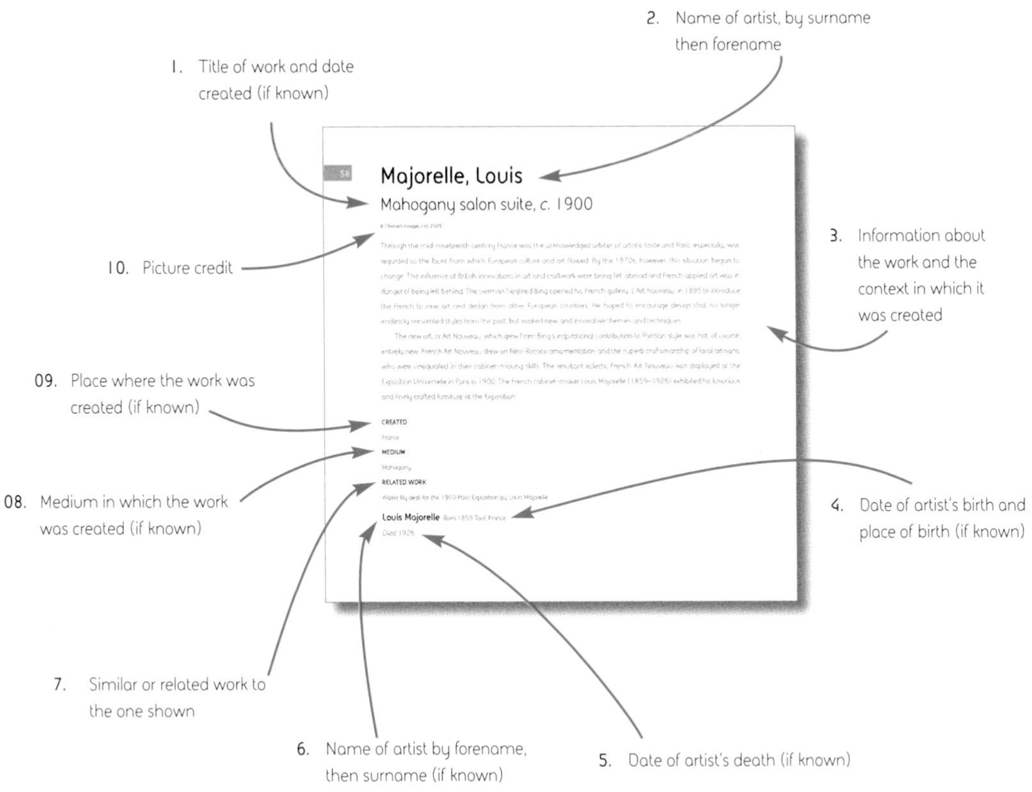
1. Title of work and date created (if known)
2. Name of artist, by surname then forename
3. Information about the work and the context in which it was created
4. Date of artist's birth and place of birth (if known)
5. Date of artist's death (if known)
6. Name of artist by forename, then surname (if known)
7. Similar or related work to the one shown
08. Medium in which the work was created (if known)
09. Place where the work was created (if known)
10. Picture credit
Majorelle, Louis
Mahogany salon suite, c. 1900
CREATED
MEDIUM
RELATED WORK
Louis Majorelle

Foreword

She was notorious in her day: reviled as decadent and grotesque, embraced as seductive and exquisite, Art Nouveau had a fashionable career mirroring the great courtesans of the Belle Epoque. Like theirs, her heyday spanned about 30 years, from fresh nubile youth in the late 1880s to elegant middle age around 1915. By the end of that time, her style was distinctly old-fashioned, overheated and outlandish by comparison with the smart, cool flapper girl of Art Deco. Yet we've never forgotten her; her insinuating tendrils continue to entangle our dreams. Looking back, we can see that all her excesses and eccentricities, however whimsical and of-the-moment they seemed, grew from the pure root of devotion to enduring beauty.

Mass production of consumer goods for an expanding middle class began in the early nineteenth century and engendered the type of historically encrusted decorative objects which progressive designers of the Arts and Crafts and Art Nouveau movements considered to be atrocities. But Art Nouveau, arising in the era of the telegraph, the illustrated newspaper and the high-quality art journal, was really the first design style to reap the benefits of rapid mass communications and publicity. This gave it a trajectory that has been familiar ever since: early adoption by an intellectual, aesthetic-minded avant garde; rapid appropriation by a wealthy, ultra-fashionable elite; a spread into mainstream popularity, devolving eventually to diluted, lower-quality versions for the low end of the market; and a fall from fashion, as the 'next big thing' comes along.

But the products of this style were too unique, too finely made and simply too beautiful to be discarded for long. After a relatively brief out-of-favour period, Art Nouveau was ripe for both scholarly and popular reassessment. Scholarly works on the style date back to at least the 1940s. In the popular imagination, Art Nouveau struck a particular chord with the counter-culture of the 1960s, when Mucha's flamboyantly nonchalant cigarette-smoking beauties became icons of rebellious and lavish-tressed youth. Psychedelic poster art adopted an idiom of dead-on Art Nouveau hommage, replete with serpentine lines and reviving a host of sinous or bulbous typefaces.

As the colourful, eclectic qualities of the 'hippie' aesthetic began to influence the mainstream, reproduction Tiffany lamps and more or less skillful neo-Nouveau handicrafts became widely popular – and led many back to the source, to a rediscovery of the incomparable originality of the period. We know that nature is the source for much of Art Nouveau's iconography; those tendrils, tentacles, wings, leaves, carapaces and seedpods are inescapable. And figures of women, with their long history of equivalence to nature in western art, are often depicted with meta-human significance and are seen as reflecting nature's moods from tranquil to malevolent. Art Nouveau artists don't show us sweeping landscapes, as a rule; no sublime mountains or misty effects of light. The natural world of Art Nouveau is marked by peculiarity and particularity; glistening scales, petals and feathers; curiosities dredged from the depths of the sea or brought from far exotic forests.

Though Art Nouveau designers sought to create interiors with a sense of harmony and serenity, individual details often throbbed and roiled with restless dynamism, a sense of Darwinian competitiveness in their depiction of fecundity, growth and decay. Even the most innocuously pretty blossoms were freighted with symbolism: poppies, lilies and roses were messages of love and death. In a world newly alert to Freudian secrets, the décor may be vegetal, but animal passions lie just below the surface.

All periods consider themselves modern, but Art Nouveau was perhaps the first aesthetic idiom of our modernity, the world we still live in – a world of ever-accelerating technological change, a largely manmade environment, an international culture. This style which bears a French name – possibly because of a Parisian shop opened by a German connoisseur – is truly international. It has roots in Japanese aesthetics, English philosophy and central-European craftsmanship, while some of its most distinguished works were produced in Italy, Belgium, Spain, Scotland and the US. Art Nouveau was the first style to be promoted through the sort of 'lifestyle marketing' which is now so ubiquitous; its philosophy of taste dictated that harmonious, aesthetically excellent interiors were within the reach of anyone willing to make an effort. Like Arts and Crafts before it and Art Deco afterwards, Art Nouveau rises to the challenge of making visual sense of modernity, and meeting that challenge with spirit, elegance and freshness. It is not surprising that this style still speaks to us so eloquently.

Alice Jurow, *2005*

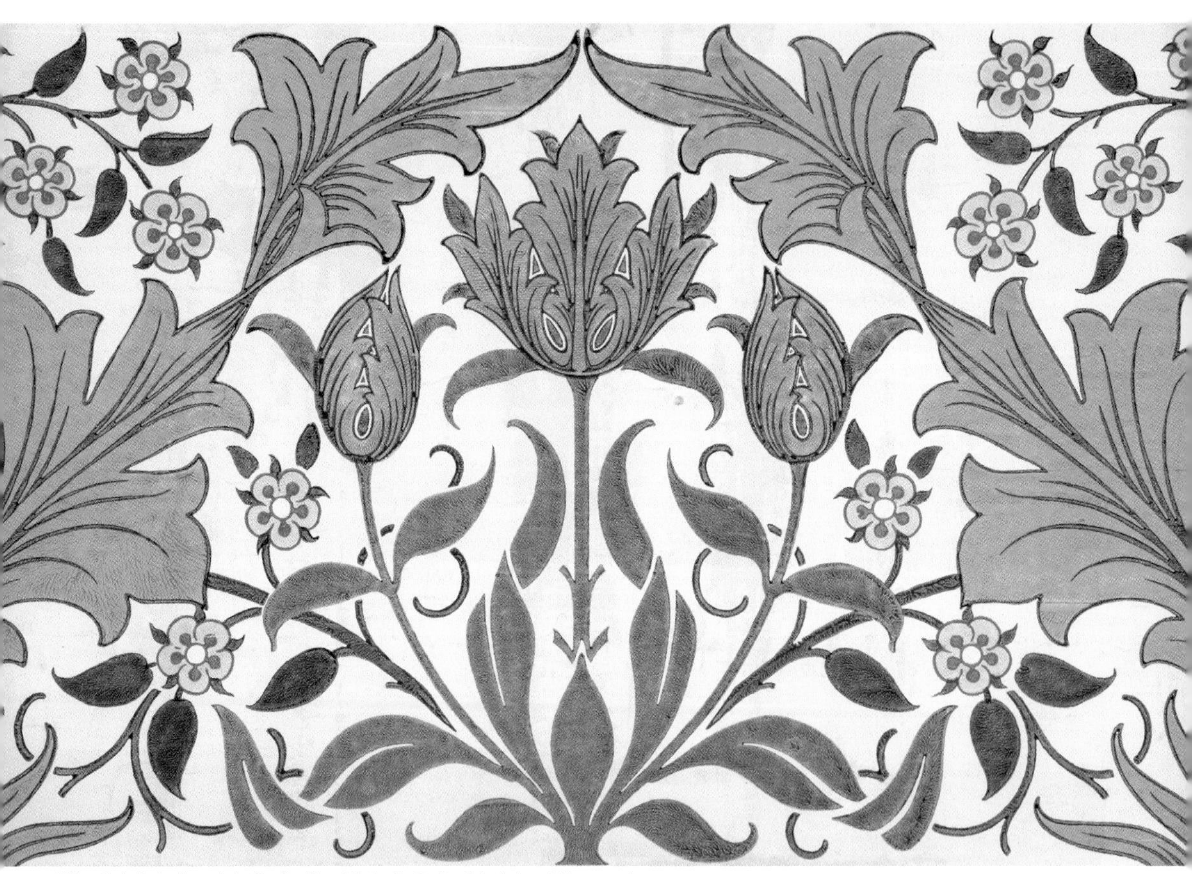

William Morris, Floral wallpaper design (detail), © Private Collection, The Stapleton Collection/www.bridgeman.co.uk

Introduction

Although the first phase of Art Nouveau celebrated skilled labour, not mass production, the movement evolved to become a widespread, international design force that eventually incorporated elements of industrial manufacture. It is therefore appropriate that the Art Nouveau movement, which was inextricably linked to industry and the growth of modern commercialism, was named by a businessman and shares its name with his retail outlet.

Siegfried Bing was born in Hamburg, but moved to Paris in 1854 to help run a branch of the family business. He dealt in Oriental art and eventually opened his own store, named L'Art Nouveau, in 1895. The name had originally been coined in the 1880s to describe the works of a group of artists in Belgium, Les Vingt (or Les XX) who aimed to reform art and its relationship with society. As it turned out, the success of Bing's store was such that the name was soon associated with the design aesthetic displayed in his Parisian emporium.

It would be a mistake, however, to assume that the sumptuous luxury found in Bing's shop in the rue de Provence was entirely characteristic of the decorative style that dominated the end of the nineteenth century. Bing and his designers arranged every room as though it were a living space, complete with furnishings, textiles and ornaments. L'Art Nouveau was unusual for its time: objects from the field of decorative arts, such as Tiffany's exquisite Favrile glassware and the furniture of Georges de Feure, were collected and displayed to complement an array of eclectic paintings, including works by the Nabis, Symbolists and Neo Impressionists. This combination of visual art was carefully planned as part of a movement to elevate the field of decorative arts and the work of the craftsmen to the same status enjoyed by fine art and artists. It became part of the Art Nouveau philosophy that the two fields should integrate, influence one another and through this lead to greater originality and innovation.

The interior of Bing's store was delicately coloured in soft pastel mauves, smoky pinks and silvery greys harmonized to create a unified whole; but the Art Nouveau style itself was far more complicated than this utterly refined aesthetic. Its roots were diverse, its influences considerable and its effects are still felt today in the buildings that shape our lives.

Art Nouveau first emerged in the early 1890s, particularly in Brussels, Paris and London. Brussels benefited from a period of considerable economic wealth and development and this led to a substantial building programme. Architects such as Victor Horta were invited to create new and innovative design projects in the city. As a result, Art

Nouveau reached a maturity in Brussels that was unmatched elsewhere. It was here that glass and iron were combined, visibly, to create light and airy interiors that carried the delicately sinuous lines of the whiplash that exemplify the Belgian interpretation of the style. In Paris the style was more conservatively interpreted, with a strong reliance on the French tradition of superb craftsmanship, particularly in cabinet-making and jewellery. Still, thanks to Paris's position as the hub of the design and art world, the city was in a prime position to disseminate the vogue through publications, exhibitions, galleries and salons.

Although England never developed the Art Nouveau aesthetic with the same aplomb as Continental Europe, it nevertheless contributed enormously to its development. The work of William Morris's workshops and Charles Ashbee's Guild and School of Handicraft revolutionized design in Britain, and their effects, alongside the social and political aspirations of the Arts and Crafts movement, were felt throughout Europe. Designers tried different media; artists turned their hands to textile design, ceramics and stained glass in an attempt to establish the value of craft and its superiority over industrial production. Medieval art provided an inspiration and the work of Pre-Raphaelites who aimed 'to study nature attentively ... and to sympathize with what is direct and heartfelt ... to the exclusion of what is conventional' was an obvious source of the cult of nature that pervaded much of the Art Nouveau aesthetic.

In Scotland Charles Rennie Mackintosh and the Glasgow School followed a different path: while still reliant on craftsmanship the Scottish designers turned their backs on historicism and endeavoured instead to create a new idiom of motif and architecture, only occasionally using local styles to influence them. The result was an astonishingly original and modern look, one which brought light into every corner of a building and united interiors with recurring Symbolist motifs, often in geometric, linear patterns.

It is widely accepted that a style, or vogue, grows in part from the ambient culture and social and political moods of a time. From the 1890s to 1915, the era of Art Nouveau, cultures across Europe had to address the question of Modernity and industrialization. It was in Vienna and Germany that this question was most firmly answered. The Austrian version of Art Nouveau was termed the Secession; in Germany it was called *Jugendstil*. In both places artists, designers and architects united to challenge the status quo and propose new solutions to questions of design.

Eventually these groups led to organizations that introduced industrial processes into their workshops and became highly influential in twentieth-century design and production methods.

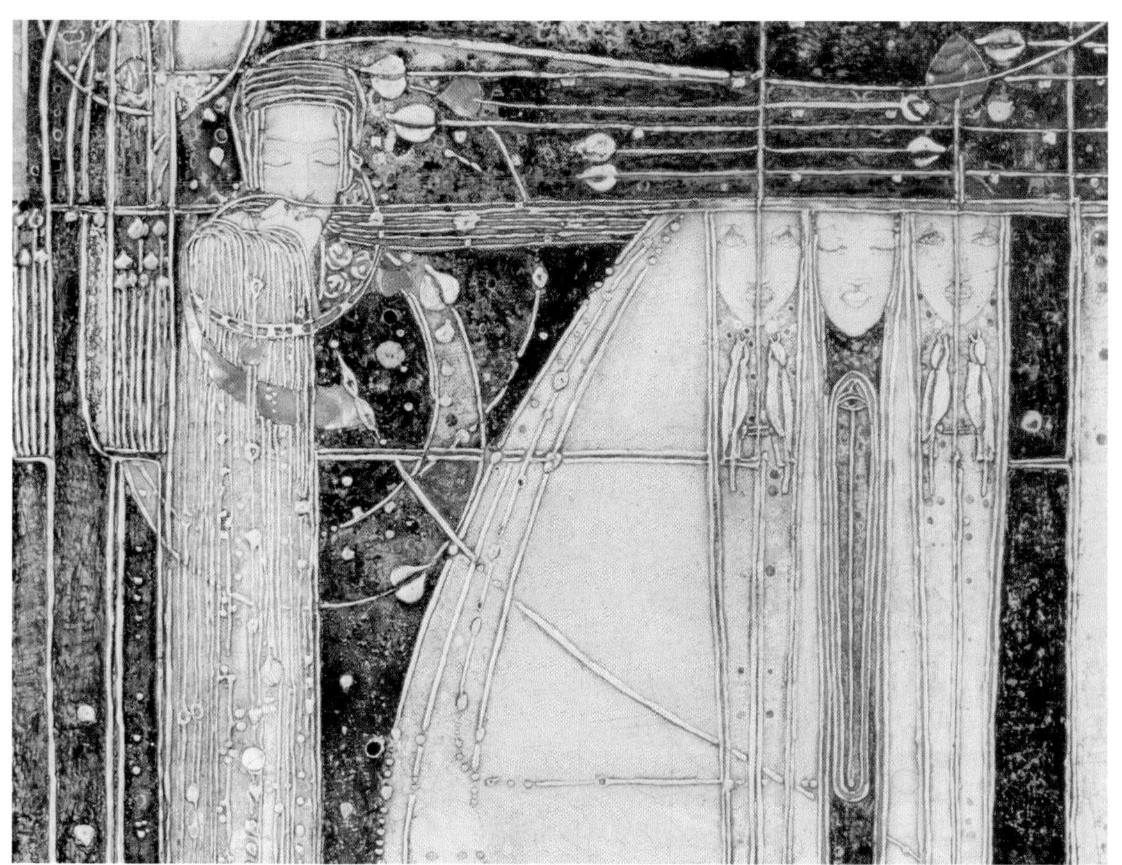

Margaret Macdonald Mackintosh, *Opera of the Seas* (detail), © The Fine Art Society, London, UK/www.bridgeman.co.uk

The New Art, or Art Nouveau, grew as a rejection of stale complacency and a dull revisiting of historicism. As the end of an exciting and eventful century approached it is not surprising that the cultural world wanted new ways to express the anticipation felt about the dawning of a new era. Like a pane of Tiffany's coloured glass held at the boundary between two centuries, Art Nouveau reflects something of the traditions of the nineteenth century, while allowing some of those influences to permeate, changed and improved, in to the twentieth. It expresses an extraordinary tension that was felt at the time, a tension between the old and the new, nostalgia and innovation, tradition and Modernism.

In Spain, Italy, Russia and the US artists and designers added to the novel and fascinating interpretations of the New Art. Every culture drew on different sources of inspiration including Gothic, Celtic, Rococo and Baroque. While historical influences were present they could not be justified unless they were approached with innovation rather than tradition. The portrayal of women in art at the turn of the century highlights another important challenge to contemporary societies. In many instances women were depicted as fantasy figures, interplaying with nature, united with it. By contrast, the gritty realism of paintings by Toulouse-Lautrec demonstrated that women could be portrayed as genuine people, involved in mundane aspects of their daily lives. This was the dawning of a new era for women, both in society and art, and the tension between the desire for the status quo and the burgeoning women's movement must have been almost palpable to avant-garde artists.

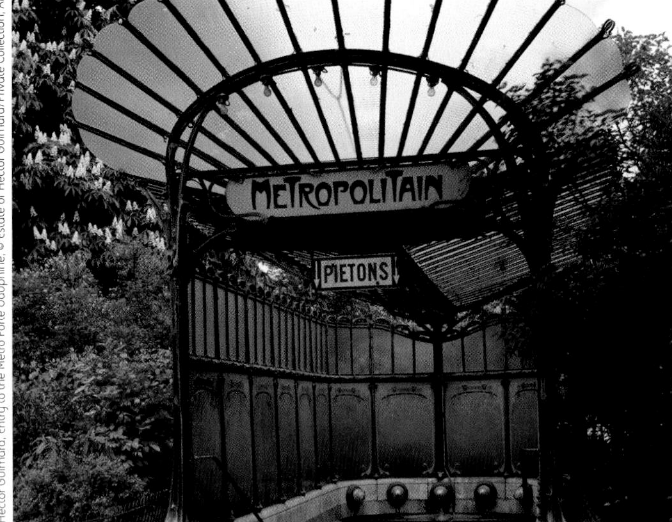

Hector Guimard, Entry to the Metro Porte Dauphine. © Estate of Hector Guimard/Private Collection, Archives Charmet/www.bridgeman.co.uk

The cult of nature, with its sinuous curves and tendrils of ivy that almost appear to take root within an item of furniture or decorative object, was a popular theme for Art Nouveau. It was through this medium that women were most often portrayed as stylized objects rather than people. Through the use of nature as an idiom, designers hoped to incorporate all aspects of life into a single object or interior: the outside was brought inside and the human relationship with the environment was explored. Symbolism, another powerful theme in Art Nouveau, was an alternative way to examine the human condition. This derived largely from a contemporary obsession with the psyche, the subconscious and the mystical. Symbols were used in the decorative arts and paintings to highlight the mythical and spiritual; artists demanded that their art be understood, not just admired. Conversely, the Aesthetes sought to remove any responsibility from art or an artist, requiring only that their work exists by value of its intrinsic beauty.

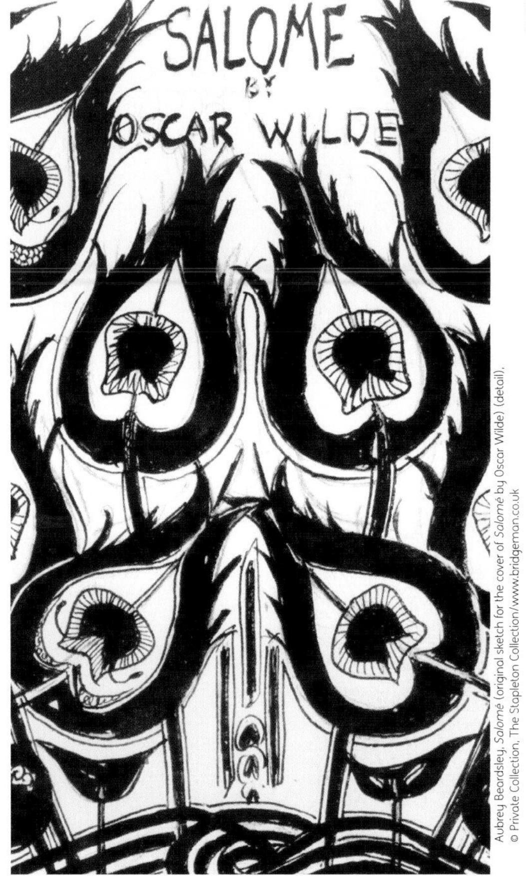

Aubrey Beardsley, *Salomé* (original sketch for the cover of *Salomé* by Oscar Wilde) (detail).

The result was a plethora of styles; Art Nouveau is impossible to define as a single aesthetic despite its short reign. Although it was, arguably, the first great international style, it showed strong regional differences and interpretations and is one of the most complex forces in the history of design. Eventually the style collapsed as the philosophies that defined it became too disparate. It did not die, however, but rather gave birth to new and exciting interpretations of Modernism that were expressed in the Art Deco movement and the work of Bauhaus. It established an enormously important precedent in the field of design, one that allows designers to apply aesthetic, social or philosophical arguments to their creative output and then challenge their customers to question the production methods, quality and artistic value of their work. Art Nouveau succeeded, eventually, in making good design an issue that involves all of us, whether we contribute to it, use it, or just enjoy arguing about it.

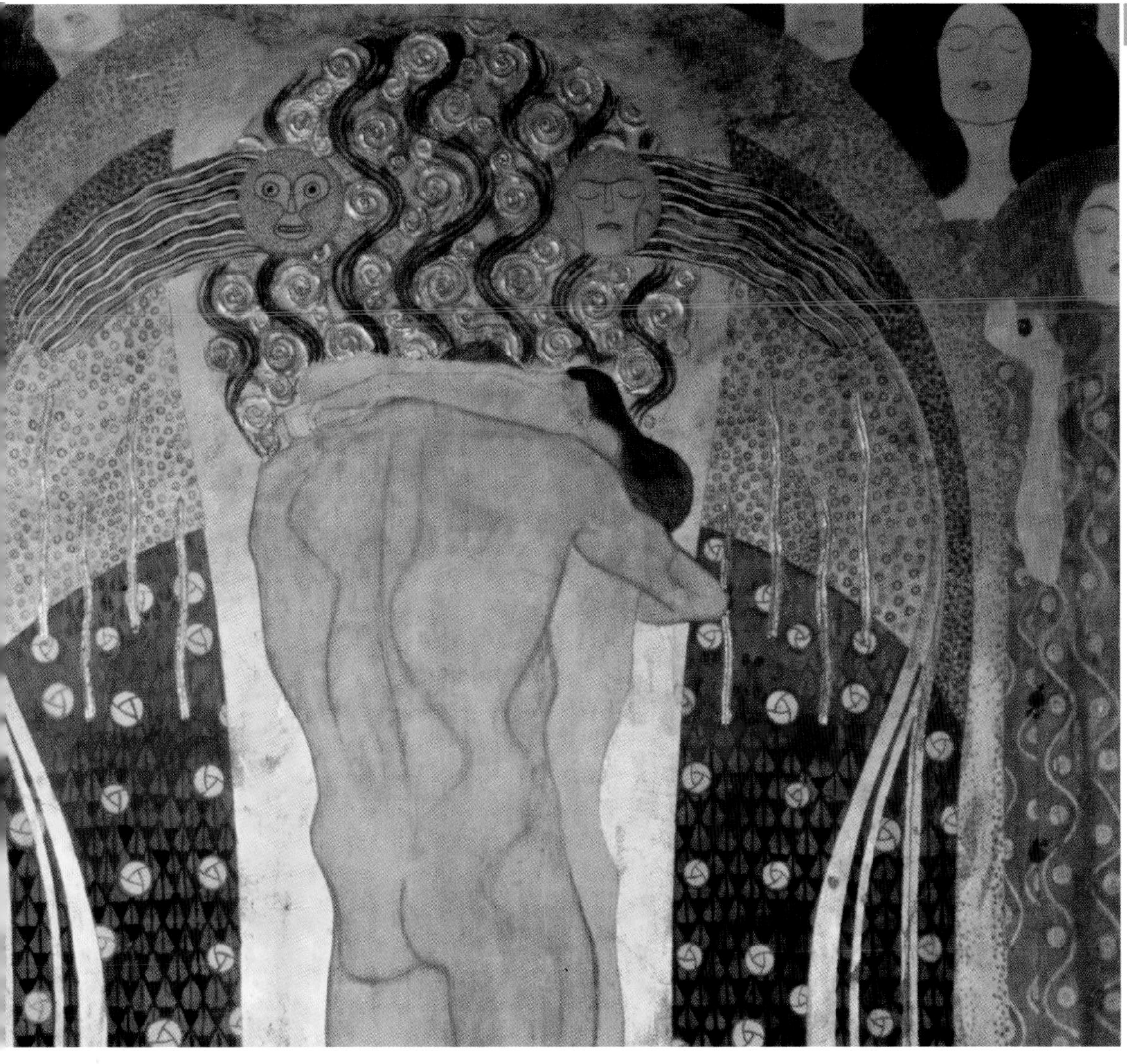

Gustav Klimt, *Here's a Kiss to the Whole World!* (detail from the *Beethoven Frieze*), © Osterreichische Galerie Belvedere, Vienna, Austria/www.bridgeman.co.uk

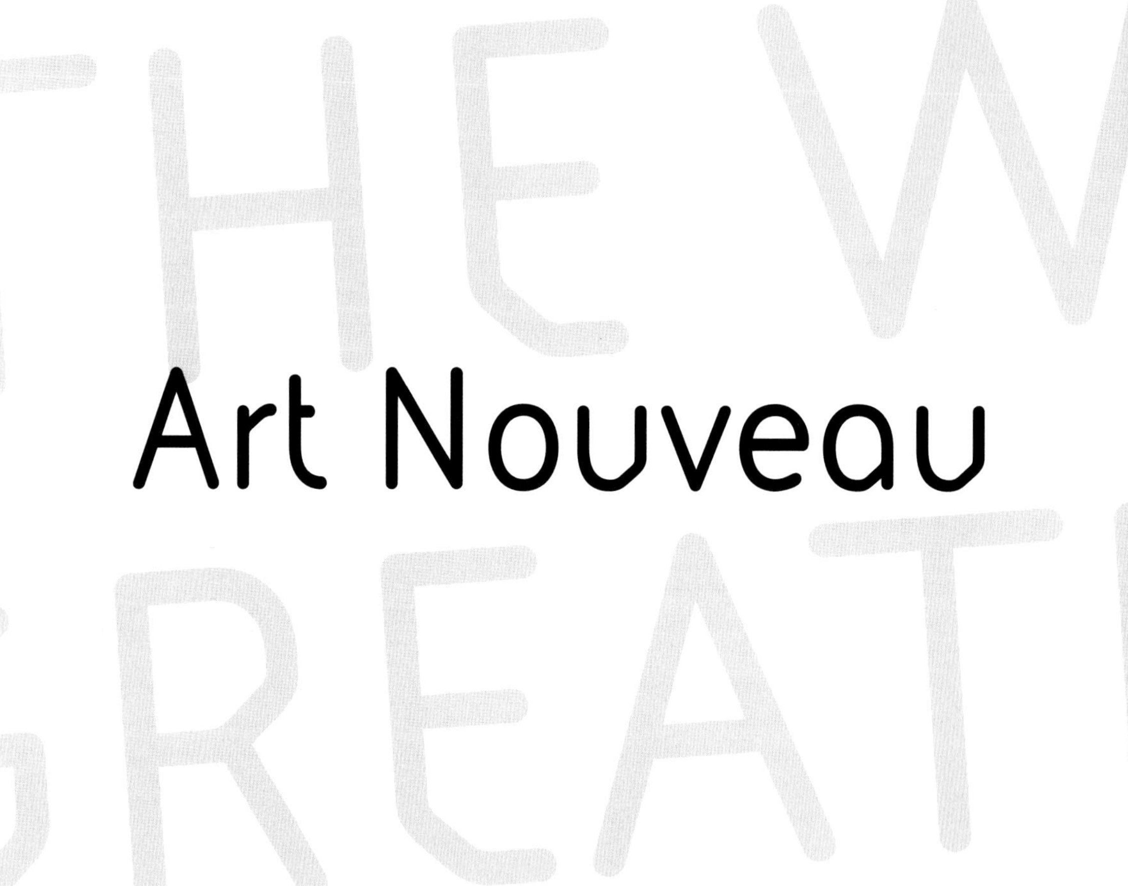

Art Nouveau

Movement Overview

Toulouse-Lautrec, Henri de

Moulin Rouge, La Goulue, from *Les Maîtres de L'Affiche, c.* 1893

Art Nouveau had as much to do with fashion as with originality and methodology; although industrial manufacturing meant that the style was disseminated through society it would mostly remain an eclectic luxury for the wealthy bourgeoisie. As such, it could have been an ephemeral fashion inspiring only local interest in Belgium and France. It proved to be more powerful; Art Nouveau survived because it rode on the crest of a surging wave of innovation and social change. Few artists of the era exemplify this more potently than Henri de Toulouse-Lautrec (1864–1901).

Born in Albi, France, artist Toulouse-Lautrec was a man of the time. He broke away from traditional methods of painting and carved his own path, inspired by contemporary artists and Japanese culture and art. He was not particularly popular in his own, short lifetime but his work stands as a testament to his observational powers. This poster depicts the star dancer of the Moulin Rouge, Louise Weber (1870–1929), who was nicknamed *La Goulue*, or 'glutton'. This first appeared as a poster in 1891.

CREATED

Paris

MEDIUM

Lithographic poster in four colours

RELATED WORK

The Englishman at the Moulin Rouge by Henri de Toulouse-Lautrec, 1892

Henri de Toulouse-Lautrec *Born* 1864 Albi, France

Died 1901

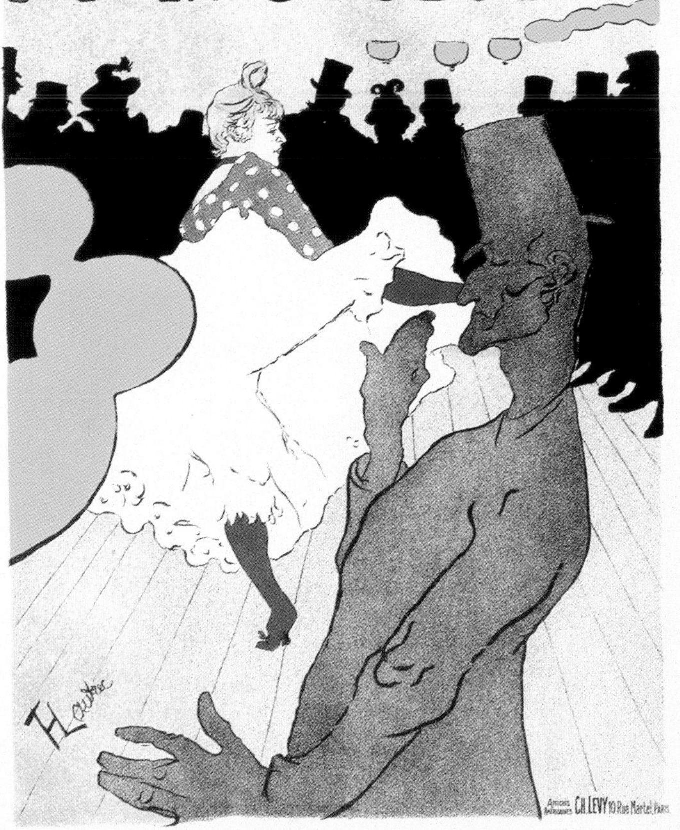
MOULIN ROUGE
MOULIN ROUGE
BAL
TOUS Les SOIRS
LA GOULUE
CH. LEVY 10 Rue Martel, PARIS

Horta, Victor

Bannister from the Hôtel Solvay, Brussels, 1894

The architectural work of Belgian artist Victor Horta (1861–1947) during the 1890s reveals many of the themes and idioms of the early Art Nouveau period. The buildings he designed were aesthetically progressive and sumptuous.

Horta was born in Ghent and trained in Brussels under the highly respected Belgian architect Alphonse Balat (1818–95) at the Ecole des Beaux Arts and was influenced by other contemporary architects, such as Eugène-Emmanuel Viollet-le-Duc. A fashionable choice, Horta was commissioned to design stores in Brussels shopping districts as well as numerous private dwellings and other commercial buildings. The Hôtel Solvay is one of his architectural projects that remains largely intact. In this unique building, Horta demonstrated his ability to create spacious and light-filled spaces that celebrated warm colours, such as the grey-green wrought iron and warm green marble he used for this staircase, which gave way to sun-burnished oranges and yellows on the floor above. Horta enjoyed the contrast caused by using materials of different textures in close proximity and often used industrial materials that were visible and even highlighted by electric lights.

CREATED

Brussels

MEDIUM

Interior design

RELATED WORK

Hôtel van Eetvelde, Brussels, 1895

Victor Horta *Born* 1861 Ghent, Belgium

Died 1947

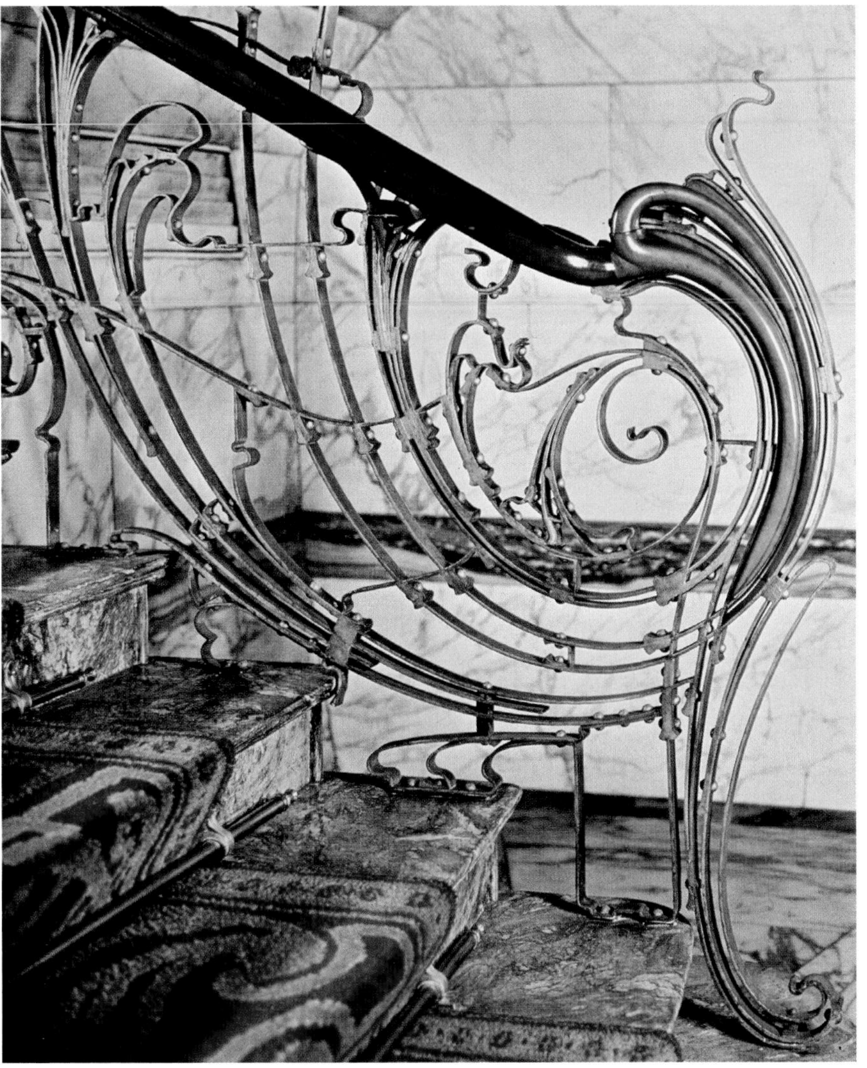

Tiffany Studios

Peacock leaded-glass window

The glasswork of Louis Comfort Tiffany (1848–1933) has come to epitomize much of the glory of the Art Nouveau movement. He combined his business skills with a real artistic flair to supply many American homes with beautiful and decorative glassware. The son of a famous jeweller, Louis Tiffany was born in New York and studied art under painters George Inness (1825–94) and Samuel Colman (1832–1920). In 1877 he helped establish the Society of American Artists. Tiffany had begun to experiment with decorative glass in or around 1875 and soon established a glass-making factory. Tiffany sought to bring colour into glass, and he studied ancient and modern techniques in his efforts to develop new ways of bringing both luminosity and vibrant colour to the medium. His glassware became internationally known, especially his Favrile glass, which was iridescent, fluid and freely shaped.

Early in his career Tiffany travelled to Europe and he visited London when the Aesthetic movement was at its height. At the time James Whistler (1834–1903) was working on his Peacock Room, which was to have a profound effect on Tiffany's development. The peacock motif was popular and recurrent throughout the Art Nouveau period.

CREATED

New York

MEDIUM

Glass and lead

RELATED WORK

Summer panel of Louis Tiffany's *Four Seasons* window, exhibited in Paris, 1892

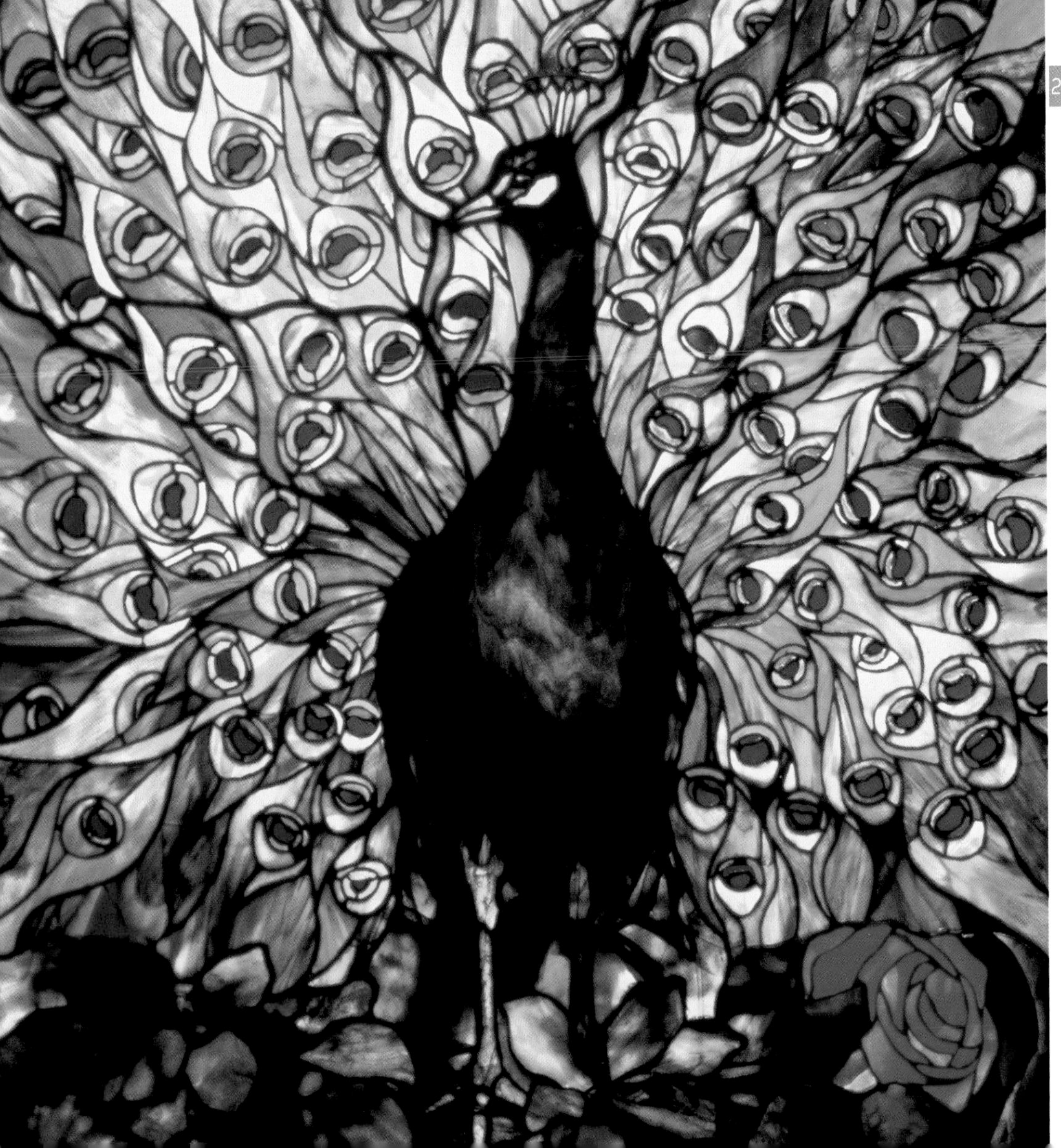

Bradley, William H.

The Chap Book (Thanksgiving edition poster), 1894

William Bradley (1868–1962) was an American graphic artist, born in Boston, who was mostly self-taught. He learnt the principles of printing when apprenticed at a printer's shop at the age of 12. He was later greatly influenced by the work of the British artist Aubrey Beardsley (1872–98), who was widely credited with significantly contributing to the Art Nouveau style, particularly in the fields of illustration and graphic design.

Bradley produced a number of designs for two Chicago publications: *The Chap Book* and *The Inland Printer*, for which he received widespread acclaim. Like Beardsley, Bradley used the contrast between black and white to great effect. His illustrations often featured large areas of flat colour, stylized figures or shapes, sharp edges between colour and fluid, whiplash lines. His pictures were enormously popular thanks to their elegance and strong visual impact. *The Chap Book* was originally produced to market a small publishing house but, thanks to its modern design and the efforts of its contributors, such as Thomas Hardy, Henry James and W. B. Yeats, its readership grew.

CREATED

Chicago

MEDIUM

Colour lithograph

RELATED WORK

The Inland Printer, cover by William H. Bradley, 1895

William H. Bradley *Born* 1868 Boston, USA

Died 1962

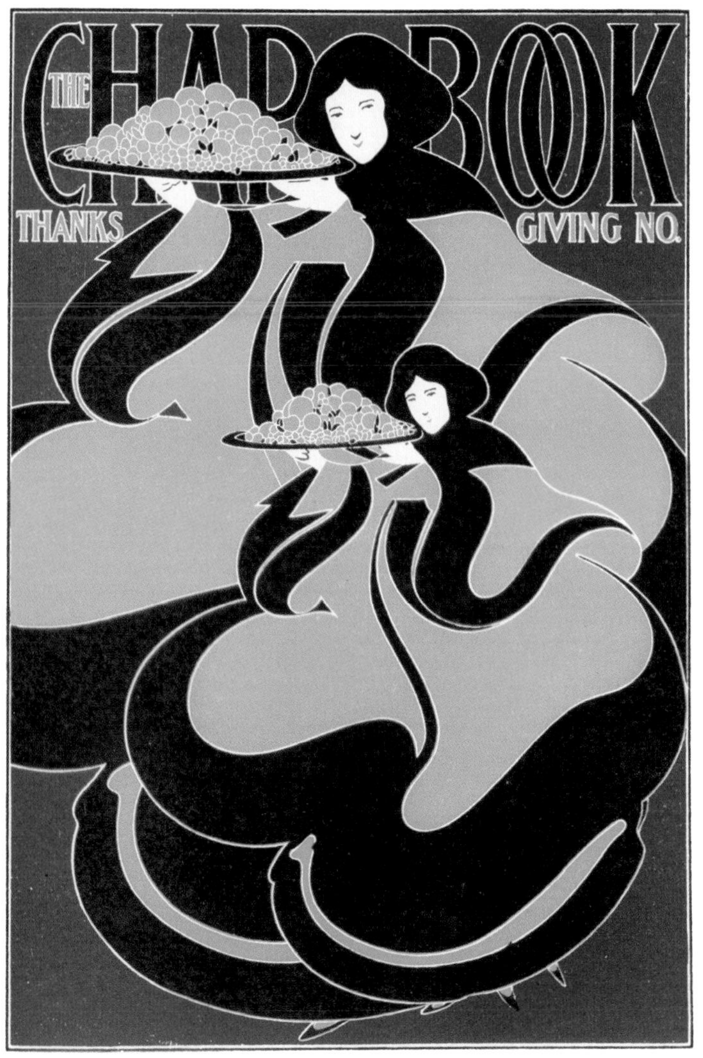
THE
CHAP BOOK
THANKS
GIVING NO.

Beardsley, Aubrey

Salomé (original sketch for the cover of *Salomé* by Oscar Wilde), *c.* 1894

Despite a short life, Aubrey Beardsley made a significant contribution to the development of British art, and the Art Nouveau movement in particular. Largely self-taught, Beardsley loved drawing from an early age. He met the English artist Edward Burne-Jones (1833–98) in 1891 and was persuaded to take drawing lessons. Beardsley became the art editor and illustrator of a new quarterly magazine, *The Yellow Book*, which was first published in 1894. It achieved immediate notoriety.

Beardsley was a friend and colleague of the great poet and dramatist, Oscar Wilde (1854–1900), and illustrated Wilde's *Salomé*. Both men were followers of the Aesthetic movement, which had arisen in late nineteenth-century England largely as a reaction to the utilitarian social philosophies that were present at the time, notably in the Arts and Crafts movement. The doctrine of Aestheticism was based on the philosophy of Immanuel Kant (1724–1804). Exponents of the doctrine believed that art existed purely for its own sake and that it need serve no political, didactic or philosophical purpose.

MEDIUM

Ink on paper

MOVEMENT

Aestheticism

RELATED WORK

Cover for a book of Ernest Dowson's verses by Aubrey Beardsley, 1896

Aubrey Beardsley *Born* 1872 Brighton, England

Died 1898

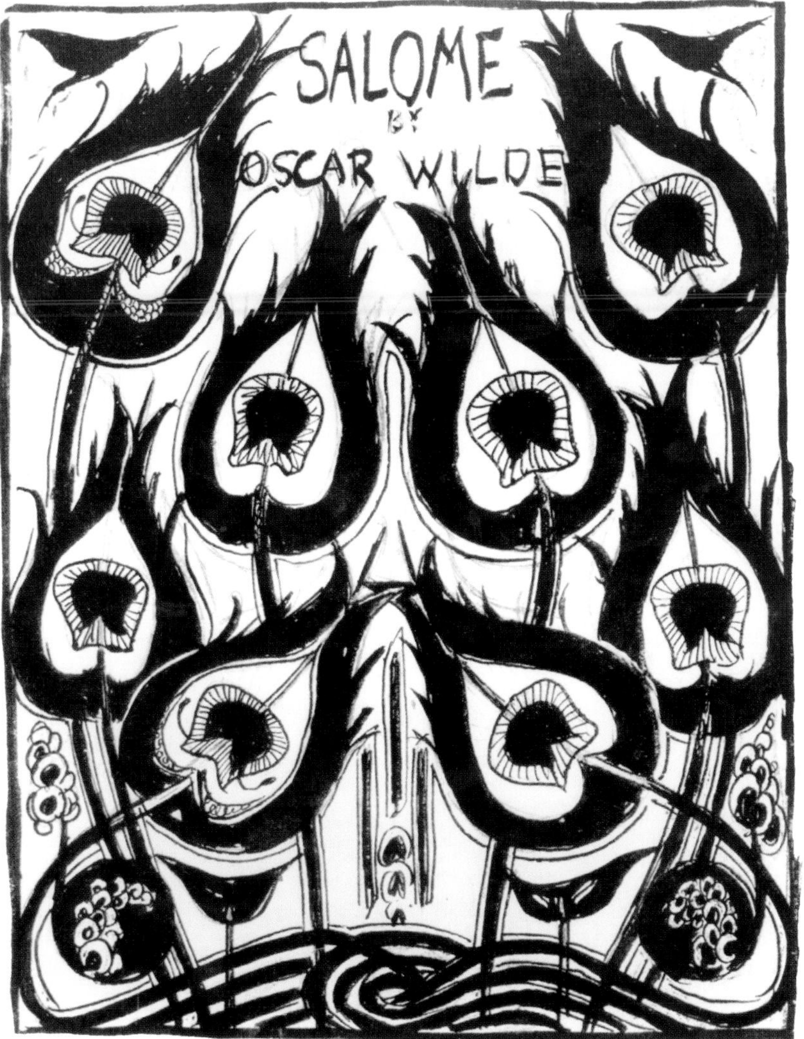
SALOME
BY
OSCAR WILDE

Wolfers, Philippe

Choker (detail), *c.* 1890s

For many designers at the *fin-de-siècle*, metal gave them the best opportunity to express Art Nouveau's fluid lines. Both ductile and tensile, metals such as wrought iron and silver could be formed into the long sinuous lines and curves so redolent of the movement.

Belgian-born silversmith Philippe Wolfers (1858–1929) concentrated less on creating the abstract designs that found favour with many of his contemporaries, and more on designs that featured natural motifs, such as irises and lilies. The natural shape of these elongated flowers perfectly adapts to the line motif. Japanese art was an important influence on Wolfers' style and he often used exotic materials to decorate his jewellery. Ivory, in particular, was in vogue thanks to the efforts of King Leopold II of Belgium who gave it, gratis, to jewellers in the hope of establishing a fashion, as his realm in central Africa, the Congo Free State, was rich in ivory. Wolfers exhibited at the 1897 Brussels Universal Exhibition and received particular praise for his pieces in ivory. Eventually Wolfers' designs became more sculptural and by 1905 he was concentrating purely on sculpture.

CREATED

Belgium

MEDIUM

Gold, enamelled and inset with rubies

RELATED WORK

Medusa: pendant in gold, opal and ivory by Philippe Wolfers, 1898

Philippe Wolfers *Born* 1858 Belgium

Died 1929

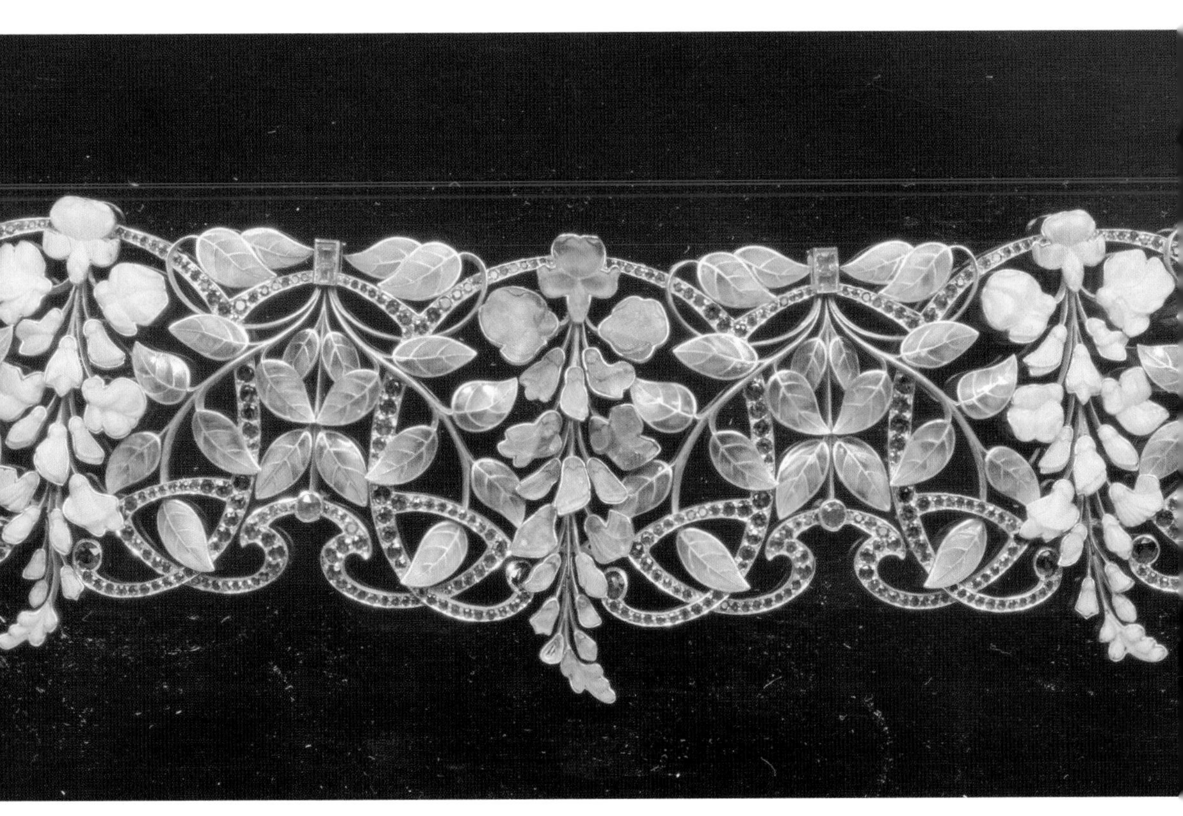

Livemont, Privat

Reproduction of a poster advertising Robette Absinthe, 1896

Early posters were printed simply, often from wood blocks or metal engravings, and rarely used colour. The expense of production precluded wide distribution of posters, until Jules Cheret (1836–1932) refined lithography. In the 1860s this French artist created a new system of lithographic printing using three stones. This method not only allowed him to put colour into a print, but to produce a variety of hues, shades and gradients of colour. Using this technology Cheret worked on an entirely new medium for artistic expression: the poster.

Posters were to become a primary method of advertising goods and publicizing events, and Privat Livemont (1861–1936) was one of the late nineteenth-century poster designers to emerge. The end of the nineteenth century was marked by increased consumerism, literacy and mobility; three elements that served to help the poster thrive as an advertising medium and an artistic force that was visible to all, regardless of income.

The cult of the poster was revived in the 1960s and 1970s, when the bold colours, stylized or simplified forms and flowing lines of the Art Nouveau poster were popular again, this time often combined with psychedelic designs.

MEDIUM

Colour lithograph

RELATED WORK

Poster of Sarah Bernhardt by Leonardo Cappiello, 1899

Privat Livemont *Born* 1861 Schaerbeek, Belgium

Died 1936

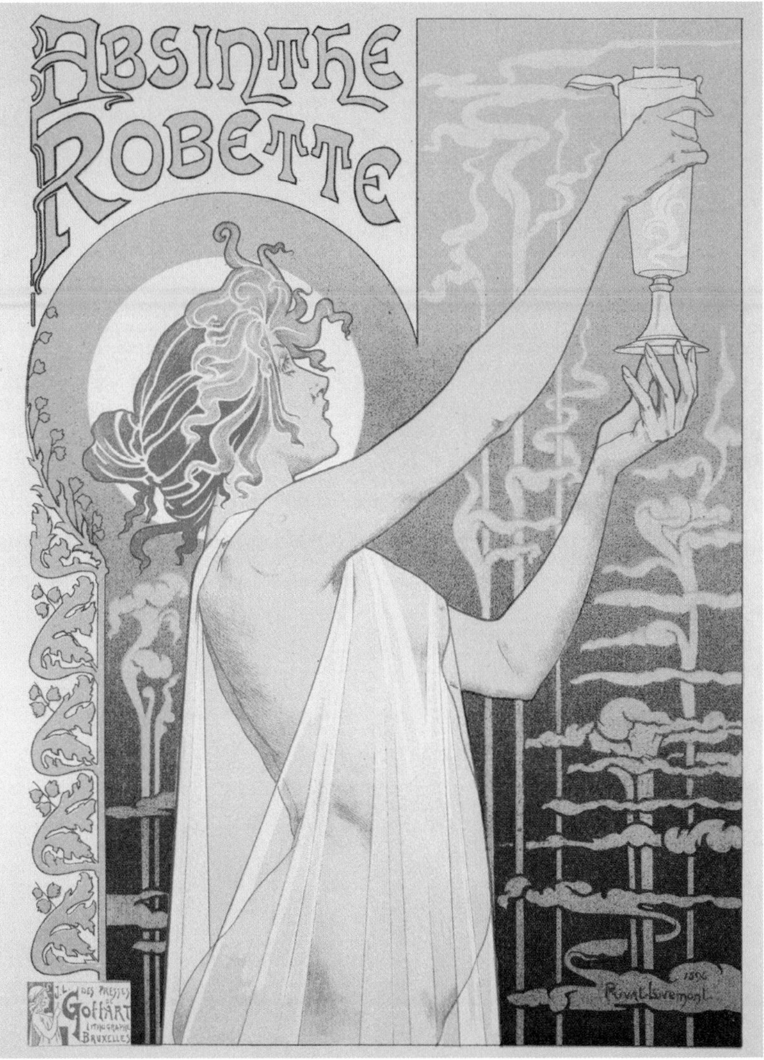
ABSINTHE
ROBETTE
J.L. DES PRESSES DE GOFFART LITHOGRAPHE BRUXELLES
1896
Rivat-Livemont

van de Velde, Henry

Desk and chair, 1896

Art Nouveau was an international movement rooted in a wide range of influences including Aestheticism, the Orient, the cult of nature, Arts and Crafts, and Gothic and Rococo Revivals. One of the most important phases in the early development of the style came about thanks to a Belgian artist and designer, Henry van de Velde (1863–1957).

Van de Velde originally studied in Antwerp before moving to Paris where he studied the works of artists such as Camille Pissarro (1830–1903) and Claude Monet (1840–1926), Post-impressionists and Symbolists. Like the English designer William Morris (1834–96), van de Velde applied his socialist beliefs to his art. Morris believed that by elevating the status of the decorative arts he honoured the integrity of the working craftsman and woman, saving them from the horror of industrialization. Van de Velde also believed that the boundary between fine and applied arts should be removed, but felt that ordinary people should be able to enjoy beautiful objects in their homes and this could only be achieved by cheaper manufacturing methods.

MEDIUM

Oak

RELATED WORK

Silver cutlery designed by Henry van de Velde, 1903

Henry van de Velde *Born* 1863 Antwerp, Belgium

Died 1957

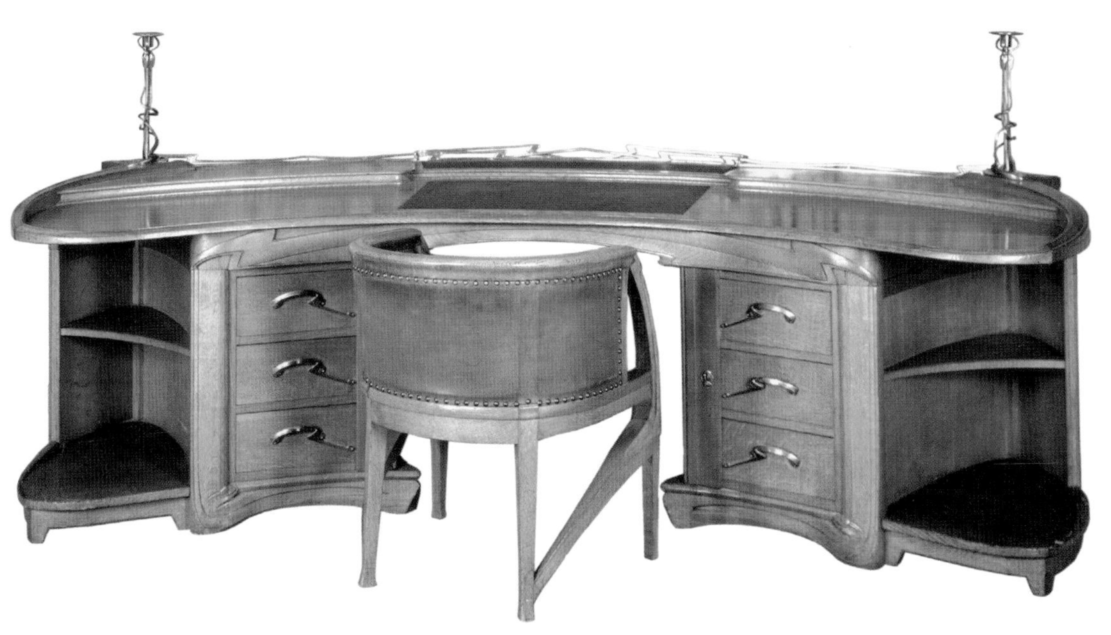

Mucha, Alphonse

Zodiac, Grand Bazar and Nouvelles Galeries, Tours, 1896

The work of Alphonse Mucha (1860–1939), a Moravian artist who trained in Paris, is said to epitomize Art Nouveau. He has become best known for his poster designs, but Mucha was an accomplished artist and designer who created interiors and designed jewellery, carpets and fabrics.

Mucha's huge contribution to Art Nouveau was complex. As an anti-rationalist, Mucha dabbled in the occult and, like many other people he was fascinated by spirituality and mysticism. His work demonstrated how the New Art came to mean different things to different groups: rationalists and anti-rationalists could both employ nature as an idiom. One used nature to signify science, the other to represent the spirit. Many of Mucha's paintings and designs incorporated both symbols and refined decorative elements. His work displayed the gentle arabesque curves so often associated with the movement; his style now seems pleasingly decorative, yet at the time it was innovative and caused a stir when first viewed. With their strong compositions, subtle colours and detailed, elegant decoration Mucha's paintings were effective as advertising posters. Mucha understood that selling a product could be best achieved by selling an idea or a promise; his posters evoked a beautiful, spiritual life, even when selling chocolate.

CREATED

France

RELATED WORK

Poster for Chocolate Amatler by Alphonse Mucha, 1900

Alphonse Mucha *Born* 1860 Ivancice, Moravia

Died 1939

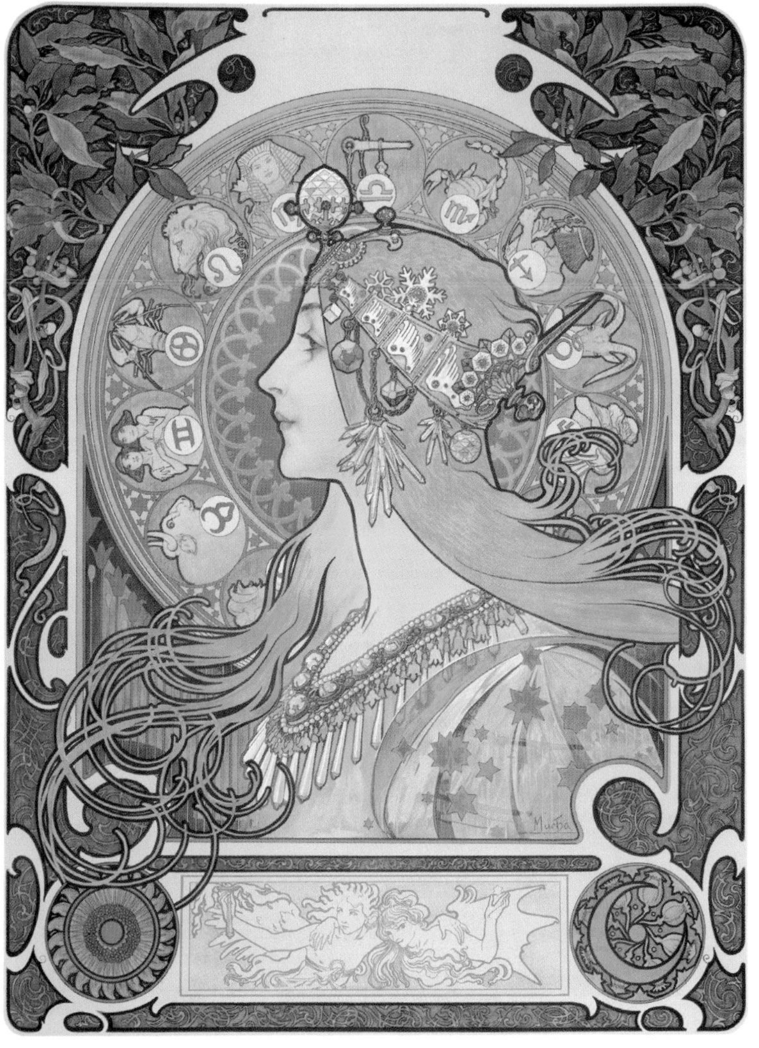
Mucha

Moser, Koloman

Cover for *Ver Sacrum*, 1898

Viennese artists were disillusioned with their city's resistance towards the emerging art movements in Europe in the 1890s. Their response to this intransigence was to distance themselves, or secede, from the traditional view of the *Künstlerhausggenossenschaft* – or *Künstlerhaus* – a body that dictated which works of art would be exhibited in the city. The Viennese Secession was established in 1897 under the leadership of Gustav Klimt (1862–1918) who believed that the *Künstlerhaus* was commercially motivated to show only Austrian work and that this had led to cultural stagnation.

By exhibiting contemporary foreign work, members of the Secession hoped to inspire other Viennese artists and crafts workers, as well as to enlighten the viewing public. They produced their own magazine of the Secession, *Ver Sacrum*, which was also displayed as part of their exhibitions; the cover of the first edition was designed by Alfred Roller (1864–1935). The magazine was published from 1898 until 1903, and the cover shown here was designed by Koloman Moser (1868–1918), a Viennese man and a leading light of the Viennese Secession. This versatile designer's works incorporated fluid and freely expressed elements, as well as geometric patterns.

CREATED

Vienna

MOVEMENT

Secession

RELATED WORK

Die Quelle design by Koloman Moser, 1901

Koloman Moser *Born* 1868 Vienna, Austria

Died 1918

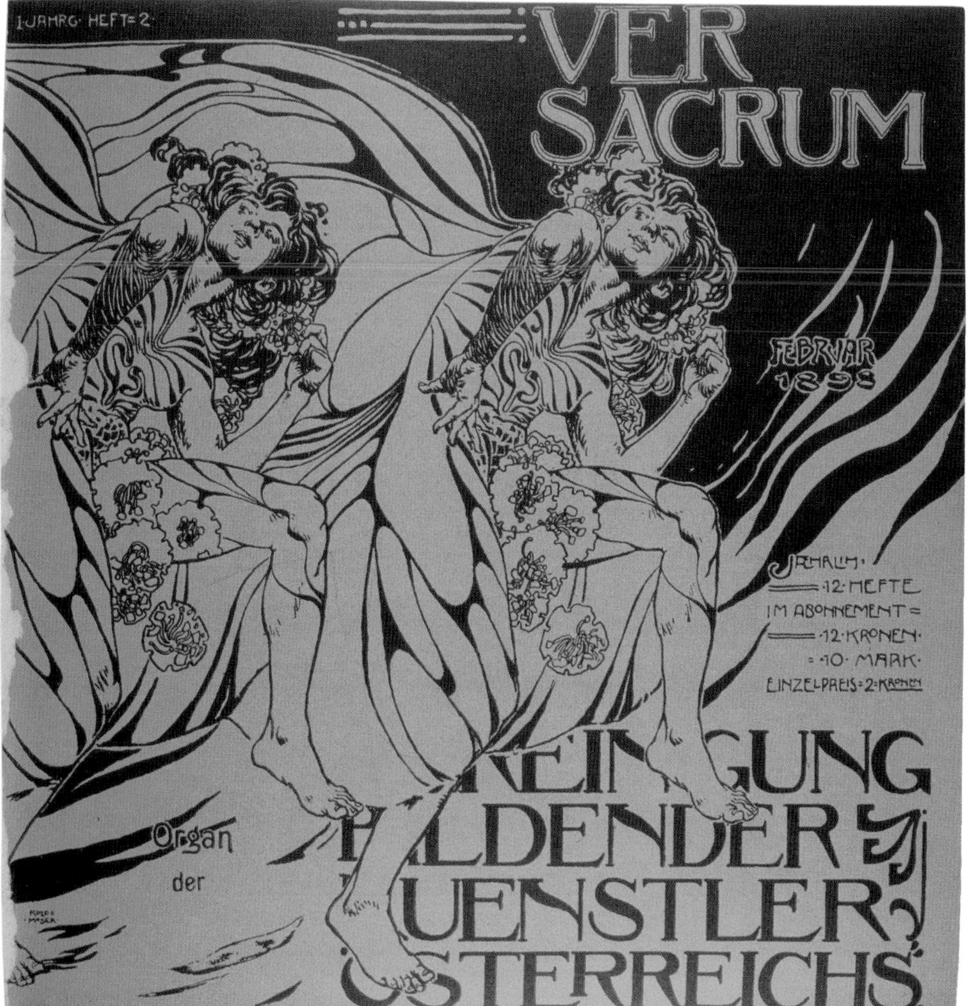
I·JAHRG· HEFT=2·
VER SACRUM
FEBRUAR 1898
12·HEFTE
IM ABONNEMENT=
·12·KRONEN·
=·10· MARK·
EINZELPREIS=2·KRONEN
Organ
der
UENSTLER
STERREICHS

Gurschner, Gustav

Table lamp, *c.* 1890s

The Art Nouveau movement was described by a contemporary sculptor as being 'an honest expression of the age', as it came at a time when society was shaking itself loose from the shackles of traditional influences and seeking inspiration for a new 'age of upheavals'. The call for reform had been loudest in Paris: from the 1870s art journals and societies had been calling for a unity of the arts, by which they meant that decorative arts should be elevated to the status of high art. Some artists, such as those who combined sculptural details in their designs for furniture, crossed boundaries even within the decorative arts and this challenged the categorization of all art forms. By the 1890s decorative arts were being exhibited in Paris, alongside high art and a wide range of sculptural styles and materials began to emerge.

In the newly unified German state the Art Nouveau movement was interpreted as a culture of youth and was known as *Jugendstil* or 'young style'. It glorified youth, and the Bavarian sculptor, Gustav Gurschner (1873–1970), often decorated his fluid sculptural creations with figures of idealized young women.

MEDIUM

Silvered metal with nautilus shade

RELATED WORK

Montadon bookcase with wooden sculptures by Rupert Carabin, 1890

Gustav Gurschner *Born* 1873 Bavaria

Died 1970

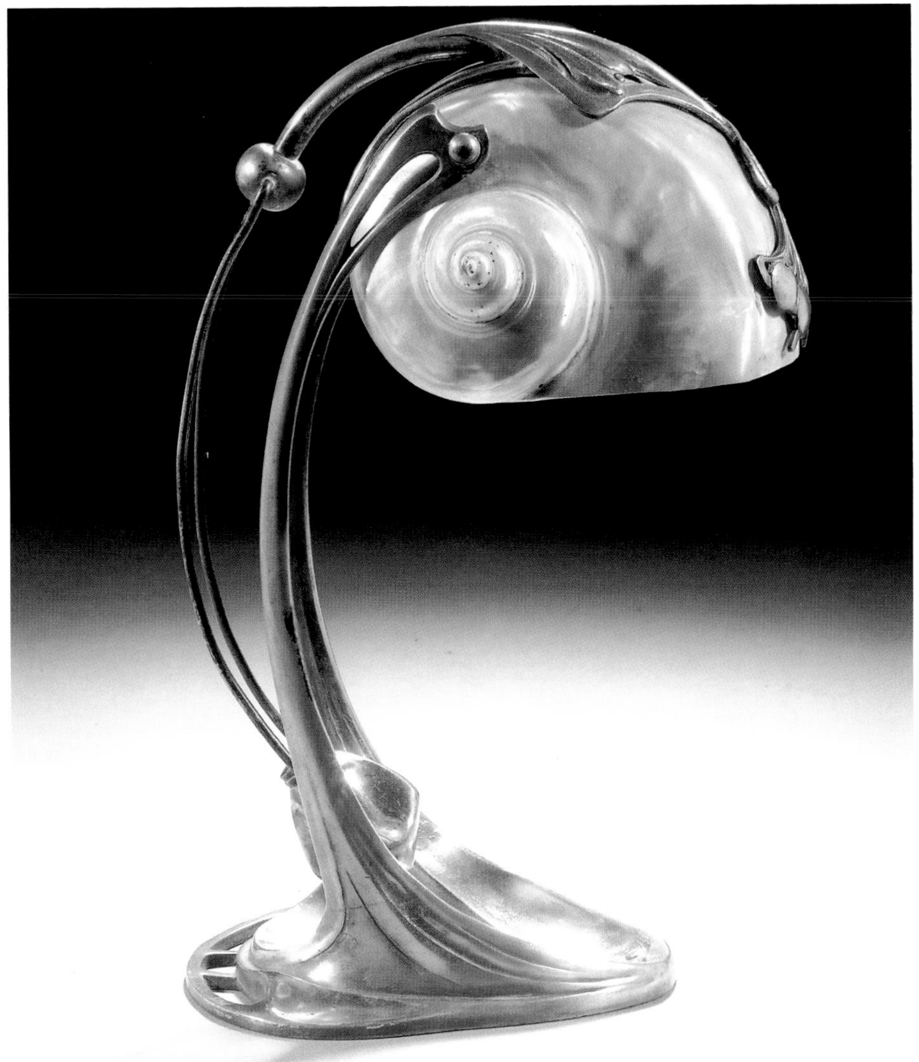

Dalpayrat, Pierre-Adrien

Mounted ceramic inkwell, *c.* 1900

The 1880s saw an exciting and new development in the lives and careers of ceramicists such as Pierre-Adrien Dalpayrat (1844–1910): they were no longer viewed as skilled craftsmen and women, but found themselves elevated to the status of artists. Designers from all arenas were experimenting in different fields, leading to an explosion of interest in crafts such as glasswork and ceramics. Traditional methods of firing and glazing were studied with new passion and improved methodologies emerged.

As in other fields, ceramics was in the troughs of historicism in the 1850s and 1860s. The influence of Japanese art, the Arts and Crafts movement and the cult of nature were all brought to bear, and by the end of the century ceramic production had undergone a radical change both in technique and style. A renewed interest in traditional crafts and materials meant that unglazed, simply glazed and rustic or naive forms were appreciated and valued. Stoneware artefacts became particularly popular because they were hard wearing and the wet clay could be easily modelled. They were also relatively cheap and thus suited the ideal of popular access to good design.

MEDIUM

Ceramic glazed in shades of purple and turquoise with stylized foliate mount

RELATED WORK

Ceramic and decorated silver inkstand by Pierre-Adrien Dalpayrat, *c.*1900

Pierre-Adrien Dalpayrat *Born* 1844 Limoges, France

Died 1910

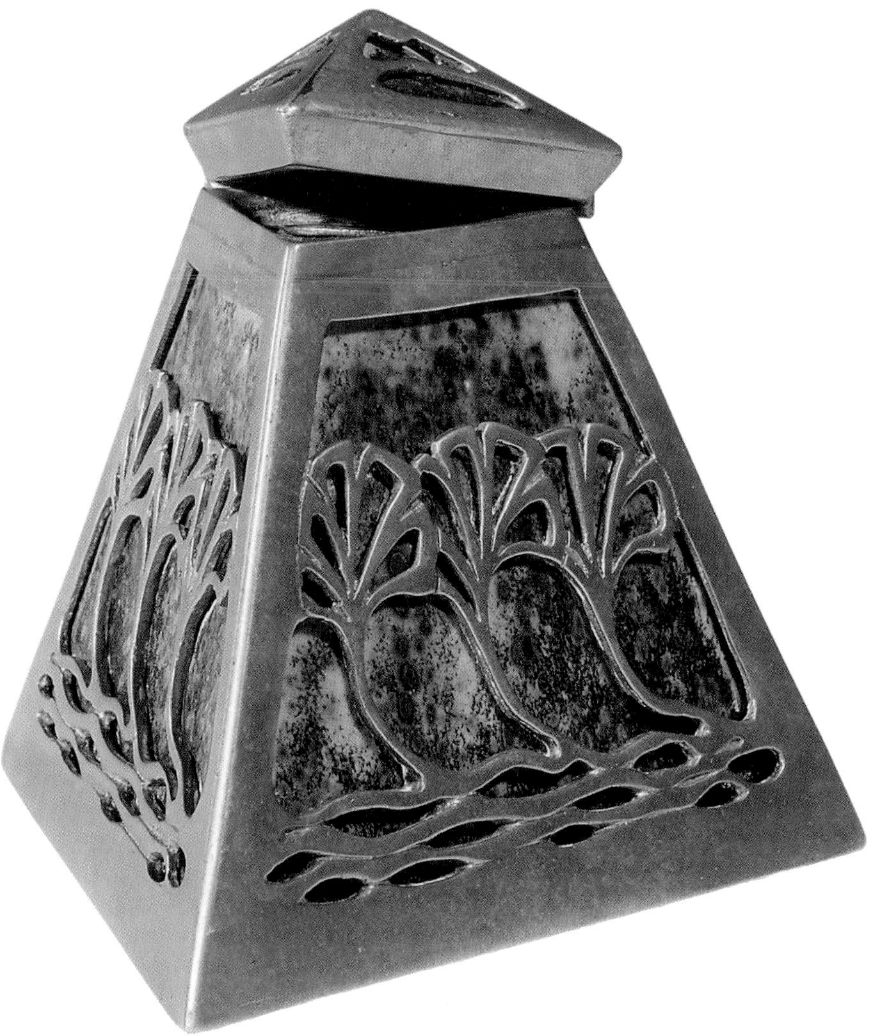

Guimard, Hector

Art Nouveau bedroom, *c.* 1900

Although Art Nouveau began in Belgium, the impetus for development of the style had moved to Paris by the turn of the century. Paris, like Brussels, was undergoing reform. The effects of industrialization and population growth had taken their toll on the great city, and progressive politicians wanted to improve the living standards for its inhabitants. Hector Guimard (1867–1942) was a French architect, decorator and furniture designer, whose radical designs thrust him into the spotlight.

Guimard is best known for the work he did on the Paris Métro. When visitors flocked to Paris in 1900 for the Exposition Universelle they found themselves entering the underground system via extraordinary entrances of woven wrought and cast iron and glass. Inspired by the French architect Viollet-le-Duc, Guimard blended new and traditional materials in plant-like forms, decorating the streets for a delighted generation. It was for his creative use of materials, and for introducing the emergent Art Nouveau to the French people, that Guimard quickly became known. He remained popular for a number of years, aided by his business acumen and self-promotion.

CREATED

Paris

MEDIUM

Interior design

RELATED WORK

Art Nouveau Synagogue at 10 rue Pavée, Paris by Hector Guimard, 1913

Hector Guimard *Born* 1867 Lyon, France

Died 1942

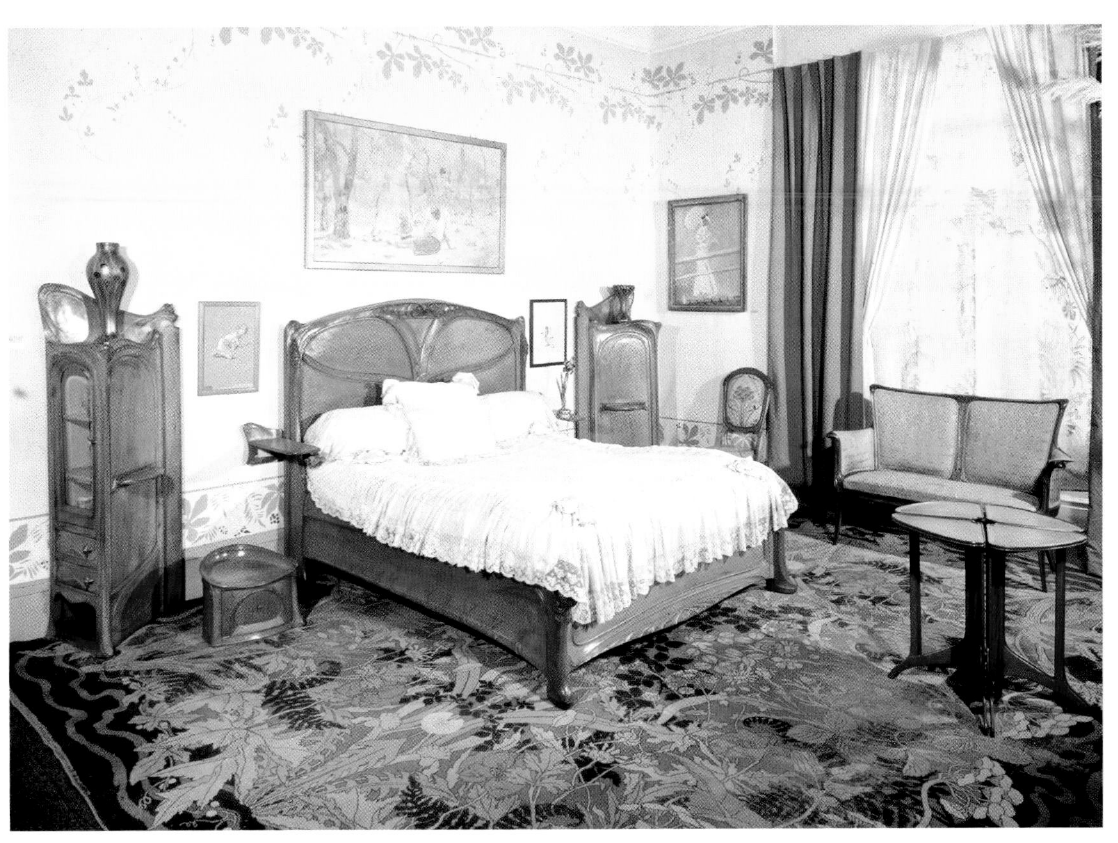

Lalique, René

Pendant

Although René Lalique (1860–1945) is most commonly associated with exquisite glassware created in the Art Deco style, his exceptional talent and extraordinary versatility predate his work in the Deco period. Like other gifted artist-designers of the day, Lalique challenged the traditional notion that one should be master of a single skill and he studied and mastered different techniques, styles and media throughout his life.

Lalique was born in Marne, France, and began his career as a jeweller. By the early 1890s he was designing for notable celebrities of the day, such as Sarah Bernhardt (1874–1934). Lalique's fine craftsmanship and fantastical designs first drew the attention of smart Parisian society in 1887, when he exhibited at the Exposition Nationale des Arts Industriels; his 'visually disturbing' jewellery caused quite a stir. Lalique's creations were often inspired by nature: extremely life-like animals and plants adorned brooches and pendants, causing some critics to call his work decadent. Lalique's success can be partly attributed to his vision that beautiful goods should be accessible to all. He often used semi-precious stones and enamel, rather than gold and diamonds, and when he worked in glass he introduced factory production methods.

MEDIUM

Gold, enamel and pearl

RELATED WORK

Peacock pendant in gold, enamel and opal by René Lalique, 1902–03

René Lalique *Born* 1860 Marne, France

Died 1945

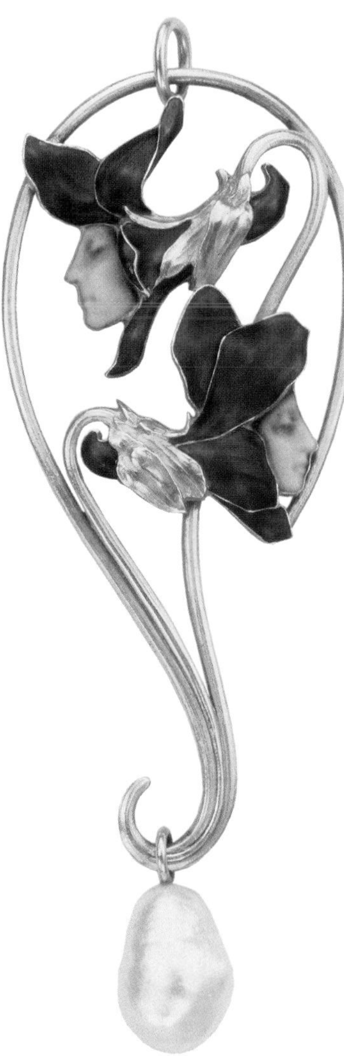

Olbrich, Joseph M.

Covered marmalade dish and plate, *c.* 1900

Joseph Olbrich (1867–1908), born in Silesia, was an influential figure in the development of the Art Nouveau style in Austria and he also helped develop the German version of the movement, known as *Jugendstil*. After studying at the Academy of Fine Art in Vienna, he worked with Otto Wagner (1841–1918) in his workshop, becoming Wagner's chief assistant in 1896 and contributing to Wagner's designs for Viennese railway stations. In 1897 Olbrich was involved in the establishment of the Viennese Secession and in 1898 he began designing the famous Secession building, which was used as an exhibition space and a meeting place for modern artists, designers and architects. In 1899 Olbrich moved to Germany at the invitation of the Grand Duke Ernest Ludwig von Hesse, who asked seven artists to come to Darmstadt and create an 'ideal habitat'. He gave them a large piece of land and enough money to construct a 'living and working world', and Olbrich designed most of the structures.

Olbrich's architectural style was both traditionally classic and modern. His structures were functional and massive and the interiors were organized freely, with movable walls and doors.

MEDIUM

Pewter and green glass

MOVEMENT

Jugendstil

RELATED WORK

Silver teapot with amethyst by Jospeh Olbrich, 1901

Joseph M. Olbrich *Born* 1867 Silesia, Austria

Died 1908

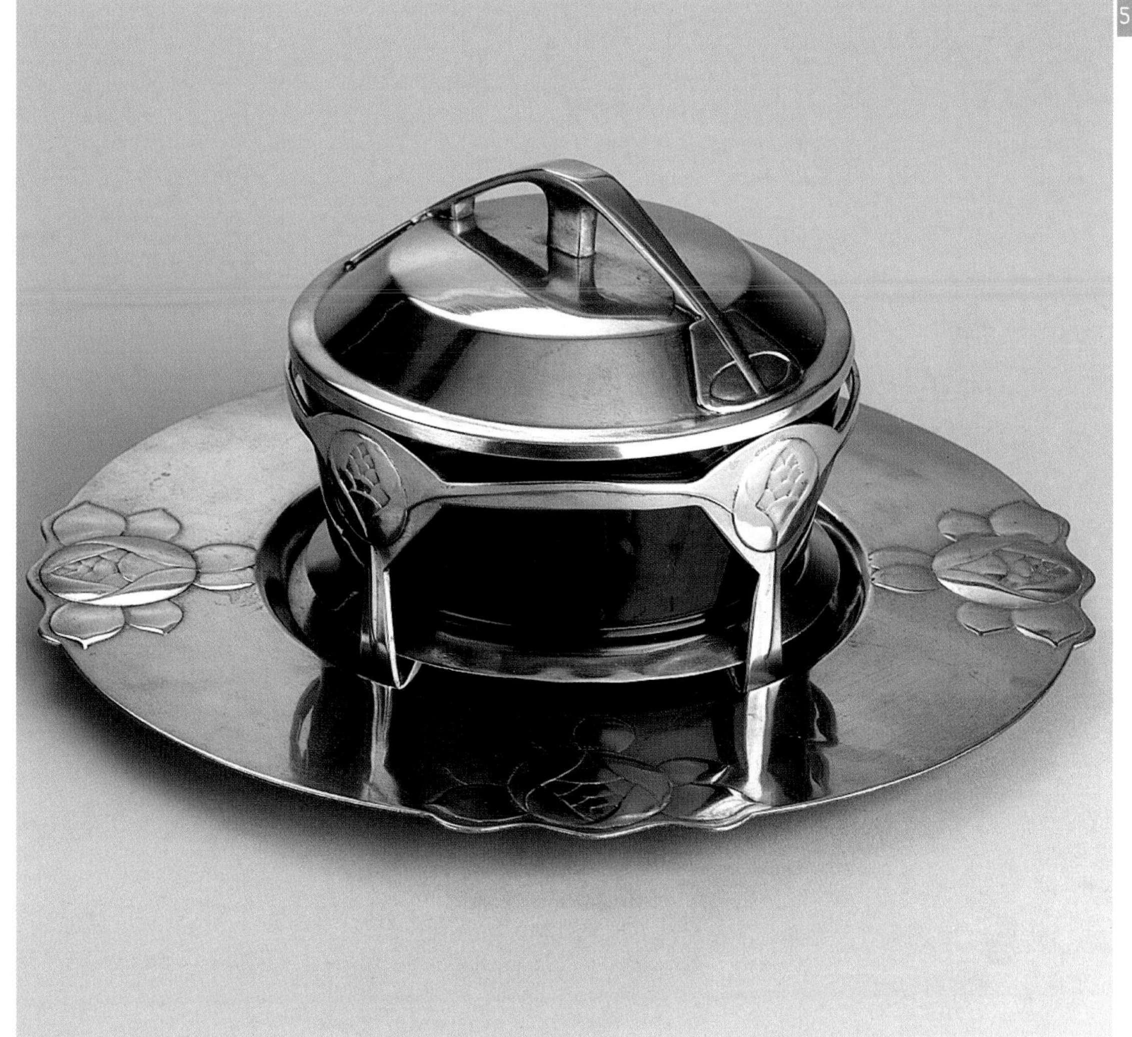

Gallé, Emile

Vase, *c.* 1900

Like his contemporary, Louis Comfort Tiffany, Emile Gallé (1846–1904) was born into a family of artisans in Nancy. His father's business was decorative glassware and ceramics (especially faïence – a type of glazed earthenware decorated in opaque colours). The business prospered and became one of the largest and most successful producers of luxury glassware in Europe.

Emile Gallé studied botany and mineralogy, and combined his technical knowledge of chemistry with a love of nature when he took over the family glassworks in the French town of Nancy in 1874. Gallé was not just a skilled technician, he was also a gifted artist and entrepreneur. He applied his artistic eye to furniture design as well as glassware, although it is for the latter that he was to achieve huge renown and praise. Gallé first exhibited his work in Paris in 1889, and through the 1890s he experimented with glassware, producing many fine works – especially cameo glass. In 1895 Gallé's glass was displayed in Siegfried Bing's (1838–1905) gallery L'Art Nouveau, alongside works by Lalique, Rodin, Pissaro, Bonnard and Toulouse-Lautrec.

CREATED

Nancy, France

MEDIUM

Coated, laminated and clouded glass

RELATED WORK

Glass vase, wheel cut, acid etched and decorated with cabochons of glass by Emile Gallé, *c.*1903

Emile Gallé *Born* 1846 Nancy, France

Died 1904

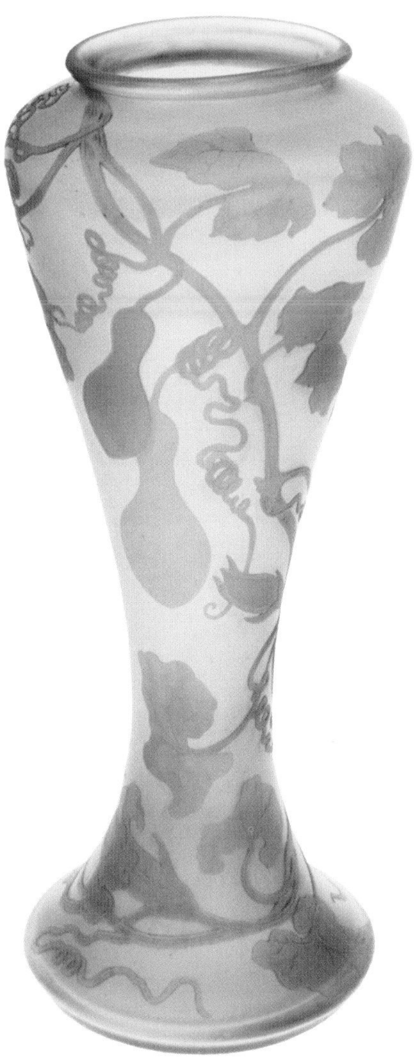

de Feure, Georges

Modern interior, 1900

The work of Paris-born Georges de Feure (1868–1943) encapsulates much of the French interpretation of the Art Nouveau movement. Work by the young artist-designer was exhibited by the businessman and art connoisseur Seigfried Bing in his sensational Parisian emporium, L'Art Nouveau, and in Bing's pavilion at the 1900 Exposition Universelle.

It was Bing's shop that was to name the entire movement eventually. He chose to show and sell work that exhibited quality, luxury and simplicity. Having dealt in Oriental work, Bing was particularly enthusiastic about arts and crafts that demonstrated refinement and sophistication, in both technique and form. Apart from furniture and interiors designed by de Feure, Eugène Gaillard (1862–1933) and Edouard Colonna (1862–1948), Bing sold the exquisite Favrile glassware of the Tiffany studios. Like many young artists of his day, Georges de Feure applied his talents to creating a design for a whole interior. He was, however, also an accomplished painter and employed symbolism and themes from nature in many of his paintings, idioms that were popular at the time.

MEDIUM

Colour lithograph

RELATED WORK

L'Esprit du Mal by Georges de Feure, 1897–98

Georges de Feure *Born* 1868 Paris, France

Died 1943

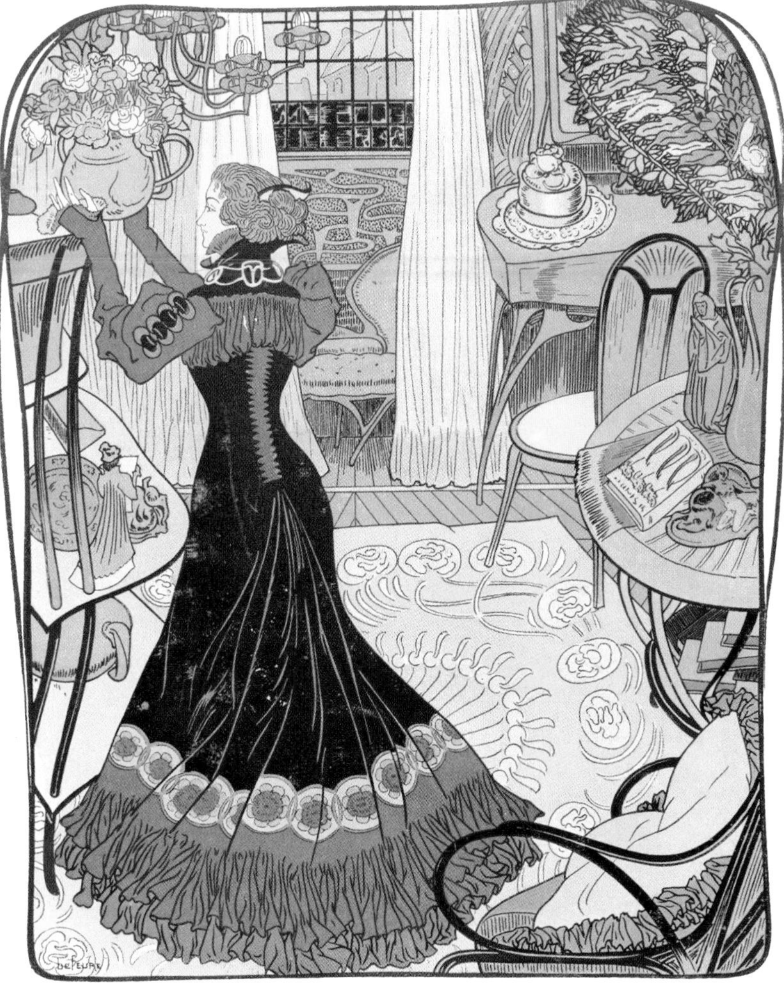
DeFeure

Larche, Raoul-François

Figural table lamp, *c.* 1900

Metal proved to be one of the most lasting and charismatic materials used by the Art Nouveau artists and designers. Wrought iron was used, particularly by French and Belgian architects, to create buildings with strong elemental lines and curves. Where once iron was thought to be base and ugly and was therefore used structurally, hidden from view, these modern architects incorporated the structural framework into the decorative form of the building.

Metal also proved to a medium that demonstrated the duality of Art Nouveau. While wrought iron required a craftsman's skill and strength, as seen in Raoul-François Larche's (1860–1912) lamp, cast iron could be produced industrially, making it more accessible to a wider audience. This duality featured in many areas of the style at the turn of the century as artists tried to reconcile the intrinsic beauty of hand-crafted items with the more practical and modern advantages of mass production. This duality continued far into the Art Deco movement. Themes employed in metalwork for architectural projects also made their way into the fine arts and bronze sculptures of the day, particularly in France.

CREATED

Paris

MEDIUM

Gilt-bronze

RELATED WORK

Comedy and Tragedy, sculpture by Sir Alfred Gilbert

Raoul-François Larche *Born* 1860 Gironde, France

Died 1912

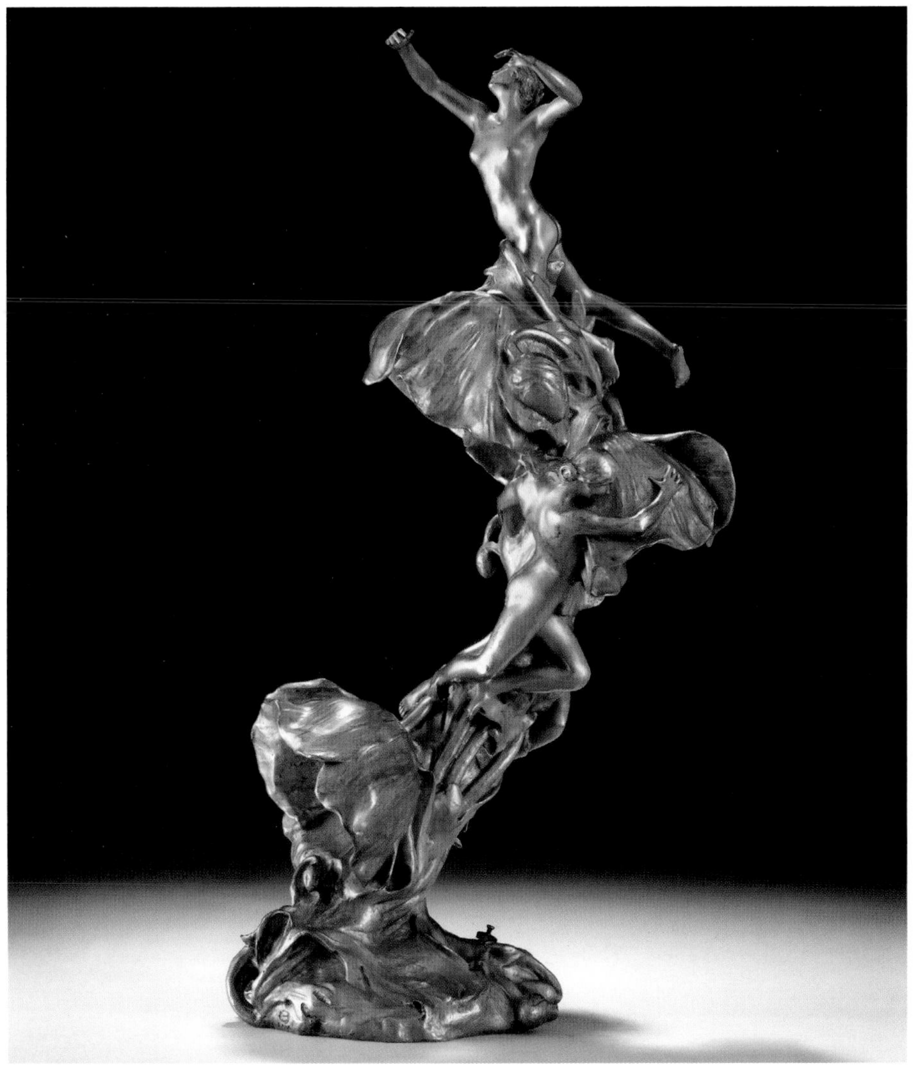

Majorelle, Louis

Mahogany salon suite, *c.* 1900

Through the mid-nineteenth century France was the acknowledged arbiter of artistic taste and Paris, especially, was regarded as the fount from which European culture and art flowed. By the 1870s, however, this situation began to change. The influence of British innovations in art and craftwork were being felt abroad and French applied art was in danger of being left behind. The German Siegfried Bing opened his French gallery, L'Art Nouveau, in 1895 to introduce the French to new art and design from other European countries. He hoped to encourage design that no longer endlessly reinvented styles from the past, but evoked new and innovative themes and techniques.

The new art, or Art Nouveau, which grew from Bing's inspirational contribution to Parisian style was not, of course, entirely new. French Art Nouveau drew on Neo-Rococo ornamentation and the superb craftsmanship of local artisans, who were unequalled in their cabinet-making skills. The resultant eclectic French Art Nouveau was displayed at the Exposition Universelle in Paris in 1900. The French cabinet-maker Louis Majorelle (1859–1926) exhibited his luxurious and finely crafted furniture at the Exposition.

CREATED

France

MEDIUM

Mahogany

RELATED WORK

Water lily desk for the 1900 Paris Exposition by Louis Majorelle

Louis Majorelle *Born* 1859 Toul, France

Died 1926

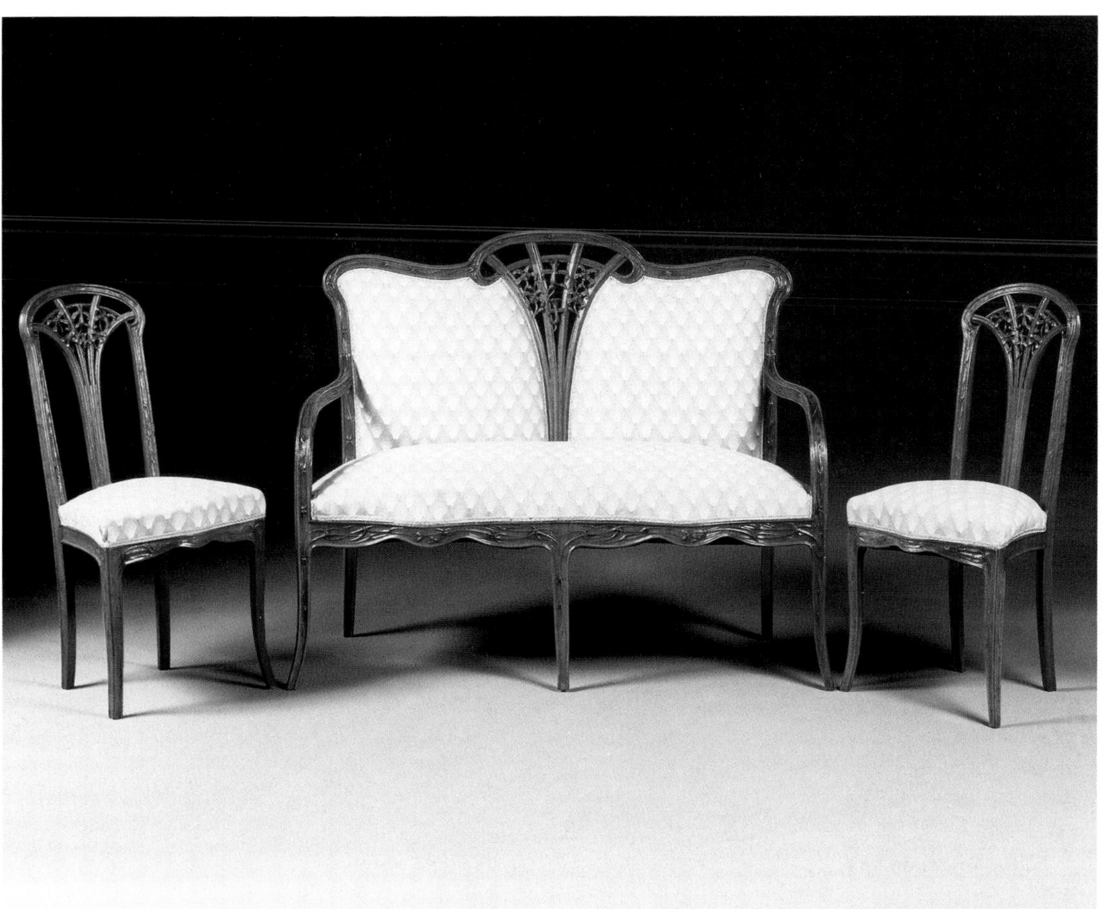

Johann Loetz Witwe Glasshouse

Selection of Loetz vases

Just as artists and designers at the *fin-de-siècle* were able to weave metal into the sinuous, free-flowing lines that became characteristic of the Art Nouveau style, so they discovered that glass was an equally suitable medium for the aesthetic of the time. Glass is malleable like metal, but it has the added qualities of transparency, translucency and hue. The style called for openness and light; in an attempt to drive out old influences and traditions, the new interiors celebrated a theme of vibrancy and freedom from clutter. As a medium, glass was highly suitable for this aim. Architects used clear glass in conservatories, or to make roofs over hallways, both in domestic houses and commercial buildings. Combined with metal struts, supports and decorations, the medium became thoroughly modern.

Exponents of the Arts and Crafts movement in Britain used stained glass to recreate medieval scenes, but elsewhere glasswork was incorporated into everyday interiors. Electric lamp fittings were becoming more commonplace and this also contributed to the demand for glass and the growth of technologies available to the designers.

CREATED

Bohemia

MEDIUM

Glass

RELATED WORK

Titania paperweight by the Johann Loetz Witwe Glasshouse, 1898–1905

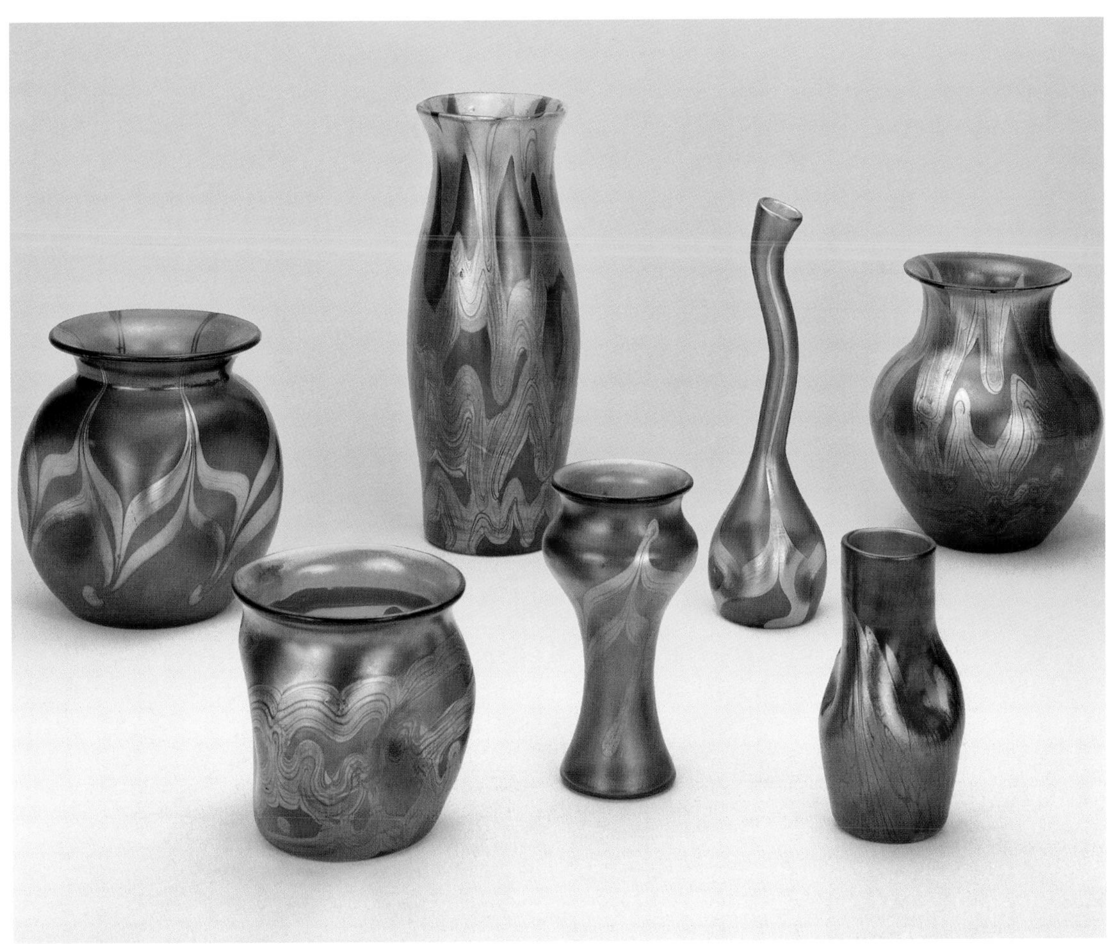

Knox, Archibald

Liberty and Co. lidded tankard, 1900

Art Nouveau was an art movement that grew hand in hand with consumerism and demands by the middle class for stylish goods at affordable prices. Avenues of smart shops were scattered across Paris and department stores were built across Europe and the US. Of all the retailers who dabbled in Art Nouveau, it was Liberty and Co., of London's Regent Street, that became synonymous with the style.

When Arthur Liberty (1843–1935) opened the doors of his shop to Londoners in 1875, he offered them artefacts from the Orient and Arts and Crafts goods. In 1890 Liberty's success encouraged him to open a second store in Paris, which produced and sold Art Nouveau objects in the English style. He also transported European artefacts to his London shop, assisting the cross-fertilization of ideas that developed the style. Liberty aimed to 'combine utility and good taste with modest cost'. The Liberty ranges of silver and jewellery adopted strong Celtic images and were made from pressed and soldered metal, but hammered to achieve a hand-crafted look. Archibald Knox (1864–1933), born on the Isle of Man, was one of Liberty's most famous designers.

MEDIUM

Silver and enamel

MOVEMENT

Arts and Crafts/Art Nouveau

RELATED WORK

Tudric tea set designed for Liberty and Co. by Archibald Knox, 1904

Archibald Knox *Born* 1864 Isle of Man

Died 1933

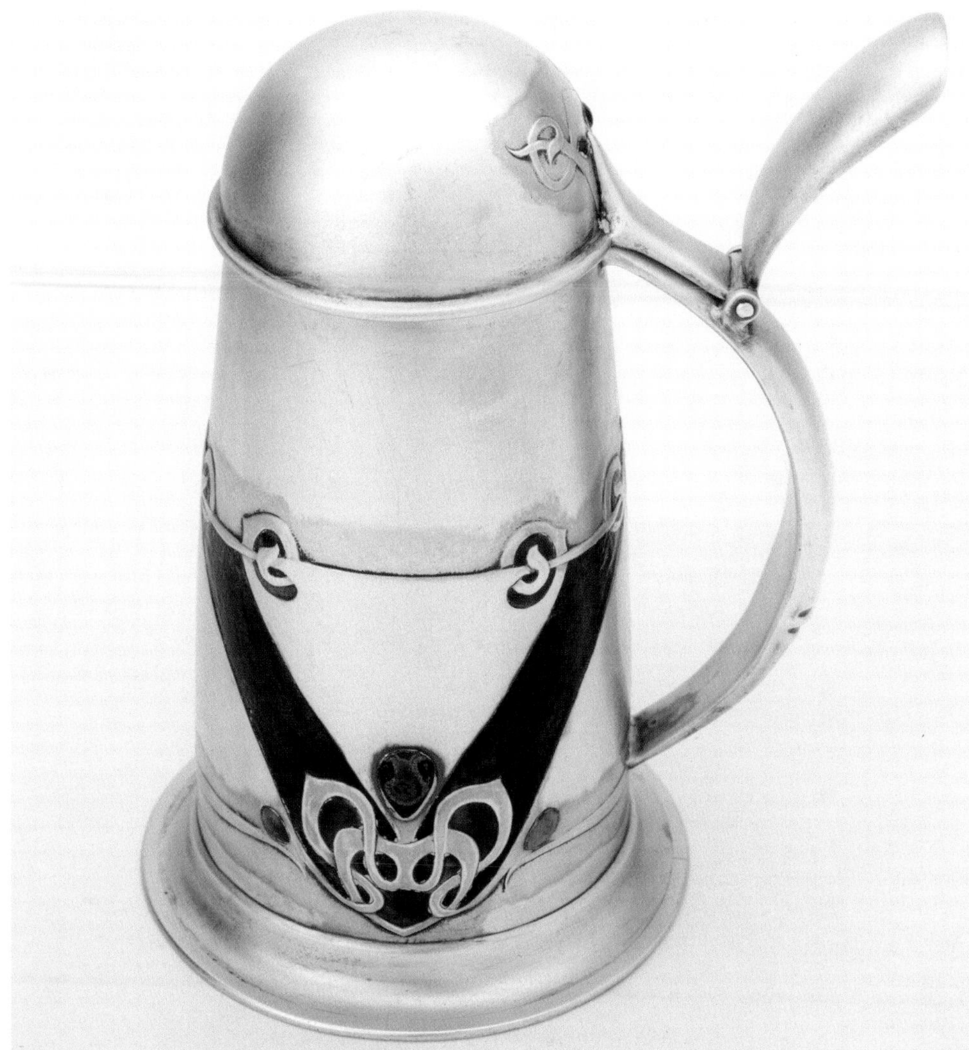

Léonard, Agathon

Female musician (produced for the Sèvres Manufactory), 1900

The Sèvres factory was first established as a porcelain works in the eighteenth century. During the 1830s and 1840s railway links were made to the town and it rapidly expanded in population and size as a result. A new nationalized factory and ceramics museum were built in 1861 and through the later years of the nineteenth century the ceramics industry of Sèvres bloomed. French artists and designers were actively encouraged to support traditional skills and crafts and there was a national movement in celebration of French design. As a result the Sèvres factory, which had previously produced porcelain goods for the luxury market, now branched out into stoneware and adopted a policy of supporting up-and-coming designers.

This statue of a female musician in French porcelain is part of a table setting designed by Agathon Léonard (1841–1923) in 1898 and shown at the Sèvres pavilion at the Exposition Universelle in Paris in 1900. The set was called *Jeu de l'Echape* (Dance of the Scarves). It was loosely based on the performances of Loïe Fuller.

CREATED

Sèvres

MEDIUM

Unglazed porcelain ceramic

RELATED WORK

Jeu de L'Echape table setting by Agathon Léonard, 1898

Agathon Léonard *Born* 1841 France

Died 1923

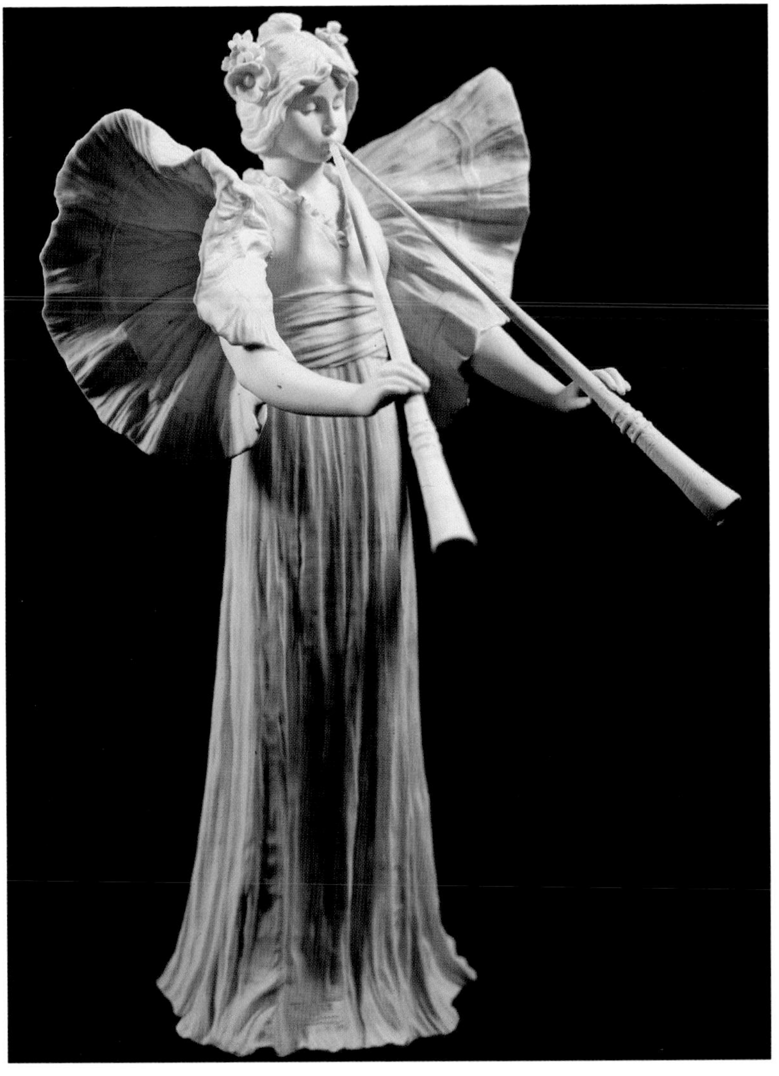

Daum Frères and Gallé, Emile

Selection of Daum and Gallé cameo vases

The French Daum Frères (Daum Brothers), Auguste Daum (1853–1909) and Antonin Daum (1864–1930), began working at the family glass factory in around 1890. The factory was in the French town of Nancy, famous for its glassware and particularly the work of Emile Gallé. Encouraged by Gallé, Antonin Daum, artistic director of the Daum Glassworks, made the business more profitable by producing art glass in preference to the domestic tableware that had previously been the backbone of their production.

The Daum brothers exhibited with some success in Chicago in 1893 and then again in 1900. By this time their individual style was evident and they were awarded a prize for their designs at the Exposition Universelle. The Daum brothers collaborated with other designers, but their output has remained in the shadow of Emile Gallé, whose work is generally considered to be finer. Daum work characteristically featured motifs from nature and techniques employed included *pâte de verre*, cameo and applied glass in high relief. In 1901 the Ecole de Nancy (School of Nancy) was established. Exhibitions of Gallé and Daum glassware were shown and became internationally famous.

CREATED

Nancy

MEDIUM

Glass

RELATED WORK

Nautilus shell cup in engraved and etched glass by Daum, 1905

Auguste Daum *Born* 1853 Bitche, France

Died 1909

Antonin Daum *Born* 1864 Bitche, France

Died 1930

Emile Gallé *Born* 1846 Nancy, France

Died 1904

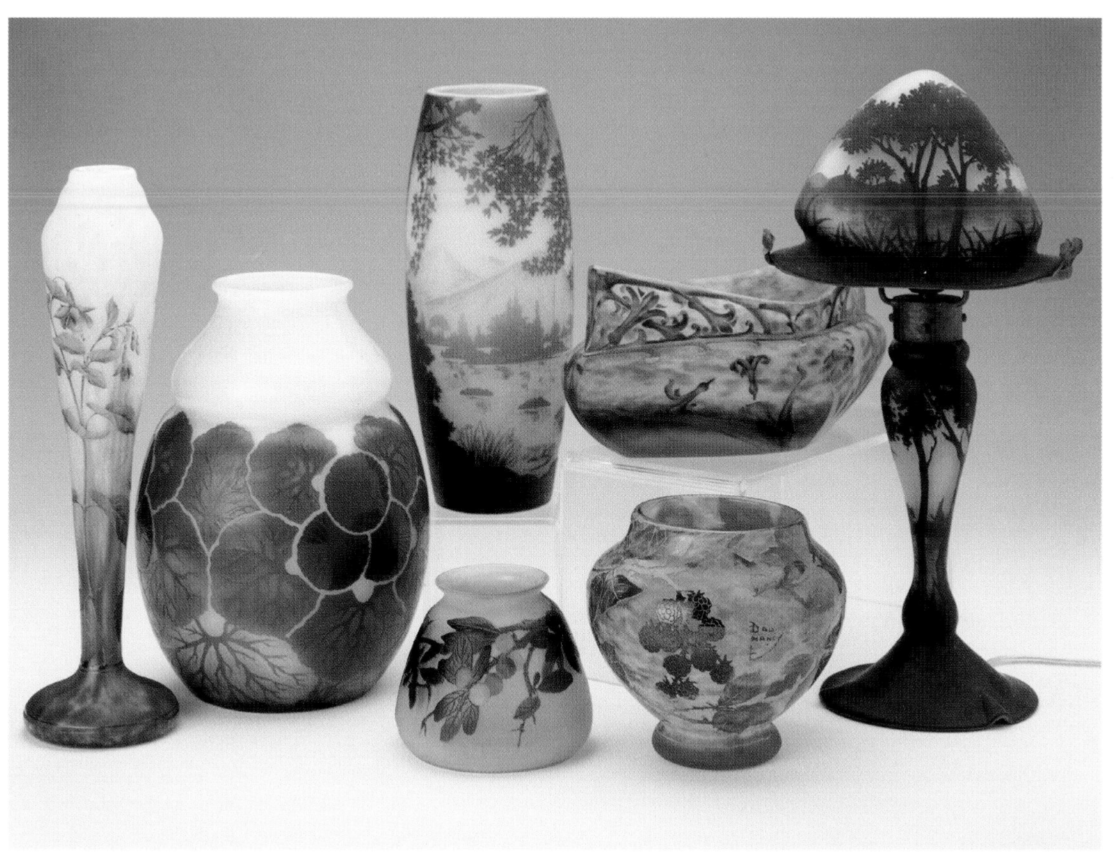

Bugatti, Carlo

Ice bucket

In 1861 Italy became a united kingdom, following a long period of Risorgimento, an ideological and literary movement to unify the country. Despite its success, this movement had done little to address the regional differences that existed: the South was largely rural, while the North was in the belated throes of industrialization. A conviction existed, however, that a new sense of nationhood was required and the quest for a new artistic identity began. In theory this conviction should have led to Italian artists embracing the Art Nouveau style and adapting it to suit their own cultural vision, as other European countries had done.

In 1902 Turin staged the largest Art Nouveau Exhibition to date, the Prima Esposizione d'Arte Decorativa Modern, with the aim of demonstrating its new art and publicizing its manufacturing industry. Critics were not entirely favourable towards the Italian style, which became known as *Stile Liberty* (after the London store) or *Stile Floreale* (after the ornate decorations inspired by nature). Italian artists were said to be either too reliant on historical and traditional aesthetics or guilty of mimicking other European Nouveau styles. The designer of the ice bucket depicted here was Milan-born Carlo Bugatti (1855–1940).

MEDIUM

Metal

RELATED WORK

Pavilion of Interiors, from Turin Exposition 1902 by Raimondo d'Aronco

Carlo Bugatti *Born* 1855 Milan, Italy

Died 1940

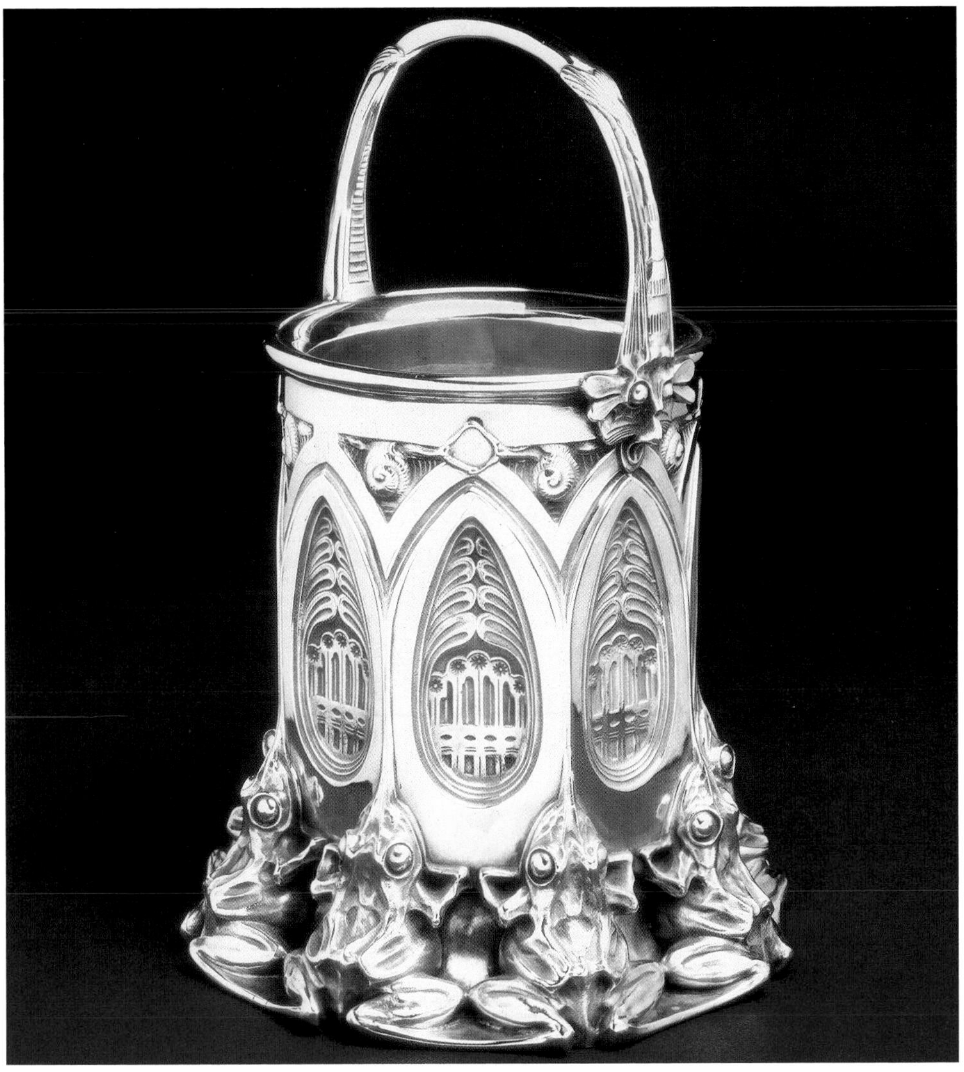

Mackintosh, Charles Rennie

Cabinet made for 14 Kingsborough Gardens, Glasgow, 1902

The art of furniture design and manufacture changed enormously through the Art Nouveau period. Many of the techniques and style idioms that were developed became core design elements of the Art Deco period (which emerged from the ashes of Art Nouveau after the First World War). The Glaswegian Charles Rennie Mackintosh (1868–1928) was an influential artist and designer of the time; his work bridged the defining aesthetics of both Art Deco and Art Nouveau. His innovation and enormous talent have left their mark on the field of decorative art in subsequent years and designs by Mackintosh are as popular today as they were 100 years ago.

Mackintosh belonged to the new breed of architect-artists who became a powerful force for Art Nouveau. His approach was holistic; he designed every element of an interior from the textiles to the furnishings and lighting. He drew on the Arts and Crafts aesthetic of superb craftsmanship and quality materials, but his designs were light, elegant and entirely new. Mackintosh often worked with his artist-designer wife, Margaret Macdonald (1864–1933).

MEDIUM

Painted oak

RELATED WORK

Small painted table with drawers for The Hill House by Charles Rennie Mackintosh

Charles Rennie Mackintosh *Born* 1868 Glasgow, Scotland

Died 1928

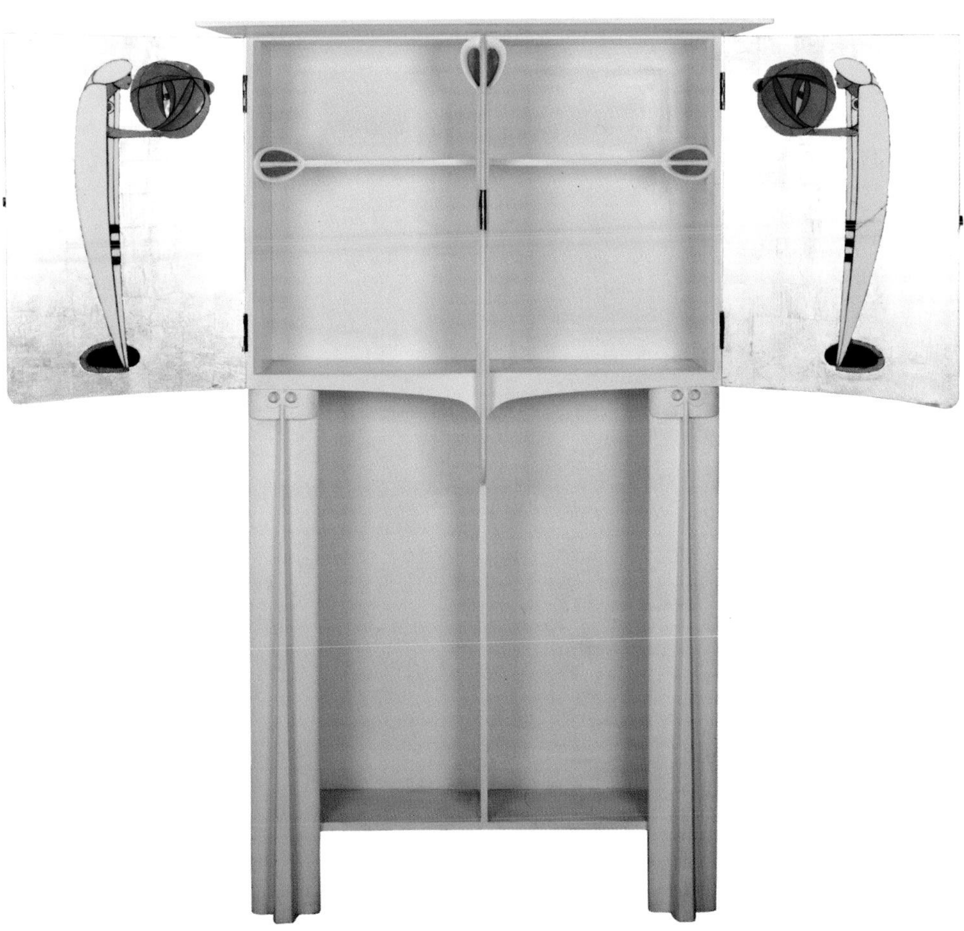

Mackintosh, Margaret Macdonald

Deutsche Kunst und Dekoration, 1902

The work of Margaret Macdonald is often overshadowed by that of her husband, Charles Rennie Mackintosh. Her work, however, was influential in the development of the Art Nouveau movement and Mackintosh himself always acknowledged the huge contribution she made to the success of his architectural designs. Born near Wolverhampton, Margaret Macdonald eventually settled in Scotland, after her family moved to Glasgow in around 1890. With her sister Frances (1873–1921), Macdonald studied at the Glasgow School of Art, which had a reputation for progressive art and for encouraging female artists. Macdonald diversified into many arenas; she was skilled in gesso work (the use of plaster of Paris, or gypsum, in painting or bas-relief), repoussé metalwork (metalwork that is raised in relief after being hammered from behind), watercolours, oil, fabric design and interior design. Margaret Macdonald's work was known across Europe and her posters were exhibited at the Munich exhibition centre, Glaspalast, in 1899 alongside work by Mackintosh, Lalique, Carl Fabergé (1846–1920) and Henry van de Velde. Mackintosh said of his wife 'I had talent, she had genius'.

Art journals, such as *Dekorative Kunst* and *Deutsche Kunst and Dekoration*, proliferated in the 1890s, helping to further the Art Nouveau movement.

RELATED WORK

The May Queen by Margaret Macdonald, 1900

Margaret Macdonald Mackintosh *Born* 1864 Tipton, England

Died 1933

Künstlerische Kostüme • Porzellane • Fotogr. Porträts • Buchgewerbe.

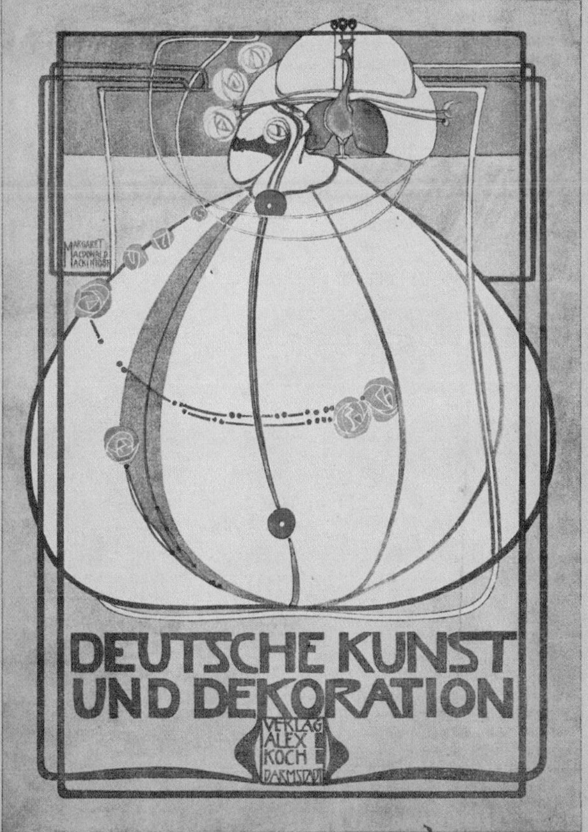

V. JAHRG. HEFT 8. MAI 1902. EINZELPREIS M. 2.50.

Wagner, Otto

St Leopold's Church of the Steinhof Asylum (*Kirche Am Steinhof*), 1902–07

Vienna at the turn of the century enjoyed the benefits of a progressive culture that supported avant-garde art and architecture. Otto Wagner was born in Vienna and studied at the Academy of Fine Arts, becoming a highly influential in the development of modern architectural styles and methods. He believed that architecture should be conducted using modern construction techniques and modern materials. With his students, Josef Hoffmann (1870–1956), Joseph Olbrich and others, Wagner contributed to the Secessionist movement in 1897 as it separated from the conservative school. The influence of this Modernist movement was not only felt in Austria, but throughout Europe and beyond.

St Leopold's Church of the Steinhof Asylum was designed and built by Wagner for the Lower Austrian Institution and Sanatorium. Although built of brick, the walls were sheathed in gleaming white marble and its copper dome was gilded. Situated on a hillside in the Vienna woods and perched above the city, the building must have made a spectacular sight. Koloman Moser designed a large feature window made of glass mosaic.

CREATED

Vienna

MOVEMENT

Secession

RELATED WORK

Post Office Bank by Otto Wagner, 1903

Otto Wagner *Born* 1841 Vienna, Austria

Died 1918

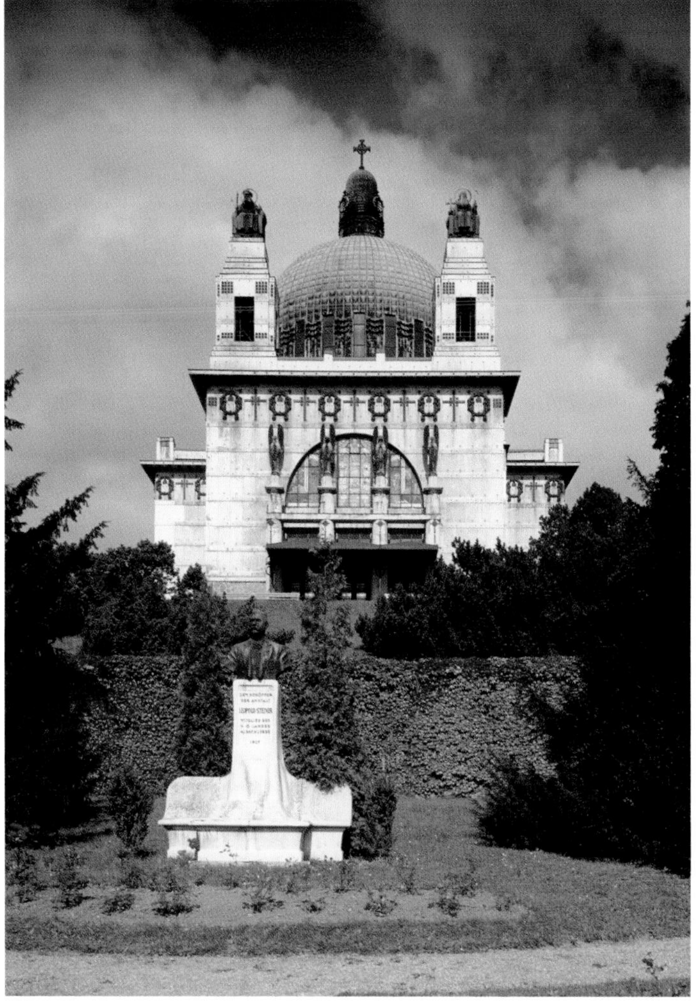

Serrurier-Bovy, Gustave

Three-fold stained screen

Gustave Serrurier-Bovy (1858–1910), born in Liège, was one of Belgium's finest Art Nouveau designers. He studied design and architecture in his home town of Liège and was particularly influenced by the work of John Ruskin (1819–1900), William Morris and Eugène-Emmanuel Viollet-le-Duc. In 1884 he established an interior design and furniture shop in Liège and sold his own furniture and imported wares. Following the success of this outlet, he was able to set up branches in Paris and Brussels.

In 1894 Serrurier-Bovy became a founding member of the Salon de l'Esthétique in Brussels and exhibited there and at other major exhibitions in Europe. With Henry van de Velde he contributed to the Congo Pavilion at the Universal Exhibition in Brussels in 1897. In 1900 he exhibited at the great world fair that dominated the French artistic cultural scene, the Exposition Universelle. Serrurier-Bovy's *Pavillon Bleu* restaurant was an extravagant Art Nouveau exhibit with a flamboyant interior, decorated with friezes embellished with bold curves and metal arabesques. Although renowned for the *Pavillon Bleu* restaurant, which was a fine example of unrestrained and imaginative Art Nouveau architecture, Serrurier-Bovy also designed furniture and metalwork.

MEDIUM

Wood and stained glass

RELATED WORK

Pavillon Bleu restaurant by Gustave Serrurier-Bovy, 1900

Gustave Serrurier-Bovy *Born* 1858 Liège, Belgium

Died 1910

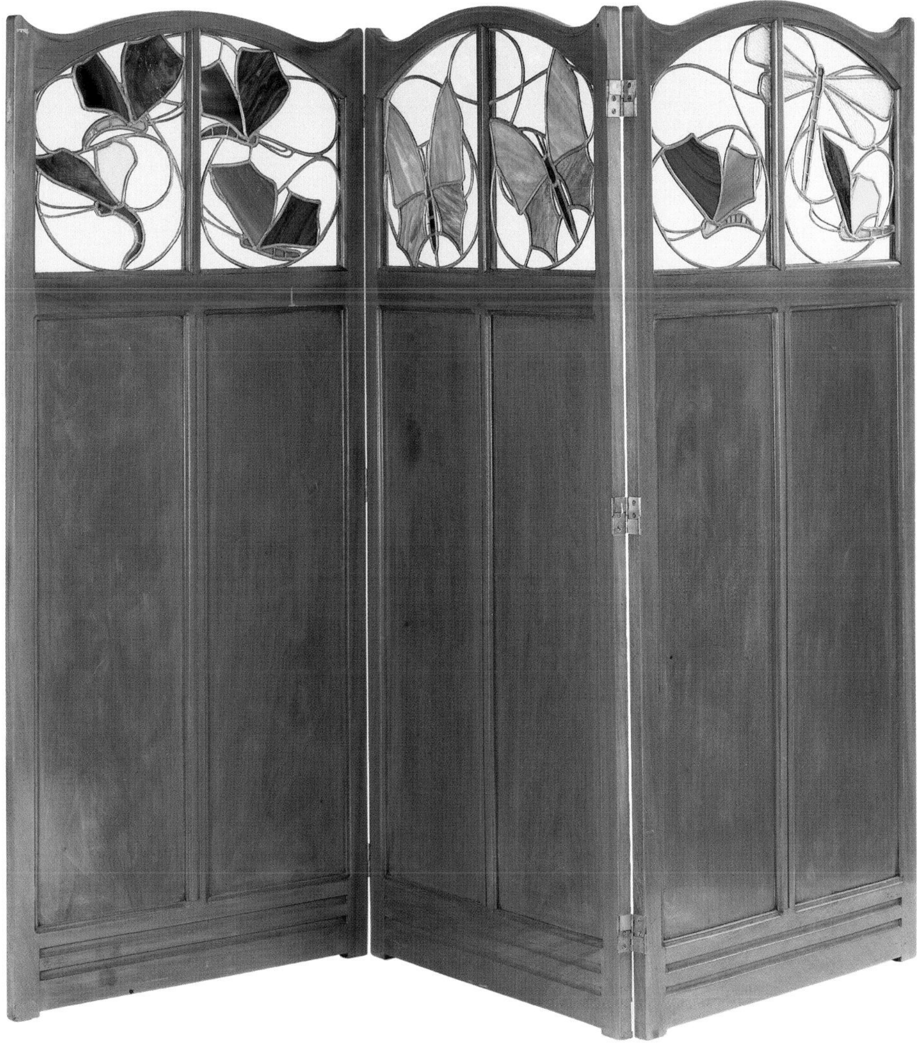

Gaudí, Antonio

Wooden corner seat from the dining room of the Casa Battló, 1904–06

One of the defining characteristics of Art Nouveau is, ironically, its sheer diversity. Although it covered a relatively short time span, the movement successfully announced a whole-hearted rejection of endless recycling and rehashing of old styles. In renouncing stale ideas, the Art Nouveau movement was receptive to all original suggestions for the applied arts. Nowhere is this more evident than in the highly individual work of Antonio Gaudí (1852–1926).

Gaudí was born in Catalonia and spent most of his working life designing in or around Barcelona. He blended elements of Continental Art Nouveau with the local Gothic architecture in his home region of Catalonia. A proud and independent region, Catalonia has always maintained its sense of individuality and separateness from the rest of Spain. Its distinctive architecture, both pre and post Gaudí, reflects this individuality. Gaudí revived the local Gothic style but added fantasy, a voluptuous sense of colour and an unrestrained love of curves and asymmetry. The results of this vision were a collection of extraordinary buildings that seem organic, appearing to merge into nature without boundary.

CREATED

Catalonia

MEDIUM

Wood

RELATED WORK

Sagrada Familia cathedral by Antonio Gaudí (unfinished)

Antonio Gaudí *Born* 1852 Reus, Spain

Died 1926

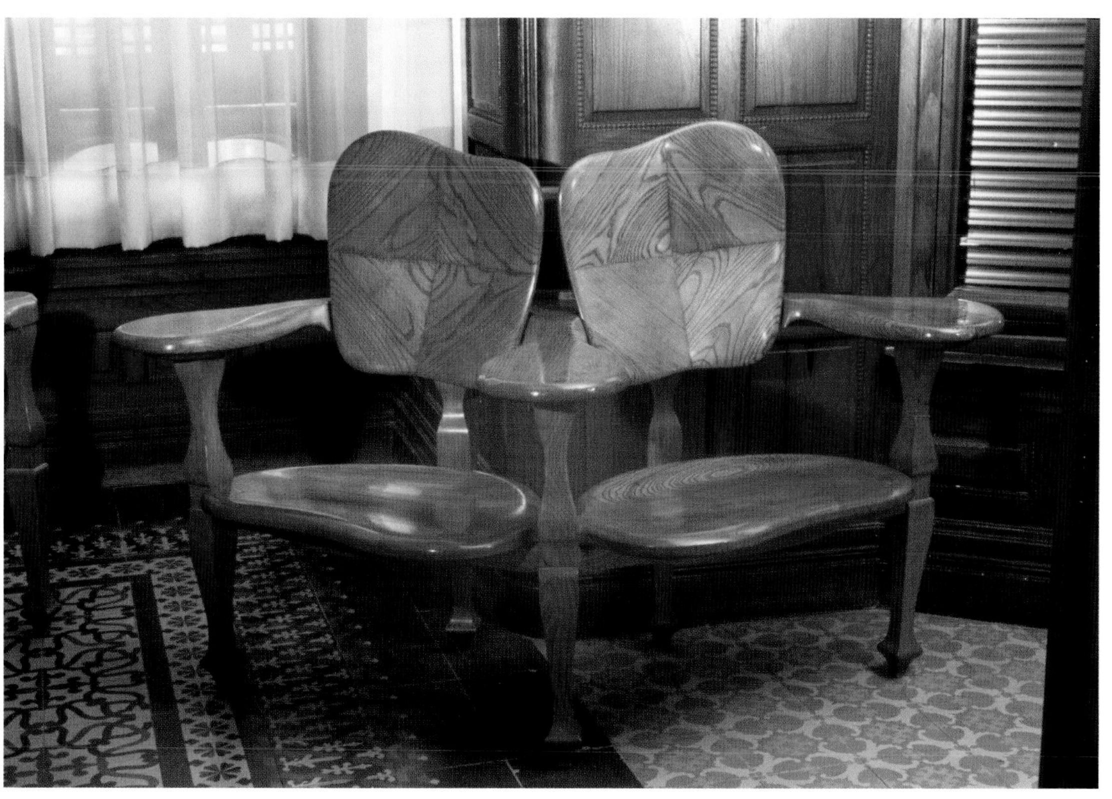

Hoffmann, Josef

Tea service, *c.* 1905

In the work of Josef Hoffmann one can see the future of design in the twentieth century. Born in Moravia, he studied and worked in Vienna at a time when the city was alive with innovation and radical change and, with his contemporaries, Hoffmann embraced modernity and developed a new aesthetic that continued to bloom well into the Art Deco era. Hoffmann trained under the great Otto Wagner, one of the few designers of the 'old school' who was able to shrug off the stagnant historicism that pervaded Vienna until the 1890s. Wagner applied new techniques and forms in architecture, applying his own maxim that 'Nothing that is not practical can be beautiful'. Under this premise, Hoffmann produced one of the most important buildings of the era: the Palais Stoclet in Brussels.

Hoffmann was appointed Professor of Architecture at the Viennese *Kunstgewerbeschule* (School of Arts and Crafts) in 1899 and he was responsible for decorating and furnishing a room at the Paris Exhibition of 1900. In 1903 he was a founding member of the *Wiener Werkstätte* in Vienna: a community that aimed to broaden public interests in luxury arts and crafts.

MEDIUM

Silver-gilt

MOVEMENT

Secession

RELATED WORK

Teapot designed for the Paris Exhibition, 1937 by Gustav Beran

Josef Hoffmann *Born* 1870 Pirnitz, Moravia

Died 1956

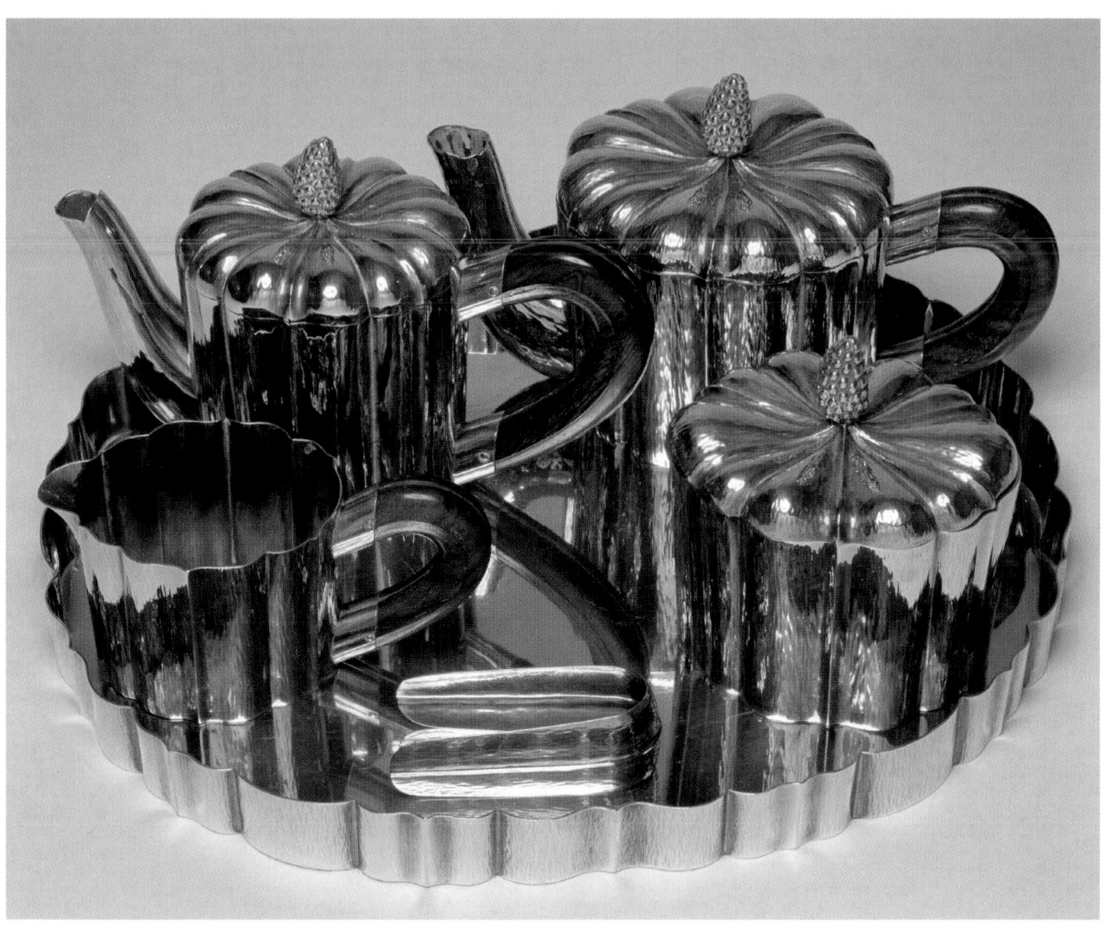

Klimt, Gustav

Fulfilment from the *Stoclet Frieze*, *c.* 1905–09

In Vienna, artists who sought to distance themselves from historicism and tradition formed an avant-garde, experimental group called the Secession, the Viennese interpretation of the Art Nouveau. Austrian artist Gustav Klimt led this organization from 1897 until 1905. Klimt's work is typical of the profound historical and ideological changes that were taking place at the end of the century, although his output was atypical in terms of style and effect. Klimt had an aesthetic ideology and understood why art needed to explore deeply into emotion and existentialism and break free of all contemporary conventions in order to do so. He achieved this by creating extraordinarily decorative murals and paintings, often lavishly coated in gold.

Klimt's most experimental work dealt with the themes of the subconscious, impulses and desires, and they aroused high feelings amongst the public and art critics. Nevertheless he received commissions for the University of Vienna and the Palais Stoclet in Brussels.

CREATED

Brussels

MEDIUM

Tempera and watercolour

MOVEMENT

Secession

RELATED WORK

The Three Ages of Woman by Gustav Klimt 1905

Gustav Klimt *Born* 1862 Baumgarten, Austria

Died 1918

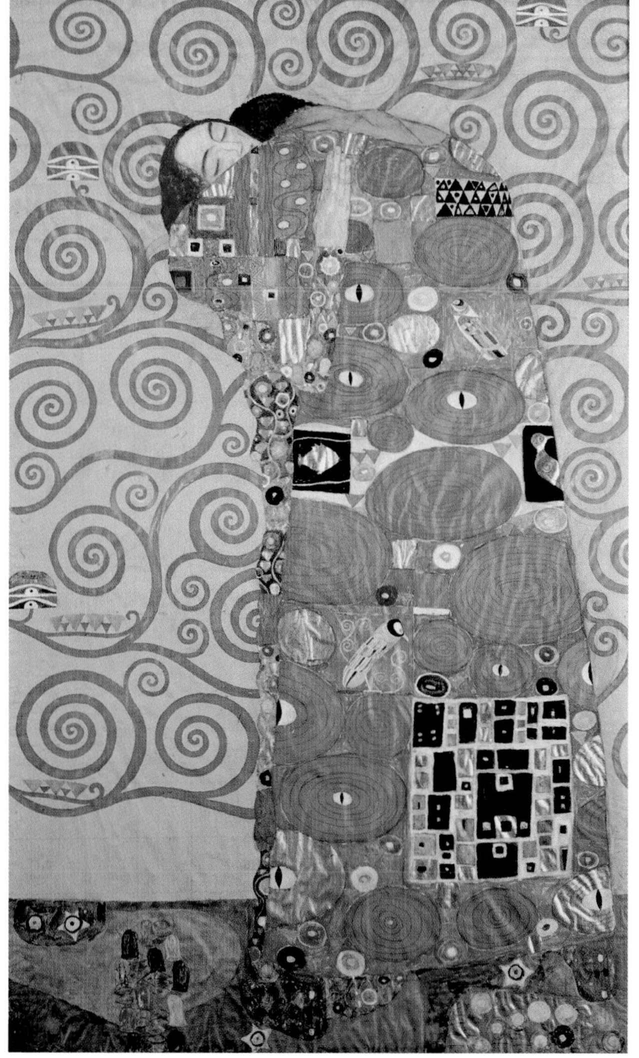

Behrens, Peter

Pitcher, *c.* 1907

Courtesty of Indianapolis Museum of Art, USA, Harold Victor Decorative Arts Fund/www.bridgeman.co.uk/© DACS 2005

Art Nouveau was a complex cultural movement; although it lasted only a brief time, from around 1890 to 1914, its influence on modern twentieth-century design was considerable. The notion that ordinary people should have access to design that not only reflected functionality, but was intrinsically beautiful too, emerged during the Arts and Crafts movement in Britain. This concept of beautiful objects developed into curves and arabesques, notable particularly in Belgian architecture, and the use of natural themes for decoration and ornamentation. In Scotland, Mackintosh restrained the lavishness of the early Art Nouveau idiom and introduced a cleaner, more geometric view. In Germany, a more practical approach was applied: *Jugendstil* artists and architects were amongst the first to propose the idea that embracing, rather than rejecting, manufacturing processes was the way to democratize the applied arts.

Peter Behren's (1868–1940) roots lay in *Jugendstil*, but his work transcended the confines of the Art Nouveau aesthetic. He became the first industrial designer of the twentieth century and his work demonstrates how good design can suit industrial mass production.

MEDIUM

Salt-glazed stoneware, blue cobalt decoration and pewter lid

MOVEMENT

Jugendstil

RELATED WORK

Electric kettle for AEG by Peter Behrens, 1908–09

Peter Behrens *Born* 1868 Hamburg, Germany

Died 1940

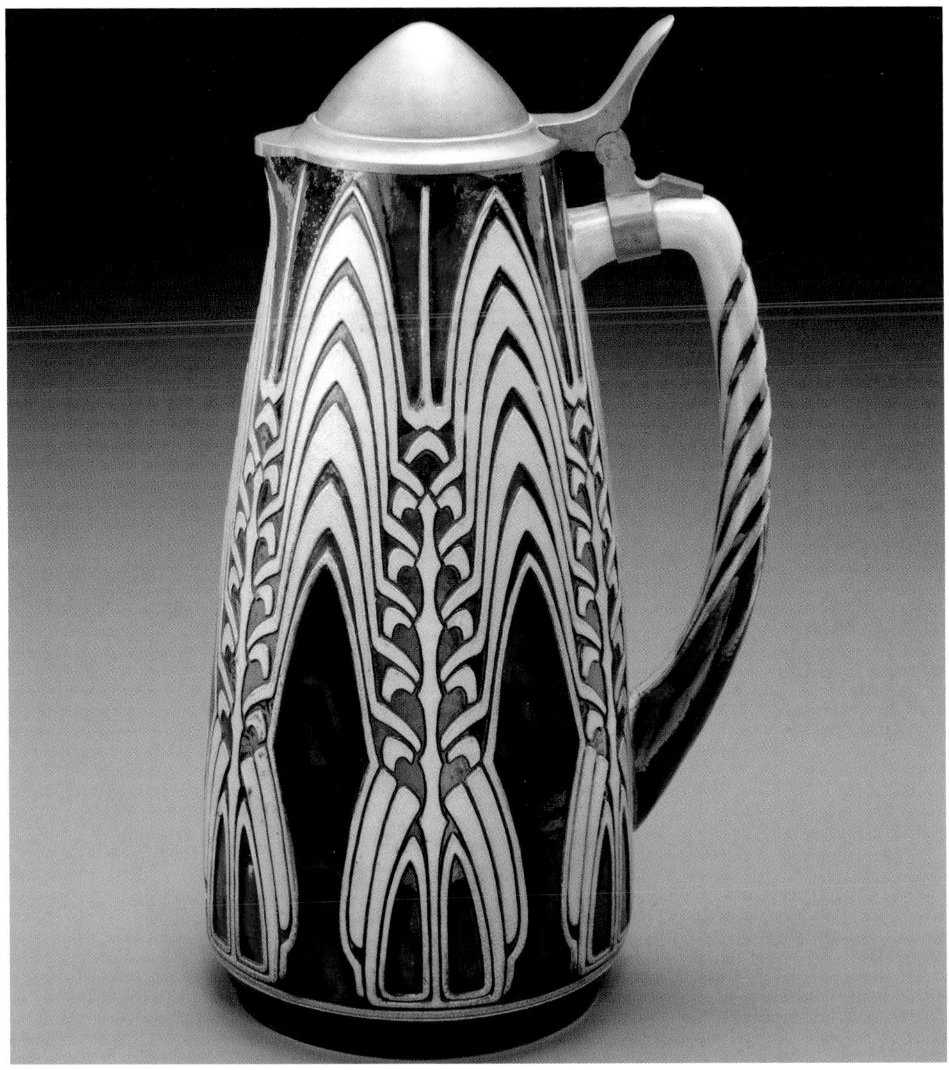

Art Nouveau

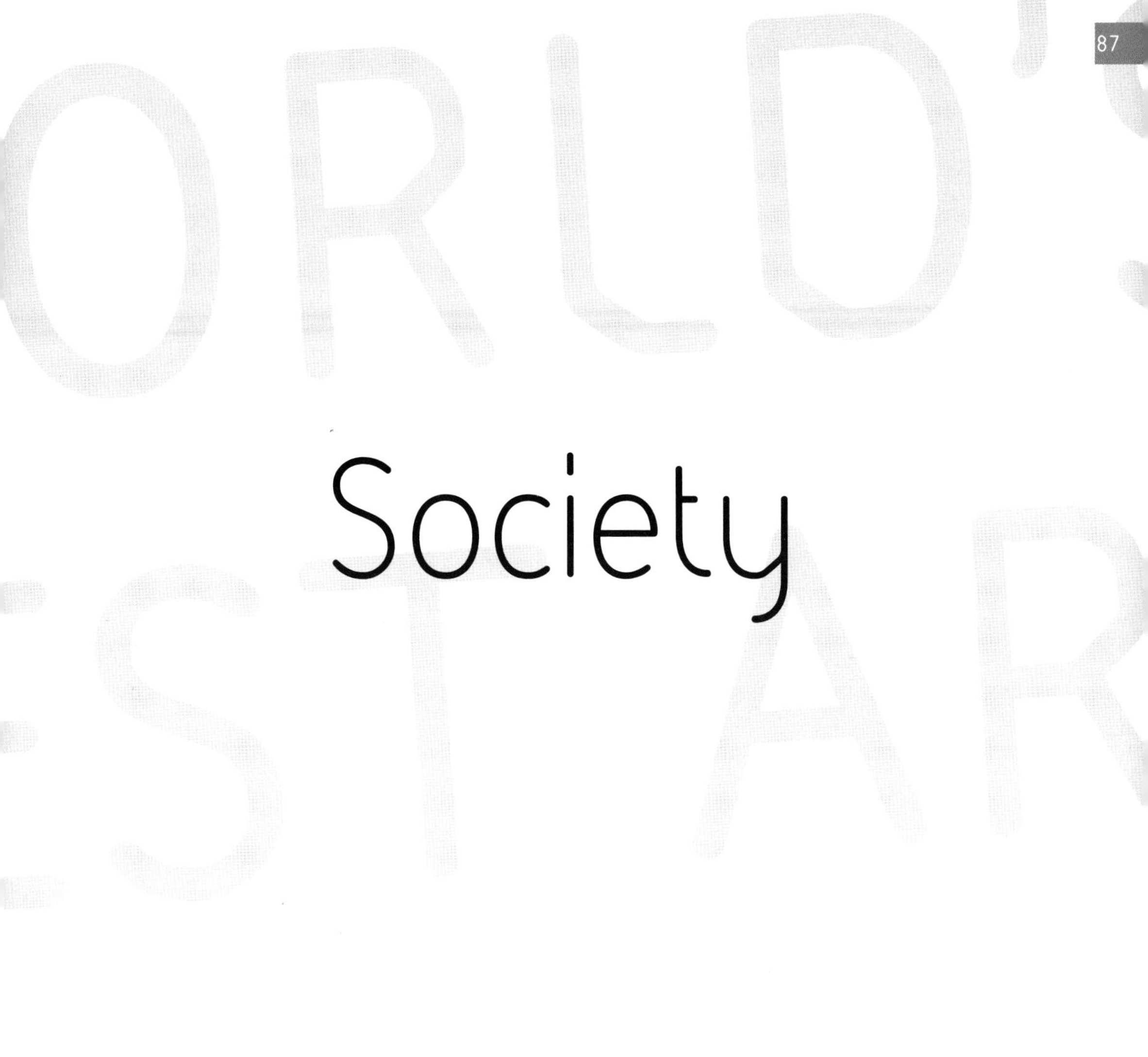

Society

Horta, Victor

View of the exterior of the Hôtel Tassel, Brussels, 1892–93

Belgium was a wealthy, colonial country at the end of the nineteenth century, ruled by Leopold II. It had taken over large areas of the Congo River basin and eventually formed a region called the Congo Free State in 1885, of which Leopold was made sovereign. Through forced labour, acts of great brutality and other atrocities, the region produced vast quantities of rubber, ivory and minerals, bringing wealth to Belgium and extreme hardship and political instability to the Congo, which remain to this day. It is now independent: the Democratic Republic of Congo.

Empowered by wealth, Leopold sought to consolidate his small nation's independence in a turbulent Europe. Belgium had remained neutral through the Franco-Prussian war of 1870–71, but as the strength of its neighbours increased Belgium needed to reinforce its own identity. One small yet significant way to achieve this aim was to build and develop its major city, Brussels. Large architectural projects were commissioned and Victor Horta (1861–1947), born in Ghent, was the beneficiary of many such projects. The Hôtel Tassel was one of Horta's first commissions.

CREATED

Brussels

MEDIUM

Architecture

RELATED WORK

Hôtel Deprez-van de Velde by Victor Horta, 1895

Victor Horta *Born* 1861 Ghent, Belgium

Died 1947

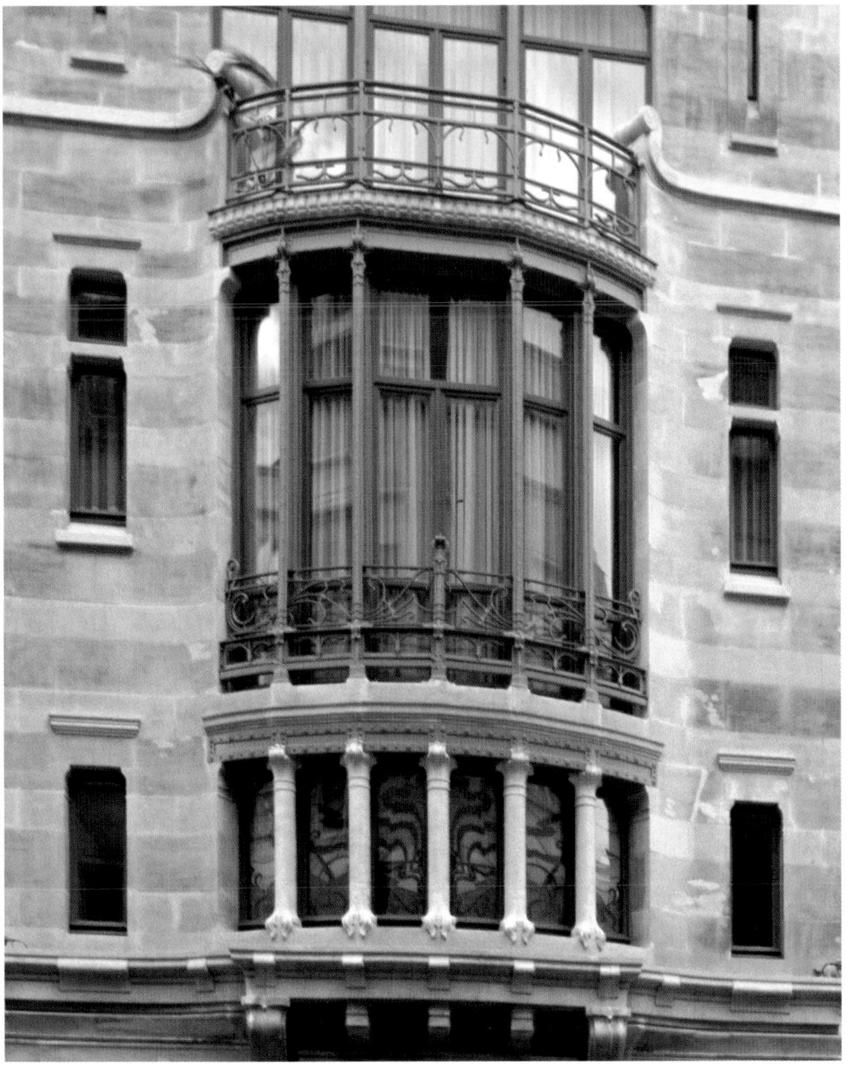

Horta, Victor

Partial view of the façade of the Musée Horta, Brussels, 1898

Victor Horta's architectural projects combined two almost diametric design aesthetics of the Art Nouveau movement. The English reforms in design rested heavily on the Arts and Crafts movement, which advocated the handcrafted medium and aimed to bring quality workmanship to all, while improving the craftsperson's lot by elevating their status to artists. The Neo-Rococo style, popular in mainland Europe, was more grand, elaborate and expensive, although there was a large market for poor machine-made imitations. Horta's designs included elements of both schools; he combined elitist Rococo ornamentation, industrially produced materials and handcrafted, expensive finishes.

The Musée Horta was originally the architect's home and studio. Built between 1898 and 1901, the design fully integrated the décor and the design of the house; structural elements such as metal arches were left exposed as features. The rooms opened directly on to the staircase, which was flooded with light from a glazed skylight. The effect was one of tranquility, beauty and an entirely modern sophistication.

CREATED

Brussels

MEDIUM

Architecture

RELATED WORK

Meeting Hall in Brussels by Victor Horta, 1896–99

Victor Horta *Born* 1861 Ghent, Belgium

Died 1947

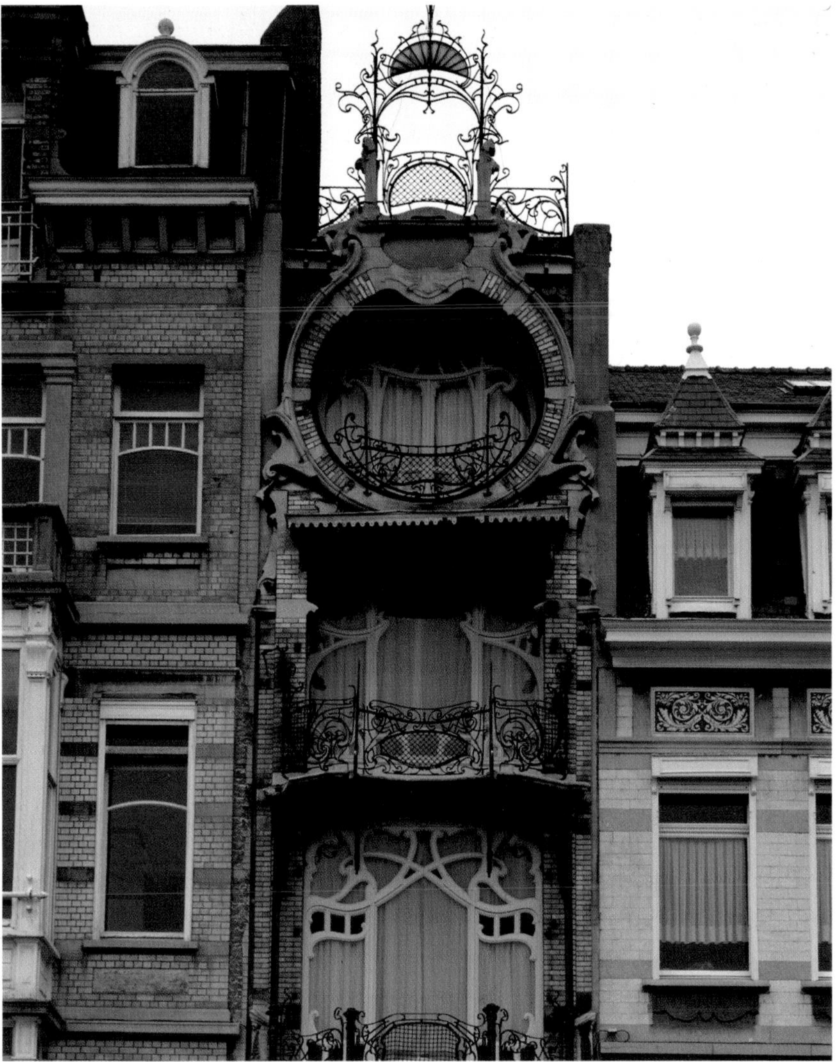

Horta, Victor

The dining room at the Hôtel Solvay, Brussels, *c.* 1894

Horta's view of architecture caused him to bring the sinuous lines of Art Nouveau into three-dimensions. The use of metal as a support enabled him to do away with some load-bearing interior walls and allow the movement of light through the interior. These supports were often left visible and ornamentation in metalwork decorates the walls, but also projects into the living space. Light fittings are a continuation of the decorative theme established by the wrought iron and, from every angle, throw light into the room. Thanks to the combination of windows and electrical light, Horta was able to play with colours and create different effects of tone and shade according to the time of day.

Large pieces of furniture are firmly rooted in their positions; wherever possible Horta avoided putting legs on furniture, preferring instead to give the illusion that they were part and parcel of the architectural structure. The sideboard and fireplace in the dining room of the Horta House are firmly set into the building and fulfill Horta's ideal of creating a unified décor and structure.

CREATED

Brussels

MEDIUM

Architecture and interior design

RELATED WORK

Grand Bazar Anspach, Brussels by Victor Horta, 1903

Victor Horta *Born* 1861 Ghent, Belgium

Died 1947

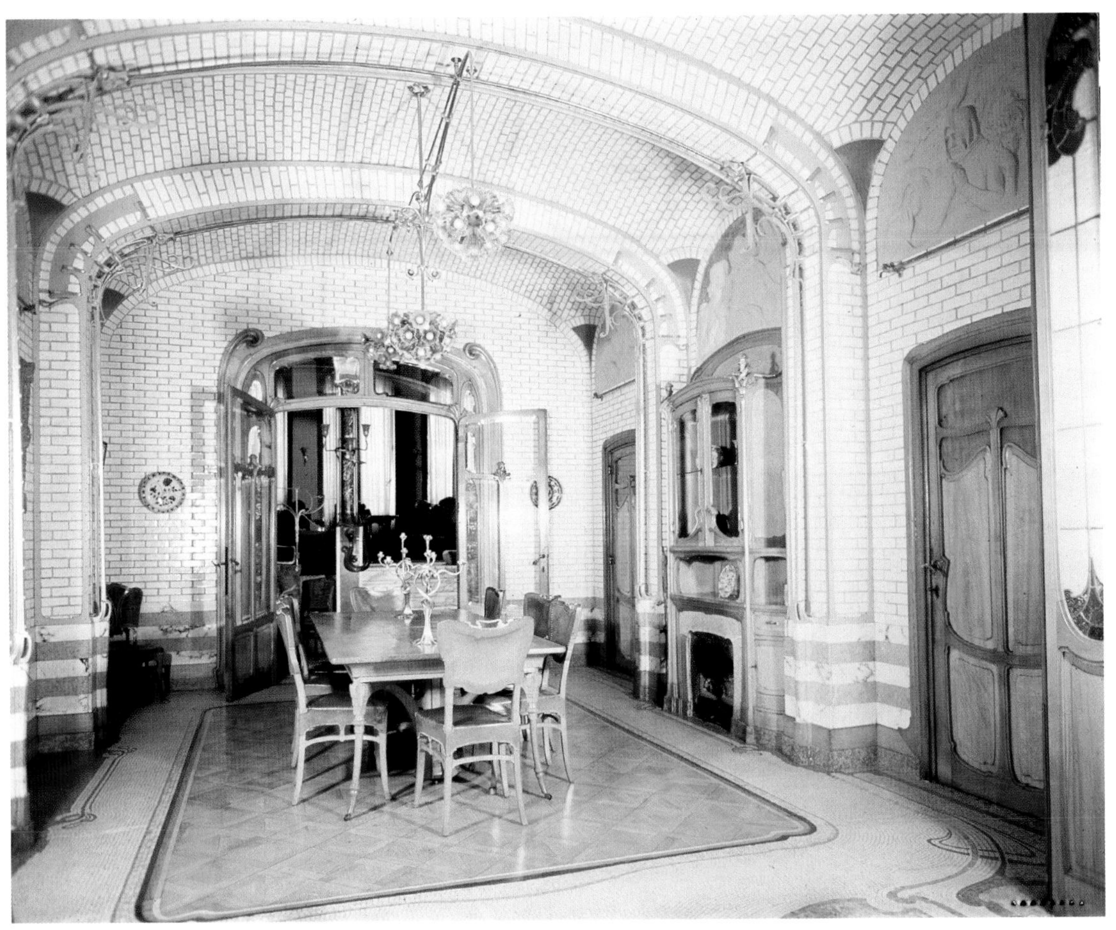

Horta, Victor

Clock, *c.* 1895

As the nineteenth century came to an end artist-decorators and architects had an entirely new set of tools, textures and techniques at their disposal, the results of industrialization and new mechanical processes that had been developed during the Victorian period. Victor Horta was one of the first architects to make full use of this new repertoire; his contribution to the media of glass and iron was particularly innovative and influential. Towards the end of his career Horta built in concrete: a relatively new material that became enormously popular later in the twentieth century.

Horta used the many components of Art Nouveau to create an entirely new architectural style for both the exterior and interior of a building. This clock is a good example: Horta took iron, a strong, sturdy and imposing material, and moulded it into feminine, intricate, delicate and fluid shapes, creating a contrast between material and form. Iron was a common feature of his interiors; it was used as a structural support but was often exposed, to harmonize with featured artefacts such as light fittings, clocks or wrought-iron banisters.

MEDIUM

Bronze

RELATED WORK

Ironwork and glass skylights at Hôtel van Eetvelde, Brussels by Victor Horta

Victor Horta *Born* 1861 Ghent, Belgium

Died 1947

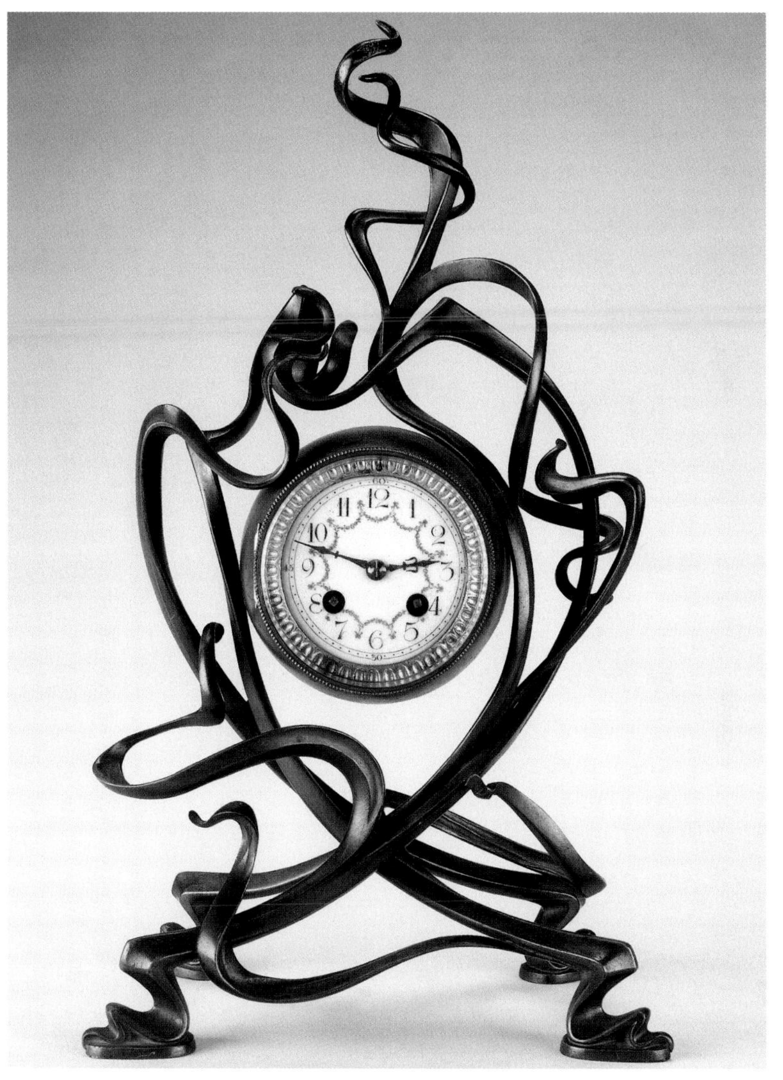

van de Velde, Henry

Poster for the Tropon Food Company, 1898

At the *fin-de-siècle* there was a general consensus that change was needed in the field of decorative arts. This meant that designers needed to take control of their domain, master different skills and media and create a synthesis between fine art and design. How they would do that, however, was a subject for much debate.

Supporters of the influential Arts and Crafts movement of William Morris (1834–96) aspired to a Utopian dream of socialism; a world where, as Morris wrote in 1877, the decorative arts fulfiled noble hopes, 'To give people pleasure in the things they must perforce use, that is one great office of decoration; to give pleasure in the things they must perforce make, that is the other use of it'. The Aesthetic viewpoint was radically different. It maintained that art need achieve no purpose other than to be beautiful. If creating art for art's sake left it beyond the means of ordinary people so be it. Van de Velde (1863–1957), like Morris, had socialist leanings. However, he aspired to bring good design to ordinary people and for the goods to be affordable, they needed to be industrially produced.

MEDIUM

Lithograph

RELATED WORK

Interior design for Havana Tobacco Company shop in Berlin by Henry van de Velde, 1899

Henry van de Velde *Born* 1863 Antwerp, Belgium

Died 1957

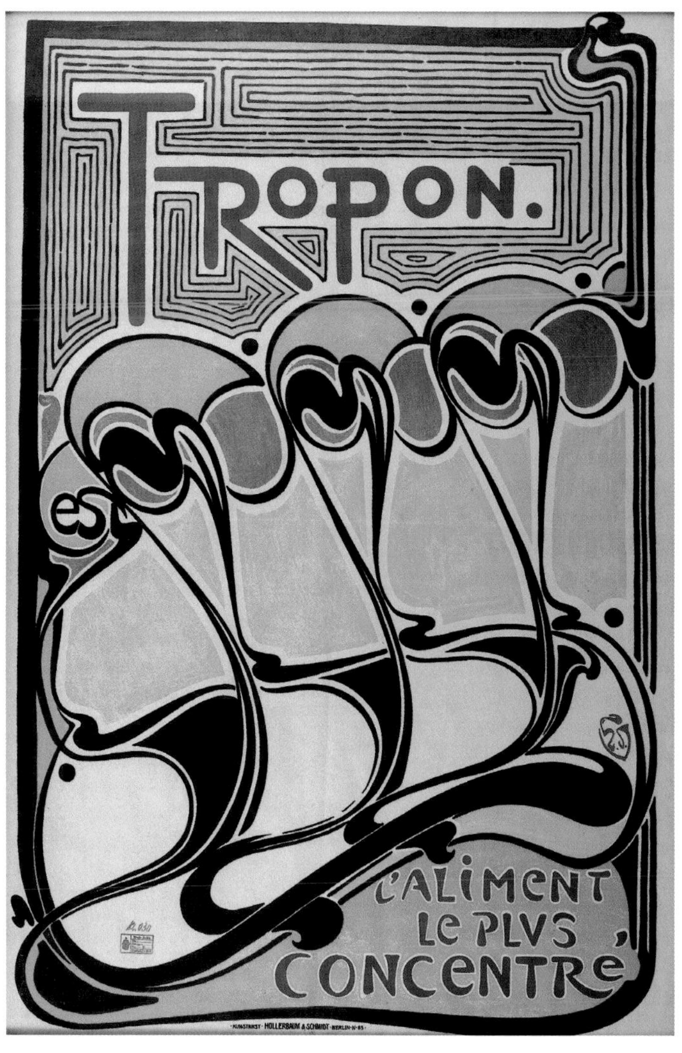
TROPON.
est
L'ALIMENT
LE PLUS
CONCENTRÉ
·KUNSTANST· HOLLERBAUM & SCHMIDT ·BERLIN·N·65·

van de Velde, Henry

Armoire, *c.* 1897

During the 1890s Brussels was the cultural and artistic centre of Europe, thanks to the work of numerous artists who had inhabited the city in the previous decade and established its reputation as an exciting arena for the avant-garde. Henry van de Velde was a Belgian designer, painter, artist and critic who belonged to the exhibition group Société des Vingt (Les Vingt or Les XX). His considerable contributions to the development of the Art Nouveau style include introducing it to a wider audience, particularly Germany.

Although he trained as a painter, in the 1890s van de Velde, influenced by the doctrines of John Ruskin (1819–1900) and William Morris, moved to other media, especially the decorative arts (including furniture design) and architecture. He left his native Belgium in 1900 and moved to Germany where he directed the School of Arts and Crafts, which eventually led to the emergence of the Bauhaus. Van de Velde was a founding member of the *Deutscher Werkbund*: a popular association that gathered the talents of artists, designers, architects and technicians in order to promote excellence in industrial production.

MEDIUM

Padouk, lilac-tinted glass and brass pulls

RELATED WORK

Bloemenwerf, Henry van de Velde's design for his own house, 1895

Henry van de Velde *Born* 1863 Antwerp, Belgium

Died 1957

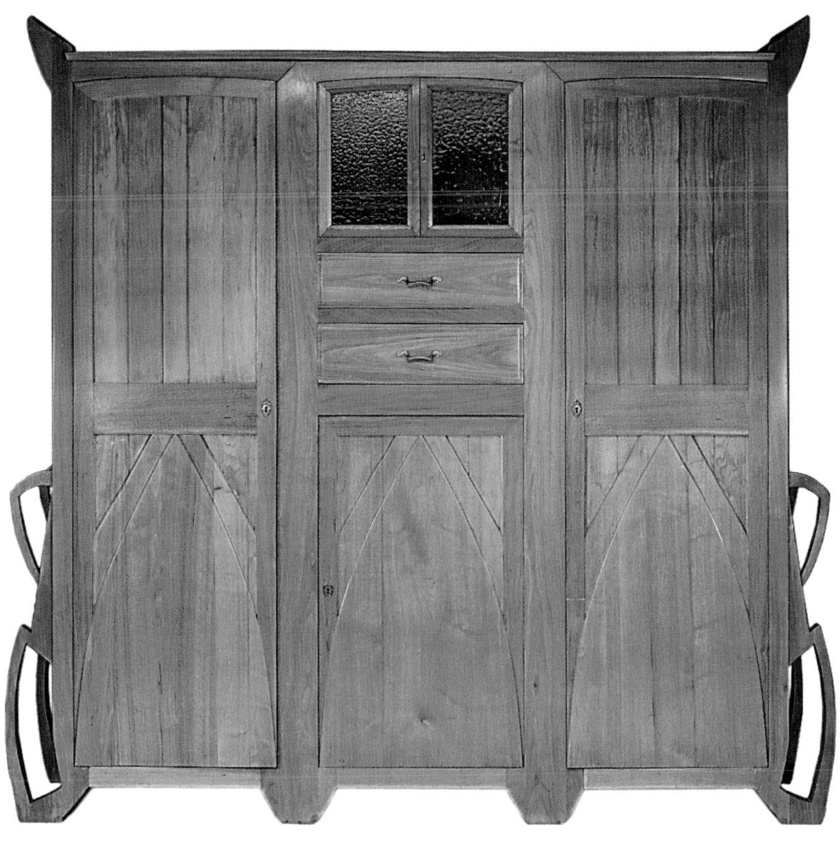

van de Velde, Henry

Fish knife and fork, 1903

Henry van de Velde was an accomplished designer who developed the Art Nouveau idiom of lines to great effect. Artists used lines in a new and exciting way for emphasis and expression; lines could control and unite form and shape within the decorative arts. Van de Velde explained it thus, '*Linie is eine kraft*' ('line is a force'), and he used lines in metalwork to express this idiom vibrantly and with sophistication. This aesthetic appealed to the European bourgeoisie, which delighted in the proliferation of retail outlets, especially department stores that dealt in luxury goods. Commercial organizations sold Art Nouveau goods to a discerning middle class and numerous art-related publications and exhibitions spread the word still further. A new era of entrepreneurship, combined with a proliferation of mechanisms for selling and publicizing luxury goods, served the market well.

Van de Velde established a design factory in a suburb of Brussels and produced jewellery and ornamental objects in silvered bronze. In 1900 he began to operate in Berlin and worked with the renowned goldsmith Theodor Müller to produce abstract items in silver of great quality.

CREATED

Berlin

MEDIUM

White metal

RELATED WORK

Candelabra in electro-plated bronze by Henry van de Velde, 1898–99

Henry van de Velde *Born* 1863 Antwerp, Belgium

Died 1957

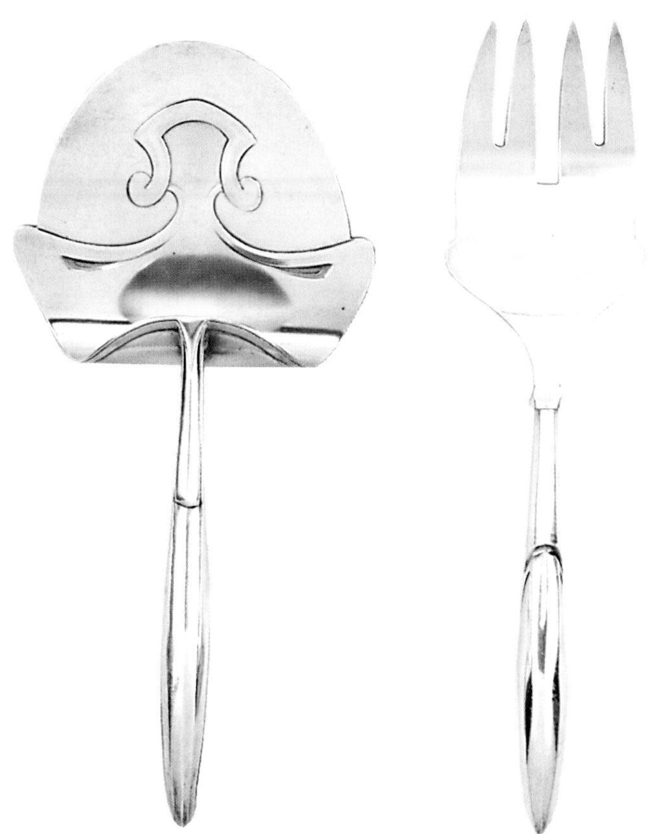

van de Velde, Henry

La Veillee des Anges textile hanging, 1893

Design at the end of the nineteenth century was perceived as a harmonious, unifying force and this applied to every element of an interior. Textiles were one particularly important element that was brought into the realm of Art Nouveau and adapted to suit this comprehensive approach. Textile designs passed between Britain and mainland Europe resulting in a cross-fertilization of ideas, but the designs of the Belgian painter Henry van de Velde, who worked in Belgium, Munich and Weimar, are now considered some of the finest of the era. They are redolent of pure Art Nouveau, or *Jugendstil* (as the movement was known in Germany), and the popular variations in style of the time. Van de Velde's work was commercially popular and his textile designs were manufactured across Europe.

This wall hanging by van de Velde is made in wool and silk and has been appliquéd by the artist and his aunt. Appliqué is a decorative technique in which pieces of contrasting or complementing fabric are overlaid and stitched. Its title translates as 'Angels wake'.

CREATED

Belgium

MEDIUM

Textile

RELATED WORK

Wallpaper in abstract pattern of sage green and pink by Henry van de Velde, 1895

Henry van de Velde *Born* 1863 Antwerp, Belgium

Died 1957

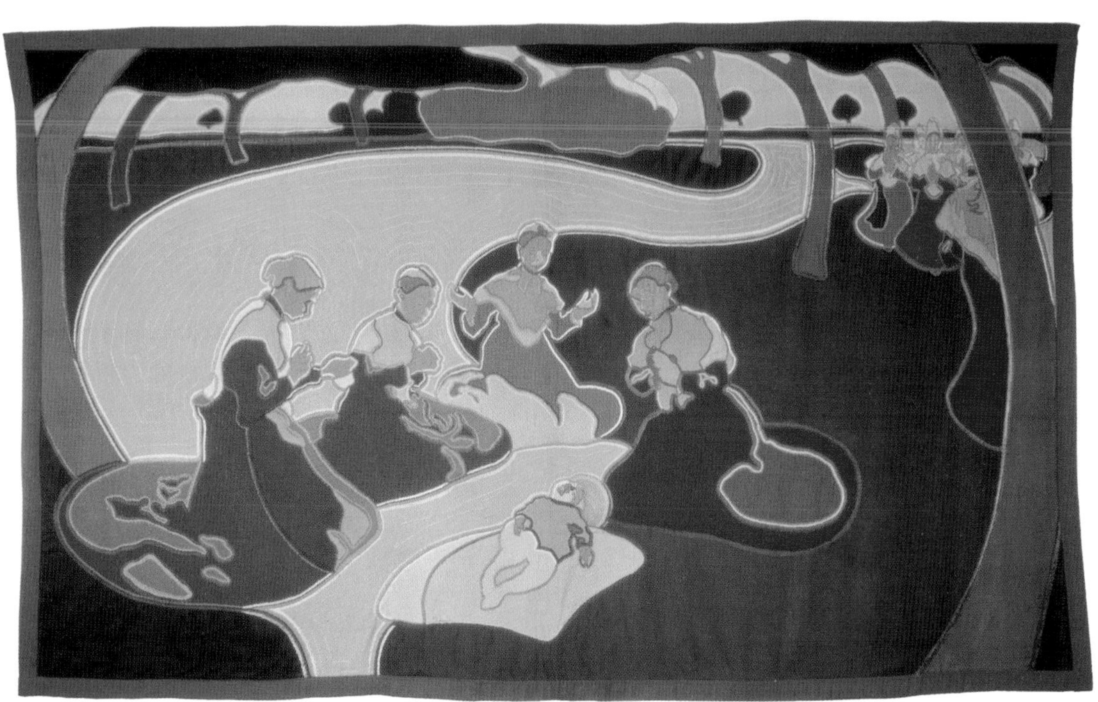

Guimard, Hector

Illustration of the entrance to Castel Béranger, 1894–98

Iron was seen as a contemporary metal and radical architects had no intention of hiding its dark, rustic qualities. The artist Paul Gauguin (1848–1903) had called for a new breed of architects who would have the engineering skill to create a new decorative art form using iron. He saw no need to hide iron behind masonry or paint: Victor Horta and Lyon-born Hector Guimard (1867–1942) shared this vision.

In Britain and Belgium architects preferred the fluidity of wrought iron, and the craftsmanship involved in producing it suited the Arts and Crafts philosophy. Hector Guimard admitted he was greatly affected by the work of Victor Horta, but he worked with both wrought and cast iron, mixing old and new techniques in his architectural projects. In the 1890s Guimard designed a block of 36 apartments at the Castel Béranger in Paris. He was given free rein and the result was an experimental façade that mixed urban and rustic influences. Guimard rejected decorative motifs from nature and instead relied on the interplay of lines to construct the first Art Nouveau house outside Belgium.

CREATED

Paris

MEDIUM

Architecture

RELATED WORK

Castel Henriette in Sèvres by Hector Guimard, 1903

Hector Guimard *Born* 1867 Lyon, France

Died 1942

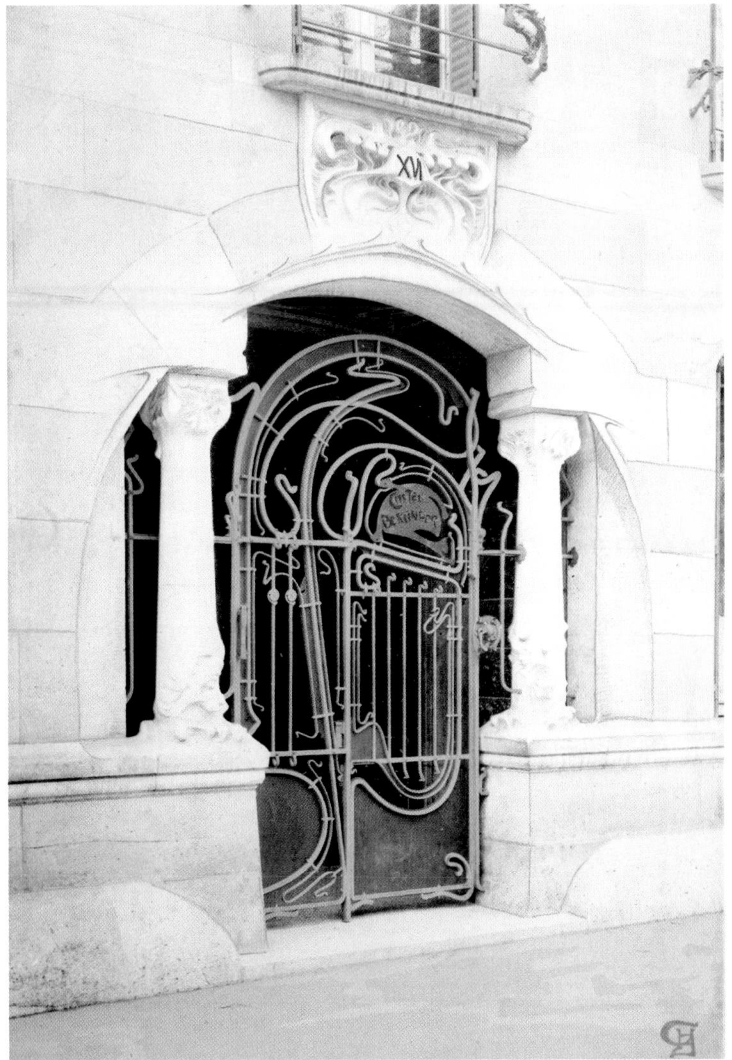

Guimard, Hector

Entry to the Metro Porte Dauphine, 1898–1901

In 1900 Paris staged a stupendous world fair: the Exposition Universelle. Millions were drawn to the lavish sights of splendid buildings, international exhibits and spectacular night-time illuminations. The Exposition aimed to demonstrate to the world that Paris had truly recovered from its ignominious siege during the Franco-Prussian war of 1870–71 and its exhibits were chosen to display progress achieved in art, industry and science. As one century melted away, a new one was beginning with panache.

The Exposition is now often associated with Art Nouveau, but although influential art dealer Siegfried Bing presented six interiors at the fair, it was not the dominant cultural style. Hector Guimard did not exhibit at the exposition but his Métro (underground train) designs were on display to the many visitors to the Fair and the city, and they have become a lasting testament to French Art Nouveau. Parisian officials recognized that a Métro system was needed in the growing city and invited designers to submit ideas for stations. Guimard's proposals were astonishingly innovative and practical. Formed from iron and glass they could be cheaply produced in pieces and erected. They quietly and elegantly proclaim their modernity and originality to this day.

CREATED

Paris

MEDIUM

Architecture (metalwork)

RELATED WORK

Monceau Station by Hector Guimard, 1898–1901

Hector Guimard *Born* 1867 Lyon, France

Died 1942

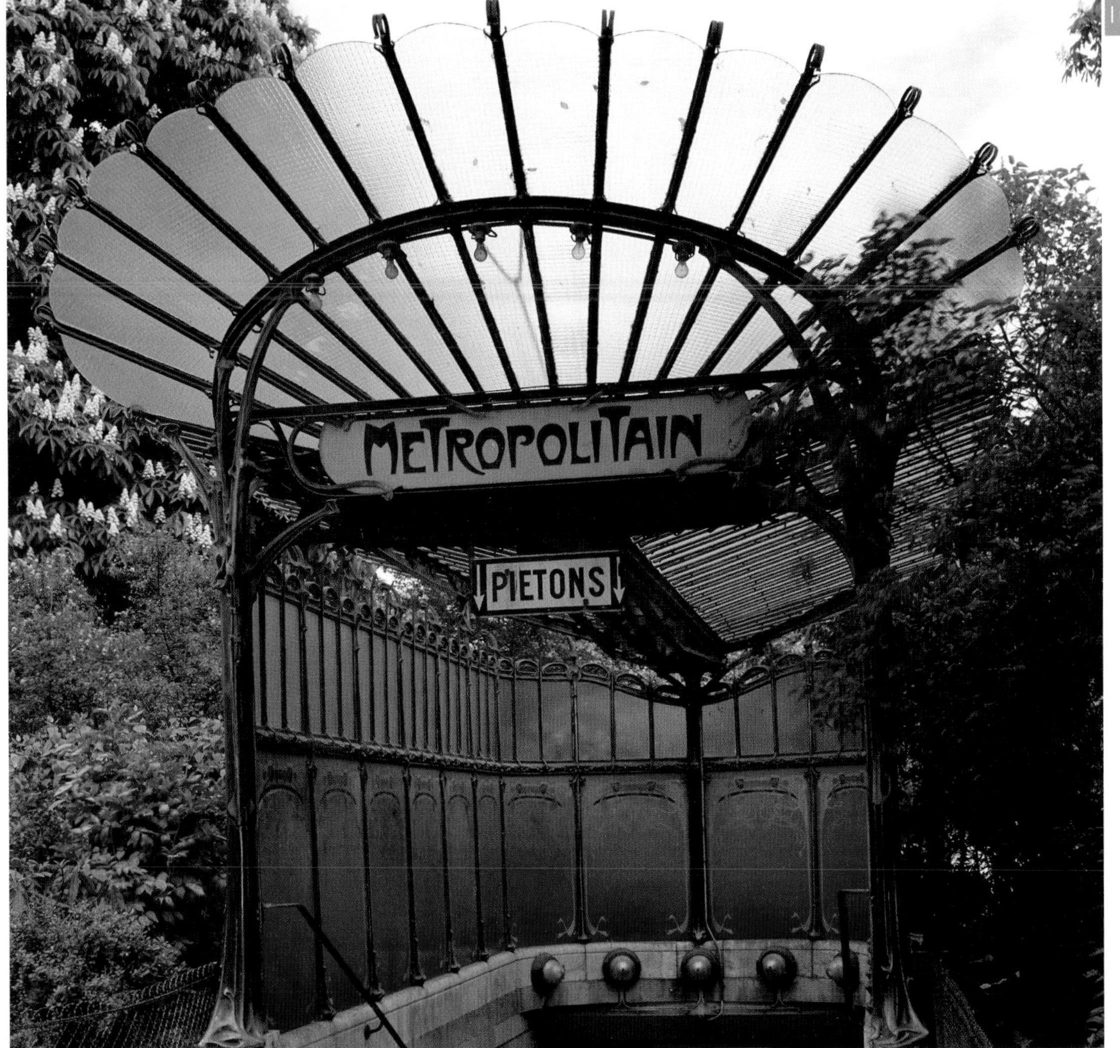
METROPOLITAIN
PIETONS

Guimard, Hector

Three-legged occasional table

The work of Victor Horta had a strong influence on Hector Guimard, as did the work of French architect Eugène-Emmanuel Viollet-le-Duc, who advocated an imaginative and adventurous use of iron and glass in buildings.

Like many other Art Nouveau designers, Guimard did not restrict his talents to one area. The prevailing philosophy was that a building, its contents and its occupants should be in harmony, and it therefore made sense for an architect to involve himself with interior design and furniture. In France designers were encouraged to draw on the elegant lines of eighteenth-century work and maintain the tradition of quality craftsmanship. French furniture designers who sought modernity managed to combine this respect for past skills and techniques with purity of form and sophistication. This three-legged table by Guimard carries the same strong and simple lines that appeared in his architecture, particularly in the ironwork of the Métro stations. The form is restrained in decoration and the tension in arrangement of the sinuous wooden legs and struts is almost palpable.

MEDIUM

Wood

RELATED WORK

Metal cup by Hector Guimard, 1900

Hector Guimard *Born* 1867 Lyon, France

Died 1942

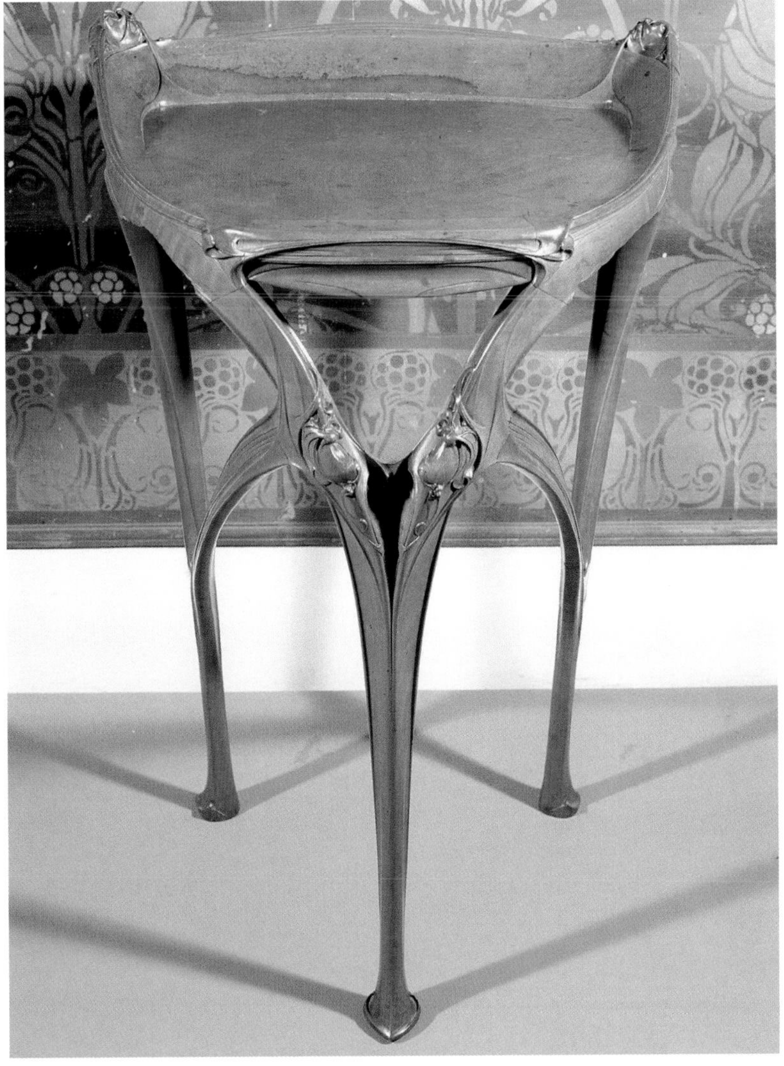

Guimard, Hector and Horta, Victor

Stopper top (Horta) and knife rest (Guimard), *c.* 1900

Artists and designers at the *fin-de-siècle* were in an unique situation. As one might expect at the end of a century, society was reviewing the achievements of previous years while looking forward with some trepidation to a new era. The world was changing at an ever-increasing rate and when Art Nouveau exploded on to the scene in the 1890s it epitomized the extravagance and modernity of the time. For some, the style marked the end of civilization and it was variously called 'revolting', 'unhealthy' and 'a disastrous epidemic'. The style overcame the critics and matured, aided by the growth of consumerism: for the first time in history a style was marketed internationally as a means of increasing industrial production and therefore national wealth.

Hector Guimard studied at the Ecole des Arts Décoratifs from 1882 to 1885 and then at the Ecole des Beaux Arts until 1889. In 1895 he visited Horta's Hôtel Tassel in Belgium and was hugely affected by the ingenuity of design he witnessed. The two architects continued to design buildings, but they also turned their attentions to the interiors and artefacts.

MEDIUM

Metal

RELATED WORK

Metal fittings for bedroom furniture by Georges de Feure, *c.* 1900

Hector Guimard *Born* 1867 Lyon, France

Died 1942

Victor Horta *Born* 1861 Ghent, Belgium

Died 1947

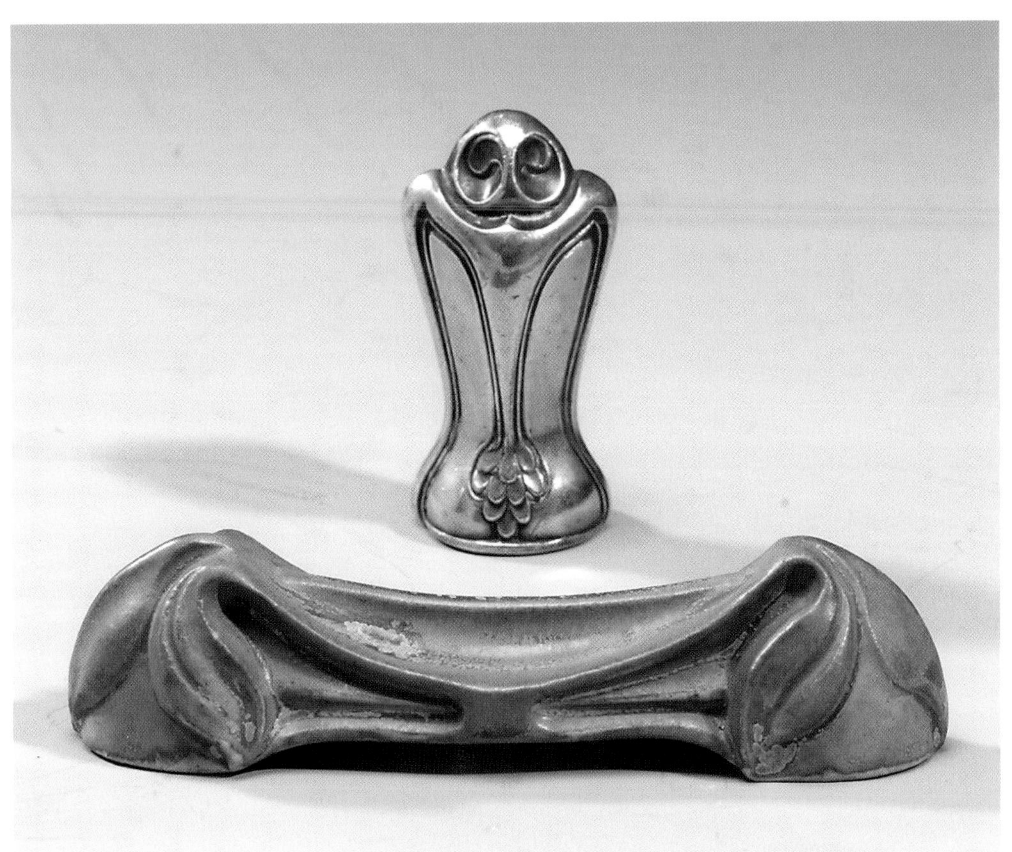

Tiffany Studios

Blue *Wisteria* table lamp

Art Nouveau proved itself to be a versatile and global style and the work of Louis Comfort Tiffany (1848–1933), who was born in New York, exemplifies these qualities. Tiffany managed to combine the design aesthetic of the Arts and Crafts movement with the business acumen of a modern industrialist. His glassware was created following years of experimentation with the medium and Tiffany and his team developed a technical prowess that was unrivalled. Yet the productions of the Tiffany Studios were also hugely popular, and although the glassware was expensive it was widespread.

North America at the end of the nineteenth century had a rapidly growing economy. It was a new continent that held vast wealth and its largely immigrant population celebrated their modernity and the new opportunities that faced them. Eschewing many of the traditional artistic practices of Europe, American society was ripe for artistic innovation and experimentation. Tiffany was to become American's foremost artistic envoy, introducing his nation's burgeoning cultural identity to Europe.

CREATED

New York

MEDIUM

Leaded glass and bronze

RELATED WORK

Poinsettia and *Lotus* lamps by Tiffany Studios

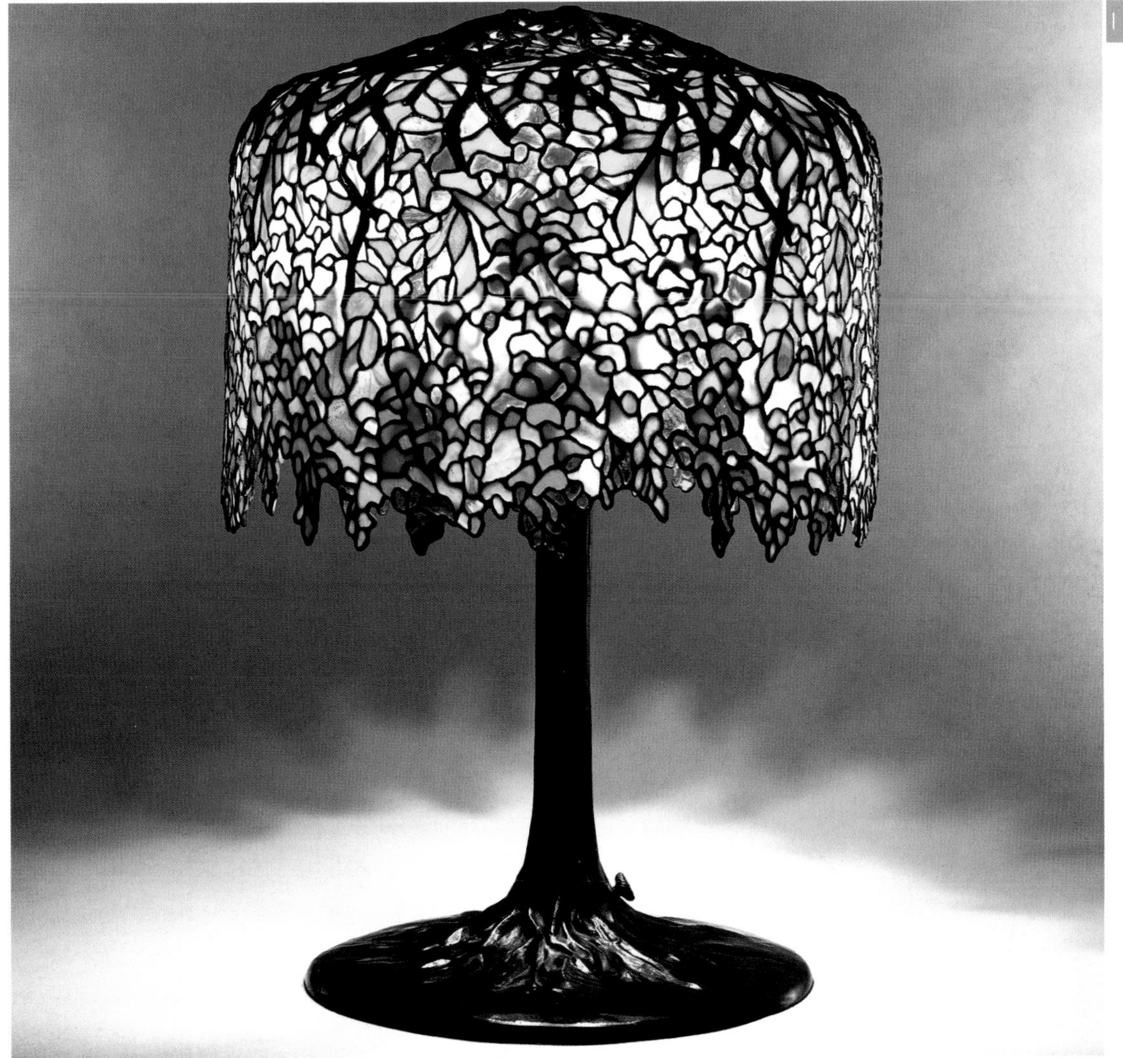

Tiffany Studios

Selection of Favrile glass, *c.* 1890

The work of Louis Comfort Tiffany reflected many of the influences affecting the society of the day. The family name was already associated with innovation; his father, Charles Louis Tiffany (1812–1902), was a jeweller and silversmith, who had established the firm Tiffany and Co. with branches in London, Paris and Geneva.

Siegfried Bing, the inspirational art dealer whose Parisian gallery L'Art Nouveau was to name an entire art movement, was a great supporter of Louis Tiffany and his work. Bing admired Tiffany's Favrile vases in particular and was impressed by the way that Tiffany had managed to incorporate design, pattern, texture and colour into the glass itself, without the traditional techniques of painting or etching. The decorations were no longer superficial, but become an intrinsic part of the artefact's form. Bing travelled extensively in the US and recognized that the newness of the nation contributed to its acceptance of modern art and techniques. He said of the Americans, 'they do not, as we (Europeans) do, make a religion of ... traditions. It is their rare privilege to make use of our aged maturity, adding to it the bursting energy of youth's prime'.

CREATED

New York

MEDIUM

Favrile glass

RELATED WORK

Tel el Amama vases in Egyptian style by Tiffany Studios

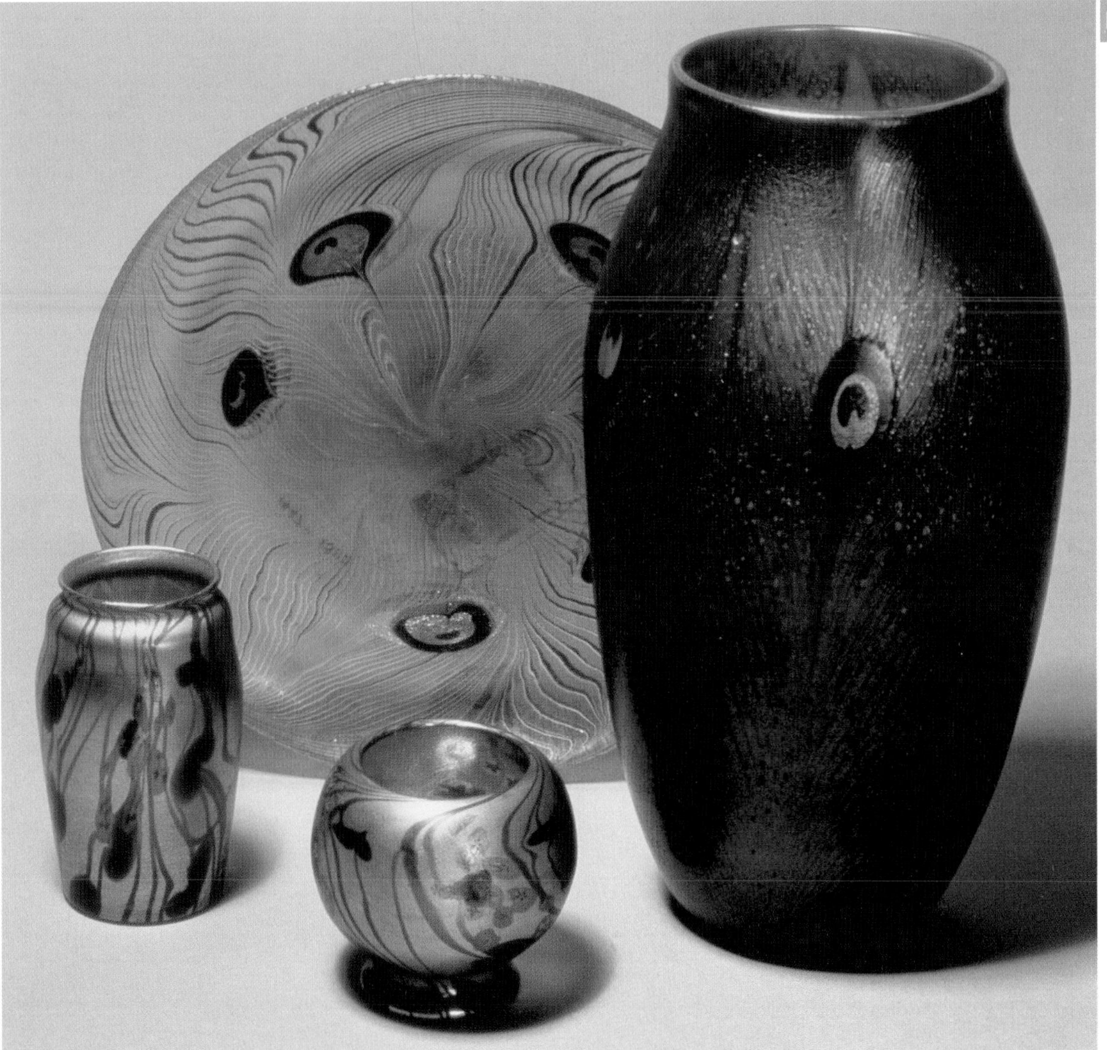

Tiffany Studios

Dragonfly table lamp

The *Dragonfly* table lamp displays all the vibrant hues and intricate design features that typify the work of Louis Comfort Tiffany. The Favrile glass was carefully coloured so that each piece was the exact shade required to emulate the gloriously loud and vibrant colours of the insect world.

As was the fashion at the time, Tiffany sought inspiration from nature for many of his designs. Typical motifs were peacocks, dragonflies, spiders' webs, feathers and the intricate patterns of leaves, tendrils and stalks. The flexibility afforded by the colour range of Favrile glass enabled Tiffany and his craftsmen to celebrate nature, but also allowed them to explore new and abstract patterns. Tiffany sought to combine form with decoration, so colour and pattern were intrinsic, not superficial. His lamps often demonstrated this unity of design, with the bases continuing the theme established by the shade. Louis Tiffany continued to work as an interior designer while his factory produced lamps and vases in Favrile glass. His output was enormous and by the end of the century Tiffany employed more than 100 craftsmen and women.

CREATED

New York

MEDIUM

Leaded glass, stone, bronze and blown glass

RELATED WORK

Daffodil lamp on bronze base by Tiffany Studios

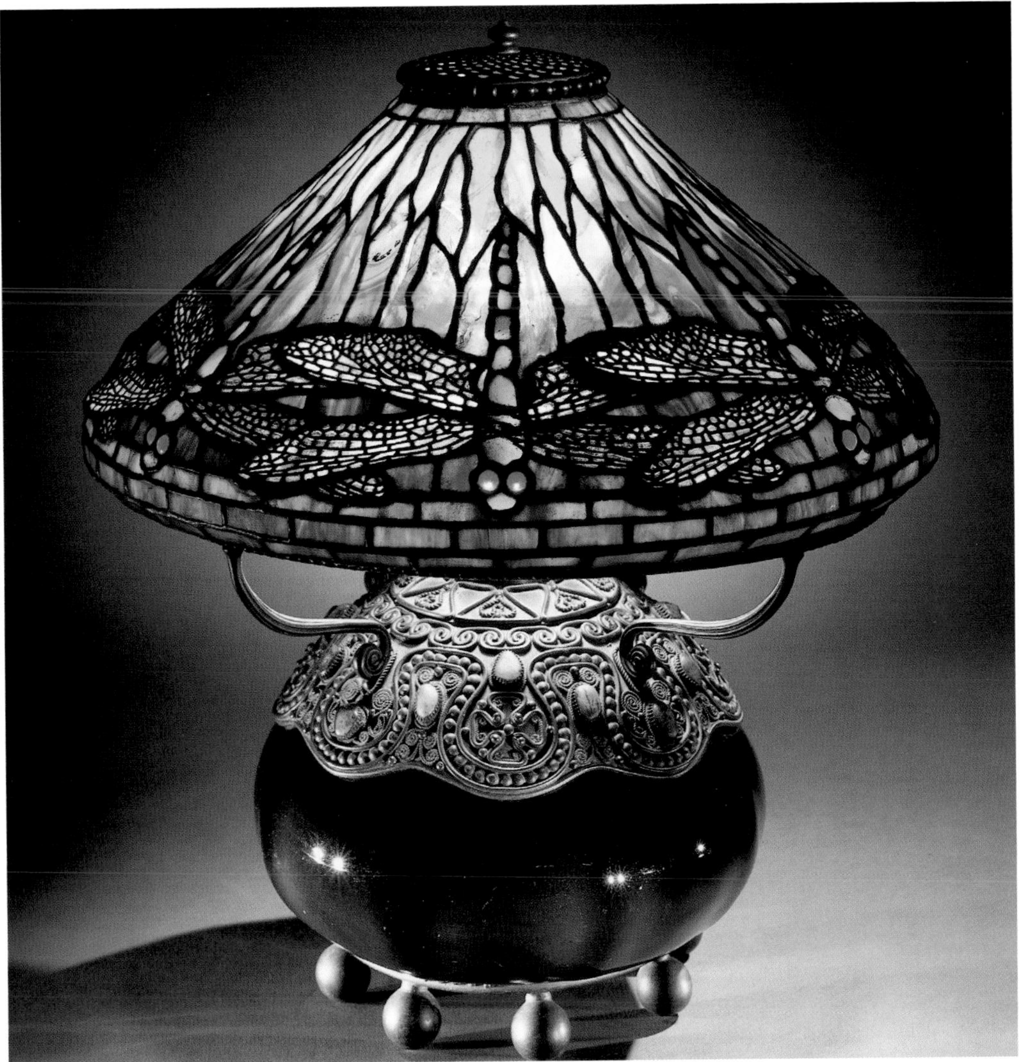

Tiffany Studios

Parakeets and Goldfish Bowl glass window, 1893

Louis Comfort Tiffany started designing interiors in 1878, when he decorated his own home in New York. Inspired by his travels through Europe, Africa and the Middle East, Tiffany was excited by the bright and bold colours that often accompanied opulent or exotic interiors. In the 1880s he collaborated on interior designs with other artist-decorators, perhaps inspired by the collaborations formed by William Morris in England. Hugely successful, Tiffany and his colleagues decorated the home of the writer Mark Twain and rooms in the White House and the Seventh Regiment Armoury in New York.

Tiffany's work in interior design and glassware was widely applauded by critics at home and in Europe. He kept abreast of the developing Art Nouveau movement with frequent visits abroad and it was during a visit to England that Tiffany met Arthur Nash. Nash was an accomplished glassworker from the Stourbridge factories; Tiffany recognized his technical skill and invited Nash to join him at his new factory in Corona, Queens. Established in 1892, the Corona factories were to become the site of Tiffany's greatest experiments and innovations in glass-making and decoration.

CREATED

Corona, New York, USA

MEDIUM

Leaded and plated-glass window

RELATED WORK

Three-panelled folding screen in leaded Favrile glass with bronze frame by Tiffany Studios *c.* 1900

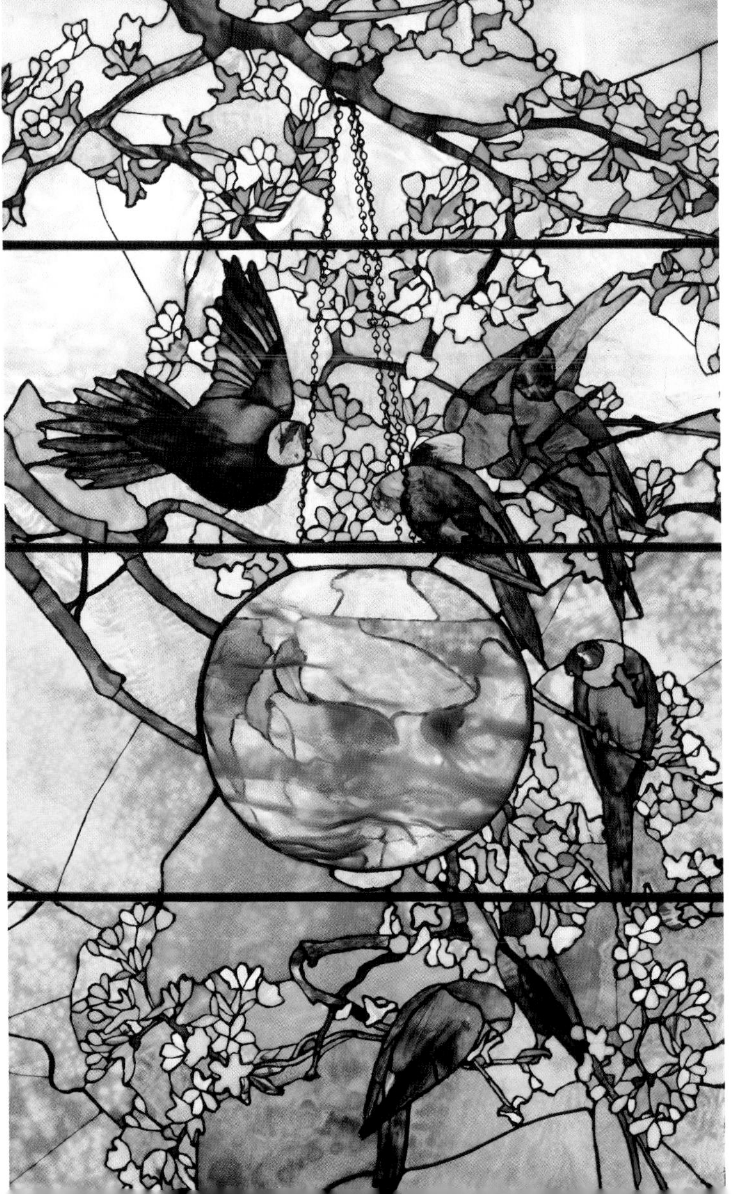

Mackintosh, Charles Rennie

The Wassail (detail), 1900

The Wassail is a watercolour completed by Charles Rennie Mackintosh (1868–1928) for a series of three gesso (bas-relief in plaster of Paris, or gypsum) panels for the Ladies' Luncheon Room at the Ingram Street Tea Rooms in Glasgow. The owner of the tea rooms, Catherine Cranston, was a supporter of the Temperance movement and opened a series of tea rooms to provide women, in particular, with a meeting place that was free of alcohol. Margaret Macdonald (1864–1933) worked with her husband on many of his design and architectural projects and there is a strong similarity between the gesso panels, attributed to Mackintosh, and work attributed to Macdonald. The architect Edwin Luytens (1869–1944) described the tea rooms as 'all very elaborately simple'.

The women in the drawings are typically elongated, almost 'pod-like'. The Glasgow style often incorporated Symbolism, a popular idiom for Art Nouveau. Symbolism concentrates on a world that exists beyond the obvious and uses symbols and images to depict the abstract, such as the exotic, erotic, occult and spiritual. The blood-red flowers were a favourite symbol for Mackintosh and Macdonald: they symbolize the fertility of women.

CREATED

Glasgow

MEDIUM

Watercolour and pencil on paper

RELATED WORK

Wall panels from Buchanan Street Tea Rooms by Charles Rennie Mackintosh, 1897–98

Charles Rennie Mackintosh *Born* 1868 Glasgow, Scotland

Died 1928

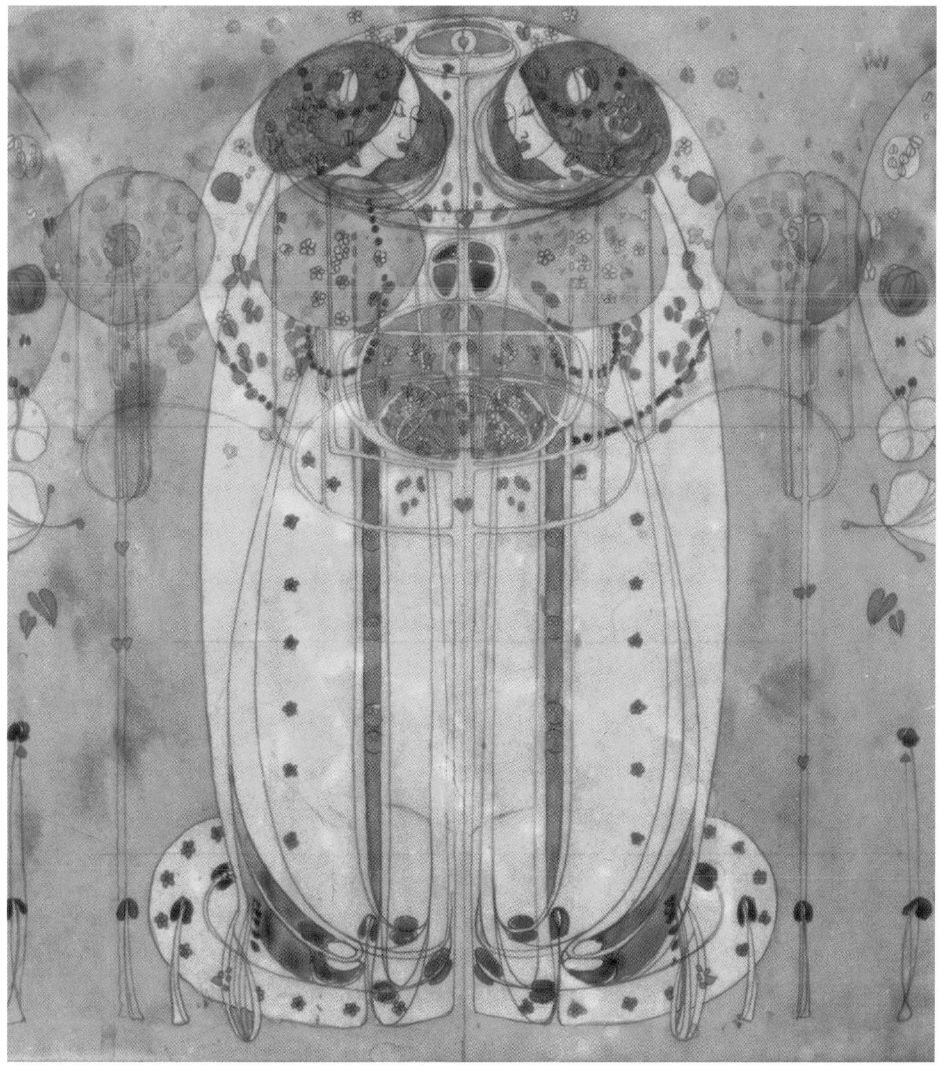

Mackintosh, Charles Rennie

Table designed for the Billiard Room at Miss Cranston's Argyle Street Tea Rooms, Glasgow, 1897

Charles Rennie Mackintosh belonged to the Glasgow School, or style. This body reflected the innovative design tradition of the Scottish city, which was further influenced by Francis Newbery (1855–1946) at the Glasgow School of Art. Women were welcomed to the school by Newbery and fully encouraged to develop their talents: it was here that Mackintosh met his artist wife, Margaret Macdonald, with whom he worked on numerous projects.

Mackintosh was commissioned to design the furniture for the Argyle Street Tea Rooms, 1897–98, and the interior designs were mostly created by George Walton (1867–1933). Miss Cranston's tea rooms provided women with a place to meet and talk. Many liberal middle-class women were vocal supporters of the Temperance movement, which promoted moderation and sobriety and argued for women's property rights. Throughout the Victorian era women held almost no economic power; at the turn of the century there was a quiet, but profound sense that women's roles and positions in society were set to change. This was not interpreted simply as a call for equality or enfranchisement, but for freedom from endless child-bearing and greater rights to health care and protection from violence.

MEDIUM

Oak

RELATED WORK

Chairs in dark-stained oak designed for 120 Mains Street by Charles Rennie Mackintosh, *c.*1900

Charles Rennie Mackintosh *Born* 1868 Glasgow, Scotland

Died 1928

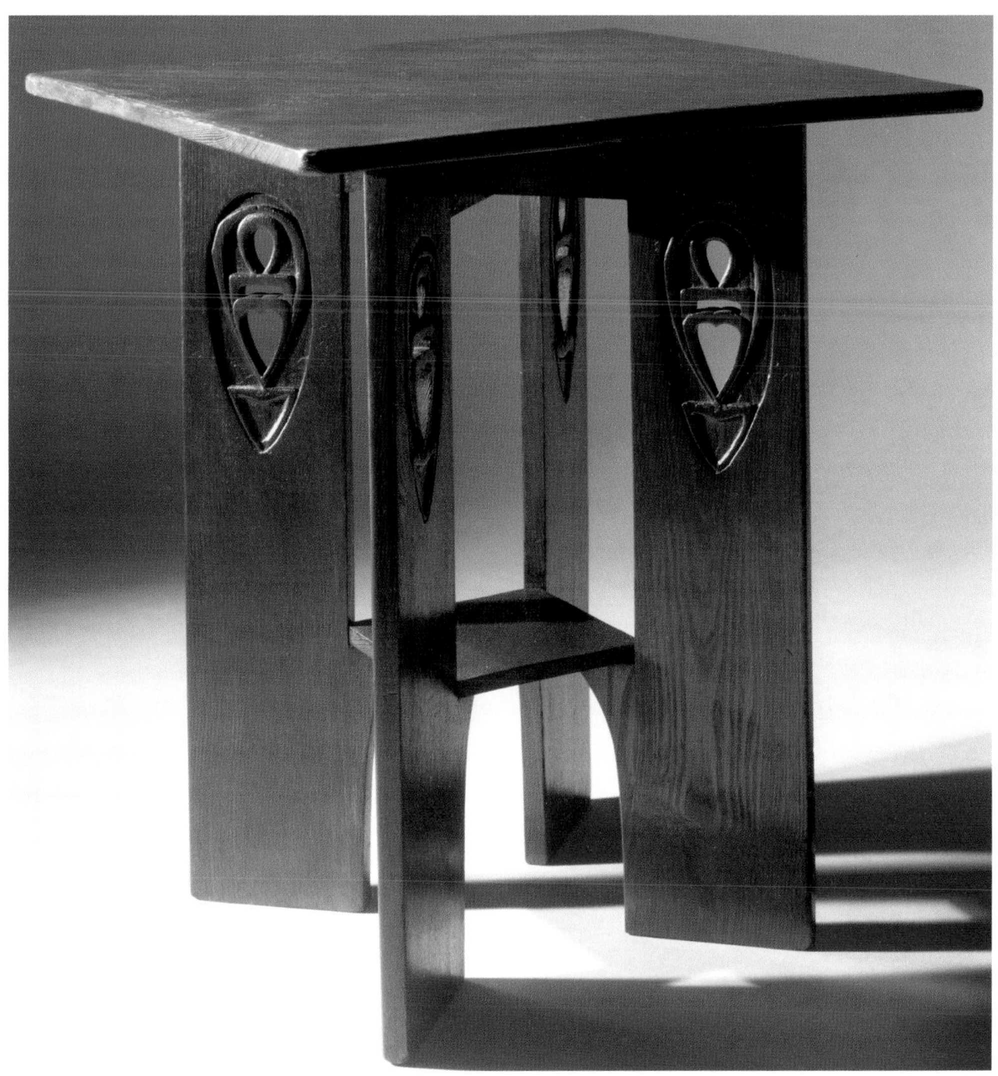

Mackintosh, Charles Rennie

Hanging shade, *c.* 1906

Charles Rennie Mackintosh and his wife, Margaret Macdonald, married in 1900 and lived at 120 Mains Street, Glasgow. They decorated the interior of the studio flat, designing every small detail from fireplaces to sugar tongs. The effect was one of light, space and elegance. In 1906 they moved to 78 Southpark Avenue and soon remodelled the house; this light fitting was one of those Mackintosh designed for his new home.

While many Victorian homes had been dark, elaborately decorated and even cluttered, the Mackintoshes sought to open up living spaces. At Southpark Avenue they enlarged the living areas by knocking small rooms into single large ones; the second floor, for example, became open-plan and was painted entirely in white. Each room had a focal point, such as a large gesso by Macdonald, or a repoussé metal decorative panel over the fireplace. The couple left the house in 1920 and sold most of the furnishings. Glasgow University has reconstructed the Mackintosh villa and re-fitted it with much of the original furniture.

CREATED

Scotland

MEDIUM

Metal and leaded glass

RELATED WORK

Light fittings designed for the White Dining Room at the Ingram Street Tea Rooms by Charles Rennie Mackintosh

Charles Rennie Mackintosh *Born* 1868 Glasgow, Scotland

Died 1928

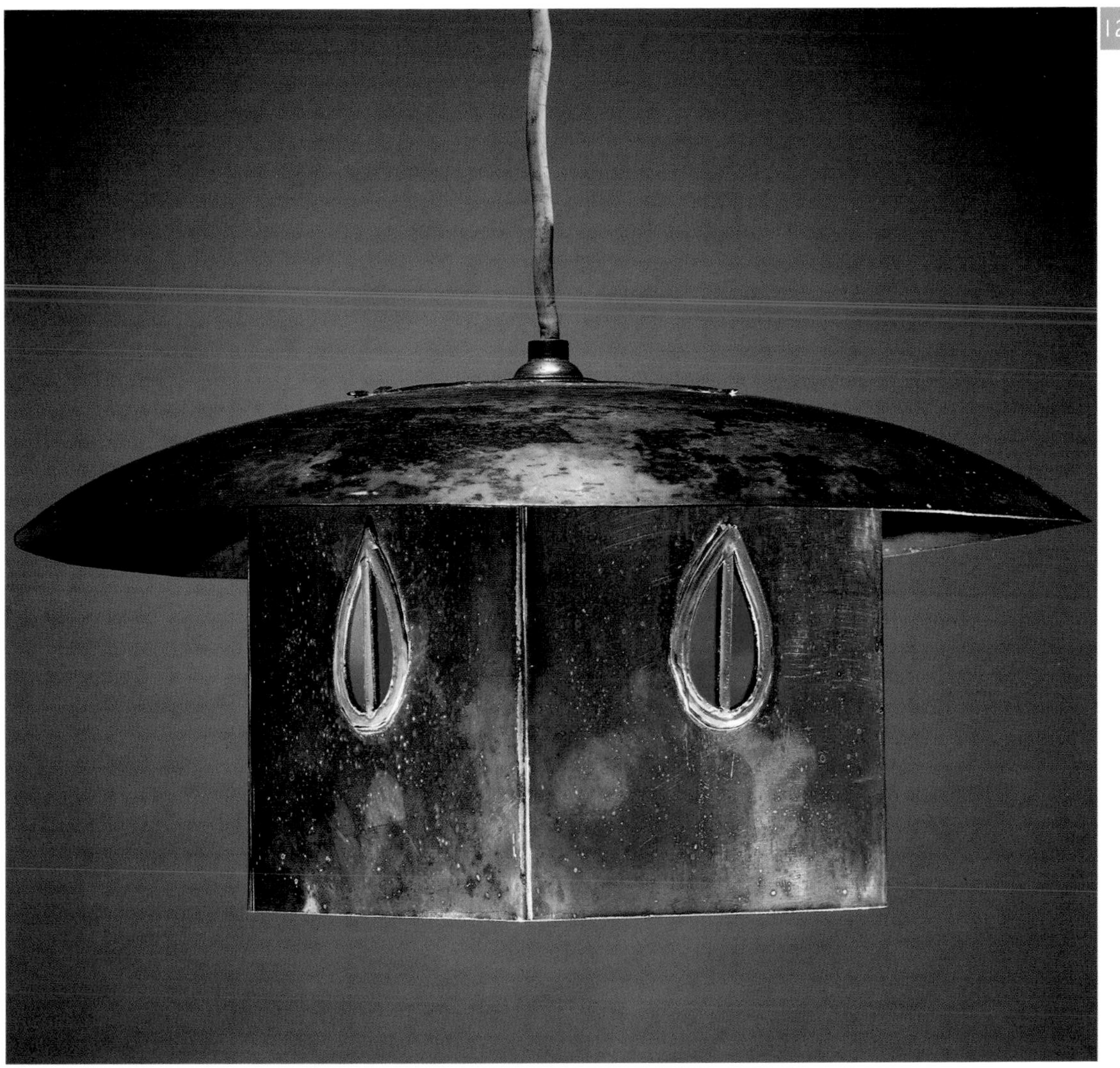

Mackintosh, Charles Rennie

Glass panel (detail), 1902

Glass was a popular medium for artists and designers at the *fin-de-siècle*. Improved technologies in colouring and staining glass meant that new effects were available to the designers. Charles Rennie Mackintosh used leaded glass, not only in windows, but also to create decorative inserts in furniture, or as panels in doors and partitions.

Mackintosh interiors are notable for their lightness. He preferred to stain his wooden furniture, or paint it in white or pastel shades. This obsession with white, clean and simple interiors has been seen as some critics as an obvious contrast to the filthy streets of the highly industrialized city of Glasgow. It would have been difficult to keep a Mackintosh interior pristine, given that heating was still a simple affair of sooty, smoking fireplaces and the air in the city would have been thick with pollution. Despite the impracticalities of his style, Mackintosh took a determined step out of the dark Victorian era. He challenged not only the prevalent historicism, but also every perspective of proportion and form that tradition had previously embraced.

CREATED

Scotland

MEDIUM

Leaded glass

RELATED WORK

Coloured and leaded-glass windows designed for the wooden partitions in the Ladies' Luncheon Room, Ingram Street Tea Room by Charles Rennie Mackintosh

Charles Rennie Mackintosh *Born* 1868 Glasgow, Scotland

Died 1928

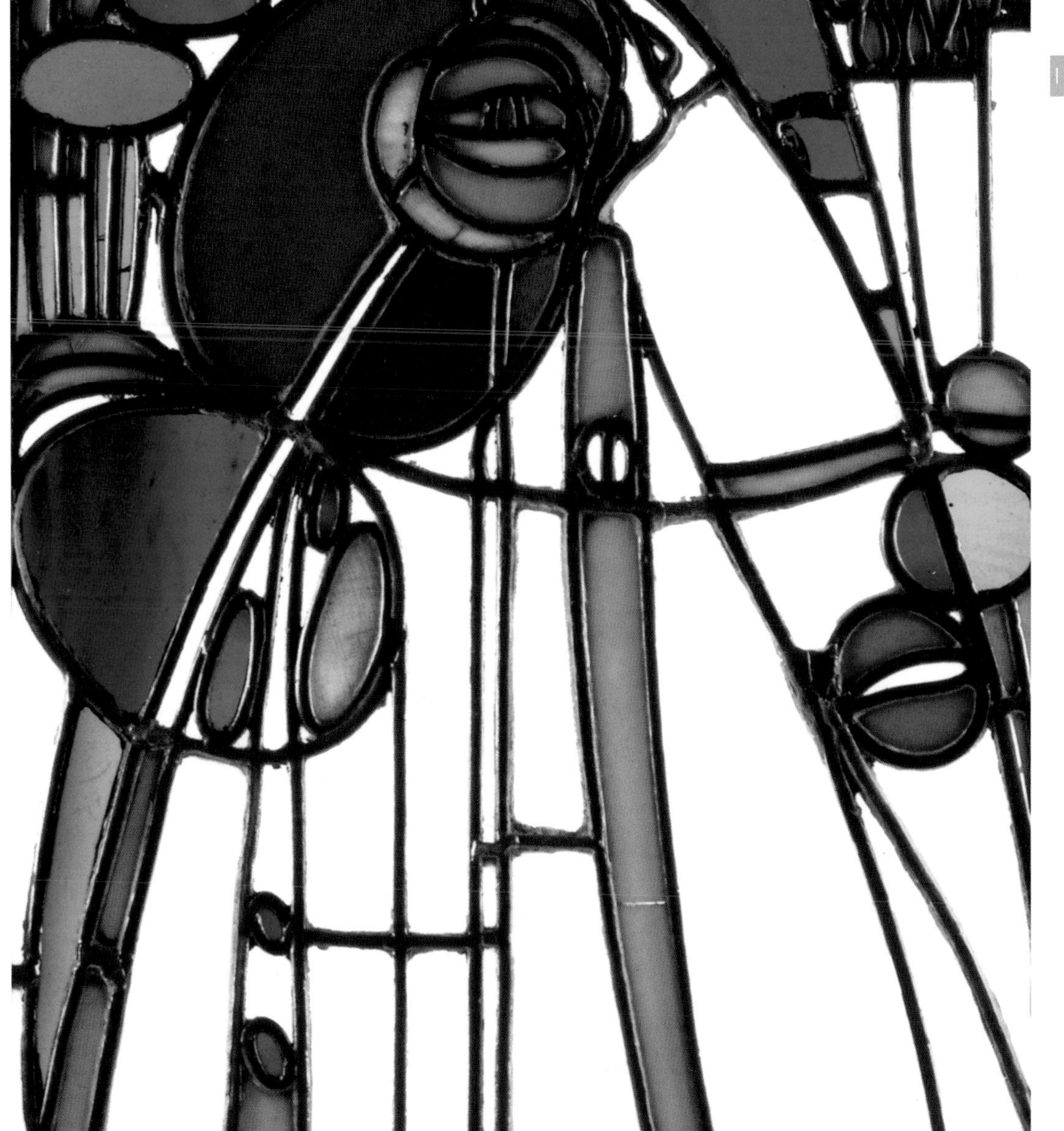

Wagner, Otto

Karlsplatz underground station, 1899–1901

During the second half of the nineteenth century the city of Vienna underwent huge changes, growing in status and population (which increased from 500,000 to two and half million in the 60 years from 1850 to 1910). Known as a city of culture, Vienna developed into a modern, thriving metropolis that embraced modernity.

The Viennese Otto Wagner (1841–1918), and his students and colleagues, Josef Hoffmann (1870–1956), Joseph Olbrich (1867–1908) and Koloman Moser (1868–1918) were instrumental in bringing about this development. Wagner's architectural work bridged the divide between Art Nouveau and Art Deco; like his Austrian colleagues, Wagner preferred to design buildings with a combination of ornamentation and clean, even austere, façades. The Viennese underground railway (the Stadtbahn) was built to Wagner's designs at the same time as Hector Guimard's stations for the Paris Métro were being constructed. Whereas Guimard's vision was one of loose, organic sinuosity, Wagner's designs were more formal, restrained and imposing. The entrance to the Karlsplatz station features a curved metal frame, demonstrating Wagner's structural rationalism, and it is decorated in repeated flower and geometric motifs.

MEDIUM

Architecture

MOVEMENT

Secession

RELATED WORK

Majolikahaus apartment block by Otto Wagner, 1898

Otto Wagner *Born* 1841 Vienna, Austria

Died 1918

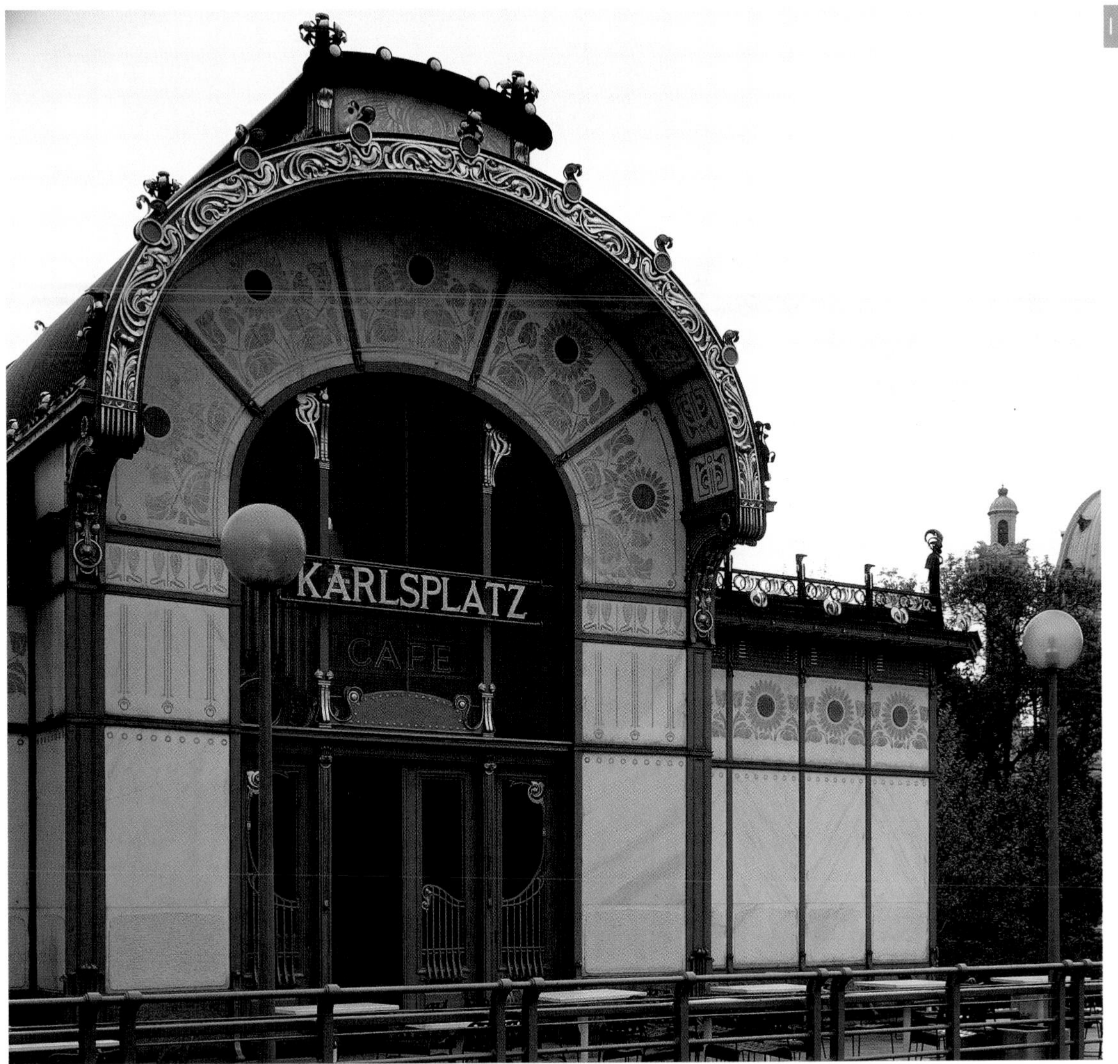
KARLSPLATZ
CAFE

Wagner, Otto

Academy of Fine Arts, Vienna (design for the Hall of Honour)

Otto Wagner produced his first designs for an Academy of Fine Arts in 1898, the year of Emperor Franz Josef's jubilee celebrations, but continued to modify and develop his ideas for the building over the next ten years. The project was never adopted but it demonstrates his vision for combining a traditional, classical style with modern elements. As with many of Wagner's architectural projects, this design demonstrated his taste for the monumental.

This Austrian architect is often lionized as one of the founding fathers of modern European architecture, but his roots lie in the traditional historicist foundation of his younger years. The design for the Academy of Fine Arts involved combining classical planning principles with monumental and modern ornamentation. The open crown structure that would have adorned the building was designed with floral decoration and would have been considered modern in its day. Wagner taught at the Viennese Academy of Fine Arts and his lectures formed the basis for an influential book on architecture, *Moderne Architektur*, which was first published in 1896.

MEDIUM

Architectural design in coloured pencil

MOVEMENT

Secession

RELATED WORK

38 Linke Wienzeile in Vienna by Otto Wagner, 1898

Otto Wagner *Born* 1841 Vienna, Austria

Died 1918

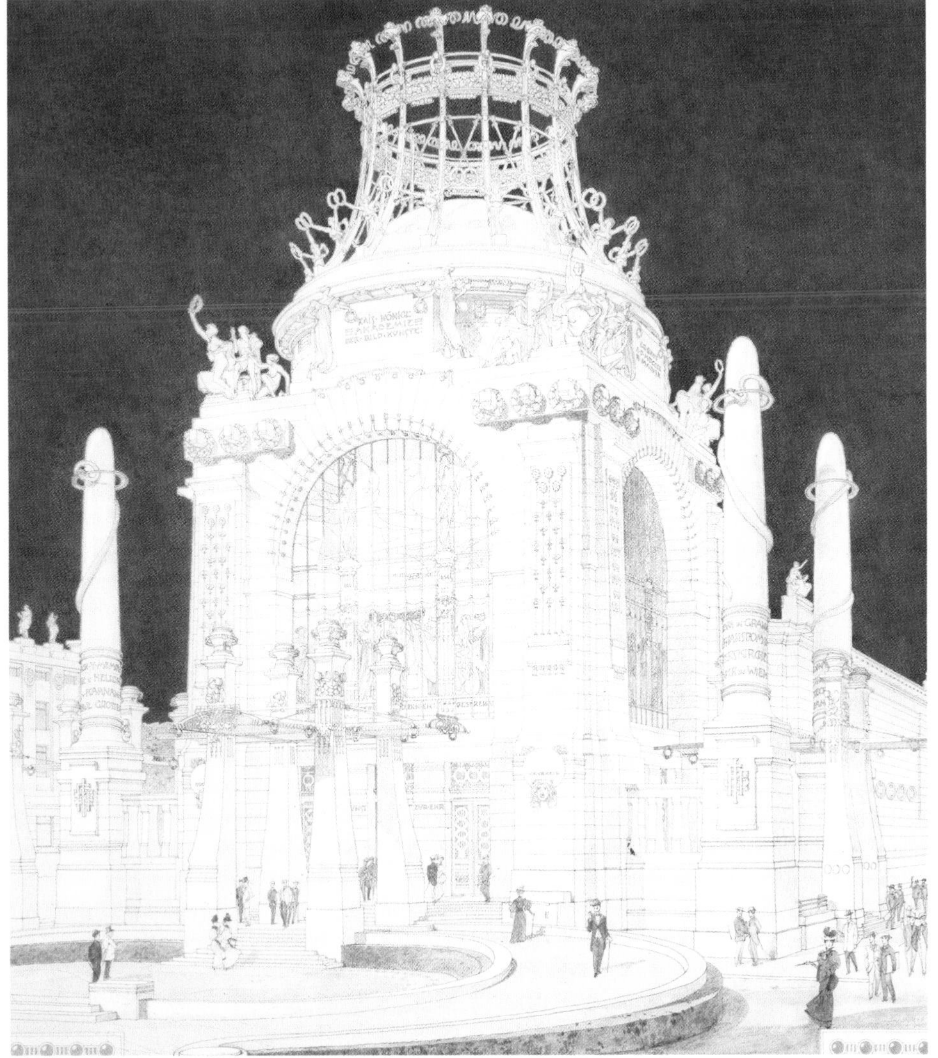

Wagner, Otto

Post Office Savings Bank, Vienna (design showing detail of the façade), *c.* 1904–06

At the turn of the century Vienna's Secessionist artists, including Otto Wagner, sought to distance themselves from the city's historicist tradition. This was a tradition that Wagner himself had studied and taught at a school of architecture in the Viennese Academy of Fine Arts, where he was appointed professor in 1894. He designed a number of residential and commercial buildings in Classical-Baroque styles through the 1890s, but he was gradually developing a progressive stance, no doubt influenced by his own Modernist students. Wagner's style became more revolutionary and he joined the Secessionist group. His lectures and writings emphasize his new approach, 'Modern forms must correspond to new materials, contemporary needs, if they are to be found suitable for mankind today.'

The Post Office Savings Bank is regarded as one of Wagner's greatest and most influential architectural achievements. The building was six storeys and built of concrete and glass in a trapezoidal shape. It was erected in two phases, 1904–06 and 1910–12, a huge glass-vaulted roof being completed in the first phase of building.

MEDIUM

Architectural design in coloured pencil

MOVEMENT

Secession

RELATED WORK

Nussdork Lock by Otto Wagner, 1897

Otto Wagner *Born* 1841 Vienna, Austria

Died 1918

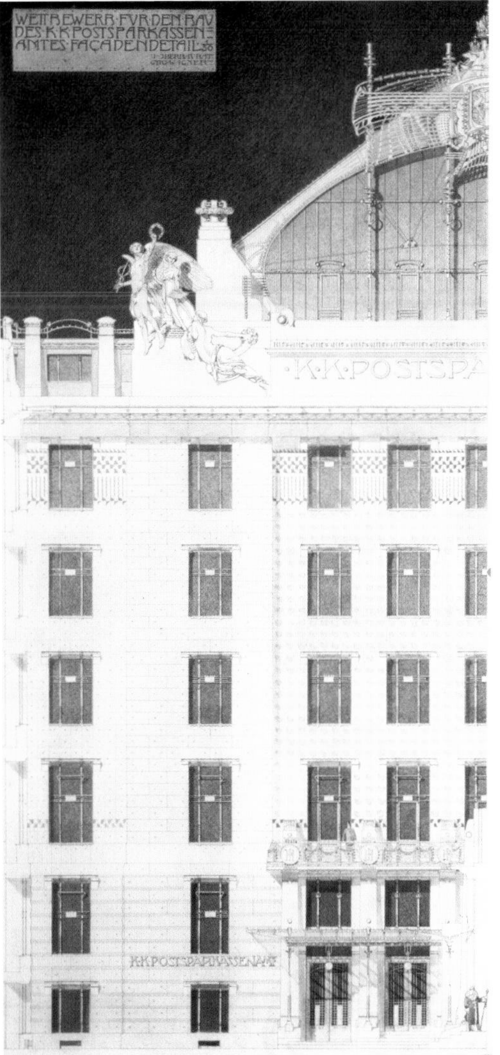
WETTBEWERB·FVR·DEN·BAV
DES·K·K·POSTSPARKASSEN
AMTES·FAÇADENDETAIL
·K·K·POSTSPA
K·K·POSTSPARKASSENAMT

Wagner, Otto

Ebonized bentwood bench, *c.* 1902

The Post Office Savings Bank was hailed as a hugely successful project and as an example of how design was moving away from the creation of structures of fixed form, towards structures that were born of necessity. Wagner believed that a building should reflect the needs of the people who used it and that modern materials were essential for modern times.

The building's main hall had a glass ceiling and glass blocks in the floor for light to penetrate rooms below. This was a ground-breaking design that allowed light to flood the building's central space. Aluminium was used in the exterior walls, as well as inside the building for furniture and fittings. The aim of the design was to integrate all aspects of the building into one functional harmony. This extended to Wagner's involvement in the design of unique items of furniture. Chairs and stools were simply designed, yet elegant not austere. They were often lightweight and easily portable, adding to flexibility in design that was seen elsewhere with the use of detachable walls in the functional office space.

CREATED

Vienna

MEDIUM

Ebonized bentwood

MOVEMENT

Secession

RELATED WORK

Armchair for the boardroom of the Post Office Savings Bank, 1904–06

Otto Wagner *Born* 1841 Vienna, Austria

Died 1918

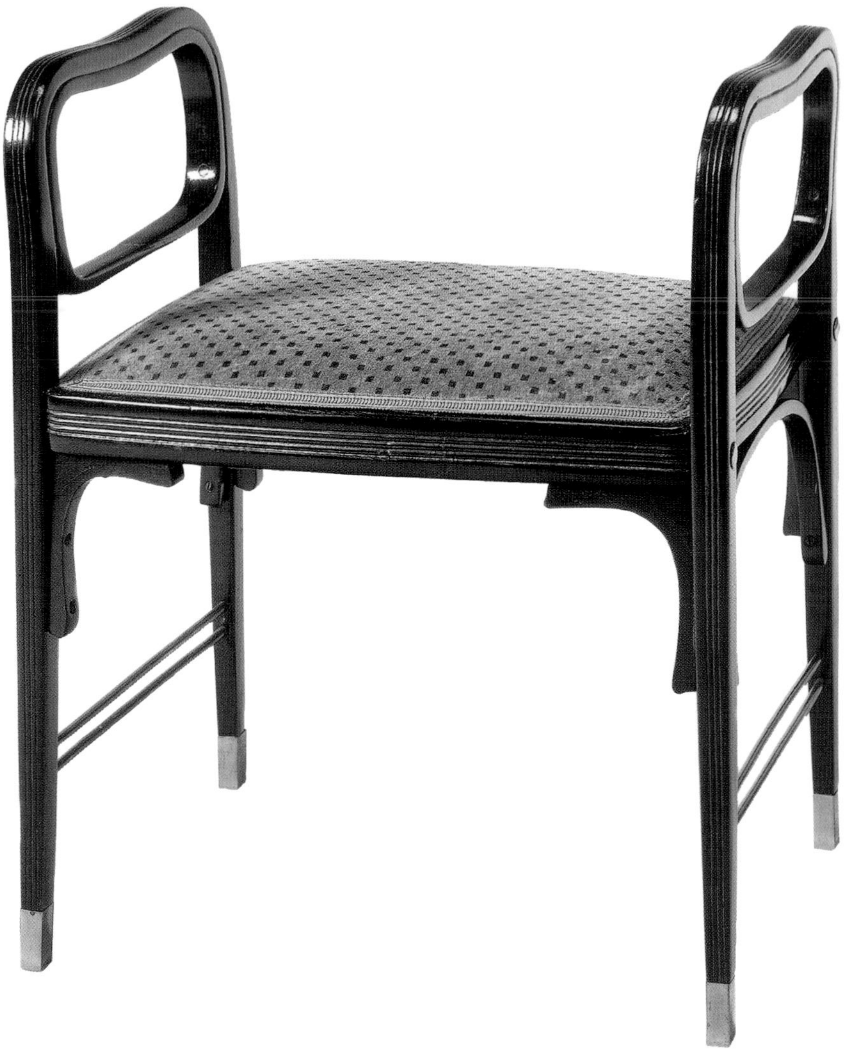

Lalique, René

Pendant brooch and chain, *c.* 1899–1902

René Lalique (1860–1945) was born in Marne, a rural region of France, but was brought up in Paris. He returned to the countryside many times and it was here that he developed his great passion for nature by observing, painting and sketching insects and flowers. His mother recognized an emerging talent and apprenticed her son to a Parisian jeweller. Lalique consolidated his learning at the Ecole des Arts Décoratifs in Paris and he also spent two years studying draughtsmanship at Sydenham College, England, in the late 1870s. While in England, Lalique would have been aware of the Arts and Crafts movement, which was a vital force in the decorative and applied arts at the time.

When Lalique returned to Paris in 1880 he knew he wanted to become a jewellery designer. Paris was the ideal place to learn: the city was renowned for its innovative jewellery design and French craftsmanship was considered supreme. His early designs were traditional in execution, materials and style, but they sold well to the members of the aristocracy who loved his diamond and gold creations.

MEDIUM

Enamel, ivory, gold and pearl

RELATED WORK

Grasshopper necklace in horn and baroque pearls by René Lalique, 1903

René Lalique *Born* 1860 Marne, France

Died 1945

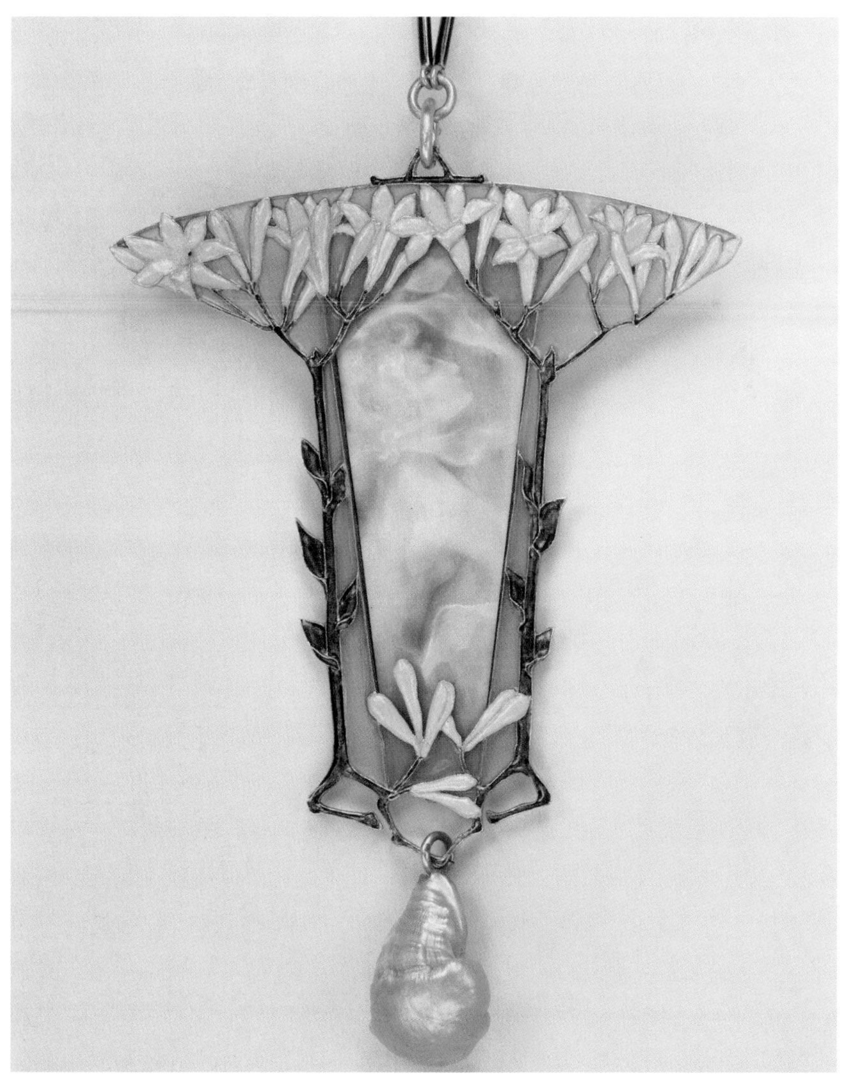

Lalique, René

Pendant brooch

In 1885 Lalique started a workshop of his own and this finally afforded him the freedom to experiment. Many of his designs featured animals and plants, often intertwined with maidens or lovers. This pendant, for example, uses sunflowers to adorn a maiden's golden face. During the 1880s and 1890s the cult of nature had fired the imagination of artists and designers. The natural world was used by rationalists and anti-rationalists. It could represent the huge, almost overwhelming, growth of scientific knowledge in the nineteenth century and it was also used to symbolize the spiritual, mystical and unexplainable elements of human existence.

Lalique, however, did not just experiment in form. He was also influenced by the socialist ideologies of the day, some of which he may have encountered during his studies in England. He aimed to create beautiful jewellery without resorting to the most expensive materials and he experimented with semi-precious stones, enamelling and glass. By 1887 Lalique's extraordinary ingenuity and technical proficiency were recognized and his designs were lauded as works of art.

MEDIUM

Gold and enamel

RELATED WORK

Beetles brooch in dark metal with tourmaline, enamel and glass by René Lalique, *c.* 1900

René Lalique *Born* 1860 Marne, France

Died 1945

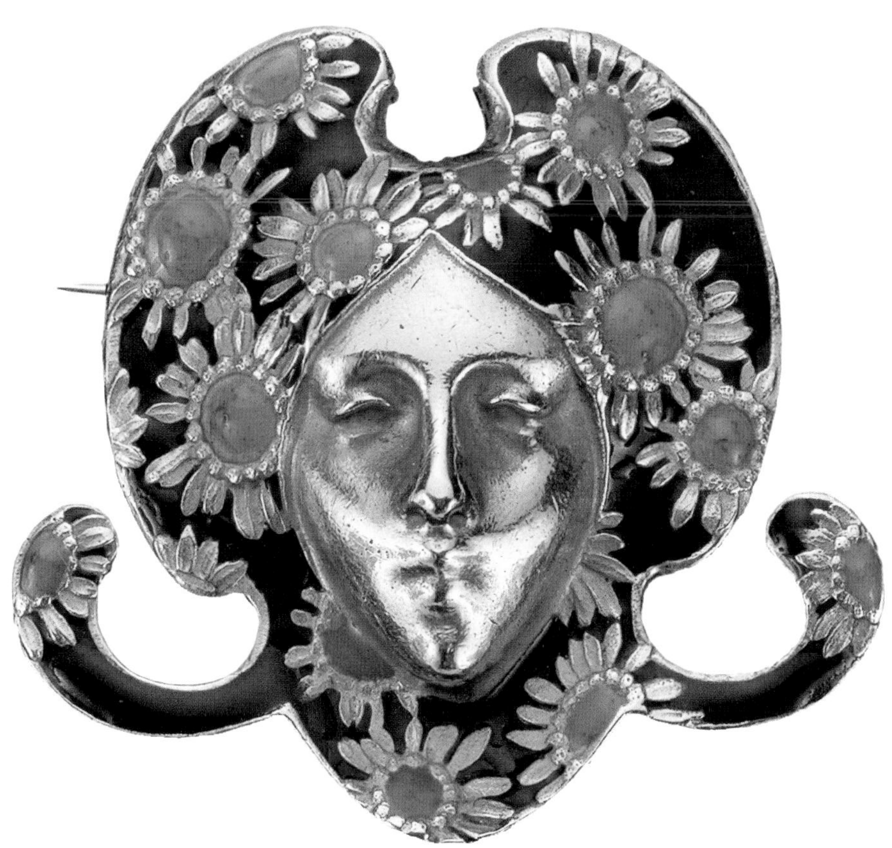

Lalique, René

Pansy plaque, *c.* 1900

Inlaid enamel work has been used for centuries to decorate jewellery. Unlike costly or rare gemstones, enamel can be manufactured, using a type of glass made from sand or flint, soda or potash and red lead. Metallic oxides are added, or the proportions of all the ingredients are changed, to produce different colours. The mixture, or flux, is heated until fusion and then poured into a mould (as in *champlevé* enamelling) or between partitions or *cloisons* (as in *cloisonné* enamelling).

Oriental enamelling had reached an extraordinarily high level of sophistication by the nineteenth century. Europeans first encountered Japanese *cloisonné* work, in any significant quantity, when the 1867 Paris Exposition took place. This technique is particularly suitable for jewellery work since it allows for fine detail and a variety of colours. Lalique found that the technique suited his designs based on nature: he used gold to create *cloisons* that could be made to represent the veins on leaves, the delicate pattern on a dragonfly's wing, or to mark the hair-like vessels that fan out through a pansy's petal.

MEDIUM

Gold, enamel and diamonds

RELATED WORK

Eagles and pine trees dog-collar plaque by René Lalique, *c.* 1900–05

René Lalique *Born* 1860 Marne, France

Died 1945

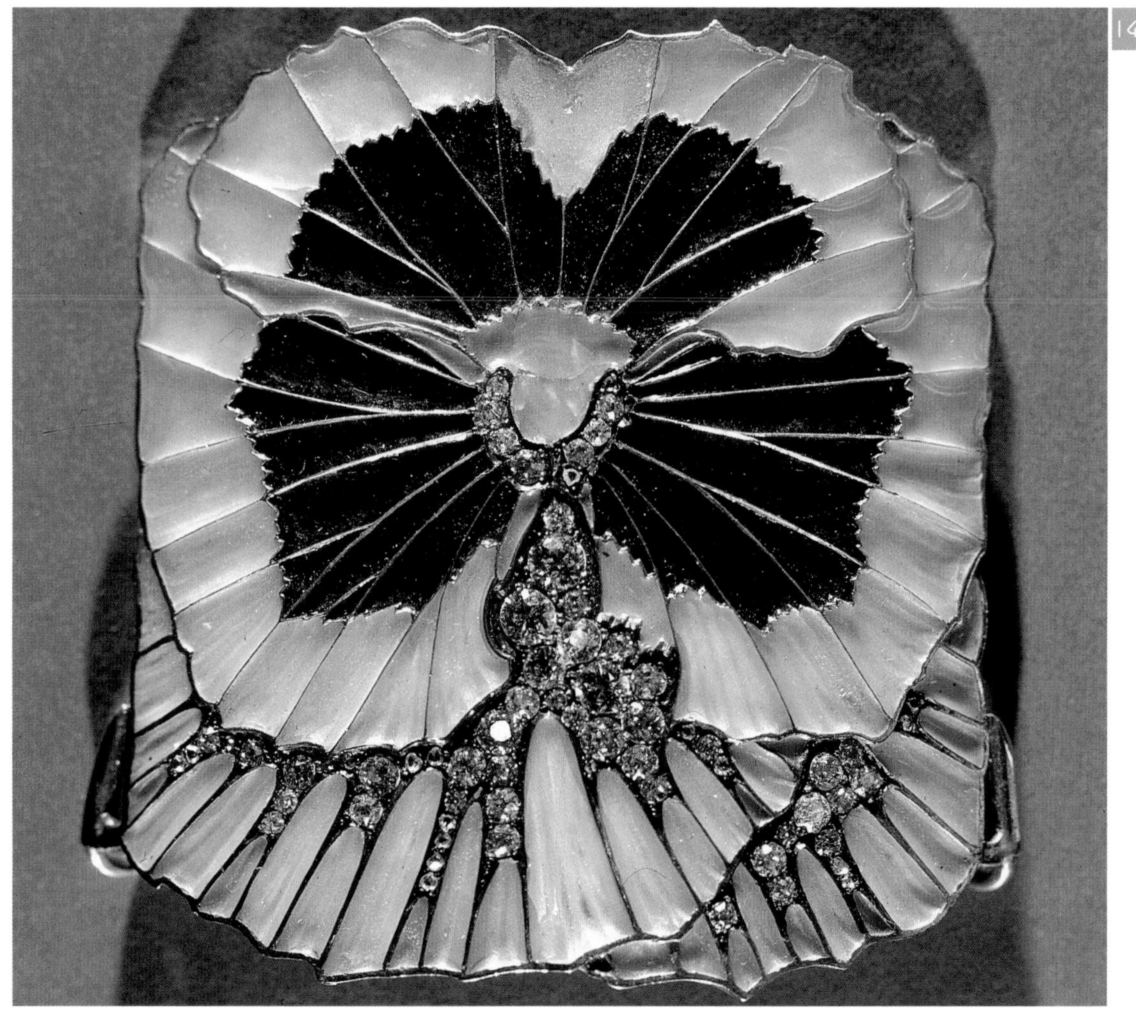

Lalique, René

Comb

René Lalique did not shy away from creating dramatic jewellery in an entirely new and extraordinary style. His motifs from nature, often sinuously entangled with erotic women, were crafted with such enormous skill that they appear almost lifelike. He was one of the greatest artists of the Art Nouveau period, and his appeal is still strong.

France was the ideal place for Lalique to experiment with his craft. French jewellery was renowned throughout the world for its originality and superb level of craftsmanship. With the benefit of increased wealth that many families enjoyed during the *belle époque*, women of the bourgeoisie had more disposable income with which to dress and adorn themselves. Women were also becoming politically aware, independent and assertive. It would be many years before women could vote, but they were becoming more vocal. Sensing the slow dawning of a new era, women rejected the fashions and accessories of the nineteenth century and sought modernity, and that meant Art Nouveau, especially Lalique's utterly original jewellery, with its erotic and decadent overtones.

MEDIUM

Gold, enamel and amethyst

RELATED WORK

Dragonfly corsage ornament by René Lalique, 1897–98

René Lalique *Born* 1860 Marne, France

Died 1945

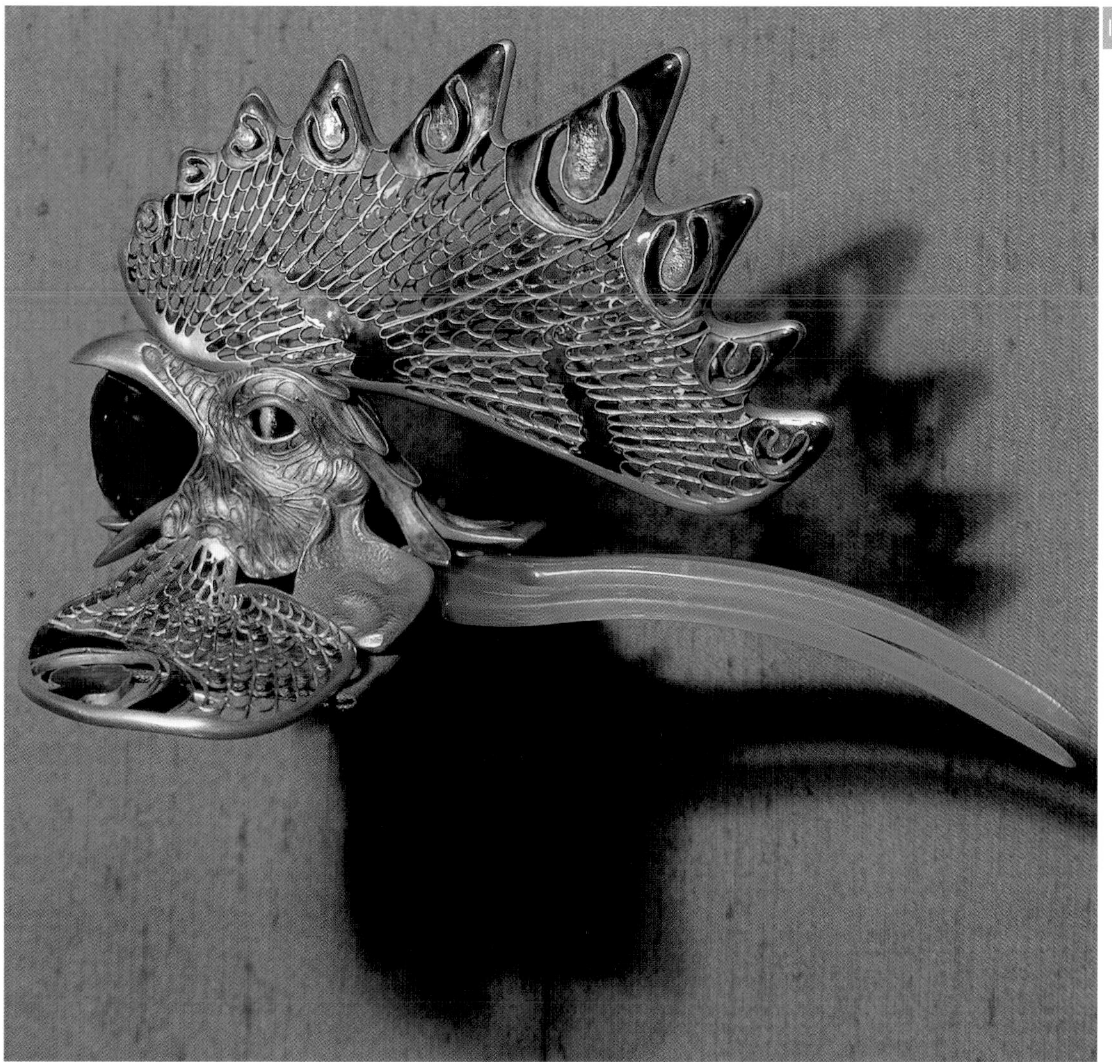

Gallé, Emile

Nenuphar side table, *c.* 1900

Although popular at its time, the Art Nouveau style went through a period of disapproval in the years following the First World War. It enjoyed a brief revival during the late 1960s, when sensuality and themes of nature were once again in vogue in the field of decorative arts. Certainly the style could be regarded as occasionally excessive, even vulgar and ostentatious. It could be argued, however, that these extreme examples of Art Nouveau were necessary as artists experimented in an entirely new field. While some, such as Emile Gallé, drew inspiration from traditional styles, such as Rococo, the overwhelming thrust of the movement was one of innovation and experimentation. Many designers aimed to move away from the influence of historicism, which had dominated the decorative arts in the nineteenth century. The cult of nature was a popular idiom for artists and designers of the day.

This side table by Emile Gallé (1846–1904) is named after the *nenuphar* giant white water lily, *Nymphaea alba*, which is used as a decorative motif. Its sinuous, flowing lines and botanical theme are typical of Art Nouveau furniture.

MEDIUM

Wood

RELATED WORK

The White Vine, dining room cabinet by Emile Gallé, 1900

Emile Gallé *Born* 1846 Nancy, France

Died 1904

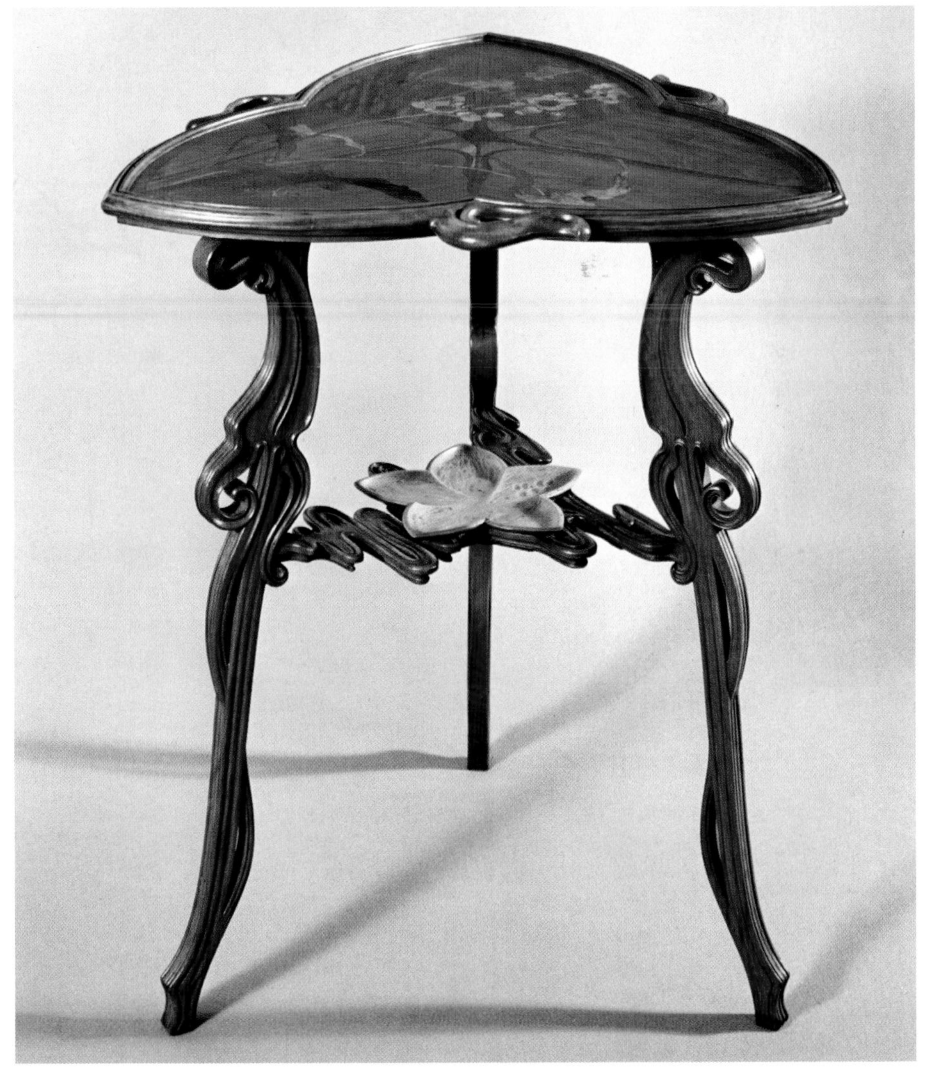

Gallé, Emile

Guyanese Forest vase, *c.* 1900

As the end of the nineteenth century approached, Europe was a mercurial place. Huge changes brought about by industrialization, war, revolution and population growth meant that those living at the *fin-de-siècle* were adjusting to a new society.

As might be expected at the end of a century, the mood was both reflective and expectant. Artists and designers eschewed the traditions of the past and paved the way for modernity as they anticipated a new era. One of the most important changes that took place at this time within the decorative arts was the concept that the style of a time was connected with the pervading social culture. In France this relationship was viewed as materialistic and rational. It was argued that a style grew out of the materials and technologies that were available to the artisans and could be both liberated or limited by these parameters. The work of French designer Emile Gallé typifies this concept. An accomplished designer and botanist, he combined his artistic skills with the technical skills of his craftsmen and women, to produce some of the most extraordinary items of furniture, glassware and ceramics of the period.

CREATED

Nancy, France

MEDIUM

Glass

RELATED WORK

Woodland Anemone vase by Emile Gallé, 1900

Emile Gallé *Born* 1846 Nancy, France

Died 1904

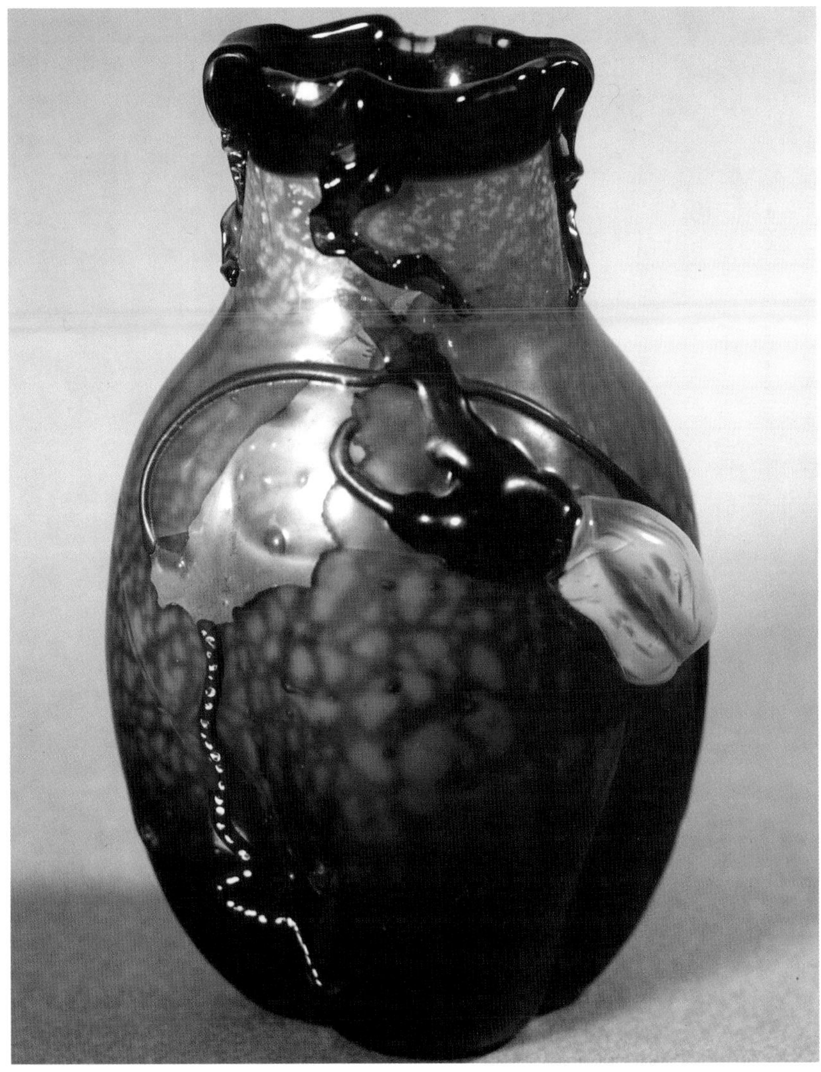

Gallé, Emile

Cup, 1889

It has been argued that Art Nouveau was less a single aesthetic than an amalgamation of various styles that emerged at the end of the nineteenth century. It is certainly true that during this period artists interpreted the movement as individuals, not collectively, and that a wide range of design styles appeared. There was, however, a general consensus among artists and designers of the day; they believed that the use of traditional motifs, designs and techniques should no longer be employed in an arbitrary fashion or purely to satisfy commercial interests. While historicism was not entirely rejected, the use of traditional models could not be justified if they simply acted as reminders of foregone days.

Emile Gallé's designs demonstrate this belief; he was not averse to historical references in his work, but they were set in an entirely new context. The use of natural forms in Gallé's work was not mere science; it was symbolic. He wrote of his decorated vases, 'It is always (a question of) the translation, the evocation of an idea by an image.'

MEDIUM

Glass vessel on a mount

RELATED WORK

The Hand, blown and decorated glass by Emile Gallé

Emile Gallé *Born* 1846 Nancy, France

Died 1904

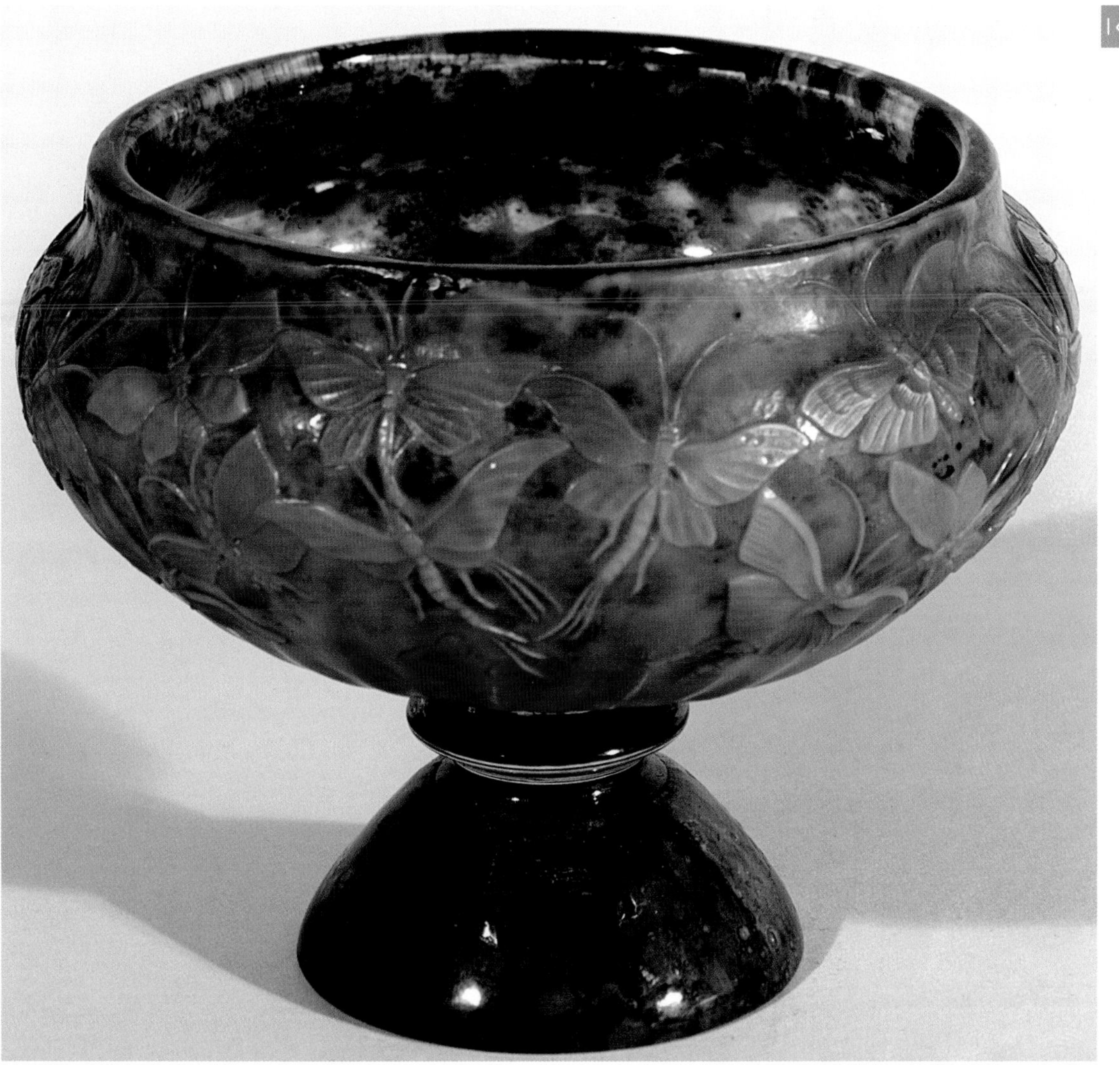

Gallé, Emile

Lamp, *c.* 1900

The nineteenth century had seen an explosion in the development of science and scientific theories, particularly in biology and zoology. Charles Darwin's thesis on the evolution of species had introduced the idea that man and nature were inextricably linked in a way that had never before been contemplated. It is unsurprising, therefore, that by the end of the century European societies were fascinated by nature and pondered how the new laws of nature that scientists were proposing might affect humanity. The relatively new field of psychology was also becoming a powerful influence on society of the day: hypnotism, suggestion and the power of the subconscious fascinated Symbolist painters and designers.

The natural world was embraced by these artists as being a suitable source of symbols for their works. Gallé described how he used corn to depict charity and goodness, olive trees for peace, figs for gentleness and grapes to symbolize the blood of the Eucharist. He sought to evoke an idea or an image by the medium of decoration and hoped that his works would provide 'an atmosphere of tranquility'.

MEDIUM

Double-layered glass

RELATED WORK

Inkcaps and lamp by Emile Gallé, 1902

Emile Gallé *Born* 1846 Nancy, France

Died 1904

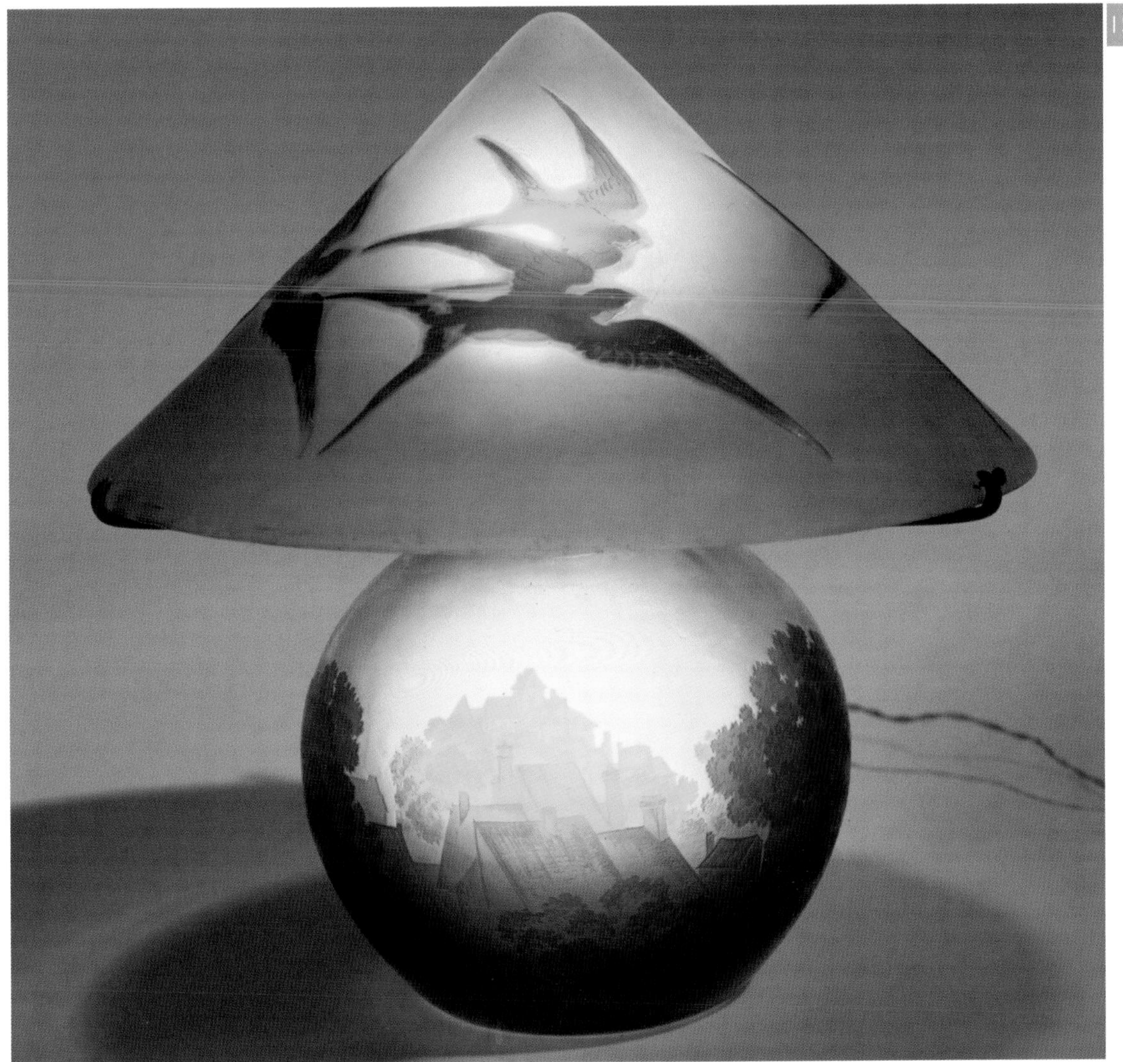

Art Nouveau

THE W
GREAT

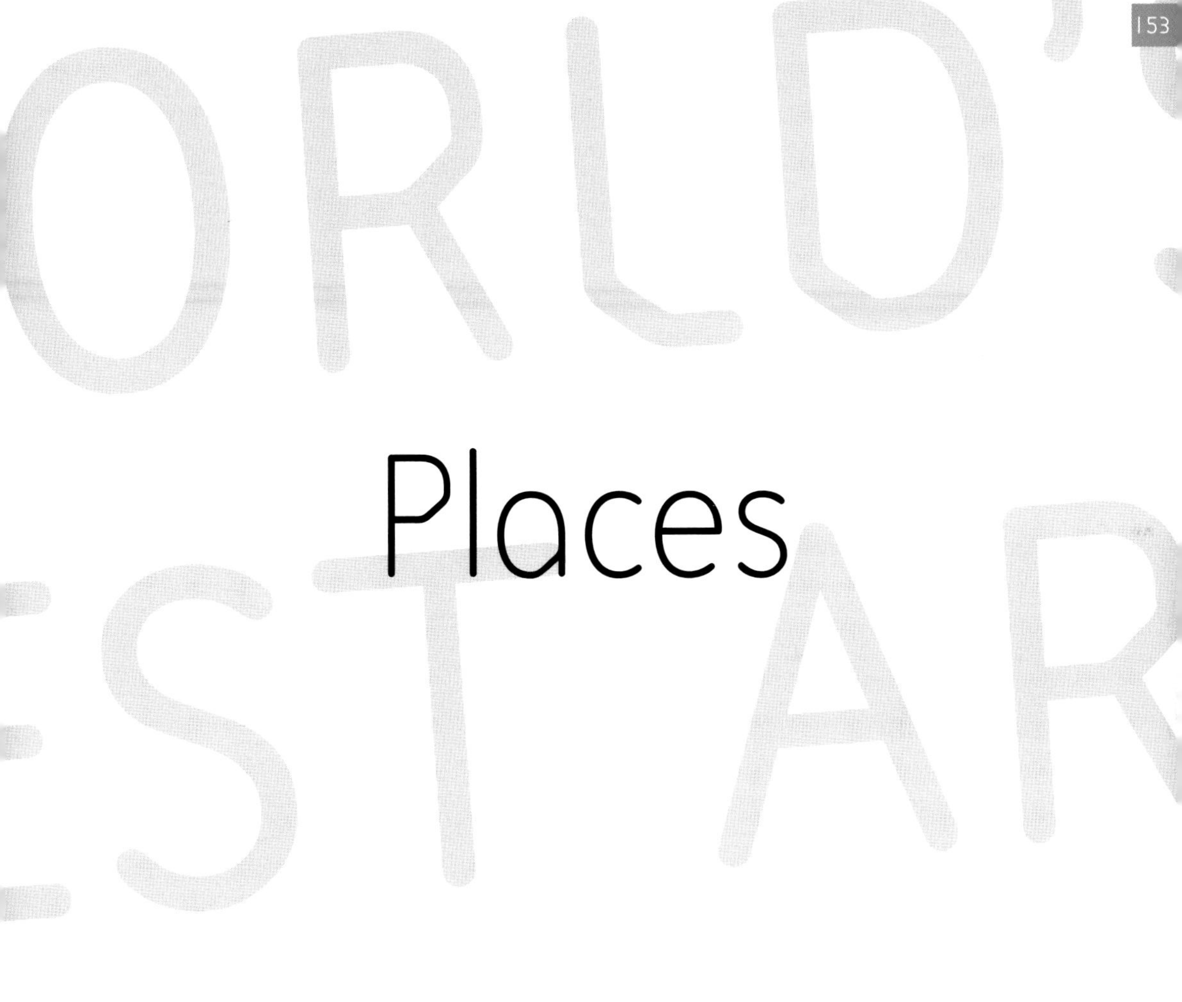

Places

de Feure, Georges

Women Surrounded by Flowers, c. 1900

Georges de Feure (1868–1943) was born Georges Joseph van Sluyters in Paris. He worked as a costumier and actor, but was fascinated by the use of Symbolism in painting. He practised interior design and began to create his own oils and watercolours, with Symbolism and women as the main themes of his work. He exhibited at the Galerie des Artistes Moderne in 1894 and was soon encouraged by Siegfried Bing to extend his talents. Bing asked de Feure to design the interiors and other elements of his pavilion at the Paris Exposition Universelle in 1900 and also to design furniture for his emporium, L'Art Nouveau in Paris.

De Feure eventually left Bing's gallery and established himself as an independent designer. He created furniture, ceramics, glass, carpets, interior designs, illustrations and paintings. His work often featured women in sensual poses, surrounded by Symbolist features, but much of it also shows a strong link to Oriental work. Siegfried Bing had imported and sold large amounts of Japanese art and promoted Japanese style during the 1870s; it was a very popular art form in Paris at the end of the century.

MEDIUM

Colour engraving

RELATED WORK

Gilt furniture from the Bing Pavilion by Georges de Feure, 1900

Georges de Feure *Born* 1868 Paris, France

Died 1943

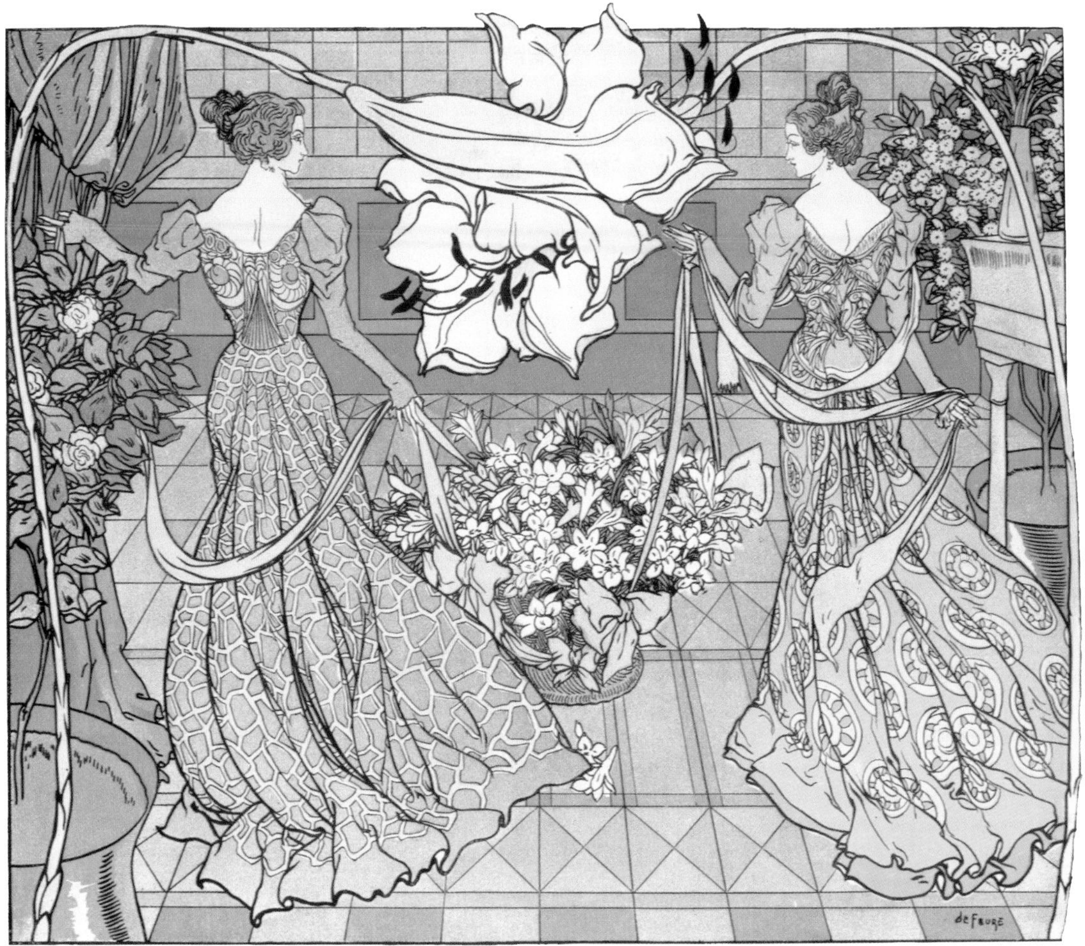
de Feure

de Feure, Georges

Porcelain vase, *c.* 1903

Symbolism was a prevalent theme of art and literature in the Art Nouveau period and often featured in the work of French artist and designer Georges de Feure, among others. Mythical, esoteric and mystical themes were often employed through the use of symbols; this represented a rejection of the Impressionists' preoccupation with light and colour and a new emphasis on the importance of the subject of the work.

The use of Symbolism in art often appeared in conjunction with the strong contours and flat colours that were adopted from Japanese prints. Stylized symbols are laid on and around the subjects of a picture, which are drawn without shadows or as simple linear designs. Decorative patterns of flowers such as lilies, adorned pictures or were used on ceramics. This style also lent itself well to posters and book covers, which became hugely popular during this period and were quickly recognized as collectable. De Feure used Symbolism in his designs for the exterior and interior of Siegfried Bing's pavilion at the Paris Exhibition in 1900. For example, women in seductive poses were used to symbolize each field of the decorative arts.

MEDIUM

Gilded porcelain

RELATED WORK

Vase des Binelles, jardinière by Hector Guimard, 1903

Georges de Feure *Born* 1868 Paris, France

Died 1943

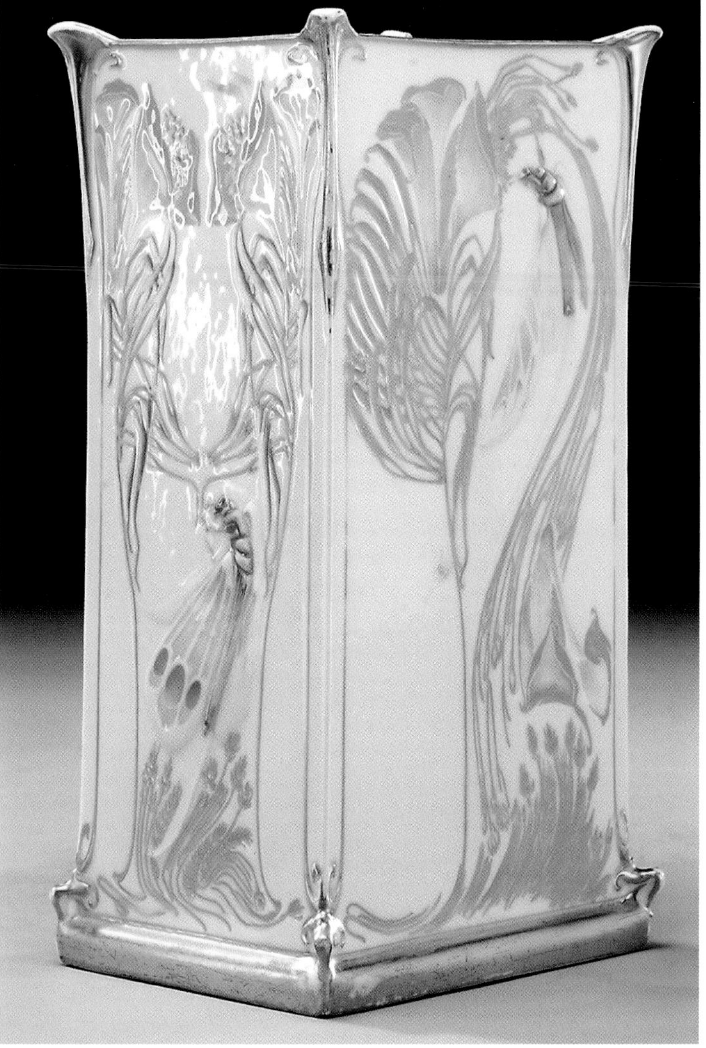

de Feure, Georges

Young Lady in Clinging Dress and Hat, 1901–02

The Art Nouveau aesthetic had many influences: one important influence in France at the end of the nineteenth century was the work of a group of artists called the Nabis. These artists, led by Paul Sérusier (1864–1927) and Maurice Denis (1870–1943), emphasized the importance of the subject of a painting, or artwork, and the relationship between the end product and the artist's vision. Thus the metaphors and symbols employed by the artist were part of his or her involvement with the work and its meaning. These artists used planes of intense colour to flatten perspective and the colour was often bound by thick black lines. The result was often similar to a stained-glass window and required the viewer to employ their imagination to look beyond the strong formalization of colours.

Paul Gauguin (1848–1903) adopted the Nabis' principles and largely through his work this aesthetic was broadcast, particularly in France. It affected the work of many Art Nouveau artists, who also sought to incorporate spirituality into their work and to challenge the viewer to seek more than a simple reading of forms and colours.

MEDIUM

Stained glass

RELATED WORK

The Daughter of Leda, oil on canvas by Georges de Feure, 1896

Georges de Feure *Born* 1868 Paris, France

Died 1943

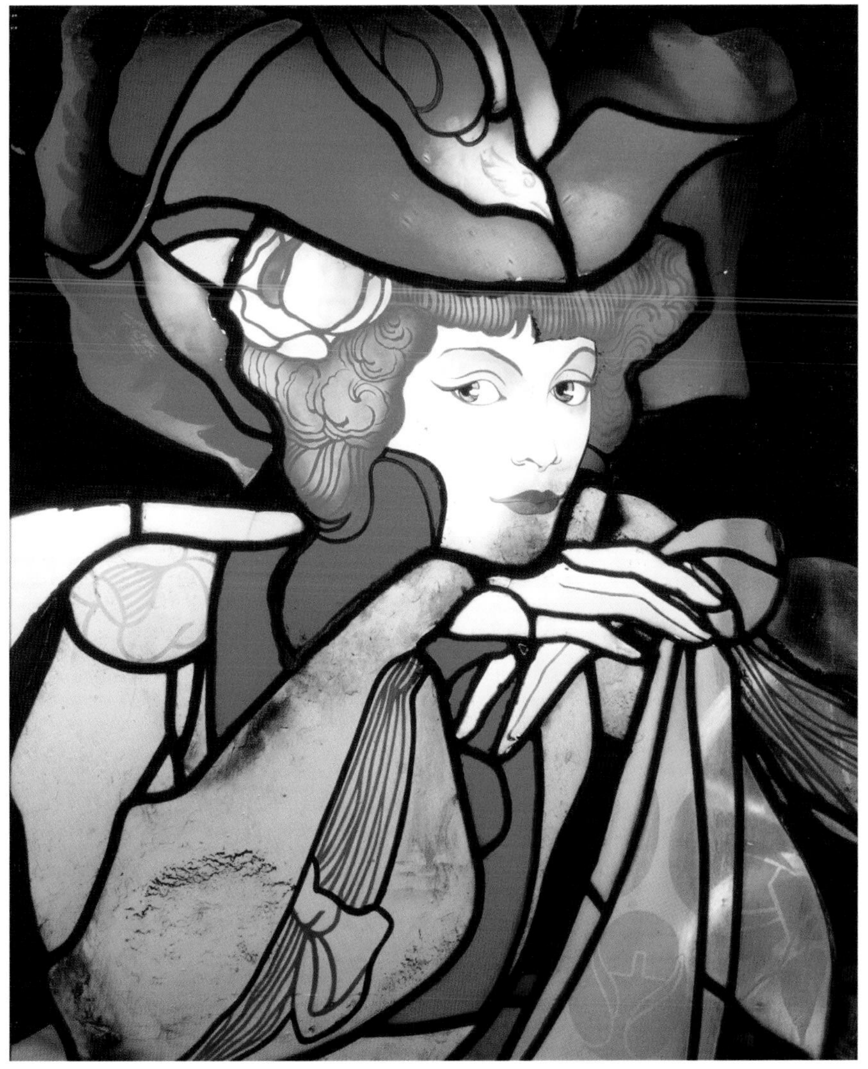

Majorelle, Louis

Nenuphar bed, 1905–09

The son of a cabinet-maker with a workshop in Nancy, Louis Majorelle (1859–1926) was destined to become a leading designer in the creation of the French Art Nouveau style. He trained as a painter and in 1877 studied at the Ecole des Beaux Arts in Paris. After his father's death in 1879 Majorelle moved to Nancy to assume responsibility for the family business, aged only 20. At the time the workshops produced furniture burdened with cherubs, scrolls and beasts in an excess of the Neo-Rococo style that was in vogue. Gradually Majorelle developed a new and restrained aesthetic.

Majorelle adhered to the principles and techniques of superbly crafted furniture made from the finest materials. He did, however, also understand the importance of introducing modern methods of production into the workshop. Majorelle's designs were very popular and he succeeded in creating a large body of work up until the First World War, when the more severe style of Art Deco became fashionable.

CREATED

France

MEDIUM

Wood and bronze

RELATED WORK

Slender cabinet in veneered oak with wrought-iron decoration by Louis Majorelle, 1900

Louis Majorelle *Born* 1859 Toul, France

Died 1926

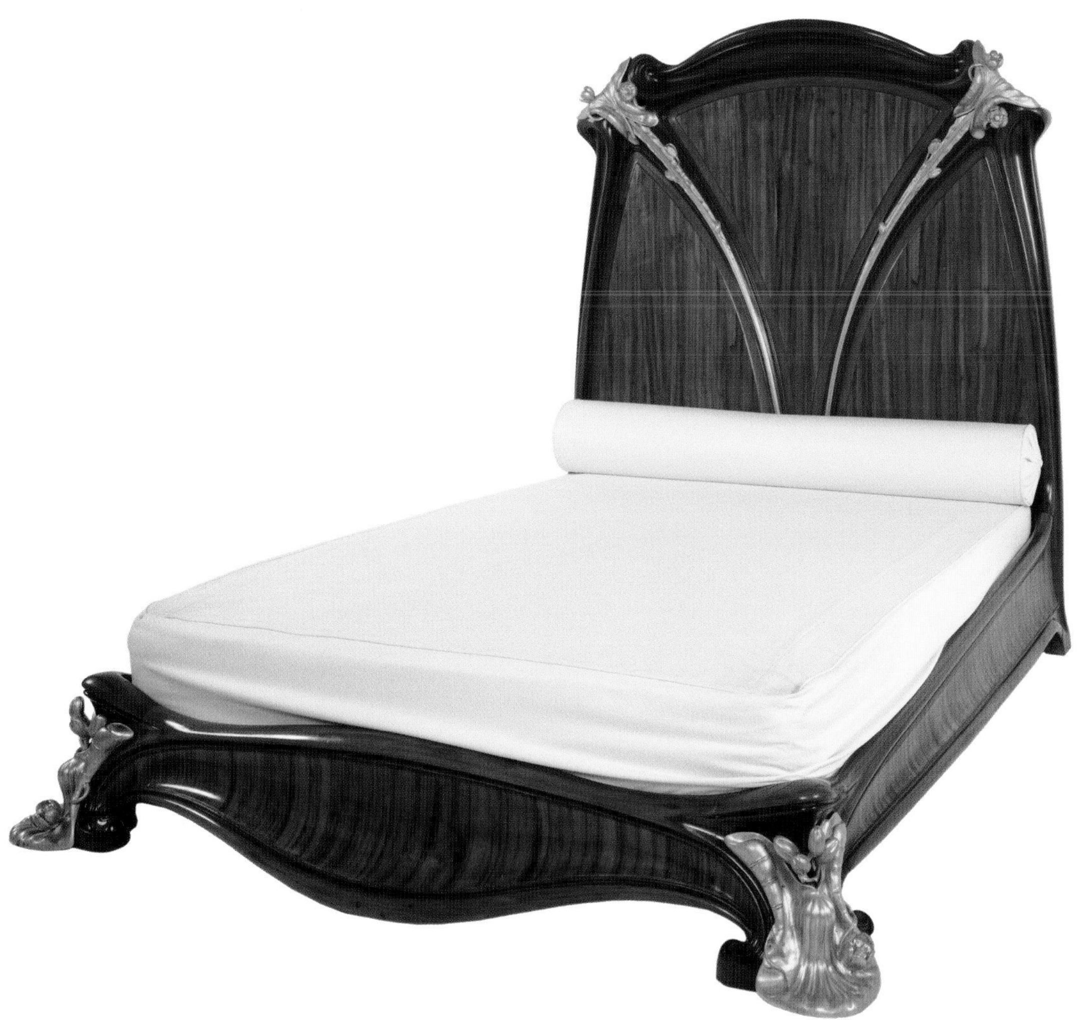

Majorelle, Louis and Daum Frères

Magnolia lamps, *c.* 1903

The 1900 Exposition Universelle of Paris was ostensibly an international event, but essentially it was an opportunity to showcase French goods and styles and display the emergent French Art Nouveau style adopted by designers such as Louis Majorelle, Emile Gallé (1846–1904) and Georges de Feure. Compared to the simplicity of form that characterized the work of other European designers, such as Joseph Olbrich (1867–1908), these French designers maintained their historical links and decorative ornament. The forms and shapes of their designs, however, were elegant and whimsical. They combined floral motifs with the luxurious quality expected of the French decorative arts.

Louis Majorelle and the Daum brothers (Auguste 1853–1909 and Antonin 1864–1930) collaborated on a number of works to combine glass and other media. The Daum brothers manufactured the glass elements, while Majorelle was responsible for the wooden or bronze elements. Here the sinuous, organically flowing bronze candelabra open into glass blooms. The nature motif is not a mere decoration for the candelabra, but is extended into the very form of the piece. This is an important development and is characteristic of the Art Nouveau aesthetic.

CREATED

Nancy

MEDIUM

Gilt-bronze and carved glass

RELATED WORK

Orchidée desk by Daum Frères and Louis Majorelle, 1903

Louis Majorelle *Born* 1859 Toul, France

Died 1926

Auguste Daum *Born* 1853 Bitche, France

Died 1909

Antonin Daum *Born* 1864 Bitche, France

Died 1930

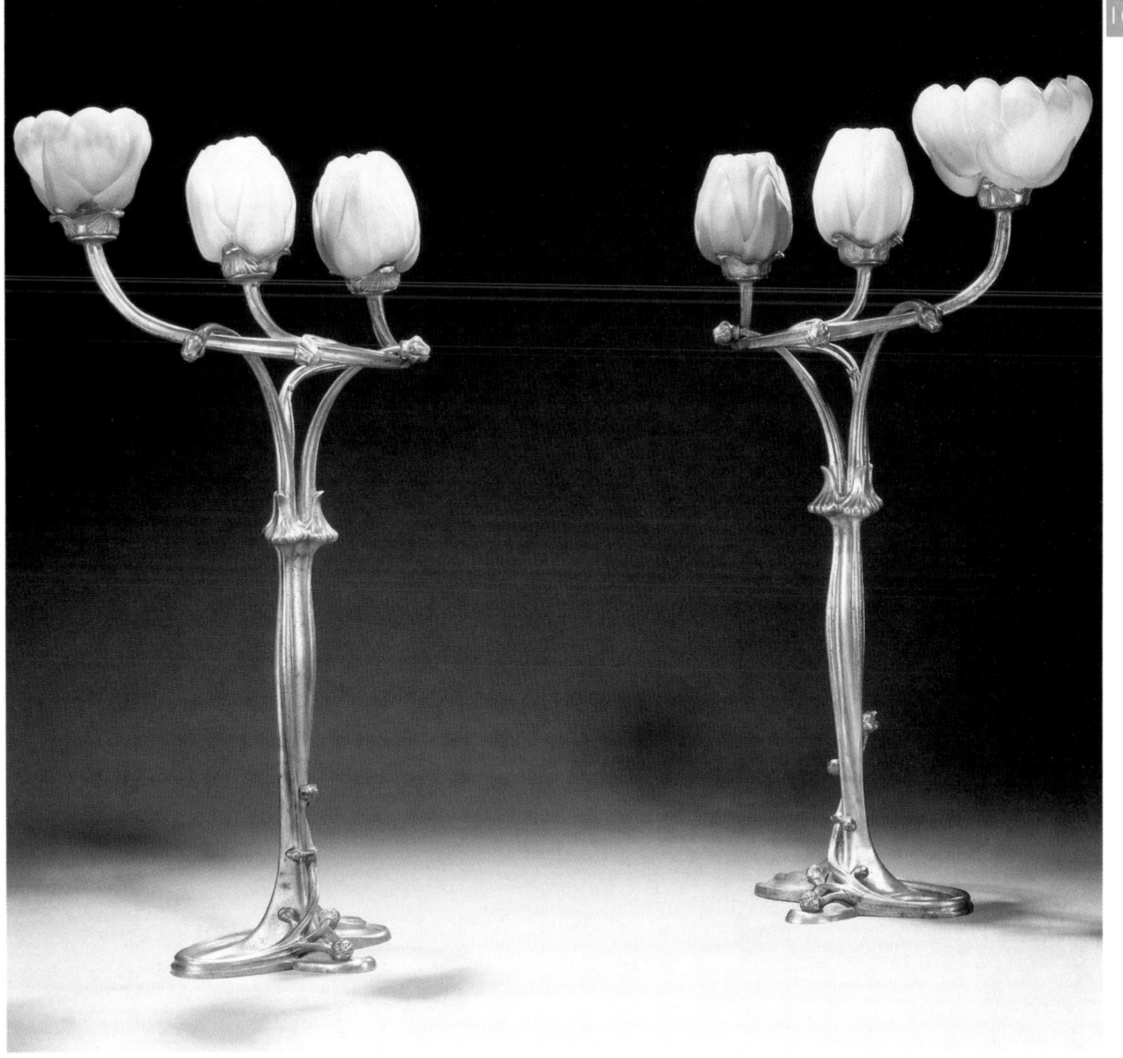

Majorelle, Louis

Fire screen

The workshop of Louis Majorelle in Nancy was a place where the synthesis of old and new methods of craftsmanship occurred. Majorelle had inherited a business that produced old-fashioned furniture the old-fashioned way. With youth and vision on his side, he set about establishing new working practices that would enable him to experiment with the Art Nouveau style and still make money. He modernized the workshop by introducing elements of machine-production, but he also maintained areas of hand labour.

Specialists continued to work by hand in wood, marquetry and bronze to create one-off items of furniture and sculpture. This meant that customers could choose between the luxurious and expensive items and the more affordable ones that had been produced, at least in part, by machines. Majorelle's output was vast and by employing different techniques he was able to lower prices. Thus the workshop generated a wide variety of goods at a range of prices. This fire screen has the soft elegant curves typical of Art Nouveau and a floral motif delicately embroidered into velvet.

CREATED

France

MEDIUM

Carved mahogany and embroidered velvet

RELATED WORK

Fire screen in ash with floral decoration by Emile Gallé, 1900

Louis Majorelle *Born* 1859 Toul, France

Died 1926

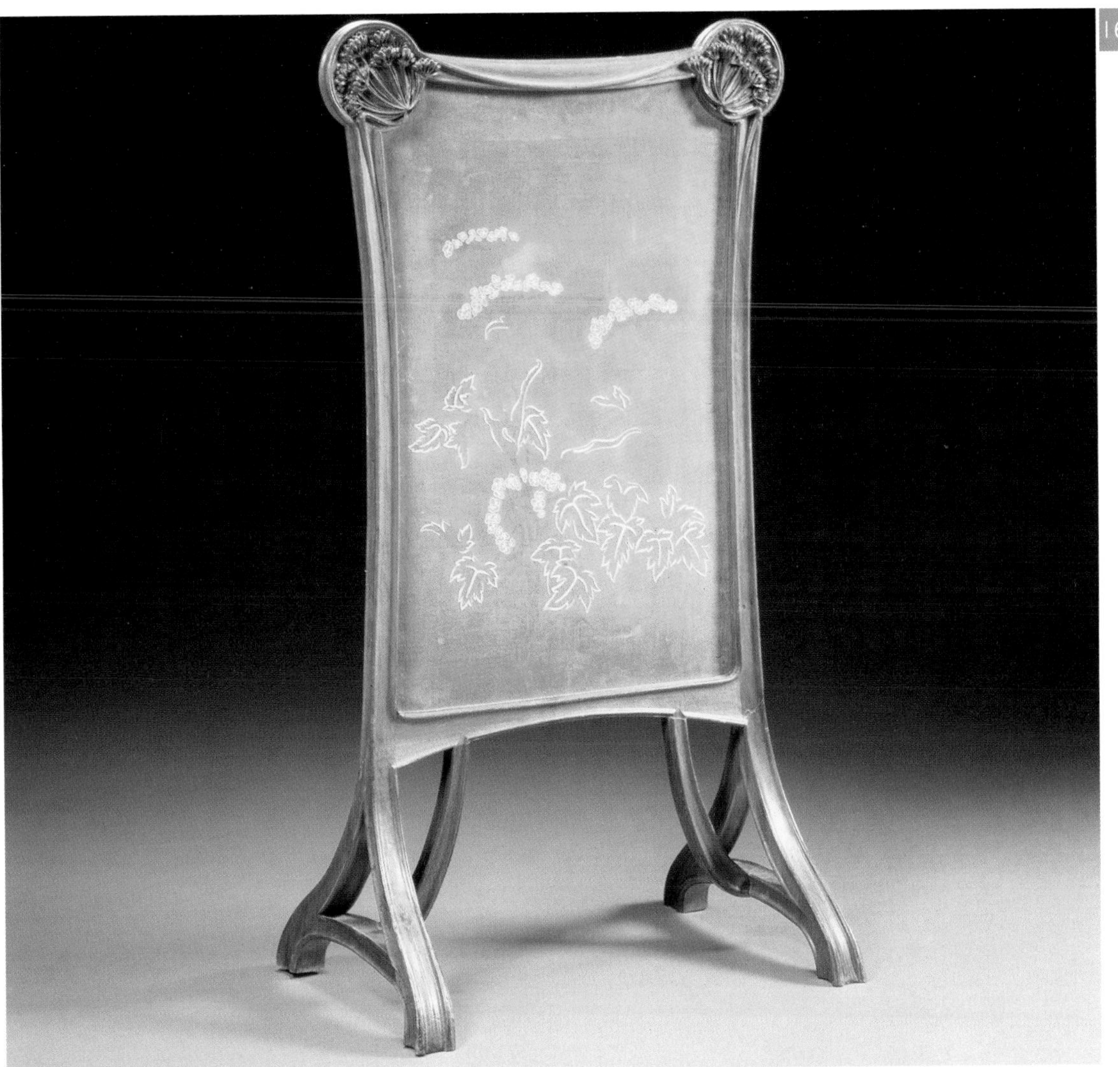

Serrurier-Bovy, Gustave

Mantel wall clock, *c.* 1905

Belgium, the home of Gustave Serrurier-Bovy (1858–1910), was the birthplace of Art Nouveau. The reason that the style was accepted here was largely to do with the many artists already in the country and especially in the city of Brussels. Avant-garde artists were welcomed in Brussels and a thriving community of international artists existed even before the style emerged. It was these artists who in turn helped to spread the Art Nouveau style to their own countries and facilitated the movement's growth and development. Art Nouveau is often cited as the first great international style; not just in recognition of its geographic distribution, but also for the wide range of influences from disparate cultures that helped to form it. It is not therefore a single style, but a collection of many.

Urban renewal in Brussels during the 1890s helped fuel the popularity of the New Art. With the advantage of wealth, many middle-class families were able to commission artists to design new buildings, interiors or furniture. Between 1900 and 1910 large parts of the city were rebuilt.

MEDIUM

Plane, lacquered brass, enamelled copper, steel

RELATED WORK

Silex range of furniture in mahogany (in kit form for self assembly) by Gustave Serrurier-Bovy, 1902

Gustave Serrurier-Bovy *Born* 1858 Liège, France

Died 1910

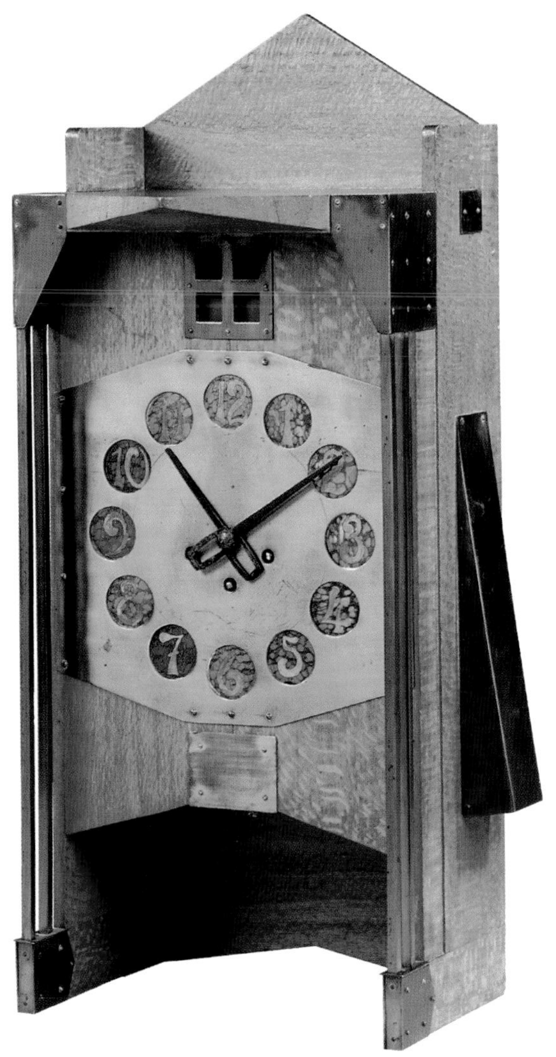

Serrurier-Bovy, Gustave

Large oak hall unit, 1898

The path that Gustave Serrurier-Bovy took, as he developed his version of the Art Nouveau style, shows how the movement matured from the 1890s to the 1900s. Like many of his contemporaries, this Belgian architect and designer had studied the traditional skills of his craft and he was aware of new and innovative work abroad. He was particularly interested in the Arts and Crafts movement of William Morris (1834–96) and the writings of John Ruskin (1819–1900), the great Victorian artist and intellectual.

Serrurier-Bovy's early designs demonstrate this interest in the philosophy of the Arts and Crafts movement. His furniture was often made of oak and showed simplicity in design and construction. He even created furniture in kit form so that it could be sold more cheaply and would therefore be accessible to more people. By around 1900, however, the artist had moved more towards the luxury market and his work became more obviously Art Nouveau than Arts and Crafts. He replaced oak with the more luxurious mahogany and added sweeping curves and stylized floral motifs. After visiting Germany in 1901 Serrurier-Bovy's furniture became straighter, more geometrical and less ornate.

MEDIUM

Oak

RELATED WORK

Metal coat stands, umbrella stands and lamps in iron and copper by Gustave Serrurier-Bovy, 1902–04

Gustave Serrurier-Bovy *Born* 1858 Liège, France

Died 1910

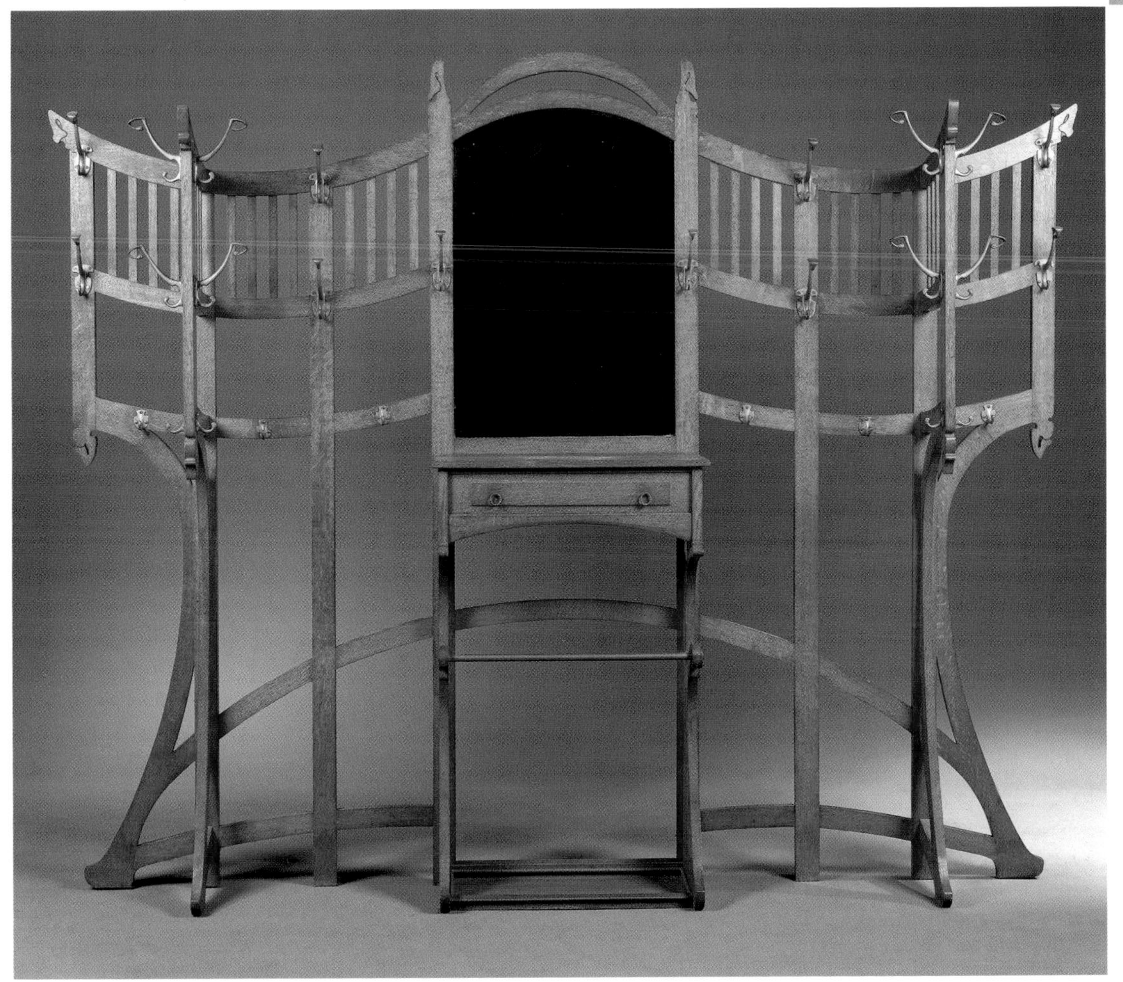

Wolfers, Philippe

Centrepiece, *c.* 1900

No other European country demonstrated the development of the Art Nouveau style better than Belgium. Here the utopian-socialist ideal of William Morris resonated with artists and architects such as Victor Horta (1861–1947); unlike Morris they did not believe that socialism precluded industrial methods of production. Exhibitions of modern art took place in Belgium regularly and, along with avant-garde groups such as Les Vingt (Les XX), they provided the opportunity for progressive designers and artists to develop the idioms of the Art Nouveau style, such as curvilinear forms.

Despite its flourishing art industry, few innovative jewellers emerged from Belgium at this time, but of these the most influential was Philippe Wolfers (1858–1929), who was born into a dynasty of Dutch and Belgian silversmiths and jewellers. Early in his career Wolfers showed a leaning towards Aestheticism. His silverware was often traditional in form but was influenced by Japanese art and featured motifs such as bamboo, flowers and fans. By the 1880s traditional forms disappeared from his designs and a true Art Nouveau aesthetic appeared, inspired by the Symbolist movement and naturalism.

MEDIUM

Metal with enamel plaques

RELATED WORK

Orchid hair ornament with gold, enamel, diamonds and rubies by Philippe Wolfers, 1902

Philippe Wolfers *Born* 1858 Belgium

Died 1929

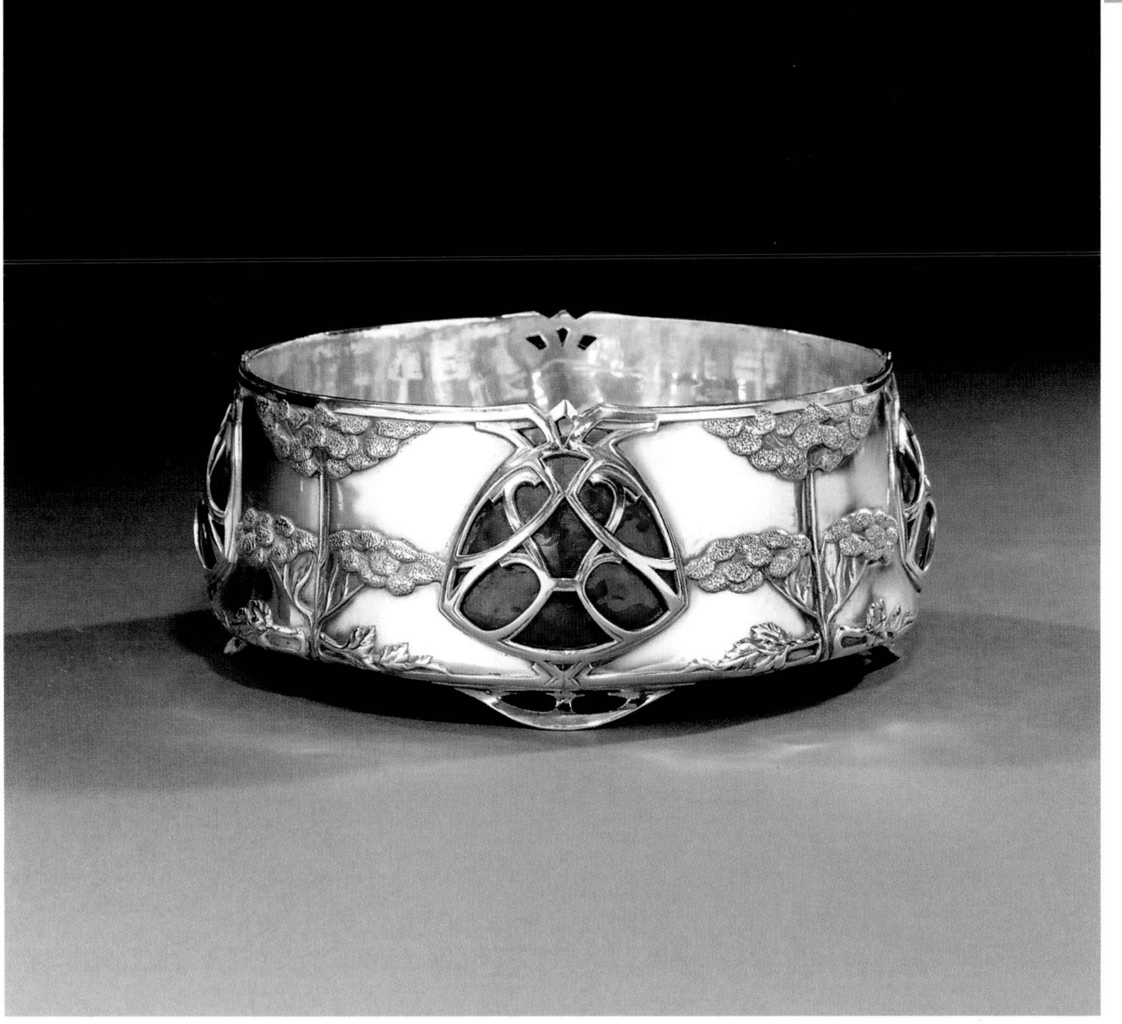

Wolfers, Philippe

Pendant

Philippe Wolfers studied at the Academie Royale des Beaux Arts in Brussels and was apprenticed to his father's firm, Maison Wolfers, at the age of 17. He was familiar with Japanese art, which had made such a powerful impression on European culture in the second half of the nineteenth century and had featured prominently in the Vienna Exhibition of 1873 and Paris International Exhibition of 1889. As a result, many of Wolfers' early pieces of metalwork and jewellery feature Japonism.

Maison Wolfers was initially a Brussels factory that sold its silverwork in Europe, particularly in the Netherlands and Belgium. Eventually the business opened its own shops and when Philippe Wolfers took over the business from his father it expanded further still. Wolfers was trained in all aspects of silversmithing, stone setting and enamelling, and used his skills to widen the range of styles that the family business produced. His own style developed from traditional to naturalist during the 1880s and 1890s. The cult of nature was a powerful influence to many artists of the day and Wolfers used images of sinuous tendrils, lilies and orchids to decorate his silverwork.

MEDIUM

Jewellery

RELATED WORK

Glass vase engraved with the figure of a bat by Philippe Wolfers, 1901

Philippe Wolfers *Born* 1858 Belgium

Died 1929

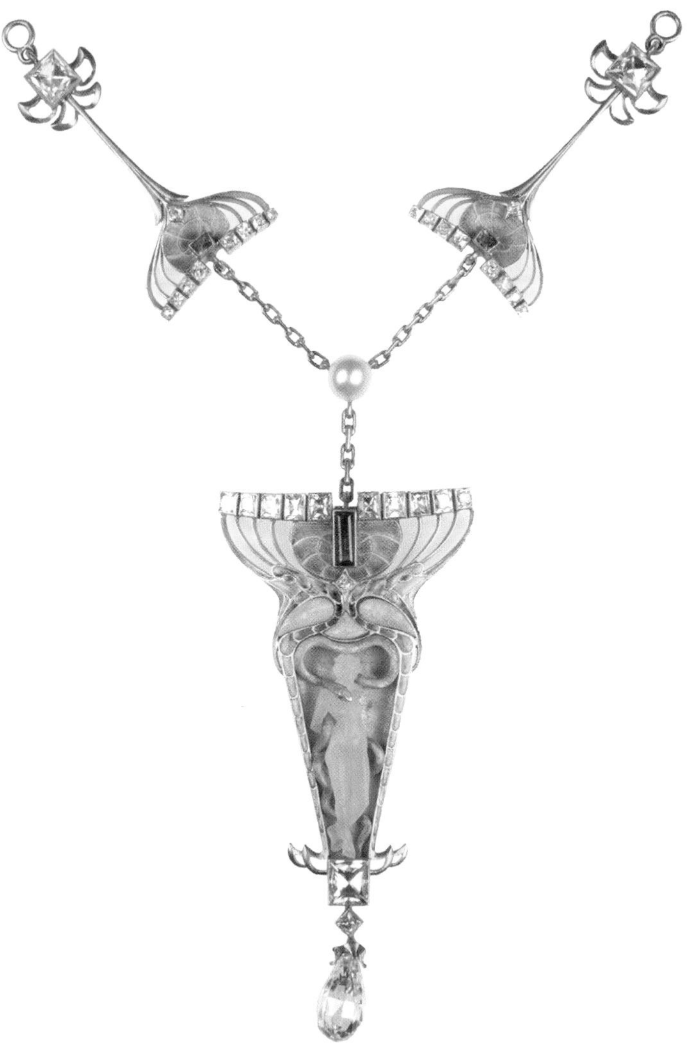

Livemont, Privat

Reproduction of a poster advertising 'Schaerbeek's Artistic Circle, the Fifth Annual Exhibition', 1897

The Belgian poster artist Privat Livemont (1861–1936) studied in Paris from 1883 to 1889 and worked there during the *belle époque*; this 'fine period' was a relatively settled and stable time during French history, from the last decades of the nineteenth century until the First World War. It was an era characterized by an era of cultural refinement, sophistication, elegance and prosperity. It was at this time that posters as cultural indicators and advertising tools came into their own, thanks particularly to the innovative work of Toulouse-Lautrec (1864–1901) and Alphonse Mucha (1860–1939).

After seven years in Paris, Livemont returned to his native Belgium and worked in Brussels and Ostende. He became one of the foremost poster artists of the Art Nouveau period in Belgium, his skill as a lithographer being perhaps greater than his innovation as an artist. Many of his advertising posters feature a scantily clad woman, normally in profile and surrounded by flowers or floral motifs. In this poster Livemont's quintessential female examines a statuette of herself. Her long and stylized hair falls in tendrils and is adorned with a metallic floral headband.

MEDIUM

Colour lithograph

RELATED WORK

Rajah, poster by Privat Livemont

Privat Livemont *Born* 1861 Schaerbeek, Brussels

Died 1936

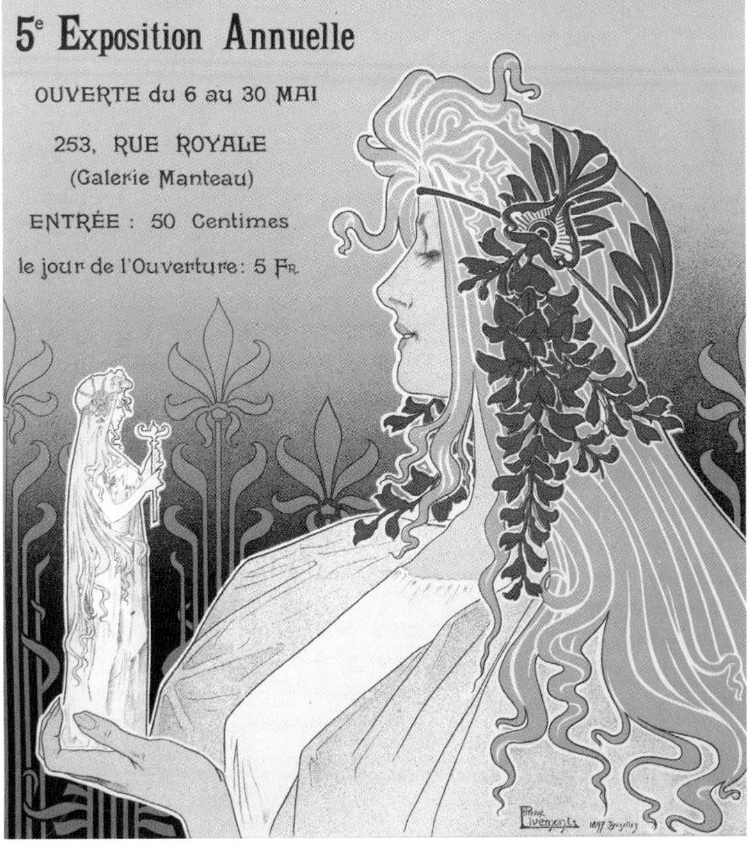
CERCLE ARTISTIQUE
de SCHAERBEEK
5e Exposition Annuelle
OUVERTE du 6 au 30 MAI
253, RUE ROYALE
(Galerie Manteau)
ENTRÉE : 50 Centimes
le jour de l'Ouverture: 5 FR.
Privat Livemont
1897 Bruxelles

Livemont, Privat

The Scent of a Rose, c. 1890

Posters of the *belle époque* came to symbolize the popular culture of the countries where they were produced. In Paris a prevailing café culture was revealed in posters advertising alcoholic drinks, such as Privat Livemont's poster for Robette Absinthe, and the posters of Toulouse-Lautrec portray the decadence of Parisian nightlife in all its splendour. Spanish posters invited the public to come and witness the traditional bullfights; in the United Kingdom and United States, literary works and circuses were advertised. Each nation adopted the poster as a medium through which stories of mundane things and extraordinary events of everyday life could be told. Feminine, romantic and stylized women amidst fussy backdrops often featured in Livemont's advertising posters: this particular image was used to sell perfume.

The proliferation of poster art from the 1880s to the First World War coincided with improved printing techniques and better distribution, which was aided by the ever-growing transport system. Competition in the market place meant that advertisers had to become canny; by the 1920s graphic designers realized that their art needed to achieve instant visual impact and brand recognition.

MEDIUM

Poster

RELATED WORK

Job by Alphonse Mucha, 1897

Privat Livemont *Born* 1861 Schaerbeek, Brussels

Died 1936

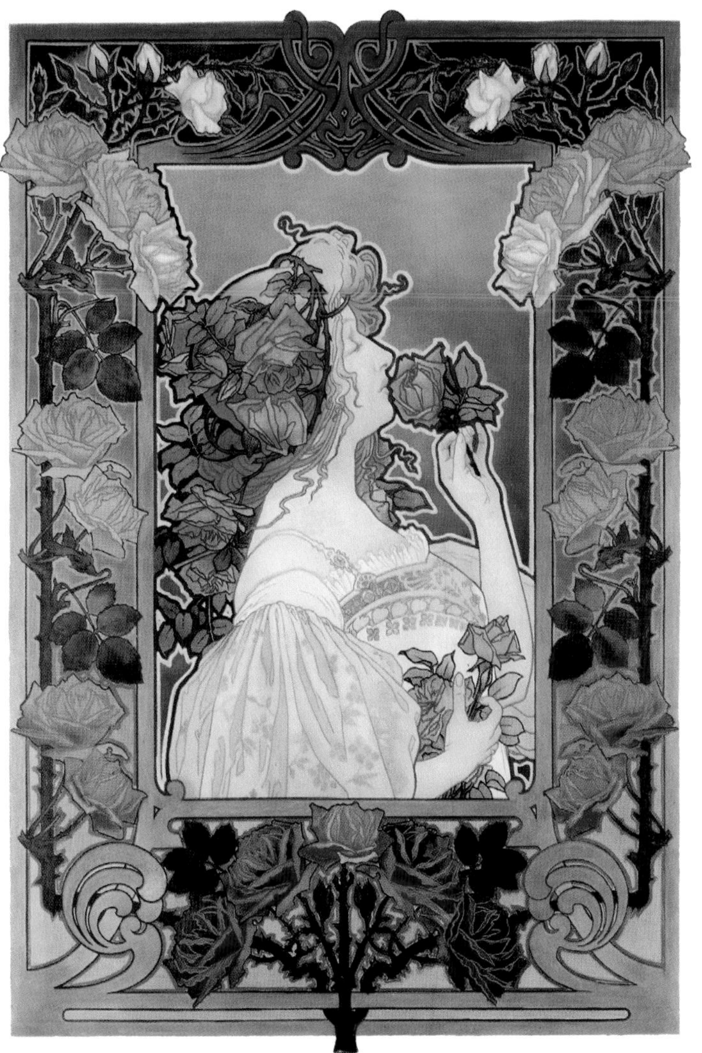

Moser, Koloman

Bentwood dressing table, *c.* 1902

The Viennese Secession movement rocked the conservative art institutions of Austria at the turn of the twentieth century. Followers of the movement, including Koloman Moser (1868–1918), rejected historicism without rejecting all elements of Classicism and many of the works from this time pay homage to the inspiration they received from the perfect proportions of Classical architecture. Music of the time went through a similar transition: Gustav Mahler had been made artistic director of the Vienna Court Opera in 1897. Mahler's music had its Classical roots set in various strands of Romanticism but its dynamic, unconventional interpretation resulted in a new musical idiom.

In 1902 the Secessionists and Mahler worked together for the Fourteenth Secessionist Exhibition (at the Secession building) in Vienna. A single theme united the show: Beethoven. A large sculpture of Beethoven by Max Klinger (1857–1920) formed the centrepiece. Max Klinger was a German painter and sculptor whose work, often gruesome and grotesque, focused on symbols, fantasy and mysticism. Gustav Klimt (1862–1918) designed a huge mural, the *Beethoven Frieze*, for this exhibition and it is regarded as one of the finest remaining works of this movement.

MEDIUM

Bentwood

MOVEMENT

Secession

RELATED WORK

Geometric plant stand in painted wood and metal by Koloman Moser, 1905

Koloman Moser *Born* 1868 Vienna, Austria

Died 1918

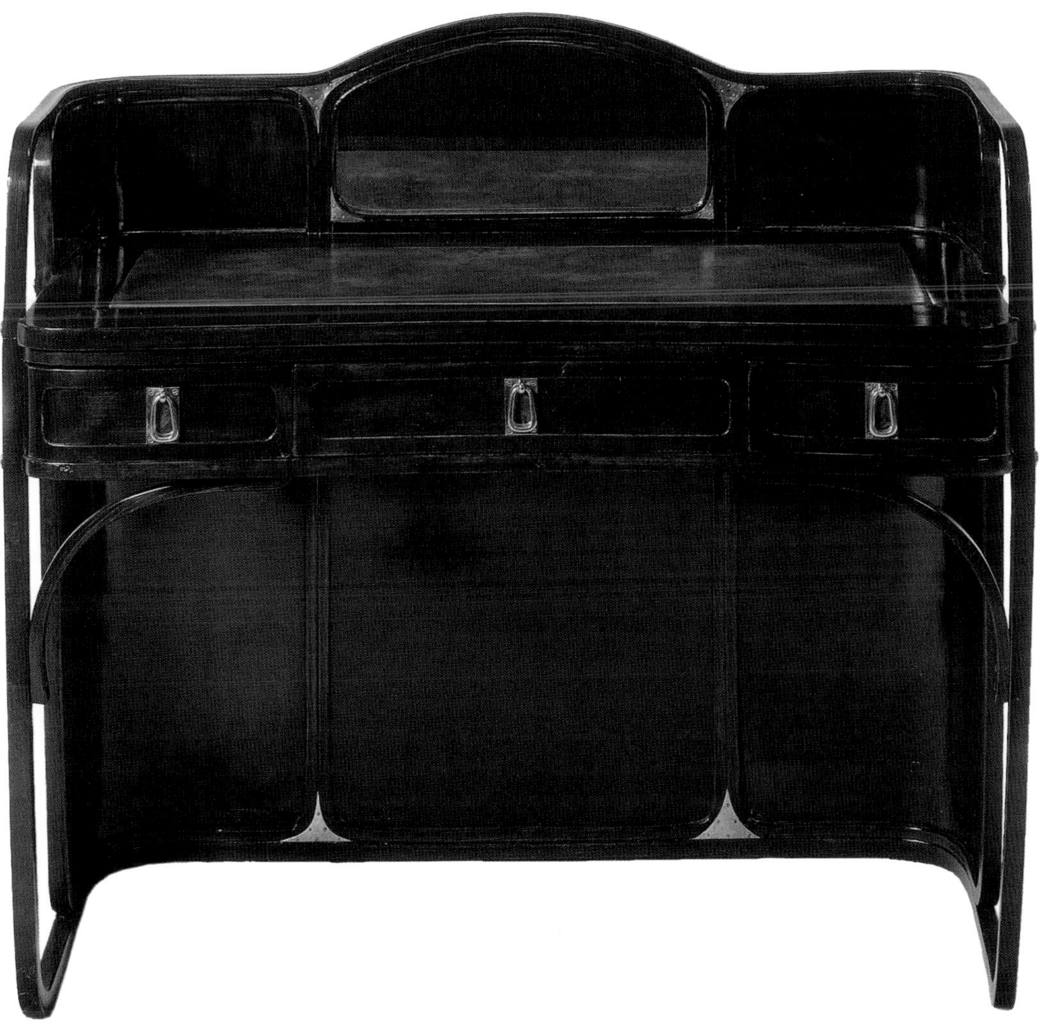

Moser, Koloman

Panel from one of a pair of *Wiener Werkstätte* white single beds

The *Wiener Werkstätte* (Viennese Workshop) was established in 1903 by Josef Hoffmann (1870–1956) and Koloman Moser. Founded on similar principles to the English Arts and Crafts movement and the London-based Guild and School of Handicraft, the *Wiener Werkstätte* aimed to preserve the skill of craftsmen and women.

Koloman Moser is widely regarded as one of the finest practitioners of applied arts in the Viennese Secession. He worked in a variety of media and on many projects, but his work in graphic design was particularly notable for its modernity. He received commissions to design stamps and banknotes and regularly contributed illustrations to the art journal *Ver Sacrum*. Moser's graphic work often featured strongly geometric patterns in black and white and rectilinear forms contrasted with curvilinear forms. Moser often worked in metal and, as seen in this panel, his decoration was frequently Minimalist. He used shiny and smooth metal that was incised so the pattern or picture became part of the form itself, intrinsic not superficial.

MEDIUM

Metal

MOVEMENT

Secession, *Wiener Werkstätte*

RELATED WORK

Presentation casket in silver with semi-precious stones by Koloman Moser, 1905–06

Koloman Moser *Born* 1868 Vienna, Austria

Died 1918

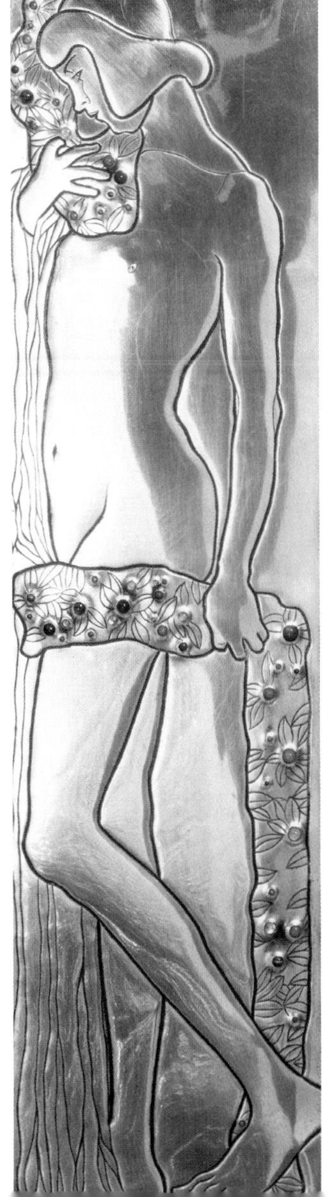

Moser, Koloman

Design for the Frommes calendar, for the 14th Exhibition of the Vienna Secession, 1902

The Viennese Secession began with 40 members and with the expressed aim of encouraging and creating art that existed as 'art for life' and did not differentiate between types of art, such as craftwork or fine art, or discriminate between affordable or expensive art. The first exhibitions showed modern foreign art and many exhibits of craftwork. More than 57,000 attendances were recorded and money donated to the cause was used to buy contemporary foreign art that was then offered for display in public places.

At the exhibition, space was given over to *Ver Sacrum*, the magazine of the Secession, to which Koloman Moser contributed. As with the German *Die Jugend* journal (of the *Jugendstil* movement), *Ver Sacrum* made clear references to youth. The name itself ('Rite of Spring' or 'Sacred Spring') comes from a mythical ritual of ancient Rome, in which young people were sent away from their homeland to spread their culture and language afar. The Secessionists set themselves a similar mission, to escape from the confines of their traditional elders in order to discover and spread their new ideas.

MOVEMENT

Secession

RELATED WORK

Front cover for *Ver Sacrum* by Koloman Moser, 1899

Koloman Moser *Born* 1868 Vienna, Austria

Died 1918

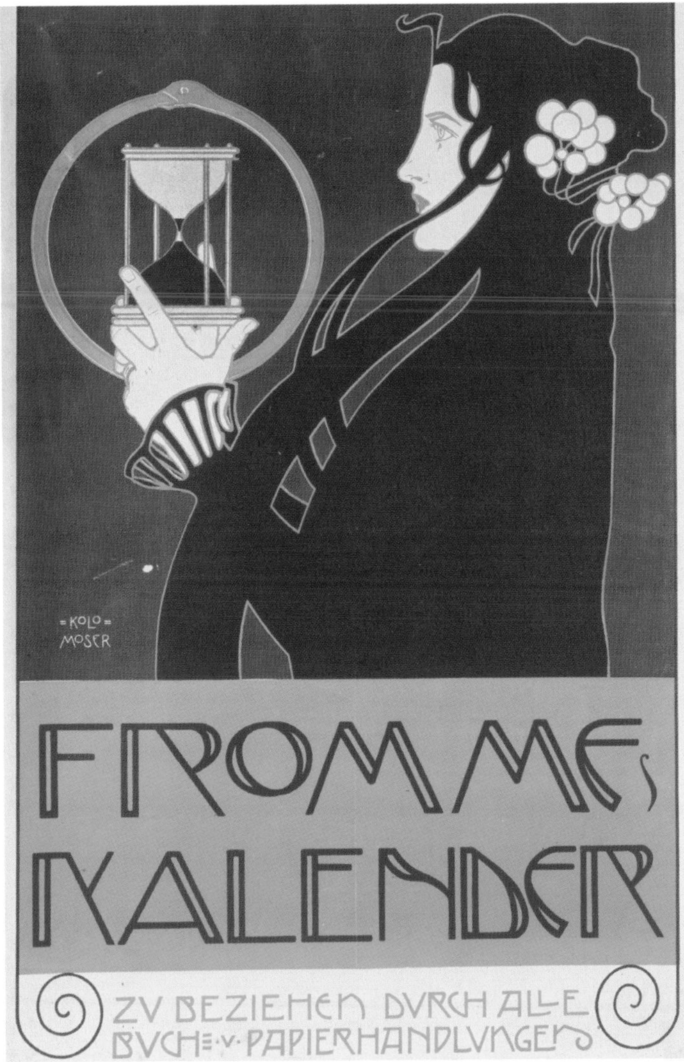

KOLO MOSER
FROMMES KALENDER
ZV BEZIEHEN DVRCH ALLE BVCHE- V. PAPIERHANDLVNGEN

Olbrich, Joseph M.

Secession House, 1898–99

The Secession House was planned, by founding members of the Viennese Secession, to be a place where modern art and crafts could be displayed. This was a very public statement of opposition to the traditional and conservative leaders of the contemporary Viennese art scene, who refused to exhibit the new foreign art to protect the commercial interests of home-grown artists and artisans. As a result of this intransigence, Viennese art had stagnated. The Secessionists sought to revitalize their colleagues through a series of exhibitions.

The building opened in 1898. It was symmetrical and monumental in style, having been largely based on ancient sacred temples. The single ornamental dome, based on a sketch by Gustav Klimt, was covered in a filigree pattern of gilded laurel leaves. Over the doorway the motto 'To the Age its Art, to the Art its Freedom' was inscribed. When visitors entered the main door they stepped into a long room that was decorated by Klimt's *Beethoven Frieze* with its scandalous erotic imagery depicted in gold paint and appliquéd materials, such as mother-of-pearl and curtain rings.

CREATED

Vienna

MEDIUM

Architecture

MOVEMENT

Secession

RELATED WORK

The Wedding Tower in Darmstadt by Joseph Olbrich, 1906

Joseph M. Olbrich *Born* 1867 Silesia, Austria

Died 1908

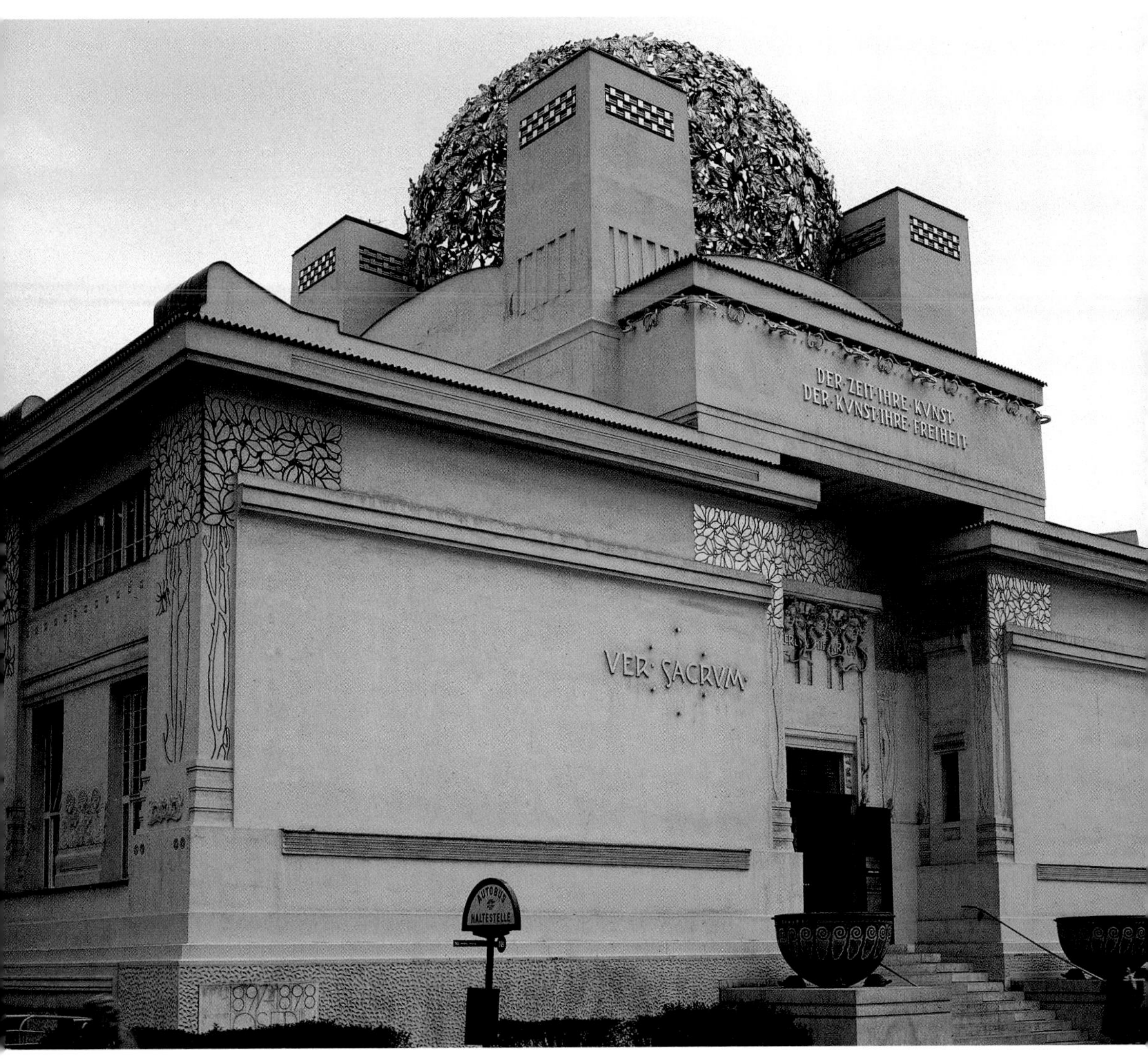
DER·ZEIT·IHRE·KVNST·
DER·KVNST·IHRE·FREIHEIT·
VER·SACRVM·
AUTOBUS
HALTESTELLE

Olbrich, Joseph M.

Study for Olbrich's House, Darmstadt (from *Architektur von Olbrich*), c. 1904–14

Olbrich's work, both in Vienna as part of the Secession movement and in Germany as part of the *Jugendstil* movement, was an attempt to integrate art into everyday life. The aim was to incorporate both the applied arts and architecture into a harmonious vision of modernity. A building and all elements of its interior, from the layout of rooms to the china and textiles, were united as a single piece of art.

Olbrich moved to Darmstadt in Germany at the invitation of the Grand Duke Ernest Ludwig von Hesse. The Grand Duke hoped to bring the Art Nouveau movement to Germany with the aid of a select band of artists who would create a colony to generate new art. This colony was a model for the future and it became known as the Mathildenhöhe. The artists built themselves houses on a hill above the city that would form the basis of an exhibition in 1901. One of the most eye-catching buildings designed for the colony was an ornate Russian Orthodox chapel with golden domes. It was built for Czar Nicholas II, who was married to Darmstadt's Princess Alexandra.

MEDIUM

Colour lithograph

MOVEMENT

Jugendstil

RELATED WORK

Ernest Ludwig House at Darmstadt by Jospeh Olbrich, 1901

Joseph M. Olbrich *Born* 1867 Silesia, Austria

Died 1908

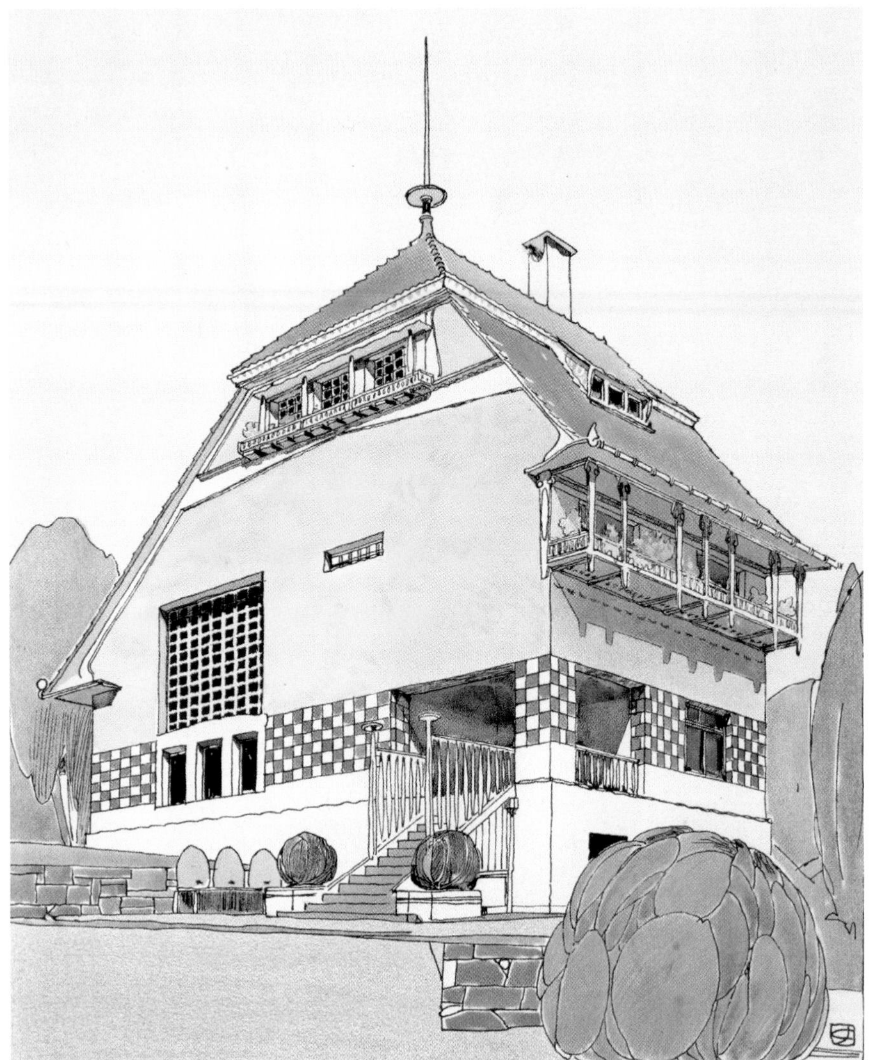

Olbrich, Joseph M.

Table, *c.* 1905

The work of the artists at the Darmstadt colony did not meet with unqualified success. The Grand Duke who patronized the colony hoped that the advent of modern art in his region would create commercial opportunities in a town with design-based industries. The hope was that artists would produce quality designs that could be translated industrially into artefacts within the means of 'citizens of not overly-abundant means'. This proved to be an impractical aspiration in Darmstadt and by 1903 the colony had mostly disbanded, although Joseph Olbrich remained to work on housing designs, with a remit to make the buildings affordable. The houses were duly designed, built and exhibited at the second Darmstadt Exhibition in 1904, but they also proved to be far beyond the financial means of the target market.

This table was designed by Joseph Olbrich for the Music Salon at the Mathildenhöhe in Darmstadt in 1905. It demonstrates a functional simplicity combined with craftsmanship. It features an inlaid pattern created using various woods and mother-of-pearl.

CREATED

Darmstadt

MEDIUM

Inlaid and ebonized maple and burr wood

MOVEMENT

Jugendstil

RELATED WORK

Corner House and Blue House at Darmstadt by Joseph Olbrich, 1904

Joseph M. Olbrich *Born* 1867 Silesia, Austria

Died 1908

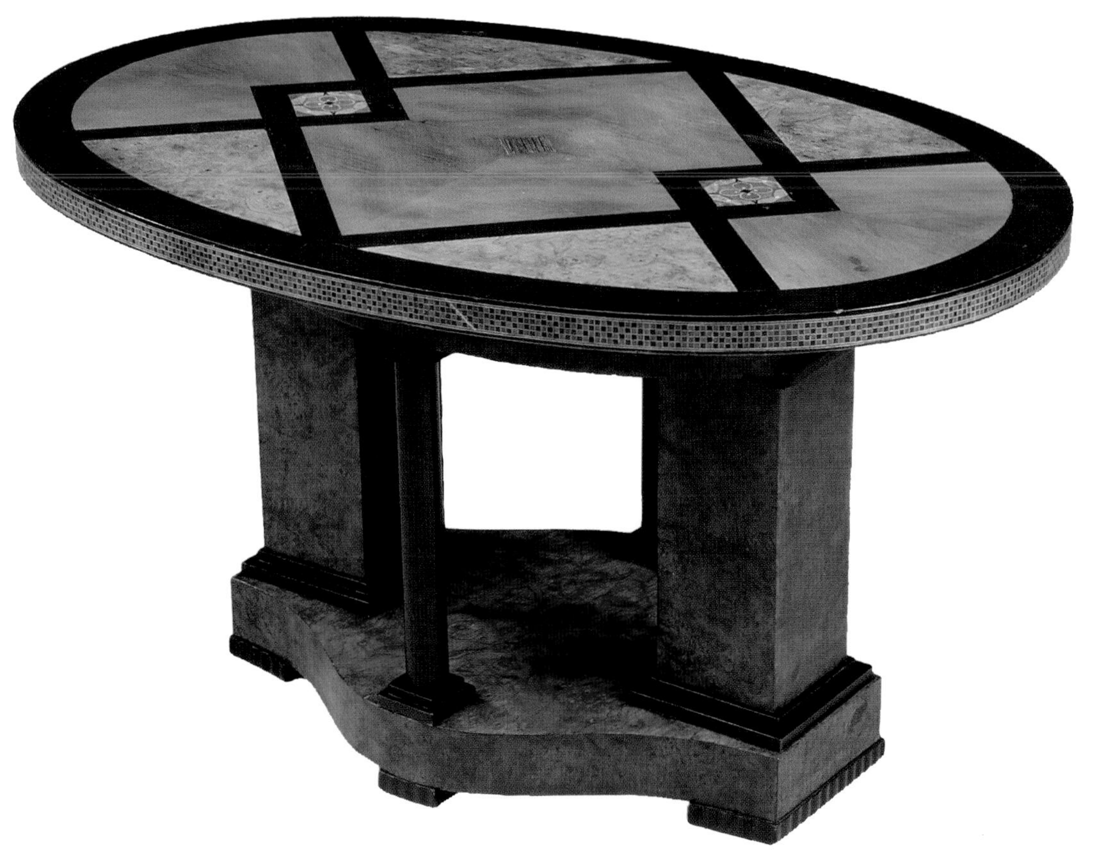

Behrens, Peter

Set of six white-metal teaspoons

Although he initially studied painting, Peter Behrens (1868–1940) eventually abandoned the medium and concentrated on graphic design and the applied arts. He settled in Munich and worked illustrating magazines and other publications; his work of the time shows him to have been a proponent of *Jugendstil*. In 1896 Behrens became a founding member of the Munich *Vereinigte Werkstätten für Kunst in Handwerk* (United Workshops for Art and Handicraft), one of several similar organizations in Germany that evolved before the more famous Austrian *Wiener Werkstätte*.

This organization resolved the underlying tension present in much of the Art Nouveau movement: how can the integrity of quality design be maintained by, or even be suitable for, mass production. For many designers the two ideas were incompatible, since the mere act of mass-producing a design reduced its status from art to fashion. The *Vereinigte Werkstätten* distanced itself from the romantic and socialist notions of William Morris and Charles Ashbee (1863–1942) and set itself a commercial goal. By 1907 it employed 600 people and was a dynamic, successful manufacturer with a strong design ethic.

MEDIUM

White metal

MOVEMENT

Jugendstil

RELATED WORK

Stoneware jug salt-glazed and with applied enamel by Peter Behrens, 1903

Peter Behrens *Born* 1868 Hamburg, Germany

Died 1940

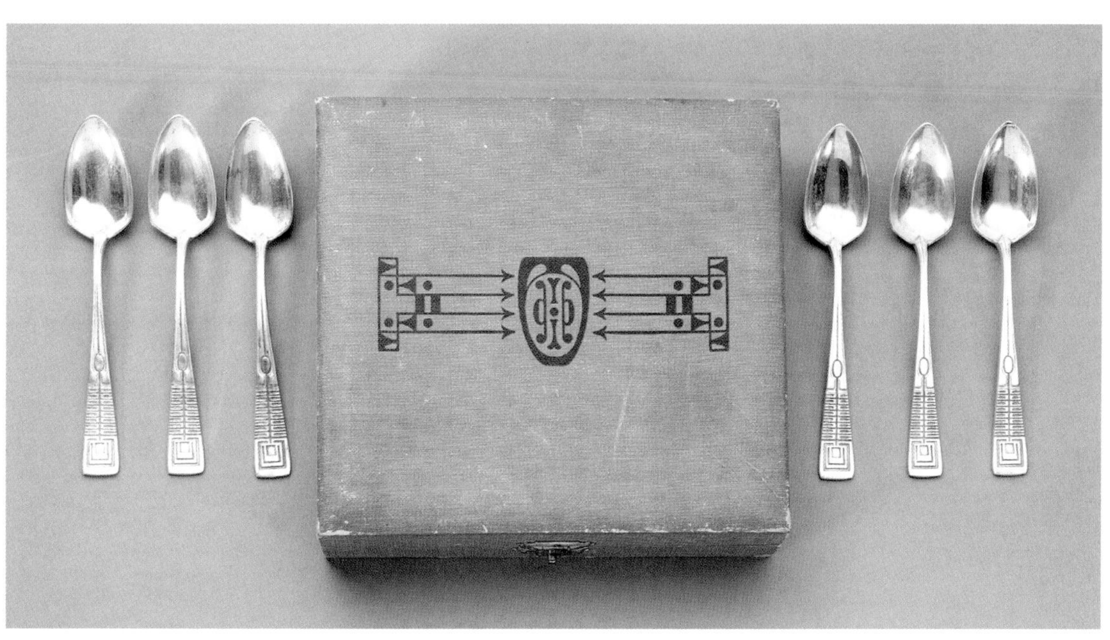

Behrens, Peter

White-painted side chair, 1901

In 1899 Peter Behrens was one of seven artists invited by Grand Duke Ernst Ludwig von Hesse to set up a cultural community in Darmstadt. The Grand Duke was Queen Victoria's grandson and when staying in England he had taken a particular interest in the works of John Ruskin and William Morris. His aim was to establish an arts and crafts community in Darmstadt and he asked a select few artists to build themselves houses at Mathildenhöhe with a view to displaying them at an exhibition.

The Behrens house incorporated both Arts and Crafts and *Jugendstil* influences and the artist designed everything in it, from the architecture to the cutlery. This chair was part of a dining-room suite from the house, which Behrens presented to the 1901 Exhibition, 'A Document of German Art'. The dining room was described as, 'sparkling white, intensified an extremely delicate combination with silver ... in some places a contrasting deep bluish red appears ... in a hundred different places, the eye meets with the same motif, but it is an eternal theme with endless variations'.

CREATED

Darmstadt

MEDIUM

White-painted wood with leather seat and copper close-nails

MOVEMENT

Jugendstil

RELATED WORK

Table lamp in bronze and coloured glass by Peter Behrens, 1902

Peter Behrens *Born* 1868 Hamburg, Germany

Died 1940

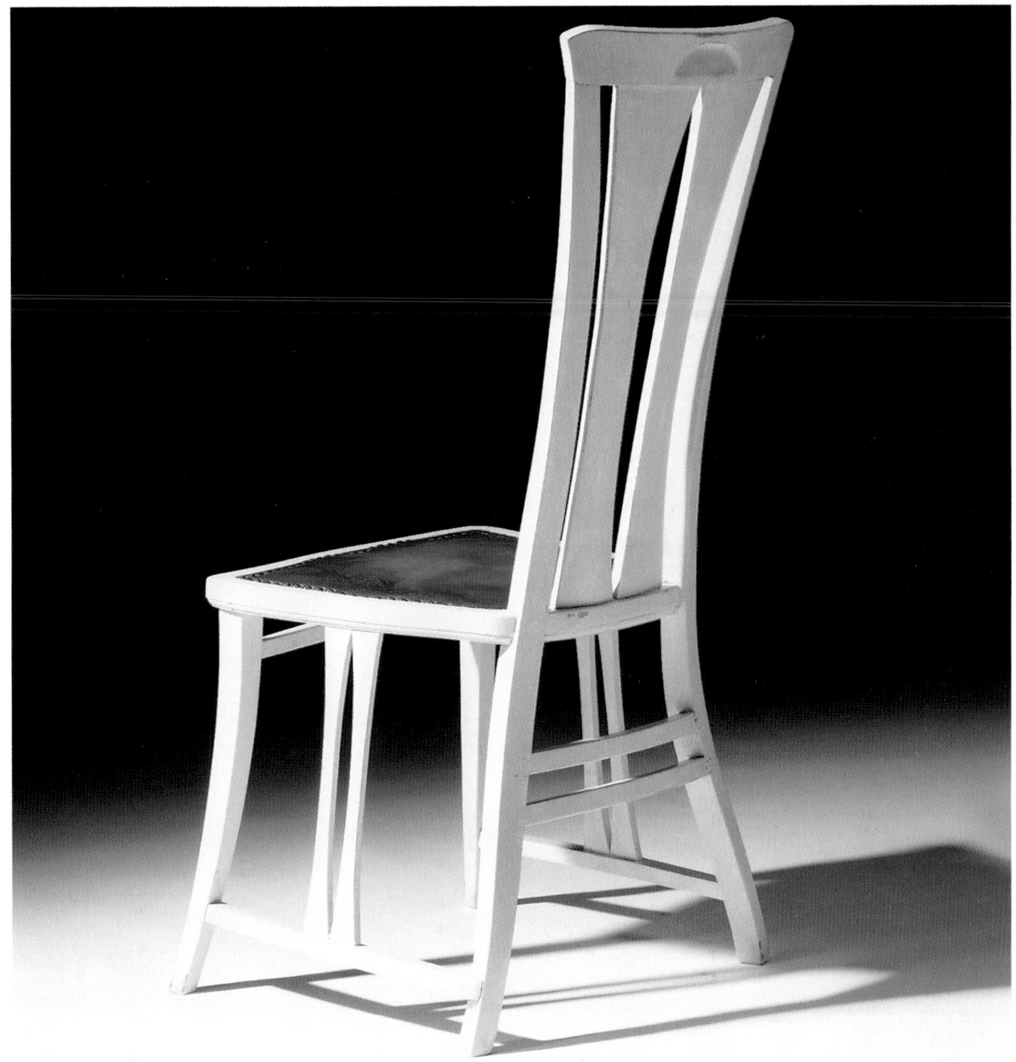

Behrens, Peter

Porcelain cup and saucer, 1901

The artists' colony at Darmstadt was not a commercial success and Peter Behrens left it in 1903 to become director of the Düsseldorf School of Applied Arts. In 1906 he was invited to take up the position of artistic adviser for AEG, a large electrical company based in Berlin, with the responsibility of producing publicity material for the company. Eventually he was awarded even greater responsibility and oversaw all design elements for the factory buildings, workers' housing and also industrial design (including kettles, fans and light fixtures).

Behrens' move to AEG was an extremely important step in the development of commercial identity and an artist's involvement with industry. Behrens pioneered the concept of corporate image and even designed a typeface for the exclusive use of the electrical giant. In 1907, while still working for AEG, Behrens became a founding member of *Deutscher Werkbund*, an umbrella organization that aimed to bring artists, craftsman and industry together. AEG joined the influential organization, as did highly influential artists of the day, including Hoffmann, Olbrich and Henry van de Velde (1863–1957).

MEDIUM

Porcelain ceramic

MOVEMENT

Jugendstil

RELATED WORK

Electric fan by Peter Behrens, 1908

Peter Behrens *Born* 1868 Hamburg, Germany

Died 1940

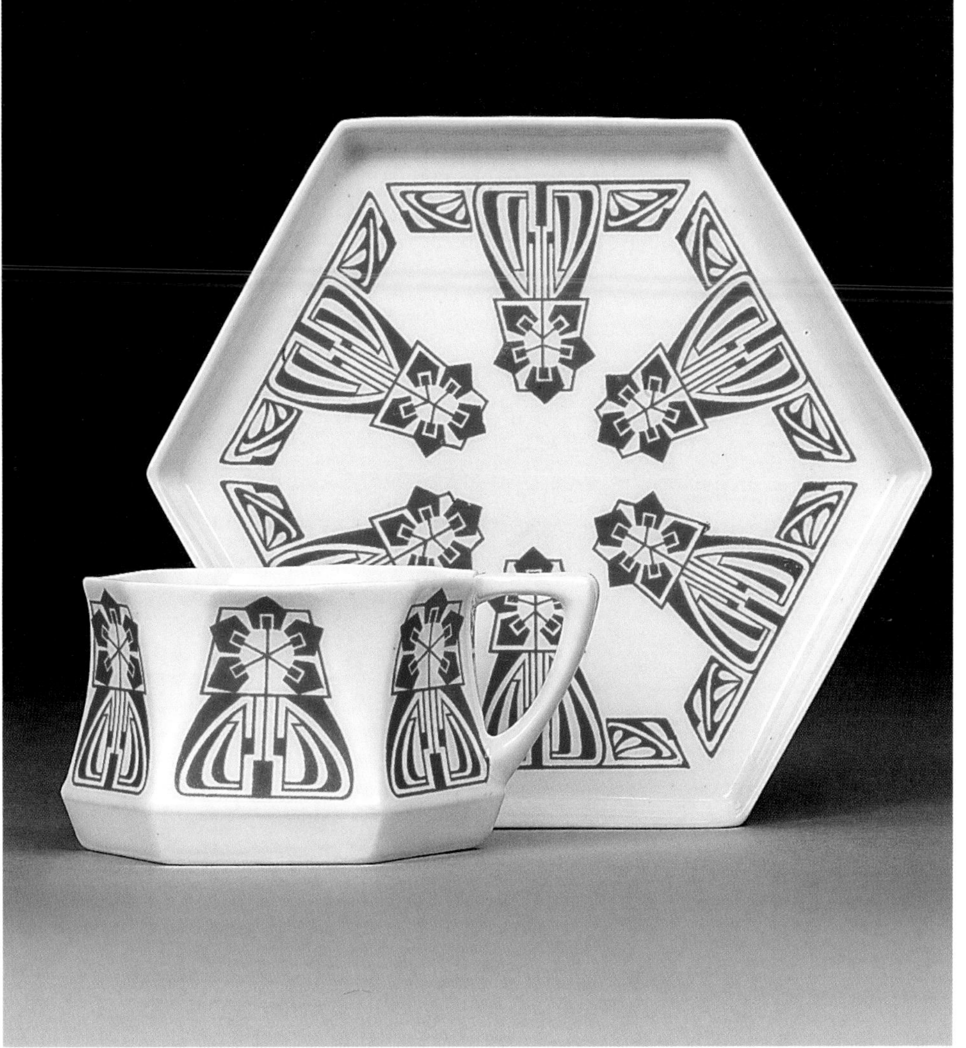

Mackintosh, Charles Rennie and Margaret Macdonald

Design for a music room, 1901

This design for a music room was not executed during Mackintosh's lifetime. It was submitted as part of an entry for a competition to produce drawings for 'A House for an Art Lover', but Mackintosh's entry was eventually disqualified as his drawings for the interiors arrived late. However, he received a special award in recognition of the originality and high standard of his work.

In 1989 building began in Bellahouston Park, Glasgow, to create Mackintosh's vision in bricks and mortar. Contemporary artists and craftsmen and women followed Mackintosh's detailed designs from his original portfolio and the project was completed in 1996. The main hall is a grand opening to the house, with wooden panelling decorated with beaten metal sections. Natural light enters through three elongated windows. The hall connects to the dining room by sliding doors, further increasing the space available for entertaining. The dining room is decorated with gesso panels and a rose motif recurs in the furniture, carpets and stained glass. The music room is long and flooded with natural light thanks to the series of double doors that open on to a south-facing balcony.

MEDIUM

Colour lithograph

RELATED WORK

Bedroom for The Hill House by Charles Rennie Mackintosh, 1902–03

Charles Rennie Mackintosh *Born* 1868 Glasgow, Scotland

Died 1928

Margaret Macdonald Mackintosh *Born* 1864 Tipton, England

Died 1933

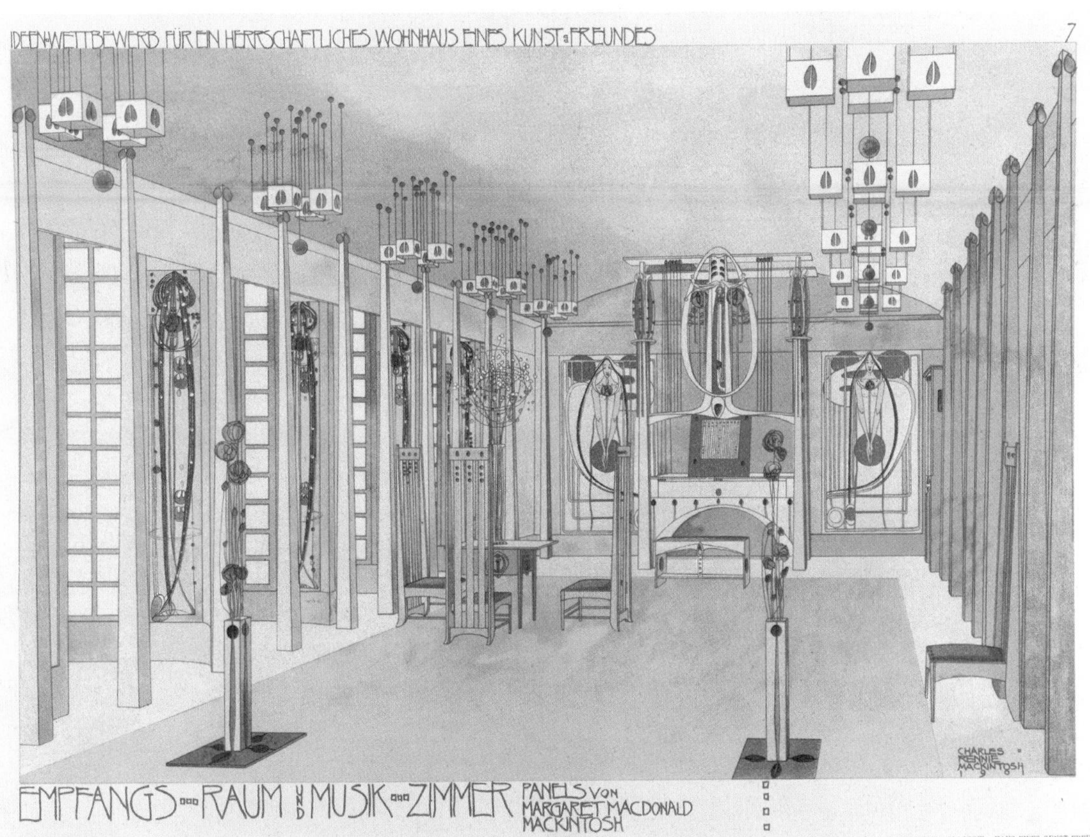
IDEEN-WETTBEWERB FÜR EIN HERRSCHAFTLICHES WOHNHAUS EINES KUNST-FREUNDES
7
CHARLES RENNIE MACKINTOSH 1901
EMPFANGS-RAUM UND MUSIK-ZIMMER
PANELS VON MARGARET MACDONALD MACKINTOSH
C. R. MACKINTOSH. GLASGOW. HAUS EINES KUNST-FREU

Mackintosh, Margaret Macdonald

Decorative panel of beaten metal, 1898–99

As the end of the nineteenth century approached, Glasgow was a hotbed of artistic invention and modernity. Charles Rennie Mackintosh, Herbert McNair (1870–1945) and their respective wives, Margaret Macdonald (1864–1933) and Frances Macdonald (1873–1921), were major proponents of a style that became known as the Glasgow School or style. They exhibited their work in London at the Arts and Crafts exhibition of 1890 and gained some fame through *The Studio* magazine, which published an entire article about them afterwards. This led to commissions and so their success grew.

The Glasgow School was remarkable because it used a more linear, restrained and geometric style than is normally associated with Art Nouveau. In many ways their style consisted of the simplistic forms rhythmically repeated, understated motifs and geometry, which are often regarded as characteristics of the Art Deco style, which grew out of the Art Nouveau movement. The designs by Margaret Macdonald and Mackintosh are often endowed with a strong sense of elegance, simplicity and harmony. Macdonald was skilled in the design and execution of repoussé metalwork, in which a decorative finish is made by hammering metal from the reverse side. Such panel work is a common feature of many interior designs by Mackintosh.

MEDIUM

Beaten metal

RELATED WORK

Decorative panel for the interior of a wardrobe by Margaret Macdonald and Charles Rennie Mackintosh

Margaret Macdonald Mackintosh *Born* 1864 Tipton, England

Died 1933

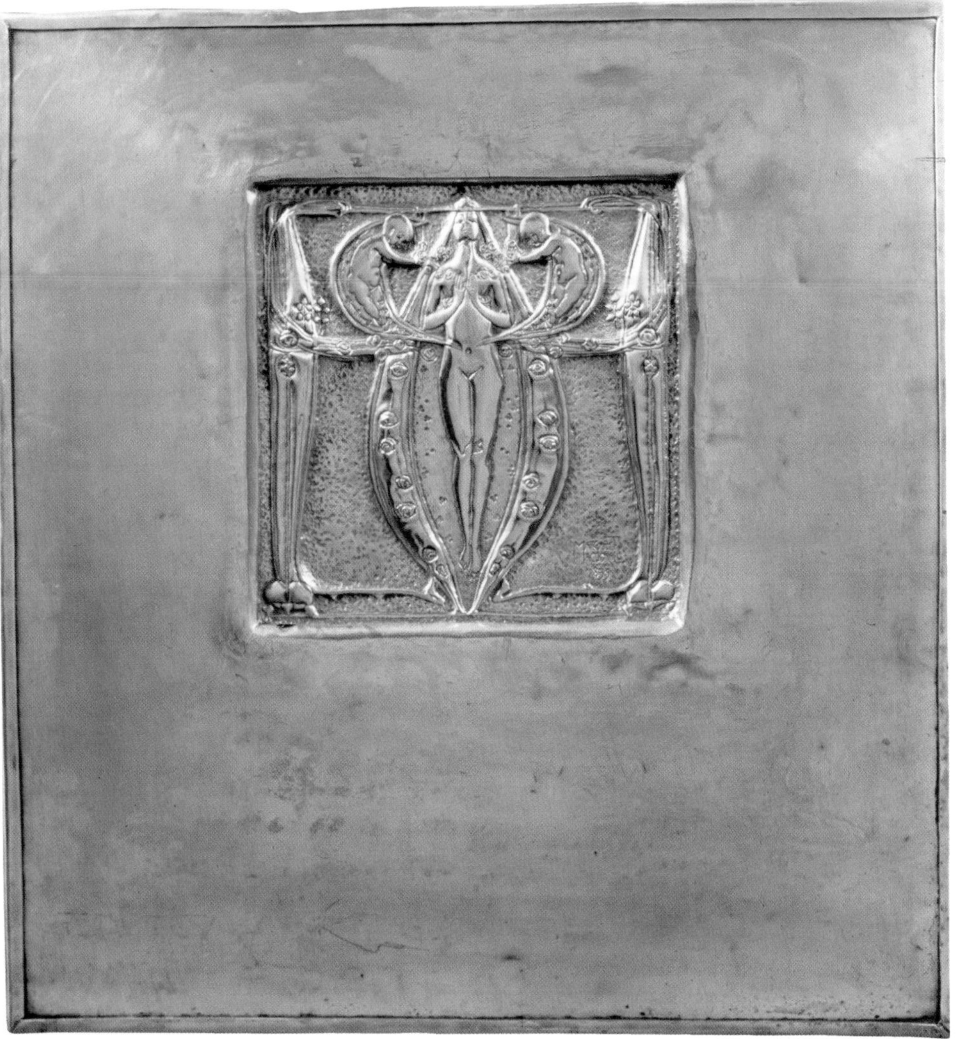

Mackintosh, Margaret Macdonald

Opera of the Seas, 1903

Glasgow is, more than any other British city, most closely associated with Art Nouveau and the developments in style that took place between 1890 and 1910. It was a growing industrial city with an economy based on the ship and locomotive industries, engineering and textiles. Many local people worked in the field of design and were highly skilled in a range of manufacturing techniques. Commercial demands were such that modern developments in style were exercised by local designers and shown at large exhibitions. While the Arts and Crafts movement centred on the individual skill of an artisan, the Glasgow style centred on the design needs of an increasingly industrial society. As such, metal and metalwork became an essential idiom for the style of the region. The influence of the wider Art Nouveau movement can be seen in the recurring theme of nature that occurred in many Glaswegian designs.

The *Opera of the Seas* is based on 'The Dead Princess' by the Symbolist Belgian poet and playwright Maurice Maeterlinck.

MEDIUM

Gesso panel

RELATED WORK

Honesty, mirror in tin and wood by Margaret Macdonald Mackintosh, 1903

Margaret Macdonald Mackintosh *Born* 1864 Tipton, England

Died 1933

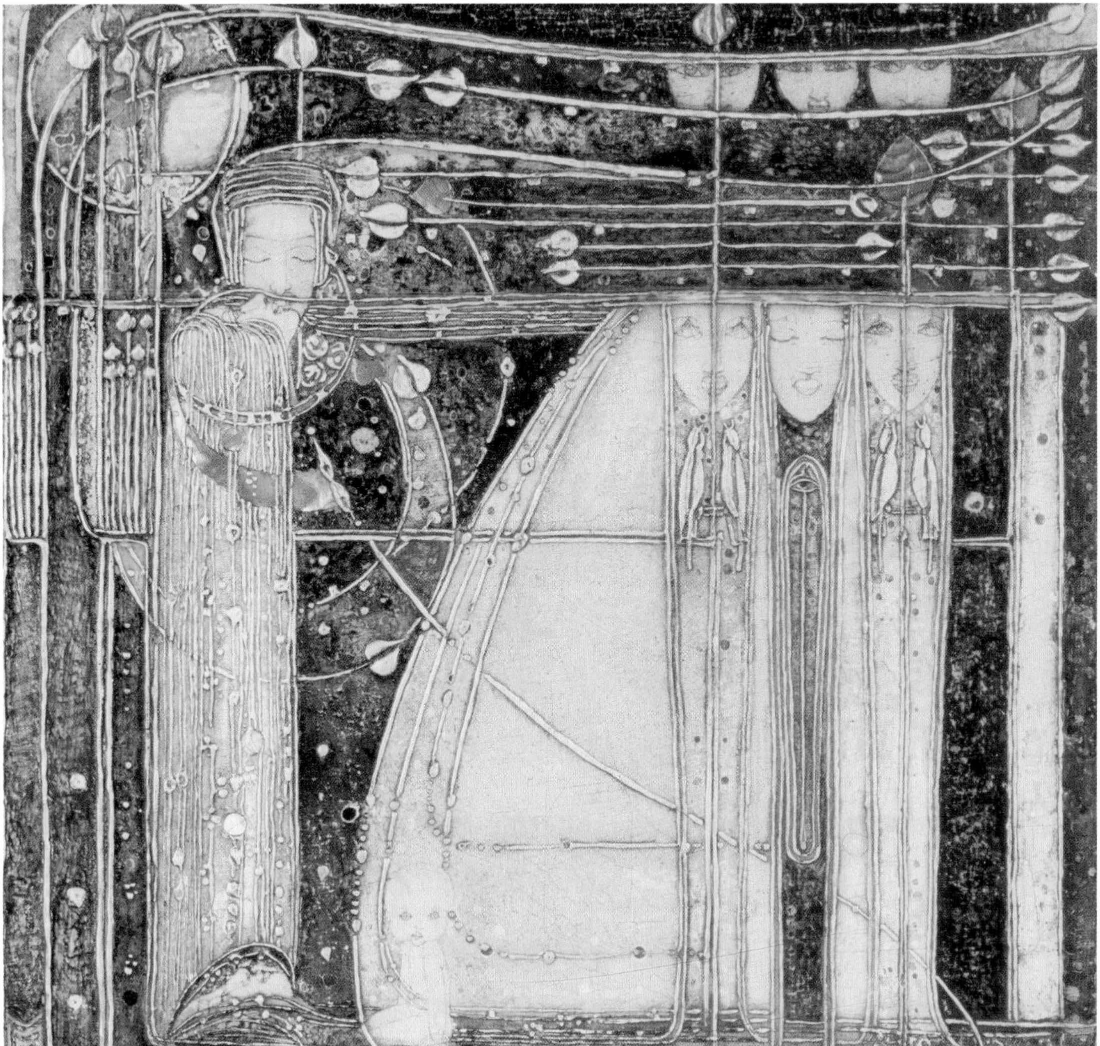

Bugatti, Carlo

Cheval glass, *c.* 1902

When Italy made its first significant inroad into the Art Nouveau movement, with the Turin Exposition in 1902, the style was already established in other parts of Europe. The Italians lagged behind and then faced the almost impossible task of introducing an original thread of modernity without being criticized for plagiarism. The exposition set Italian designers three main aims: to create art based on nature that rejected historical influences, to create democratic art and to produce unity in interior design, such that all elements should harmonize. There was widespread disappointment at the Turin Exposition that Italian artists had not managed to create their own national style. Their superb craftsmanship was, however, acknowledged and the work of Carlo Bugatti (1855–1940) was selected for special praise for its originality. In general, though, the Italians had put together an impressive collection of decorative arts, given the political and social constraints that existed in the newly united country.

A cheval glass is a full-length mirror that tilts in its frame. This mirror is decorated in embossed leather and vellum (parchment made from the hide of a young animal).

MEDIUM

Glass, painted vellum and embossed leather

RELATED WORK

Snail-shaped chair in tropical wood by Carlo Bugatti, 1902

Carlo Bugatti *Born* 1855 Milan, Italy

Died 1940

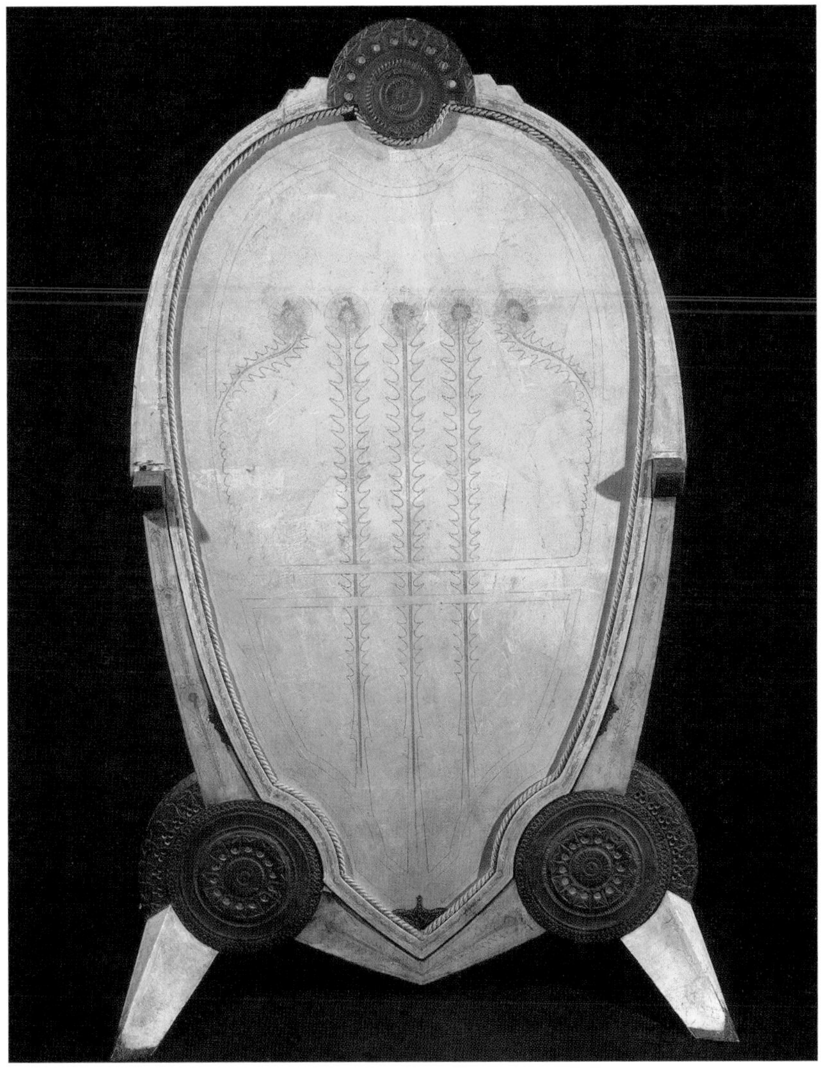

Bugatti, Carlo

Three-handled cigar bowl and sweetmeat dish, *c.* 1900

Italian artists struggled to make a mark in international circles with their interpretation of the Art Nouveau aesthetic. The names given to the Italian New Art hint at possible reasons. *Stile Floreale*, for example, describes the highly ornate decorations in natural themes that Italian furniture often bore. Many critics noted with dismay that the nature motif was applied purely to decoration, but was not incorporated into the form of the piece. *Stile Liberty* was the other name used; that the Italians drew inspiration from an English retail outlet, which aimed to disseminate its version of Art Nouveau around Europe, was telling.

There were exceptions to this generalization, however, and one of the most important and innovative of the Italian designers was Carlo Bugatti. He drew inspiration from Gothic, Oriental and Moorish cultures and the French architect Eugène-Emmanuel Viollet-le-Duc (1814–79), who instigated the Gothic Revival and advocated the use of iron and glass. Bugatti's work was geometric or organic, but powerful in its simplicity with a variety of textures and colours. His prodigious output included furniture, textiles, silverware, jewellery, musical instruments and even a bicycle.

MEDIUM

Metal

RELATED WORK

Cobra chairs by Carlo Bugatti, *c.* 1902

Carlo Bugatti *Born* 1855 Milan, Italy

Died 1940

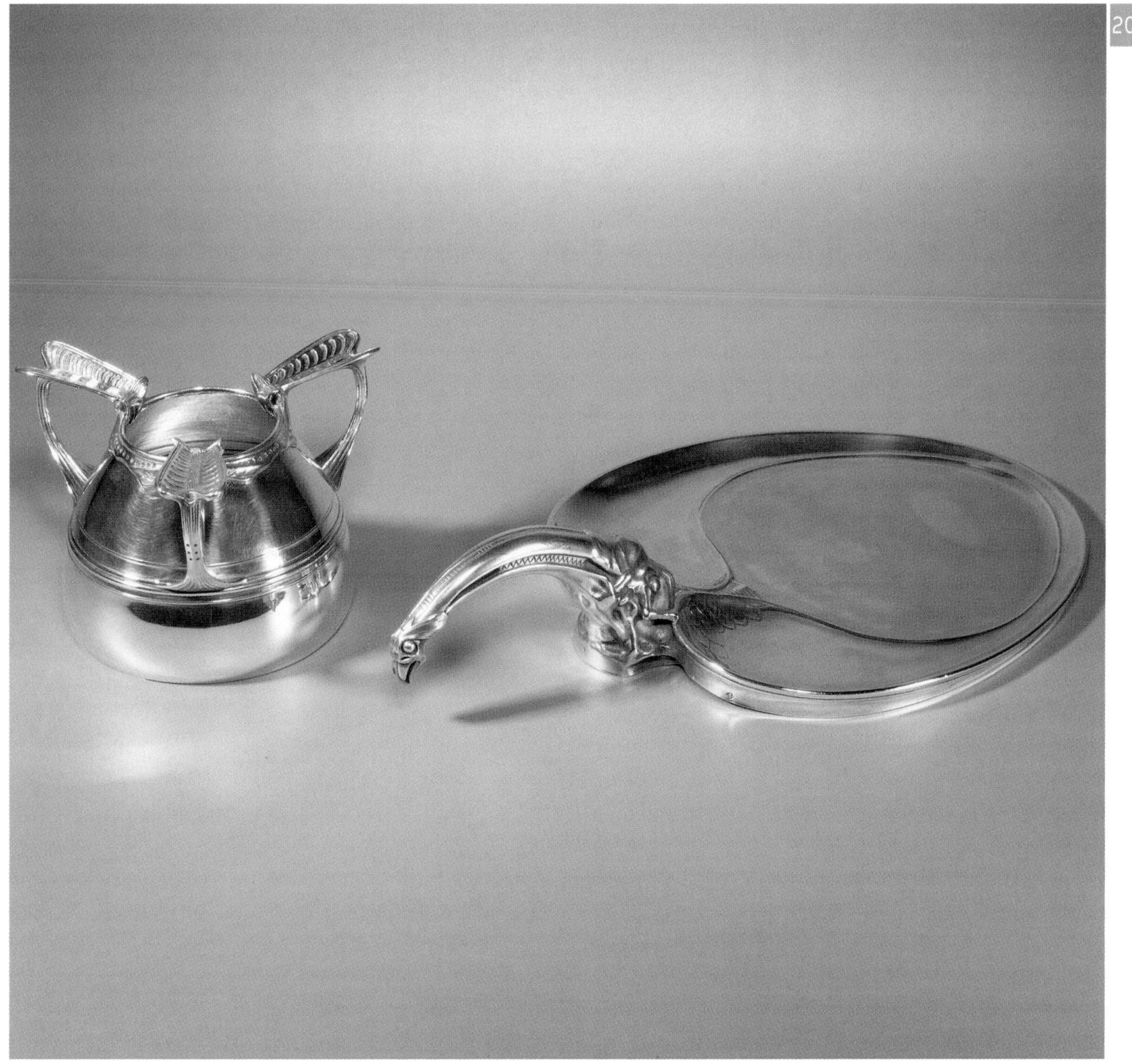

Entrance Door (designer unknown)

Villino Ruggieri, Pesaro

The development of an Italian Art Nouveau aesthetic was hindered by the regional nature of the new nation and it never developed into a truly national style. *Stile Liberty*, as it was known, appeared in many manifestations: Austrian and German art and culture had a dominating influence on parts of the country, leading to the adoption of the Secessionist ideology, particularly in Turin. Even in this industrial city, however, Secessionist-style buildings formed from geometric blocks appeared alongside others that were lavishly decorated with the floral lines and arabesques more reminiscent of Brussels architecture.

Like other Art Nouveau artists, Italian designers and architects were receptive to influences from around the world. Oriental and Islamic motifs and styles were popular, but much of the innovative Italian design at this time was commissioned by wealthy industrialists who embraced the modern style enthusiastically, but little of it trickled down to the common artefacts that the less well-off might enjoy. For this reason the *Stile Floreale* was never seen as a democratic design movement, although the impact of Italian designers on later styles and their interpretation of the Art Nouveau aesthetic are areas that have often been underestimated.

CREATED

Pesaro, Italy

MEDIUM

Architecture

RELATED WORK

Villa Broggi-Caraceni in Florence by Giovanni Michelazzi, 1910–11

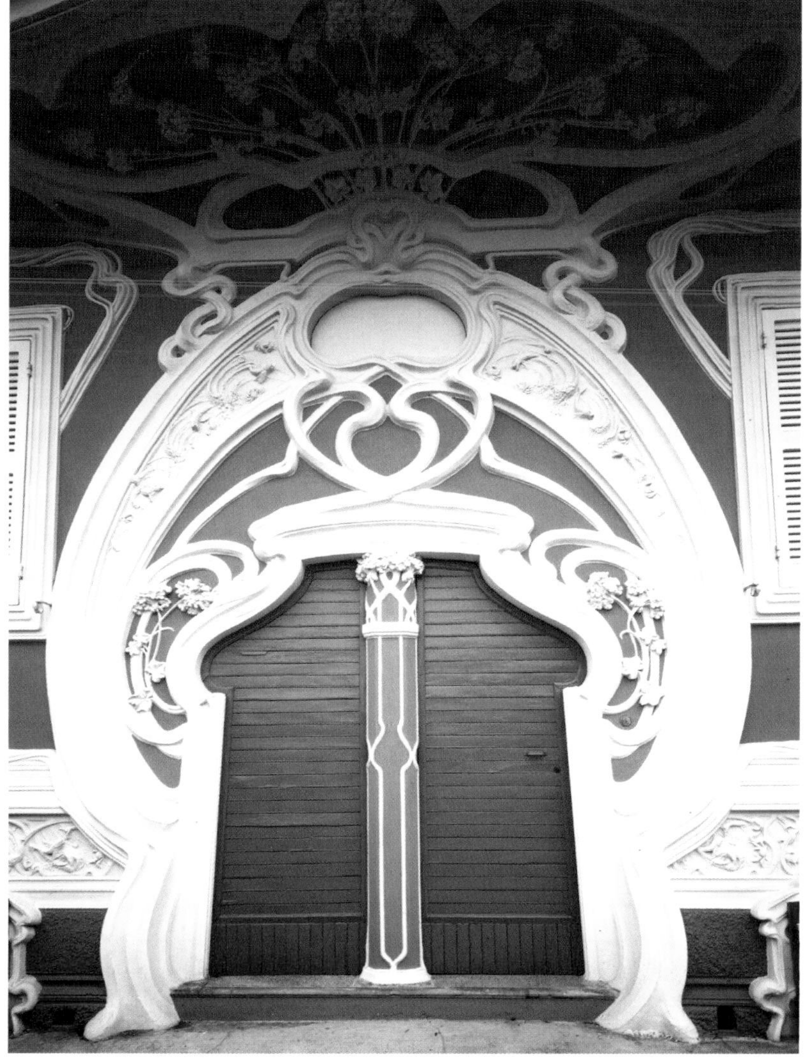

Gaudí, Antonio

Exterior of the Casa Battló apartments, 1905–07

Antonio Gaudí (1852–1926) was born the son of a coppersmith in rural Catalonia. He studied at the Provincial School of Architecture in Barcelona, finally leaving in 1878. His early work reflected the *Mudéjar* design style that was common in Spain: this was an eclectic mixture of Muslim and Christian art that was characterized by colourful bricks and tiles with floral and reptilian designs. By 1900 Gaudí's individual and original style was emerging. His architectural projects were designed in such a way that they appeared to defy normal rules of gravity and thrust: supporting structures were often hidden from view, leaving balconies suspended. It was said that his buildings appeared to emerge from the ground and grow organically, 'like a tree' Gaudí himself noted. This has become known as 'equilibrated', that is, architecture designed to stand on its own without internal bracing.

The Casa Battló apartments were first built in 1877 but remodelled by Gaudí between 1905 and 1907. The façade, in particular, demonstrates the equilibrated technique with which Gaudí became associated. This façade had rectangular windows that did not conform to Gaudí's organic, fantastical style.

CREATED

Barcelona

MEDIUM

Architecture

RELATED WORK

Casa Vicens by Antonio Gaudí, 1878–80

Antonio Gaudí *Born* 1852 Raus, Spain

Died 1926

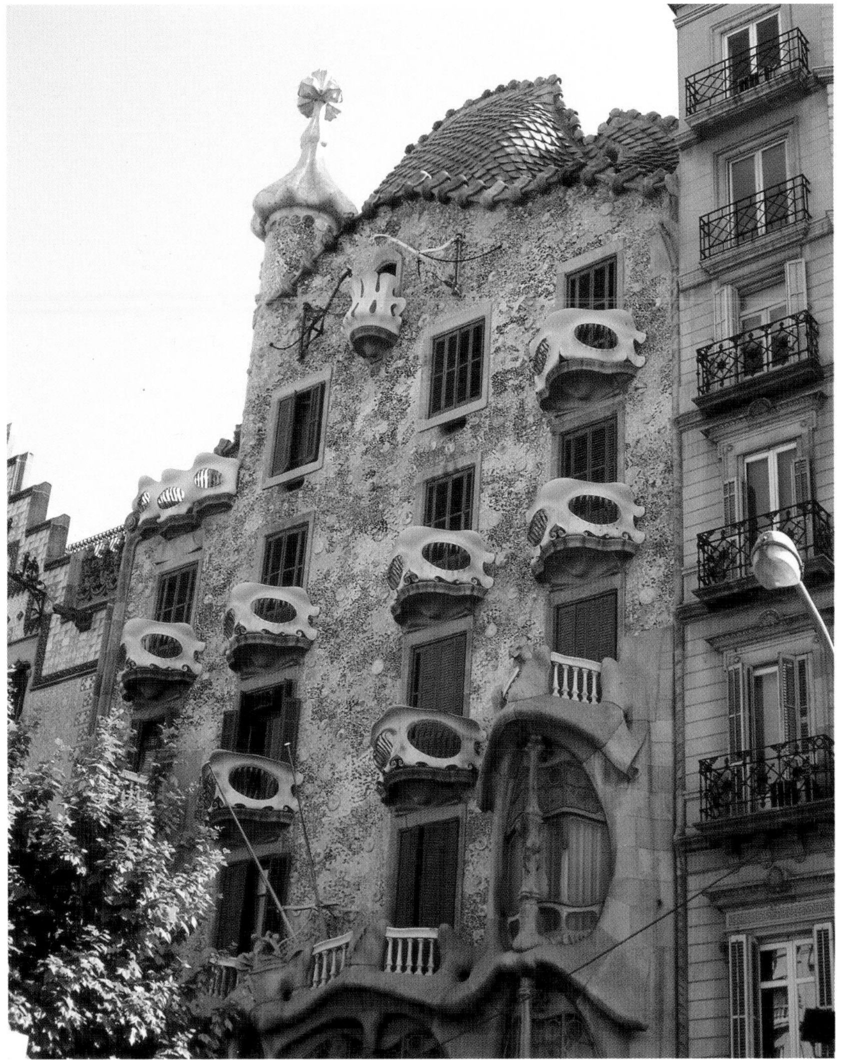

Gaudí, Antonio

Detail of the Casa Mila or La Pedrera, 1905–11

Gaudí was restricted in his designs for the exterior of the Casa Battló apartments, because he was remodelling an existing building. He used stone cladding to superimpose his own fluid plane on to the masonry, while coloured tiles on the walls and on the roof serve to distract the eye and contrast with the symmetrical architecture that surrounded the apartment block.

When Gaudí designed the Casa Mila, however, he was able to start from scratch and the resultant building reflects his organic and visceral style throughout. The façade reminded locals of a quarry, with its stone walls that appear to have had holes gouged from them by millennia of weathering. Thus they named it La Pedreda ('The Quarry'). The balconies are made from ironwork that is moulded into fantastical intertwined plants. Like a natural rock formation, the Casa Mila appears to have been adapted as living quarters, rather than to have been designed with functionality in mind. The interiors are similarly astonishing; fireplaces are carved out of the walls, which in turn meld into the ceilings in one continuous plane, as one would expect in a cave.

CREATED

Barcelona

MEDIUM

Architecture

RELATED WORK

Güell Park by Antonio Gaudí, 1880s

Antonio Gaudí *Born* 1852 Raus, Spain

Died 1926

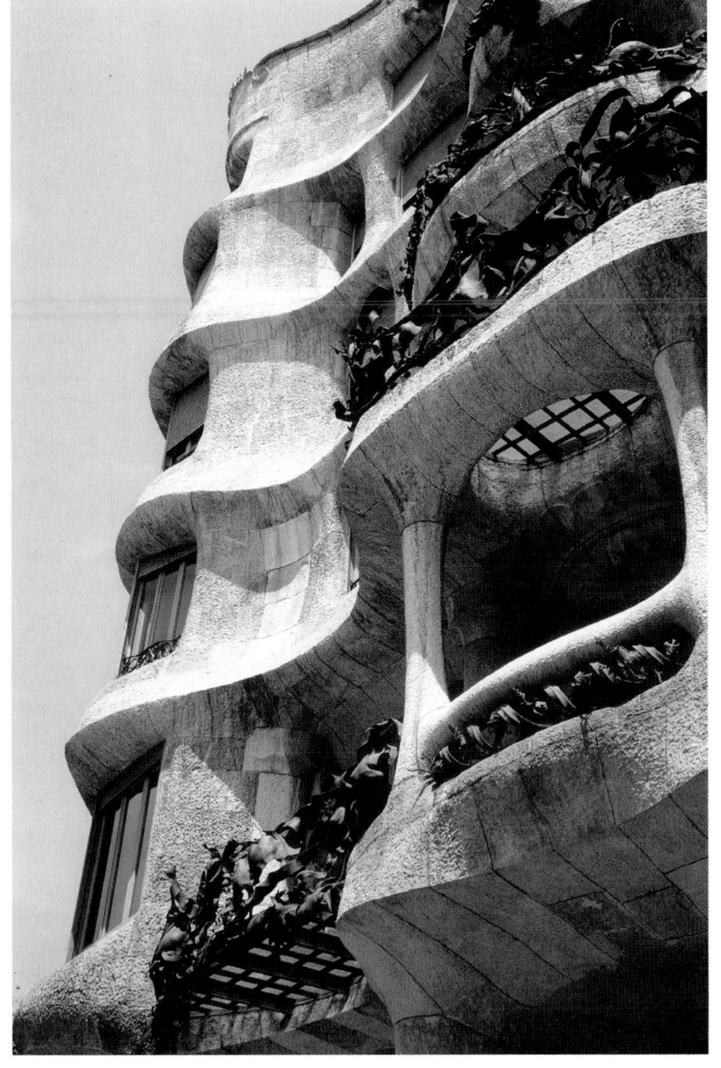

Gaudí, Antonio

Padouk armchair, *c.* 1902

Gaudí is best known for his startling architectural designs and uncompromising vision for organic buildings. He did, however, also design furniture. In fact, his first design commission was for a display cabinet that was required in the Spanish pavilion at the Exposition Universelle in Paris in 1878. The cabinet won Gaudí a silver medal and the attention of a wealthy Catalonian count who would become one of his patrons. When Gaudí completed architectural projects for his patrons they quickly noticed that their furniture looked quite out of place in his weird and wonderful interiors, so they would commission him to design furnishings in a similar style. During the Spanish Civil War much of Gaudí's furniture was destroyed, but the pieces that remain demonstrate how Gaudí's design vision was all encompassing.

This chair by Gaudí has the flowing decorative lines associated with his architecture. He respected the skills required to manipulate wood and allowed the joinery to show as part of the design. He had an ergonomic approach and demanded that his furniture be as comfortable as it was beautiful.

CREATED

Catalonia

MEDIUM

Wood

RELATED WORK

Battló bench by Antonio Gaudí, 1906

Antonio Gaudí *Born* 1852 Raus, Spain

Died 1926

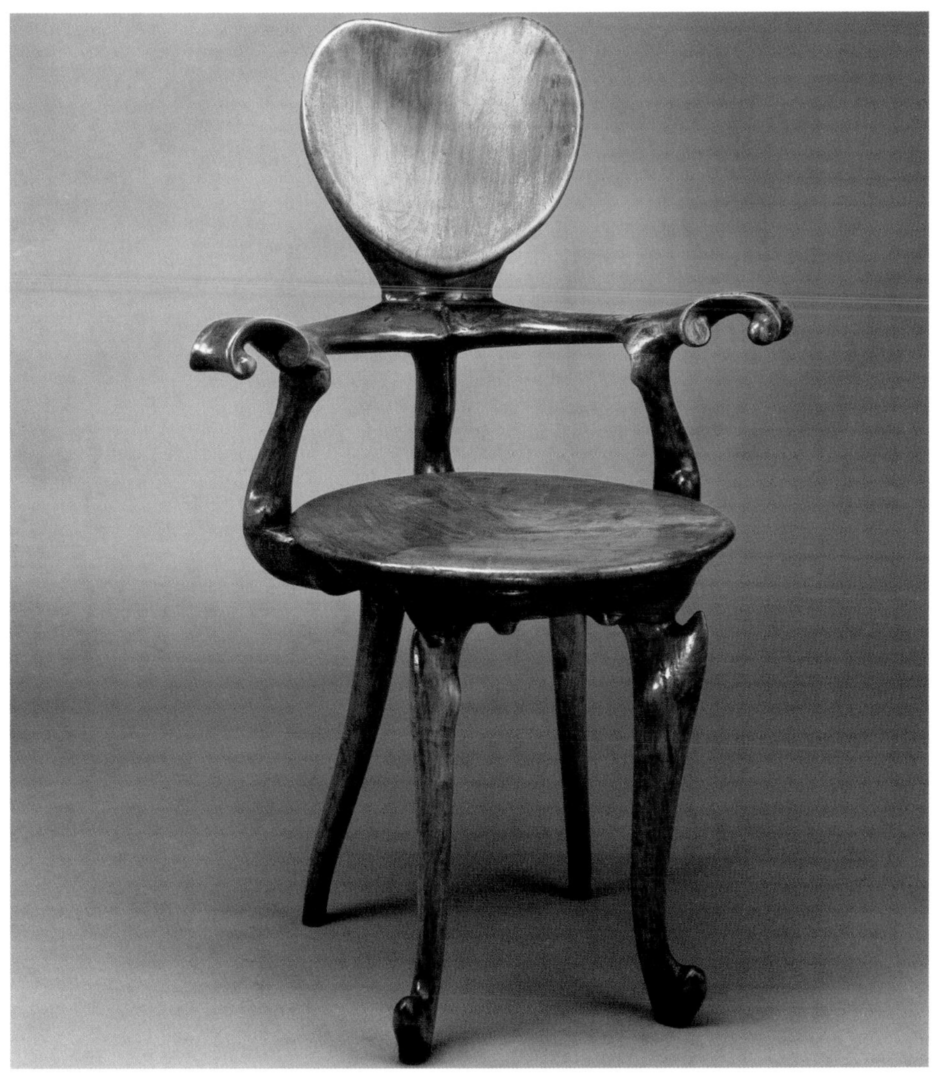

Bradley, William H.

Reproduction of a poster advertising 'When Hearts are Trumps' by Tom Hall, 1894

At the end of the nineteenth century consumerism was gaining momentum, supported by society's desire for modernity and the commercial mechanisms that supported it: industrialization, mass advertising and exhibitions. Aided by the growth of literacy, printed media had moved into a new realm. New methods of printing, including colour lithography and photomechanical reproduction, resulted in an explosion of printed materials that could be relatively inexpensively produced. For the Art Nouveau artist this presented enormous opportunities to generate art that could, literally, be spread around the world. From wallpapers to art magazines and advertising posters, printed material was able to carry the stylistic messages of an entire movement into homes, business and the streets. This was one of the crucial ways that the New Art was able to become the first truly international style.

This design by William Bradley (1868–1962) was used both as a book cover and as a poster, produced by publishers to promote Tom Hall's book. Art Nouveau posters were recognized as works of art even in their day and publishers often produced extra copies to sell to collectors.

MEDIUM

Colour lithograph in vermilion and green

RELATED WORK

Poster for Victor Bicycles by William H. Bradley, 1897

William H. Bradley *Born* 1868 Boston, USA

Died 1962

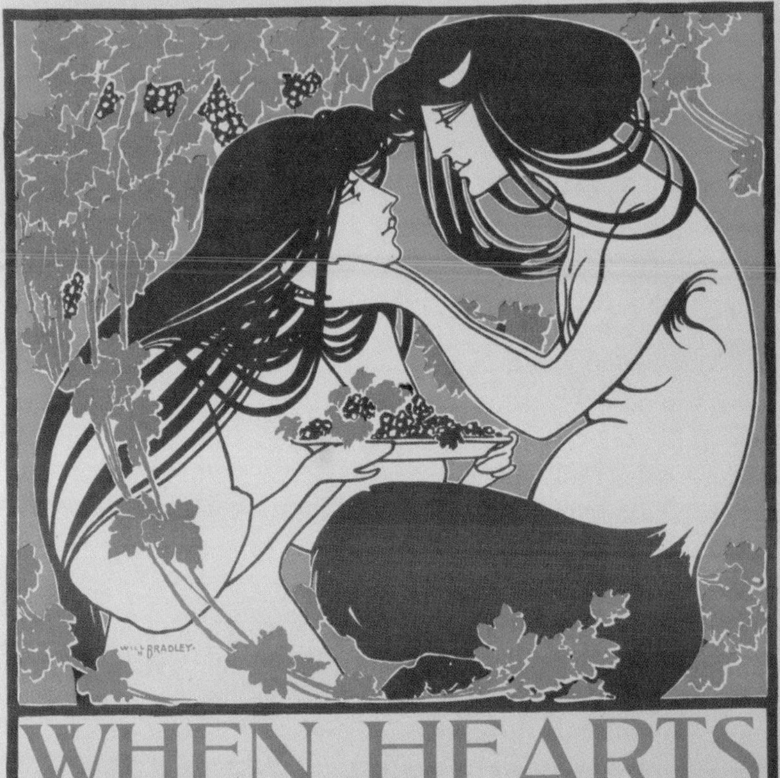
WILL H BRADLEY
WHEN HEARTS
ARE TRUMPS
BY TOM HALL

Bradley, William H.

The Modern Poster (Peacock), 1895

The second half of the nineteenth century saw the USA rise from the ashes of civil war and emerge with a booming economy. The population was growing in size and in relative wealth and a new identity and nationhood developed. Critics of the day hoped that a new cultural identity would also emerge. Much of the American population came from immigrant stock, often from Europe, and there had been a tendency to perhaps view the traditional cultures of Europe as superior in art and design, but as consumerism grew, so Americans began to develop their own tastes and sought out innovative work.

By the 1880s a new wealthy middle class was established. Extravagant spending and conspicuous displays of wealth became fashionable, fuelling the luxury-goods market. A new spirit of modernity encouraged Americans to seek the innovative. Designers such as Louis Comfort Tiffany (1848–1933) struck out into new territory; they were no longer copyists, but creators. Poster art, in particular, offered designers a relatively inexpensive way to promote their own aesthetic development. William Bradley's posters helped bring Art Nouveau to the urban population of his native America.

CREATED

USA

MEDIUM

Colour lithograph

RELATED WORK

Covers and posters for *The Chap Book* by William H. Bradley, 1894–98

William H. Bradley *Born* 1868 Boston, USA

Died 1962

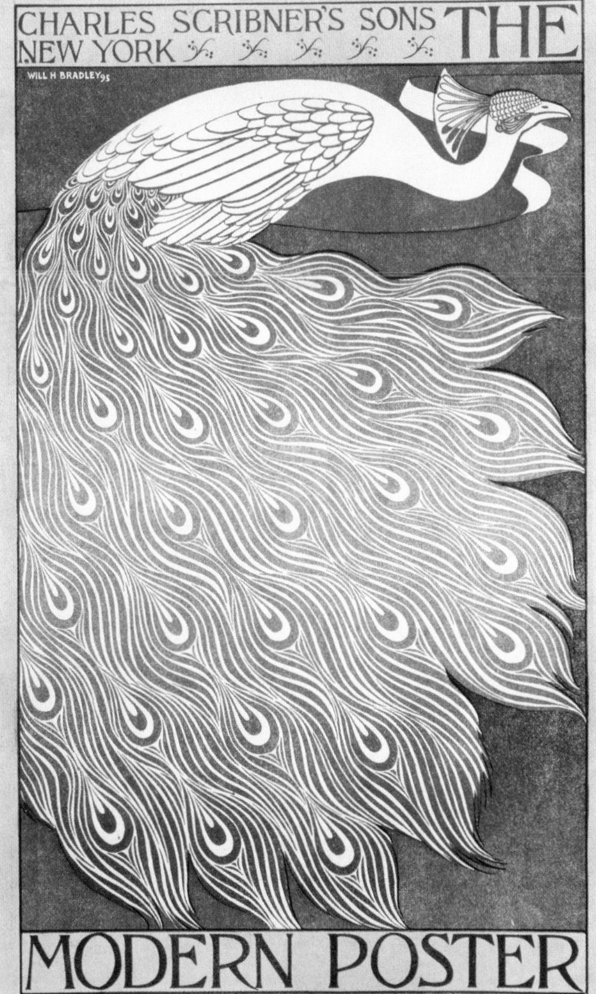
CHARLES SCRIBNER'S SONS
NEW YORK
THE
WILL H BRADLEY 95
MODERN POSTER
ONLY ONE THOUSAND COPIES
PRINTED OF WHICH THIS IS NO

Bradley, William H.

The Echo (front cover)

As the twentieth century approached, the USA was primed and ready for an expansion of the Art Nouveau; its population sought a new cultural identity and there was wealth to support its manifestation in decorative design. Influenced by the Arts and Crafts movement in England and other European art aesthetics, American designers rejected traditional styles that endlessly harked back to previous eras. They were looking for something modern, innovative and exciting. Siegfried Bing, the prominent art dealer, recognized this spirit and energy when he toured America from 1891 to 1894 to produce a report on the state of American art. Bing recognized that Americans, unlike Europeans, were not shackled by the past; they alone were living and designing purely for tomorrow. As a result of Bing's report, Europeans paid closer attention to the development of American design and it was regularly featured in the many art journals produced at the time.

It was in poster art and graphic design that American designers were particularly innovative. Although criticized for being 'disturbing', 'corrupting', 'frivolous' and transitory, graphic art of the time was effective as a marketing tool, and remains popular.

CREATED

USA

RELATED WORK

Design for a cupboard by William H. Bradley, 1891

William H. Bradley *Born* 1868 Boston, USA

Died 1962

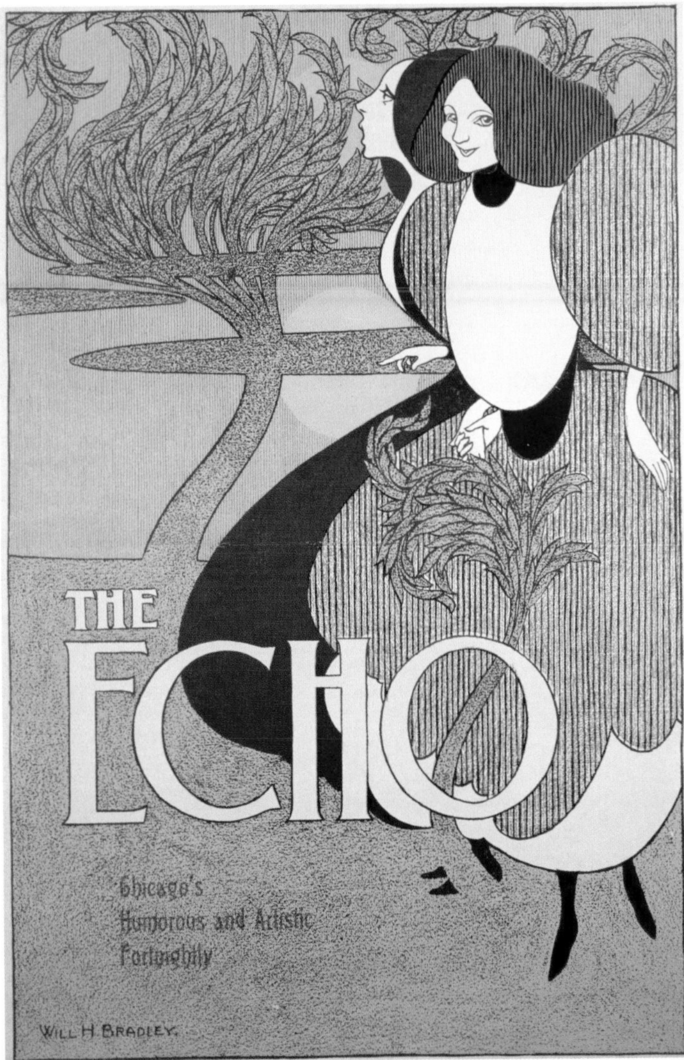
THE
ECHO
Chicago's
Humorous and Artistic
Fortnightly
WILL H. BRADLEY.

Knox, Archibald

Biscuit box, *c.* 1903

Archibald Knox (1864–1933) was born on the Isle of Man and it was his birthplace that inspired Knox to design some of the most important silverware of the British Art Nouveau period.

Knox trained as an artist at the Douglas School of Art and studied Celtic ornament, even writing papers on the Celtic crosses of the island. In 1897 he moved to London and began to teach design, but soon afterwards began working part-time on his own line of silverware objects. Knox was soon to be employed by the London retailers, Liberty and Co., to design beautiful but affordable objects. Like Liberty's other designers, Knox's name did not appear on his designs; anonymity was always maintained and once records had been destroyed in the Second World War, there was no way to be sure which designers had worked on which projects. It is known, however, that Knox was greatly inspired by Celtic ornaments, Manx carvings and ancient landscapes of his island home. His metalwork, in silver and pewter, featured traditional Celtic emblems such as interwoven stems and leaves, or stylized images from nature reworked into a new form.

MEDIUM

Pewter and enamel

MOVEMENT

Arts and Crafts/Art Nouveau

RELATED WORK

Cymric jewel box in silver with enamel and turquoise by Archibald Knox, *c.* 1900

Archibald Knox *Born* 1864 Isle of Man

Died 1933

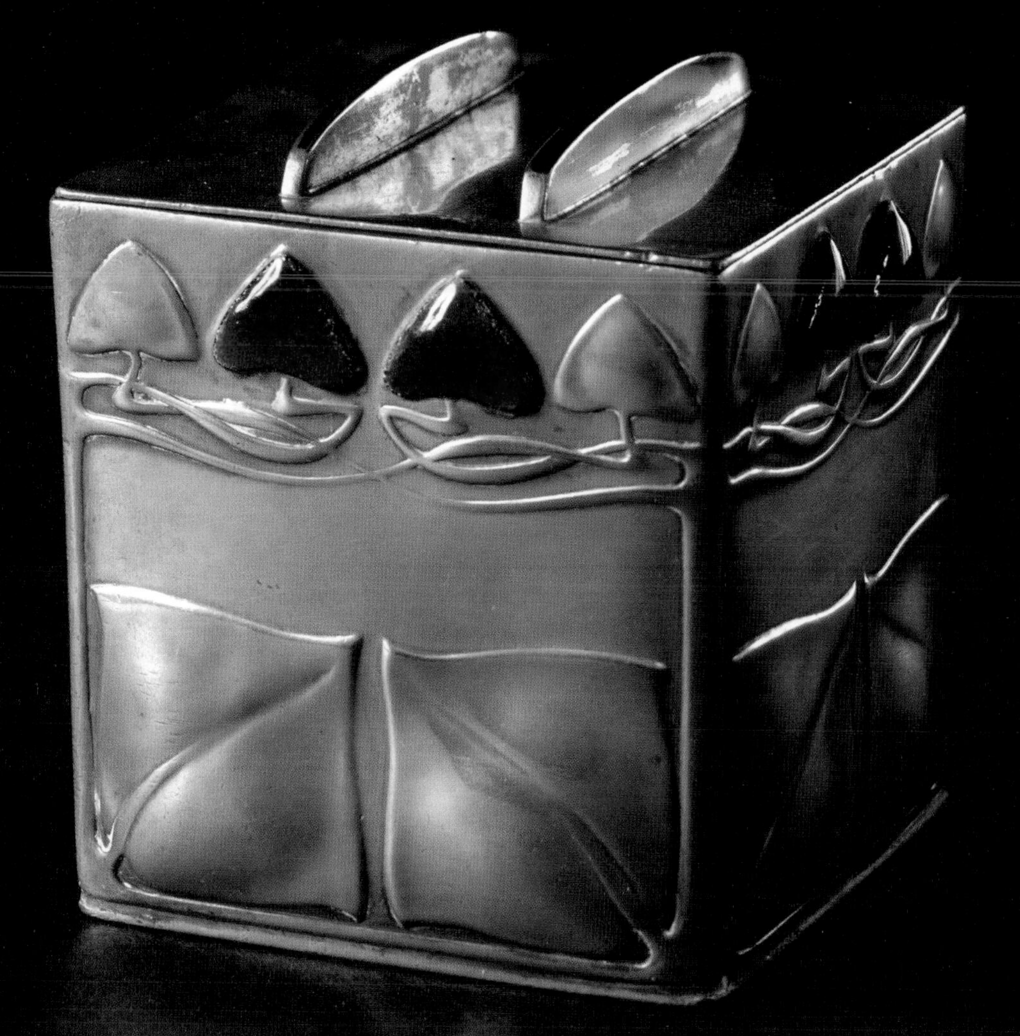

Liberty and Co.

Range of metalware

Industrial processing meant that the Art Nouveau style, more than any before, could be disseminated across a society. Metalware in particular could be produced relatively inexpensively and suited many popular idioms of the style. Cutlery, jewellery, furniture fittings and even biscuit tins were mass-produced so that the lower middle-classes could enjoy owning a piece of 'designer ware'. Naturally this mass production meant that the pieces were often poor copies and lacked the refinement and elegance of the handcrafted pieces that wealthier consumers could enjoy. It is the widespread dissemination of the Art Nouveau style and its exploitation by industry that partly led to its demise: once a style is accessible to all it is no longer desirable to the few, and it is the few who dictate whether something is in vogue, or passé.

So it was that Arthur Liberty walked a fine line when he decided to open a shop, Liberty and Co. in London's Regent Street, with the expressed aim of creating quality furniture, fabrics and silverware that were affordable to the middle classes. Liberty's (as it became known) proved a successful commercial venture: it was viewed as a setter of fashion for an aspirational populace.

MEDIUM

White metal, silver and enamel

RELATED WORK

Daffodils fabric designed by Lindsay Butterworth for Liberty

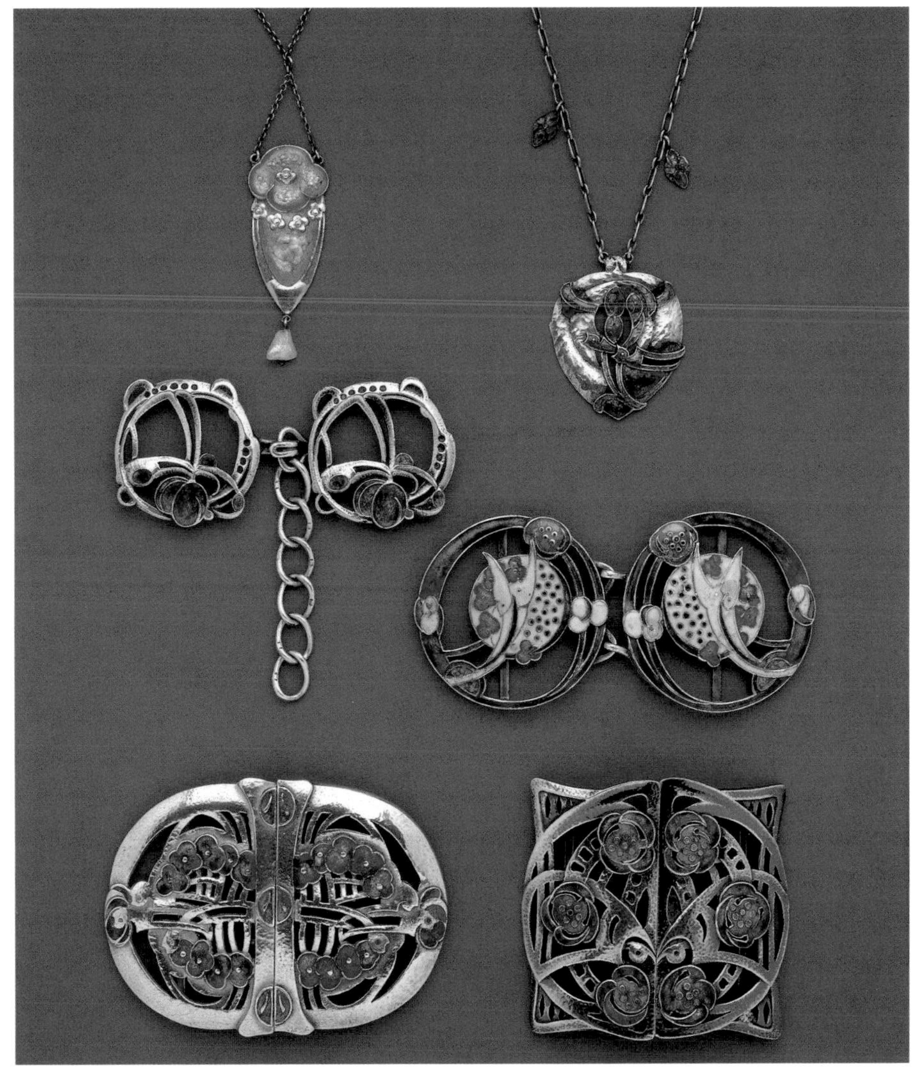

Liberty and Co.

Woman's cloak, *c.* 1900–05

The store founded by Arthur Liberty in 1875 on London's famous Regent Street had an enormous impact on the development of the Art Nouveau style and through the years its wares have often mirrored the pervading cultural and artistic trends. At first Liberty imported fine Oriental goods, Japanese objets d'art, carpets and fabrics in particular, reflecting the English taste for the Orient and Aestheticism. When Archibald Knox joined the firm at the turn of the century, he helped fuel a revival in Celtic art and pewter, which spread to the Continent. In many instances Liberty opted for a more restrained version of the Art Nouveau style than was seen in mainland Europe. Tempered, even constrained, the New Art here was often understated.

When he first opened his doors to members of the British public, Liberty offered them fine fabrics for dressmaking and furnishings. The quality of the fabric began to decline, so he sourced woven material from elsewhere then used printers working at Merton Abbey, near the William Morris buildings, to print his patterns. In 1884 he opened a costume department and Liberty fabric, to this day, remains popular and iconic.

MEDIUM

Textile

RELATED WORK

Lotus Collection, fabrics designed for Liberty in 1960

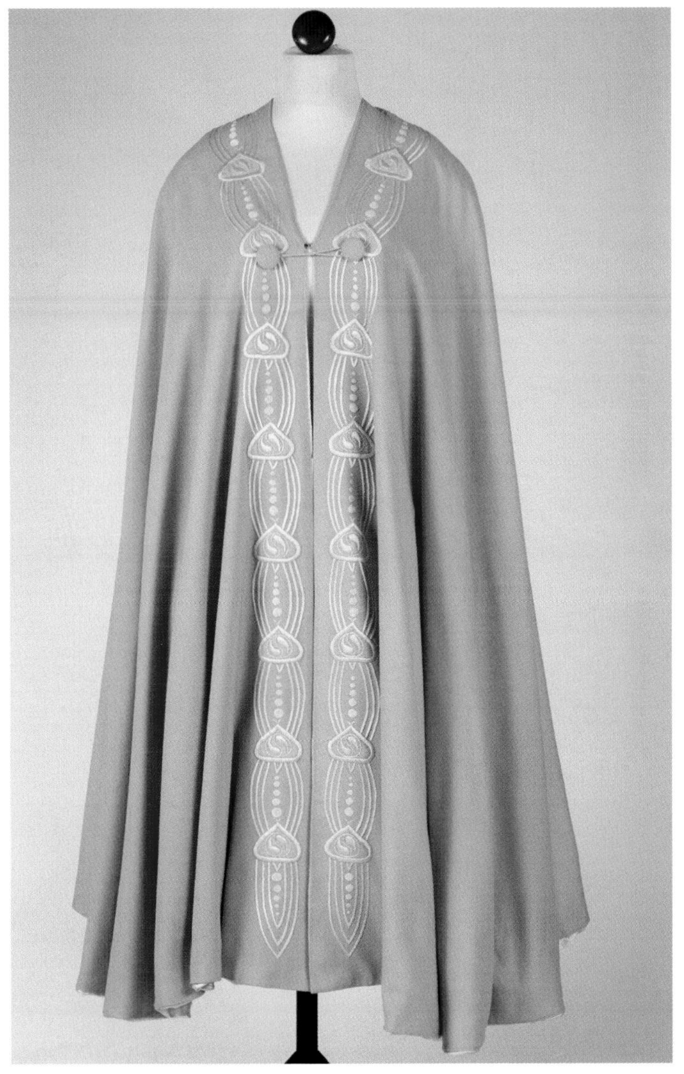

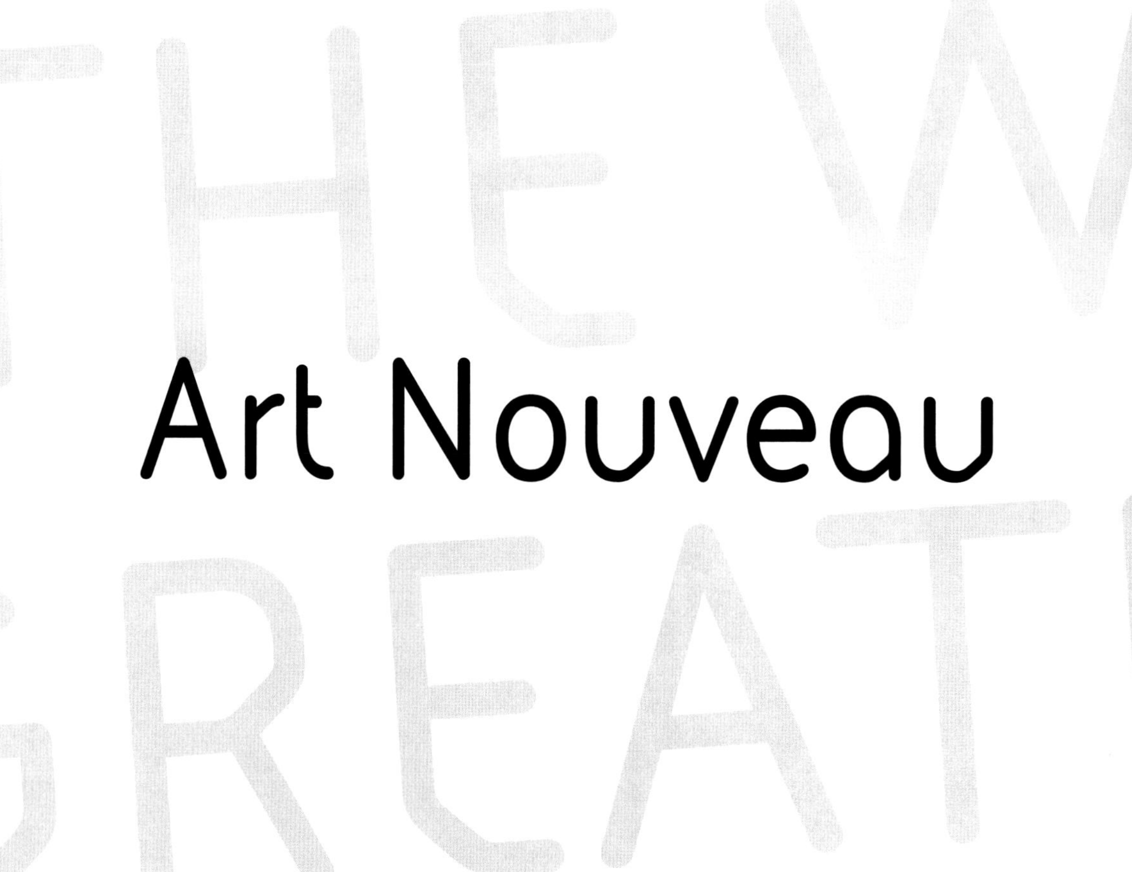

Art Nouveau

Influences

Morris, William

Floral wallpaper design

William Morris (1834–96) was born to a wealthy middle-class, evangelical family in rural Essex. Although intended for the church, Morris discovered a different calling while at Oxford University: art. He was greatly affected by the socio-political works of John Ruskin (1819–1900) and Charles Kingsley and, had he not fallen in with a group of artists and poets, he might have followed their literary path. Instead Morris was introduced to Dante Gabriel Rossetti (1828–82), the leader of the Pre-Raphaelite School, by his college friend Edward Burne-Jones (1833–98), and decided to become a painter.

Intrigued by a revival in Gothic architecture, Morris commissioned a house to be built in the medieval style. It was during the building that he discovered that the 'minor arts', as he called them, were in a poor state. He decided to set up a firm to promote the decorative arts. Supported by artists such as Rossetti, Burne-Jones and Ford Madox Brown (1821–93), Morris established the Arts and Crafts movement. The movement had socio-political aims and these, along with some design elements of the Arts and Crafts, were to affect and influence Art Nouveau.

MOVEMENT

Arts and Crafts

RELATED WORK

Bachelor's Button wallpaper by William Morris, c. 1902

William Morris *Born* 1834 Walthamstow, England

Died 1896

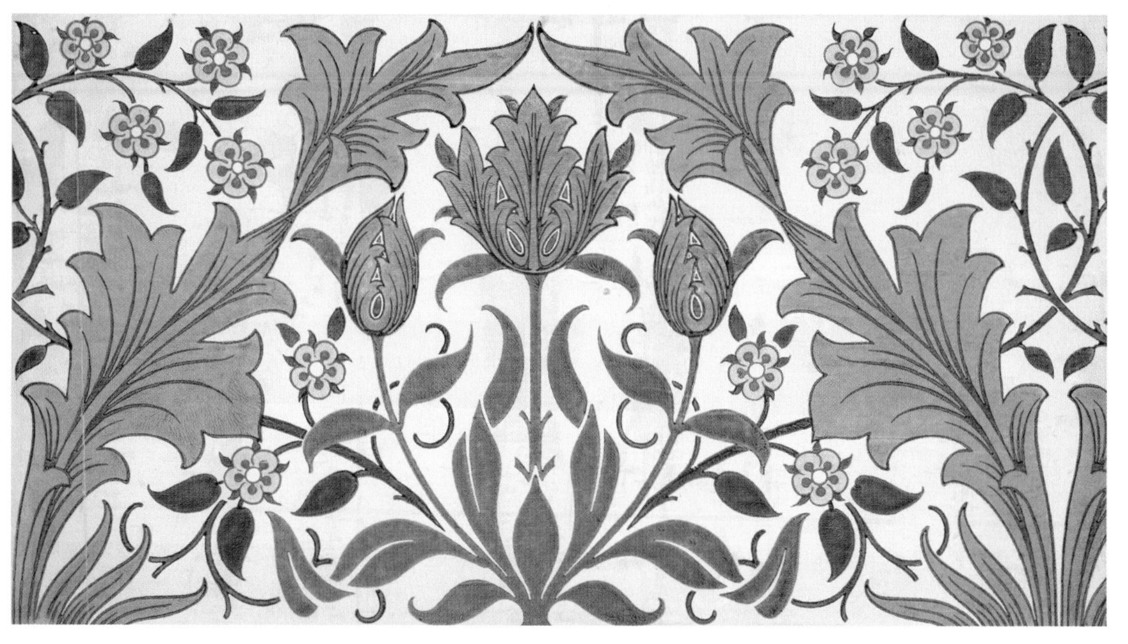

Morris, William

Foliage tapestry, *c.* 1887

William Morris had a considerable influence on the development of Art Nouveau. One of his core beliefs was that high art and the decorative arts were needlessly divided, producing a stagnant and dull period in high art and the trivialization of the decorative arts. This belief was central to the Arts and Crafts movement, as well as Art Nouveau and Art Deco.

Morris was also motivated by the goal of improving working conditions for artisans. At this time in England the fashion was for highly elaborate, decorated furniture and fittings that were made by machine, often of poor quality and dubious taste. Morris believed that this trend was having a devastating effect upon the labour force; people were losing their craft skills and had to work in appalling conditions in factories. He set up workshops in Merton Abbey, seven miles outside London, where his craftspeople applied their skills to a range of métiers, such as textiles, ceramics and printing, in a pleasant and safe environment.

CREATED

Merton Abbey, England

MEDIUM

Textile (tapestry)

MOVEMENT

Arts and Crafts

RELATED WORK

Forest tapestry by William Morris, 1887

William Morris *Born* 1834 Walthamstow, England

Died 1896

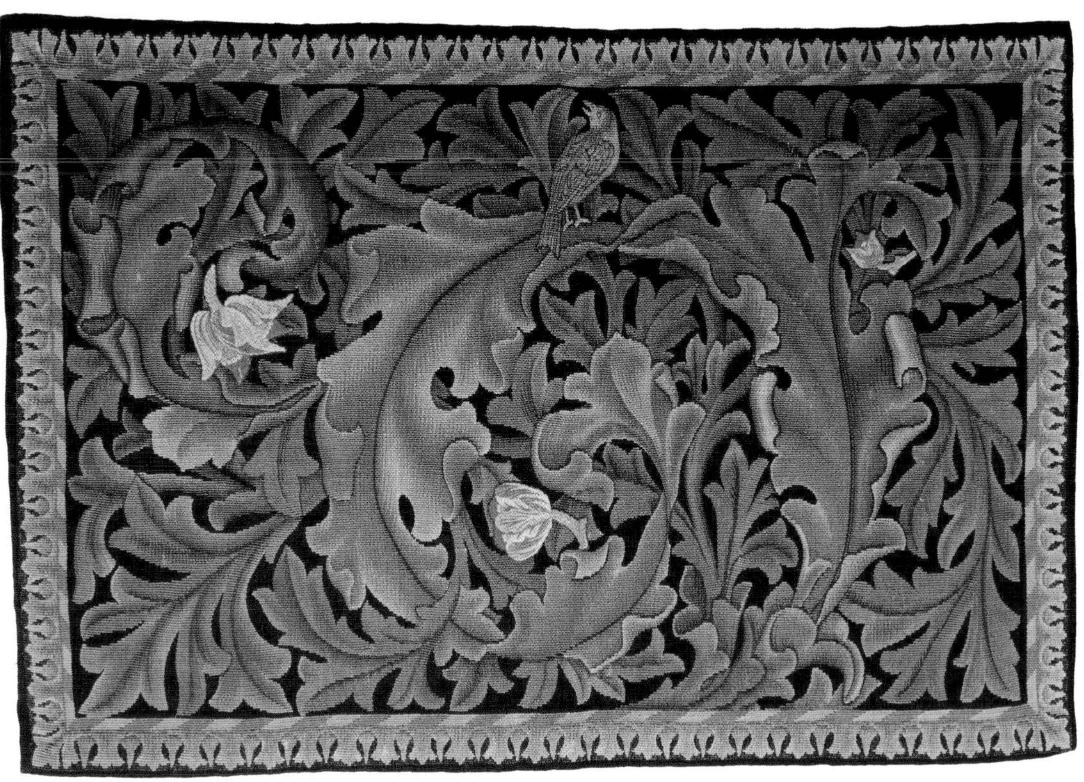

Mackmurdo, A. H.

Chair, *c.* 1883

Arthur Heygate Mackmurdo (1851–1942) was an English artist who studied under John Ruskin, the noted and influential critic and theorist. Ruskin developed the theory that a relationship exists between art and nature, and this was to become intrinsic to the Art Nouveau movement and the development of the Pre-Raphaelite Brotherhood of Dante Gabriel Rossetti.

Mackmurdo toured Italy with Ruskin and was encouraged by him to study architecture, but it was for his involvement in the decorative arts that Mackmurdo is best remembered. In 1882 he set up the Century Guild, a co-operative society of artists and craftsmen, including Selwyn Image (1849–1930), who designed the title page for the guild's magazine, *Hobby Horse*, and William de Morgan (1839–1917), the most famous designer of pottery tiles in the Arts and Crafts style. The Century Guild promoted different media, from typography to tapestry, and aimed to unite a variety of métiers and elevate handicrafts to the status of high art. The styles developed were eclectic and in many instances can be seen as forerunners to the asymmetrical curves and swishes of Art Nouveau.

MEDIUM

Mahogany, with inset mahogany fretwork panel

MOVEMENT

Aestheticism

RELATED WORK

Oak writing desk by A. H. Mackmurdo, 1886

A. H. Mackmurdo *Born* 1851 London, England

Died 1942

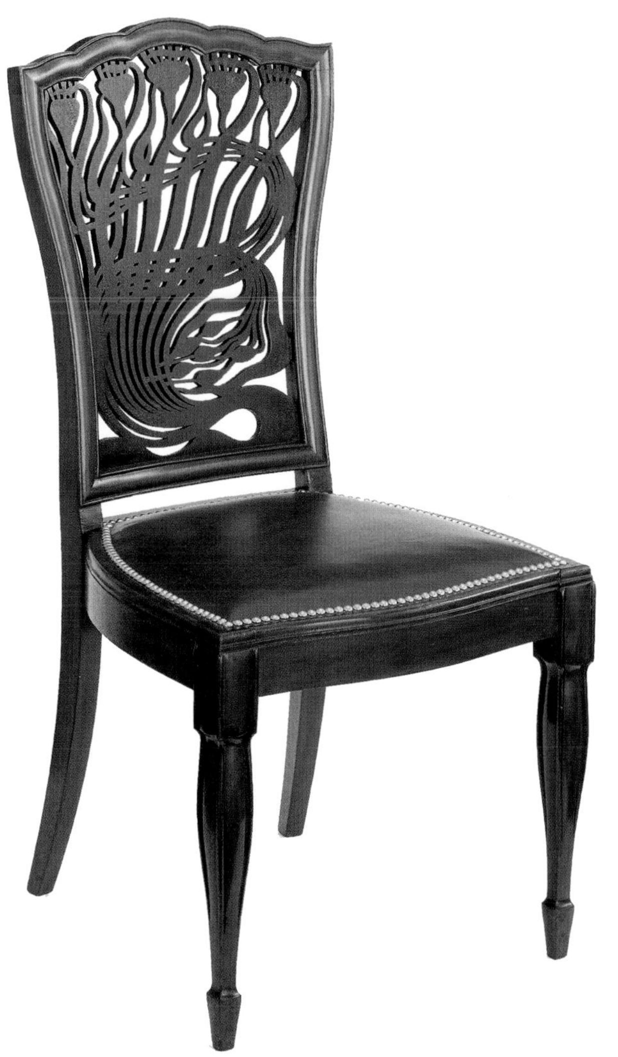

Mackmurdo, A. H.

Title page to *Wren's City Churches*, 1883

A friend of William Morris, Arthur Heygate Mackmurdo also subscribed to the belief that all branches of art ought to be in the sphere of the artist rather than the craft worker. Whereas William Morris had aspired to make artists out of craftsmen, Mackmurdo wanted to make tradesmen out of artists while elevating handicrafts to the same position as high art. He founded the Century Guild as a collection of artists who would learn different technical skills in the field of decorative arts.

The Arts and Crafts movement was founded on a similar footing but had a social mission, to restore the dignity to labour after it had been crushed by industrialization and commercialism. Members of the Century Guild did not stand on a socialist mission; they believed that art and design could be produced for their own sake and need have no utilitarian values or have any obvious relationship with society. This frontispiece to Mackmurdo's *Wren's City Churches* is illustrated in flaming, swathing curves that are clearly a forerunner to those that typify the Art Nouveau style.

MOVEMENT

Aestheticism

RELATED WORK

Screen by A. H. Mackmurdo, 1884

A. H. Mackmurdo *Born* 1851 London, England

Died 1942

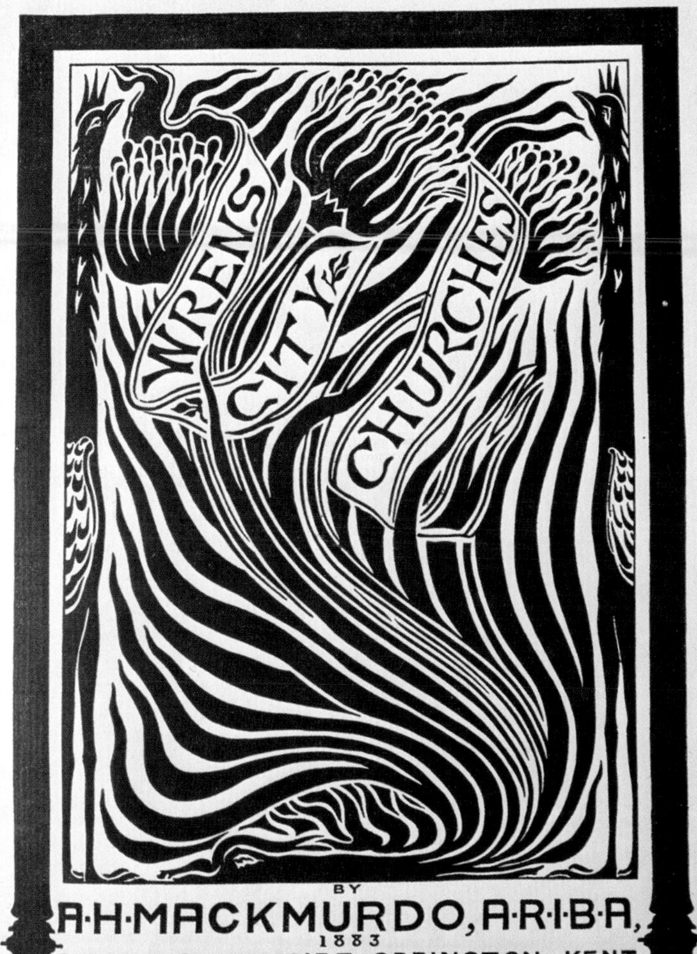
WREN'S
CITY
CHURCHES
BY
A·H·MACKMURDO, A·R·I·B·A,
1883
G.ALLEN, SUNNYSIDE, ORPINGTON, KENT.

Blake, William

Title page from *Songs of Innocence*, 1789

In England the Art Nouveau movement stemmed in part from the Arts and Crafts movement, which in turn had been influenced by the Pre-Raphaelites and other earlier British artists. One of the most important influences on the British New Art was the London-born visionary poet and artist, William Blake (1757–1827).

Blake was a man apart: deeply religious he lived in a mystical, fantastical world of his own creation. Blake rejected the art of the traditional academies and refused to draw from life. Instead he relied upon an inner eye and drew images from his mind. Unlike many contemporaries Blake did not particularly value the faithful reproduction of form and colour; to him the effect of a painting was more important than the detail. Blake wrote and illustrated books in the medieval tradition. In the *Songs of Innocence* Blake took rhymes and ballads of contemporary street children and turned them into magical, lyrical poems. In 1794 he published a single volume containing *Songs of Innocence* and *Songs of Experience*, which aimed to show 'the two contrary states of the human soul'.

MEDIUM

Relief etching tinted with watercolour

MOVEMENT

Romanticism

RELATED WORK

Pity, watercolour by William Blake, 1795

William Blake *Born* 1757 London, England

Died 1827

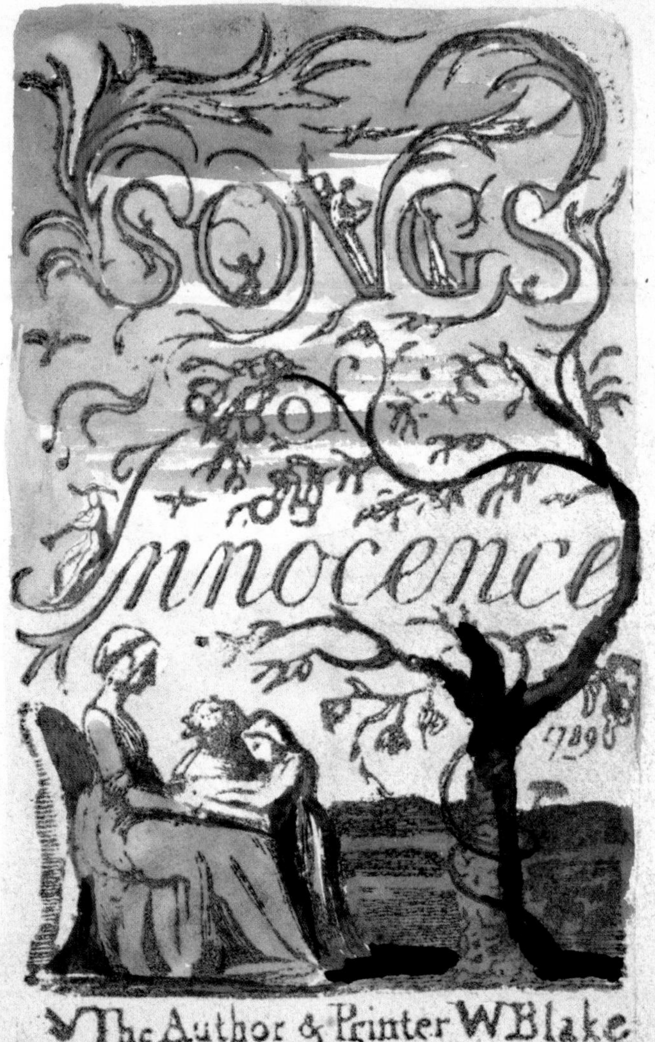
SONGS
of
Innocence
1789
The Author & Printer W Blake

Blake, William

Infant Joy from *Songs of Innocence*, 1789

William Blake broke with tradition when he produced his extraordinary paintings and lyrical, epic poems. He stressed the importance of the imagination over observation, an ideal that appealed to the Pre-Raphaelites and one that has been a major influence on many artists since. Blake drew Biblical scenes and illustrated the works of Dante and Milton in fantastical style, as well as illustrating his own great works.

The *Songs of Innocence* and *Songs of Experience*, when published together, featured 54 plates, etched in relief with touches of white line-work in some of the designs. Blake's artwork did not just comprise figurative and dream-like images but, in the *Songs* book were inspired by medieval illuminated manuscripts. Decorative patterns and curves adorn the pages and these idioms were developed in Art Nouveau. Although Blake died in poverty and neglect, his extraordinary body of work unappreciated in his lifetime, the enormity of his achievements is now acknowledged. In 1847 Blake's work was rediscovered when Dante Gabriel Rossetti bought one of his notebooks. Blake became a principal source of inspiration in Rossetti's art and that of his Pre-Raphaelite contemporaries.

MEDIUM

Relief etching tinted with watercolour

MOVEMENT

Romanticism

RELATED WORK

The Ancient of Days, metal cut with watercolour by William Blake, 1794

William Blake *Born* 1757 London, England

Died 1827

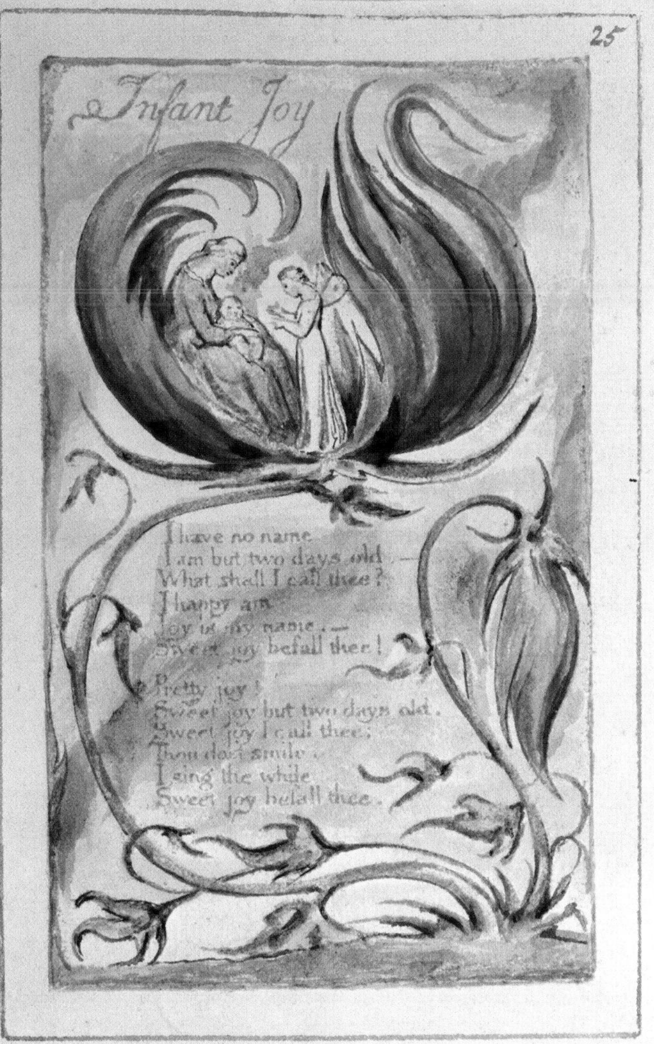
25
Infant Joy
I have no name
I am but two days old.—
What shall I call thee?
I happy am
Joy is my name.—
Sweet joy befall thee!
Pretty joy!
Sweet joy but two days old.
Sweet joy I call thee;
Thou dost smile.
I sing the while
Sweet joy befall thee.

Crane, Walter

Book jacket design for *A Floral Fantasy in an Old English Garden*, c. 1890s

Walter Crane (1845–1915) was a founding member of the Arts and Crafts movement, along with William Morris and Edward Burne-Jones. He was the son of a moderately successful miniaturist, Thomas Crane (1805–59), and was apprenticed at the premises of the engraver William Linton (1791–1876), whose endeavours to promote the cause of parliamentary reform were to profoundly affect the young man. Crane studied the works of the Pre-Raphaelites, John Ruskin, the historian Thomas Carlyle, whose writings inspired many social reformers of the era, and others. By the 1860s Crane was deeply involved in politics and had become a member of the Liberal party. He met William Morris in 1870 and over the next ten years worked mainly as a children's book illustrator. In 1881 Morris began production of Arts and Crafts artefacts at his factories in Merton Abbey, south-west of London. Like Morris, Crane loathed the modern systems of manufacture and felt that the processes were demeaning to the workers. He was one of the many talented artists who worked for Morris and contributed to designs of tapestries, among other items.

MEDIUM

Colour lithograph

MOVEMENT

Arts and Crafts

RELATED WORK

The Capitalist Vampire, illustration by Walter Crane, 1885

Walter Crane *Born* 1845 Liverpool, England

Died 1915

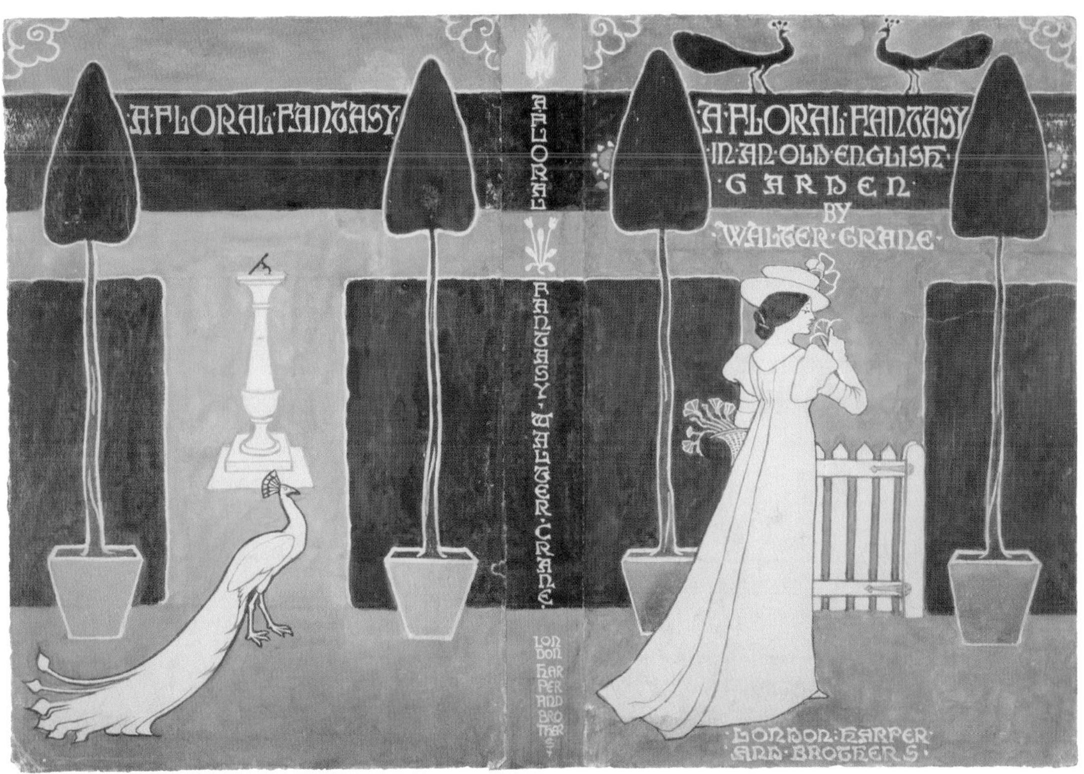

·A·FLORAL·FANTASY·
A·FLORAL FANTASY·WALTER·CRANE·
LONDON HARPER AND BROTHERS·
·A·FLORAL·FANTASY
·IN·AN·OLD·ENGLISH·
·GARDEN·
BY
·WALTER·CRANE·
·LONDON·HARPER·
·AND·BROTHERS·

Crane, Walter

Lilies of the Vale from *Flora's Feast*, 1901

Walter Crane was a contemporary of William Morris and, like Morris, aimed to promote the decorative arts and revive craft traditions. Both men felt that industrialization had damaged the nation's handicrafts and degraded the men and women who worked, almost slavishly, in factories.

In 1884 a group of young architects formed the Art Workers' Guild. This body of men aimed to raise the status of applied arts and challenge the traditional notions of architecture. Walter Crane was one of the designers who joined the guild. By 1888 some members of the guild, including Crane, had joined another, more militant group, the Arts and Crafts Exhibition Society. This society exhibited work of their own artists, designers and architects and those who belonged to like-minded guilds or fraternities. While the exhibitions were not always successful (declining quality of the work meant that the annual shows became triennial) they provided an arena in which innovative design could be displayed. Crane is best known for his illustrations, although he also exhibited paintings at the Royal Academy and in other London art galleries.

MEDIUM

Colour lithograph

MOVEMENT

Arts and Crafts

RELATED WORK

Illustrations for *Grimm's Fairy Tales* by Walter Crane, 1882

Walter Crane *Born* 1845 Liverpool, England

Died 1915

The little Lilies of the Vale,
White ladies delicate & pale;

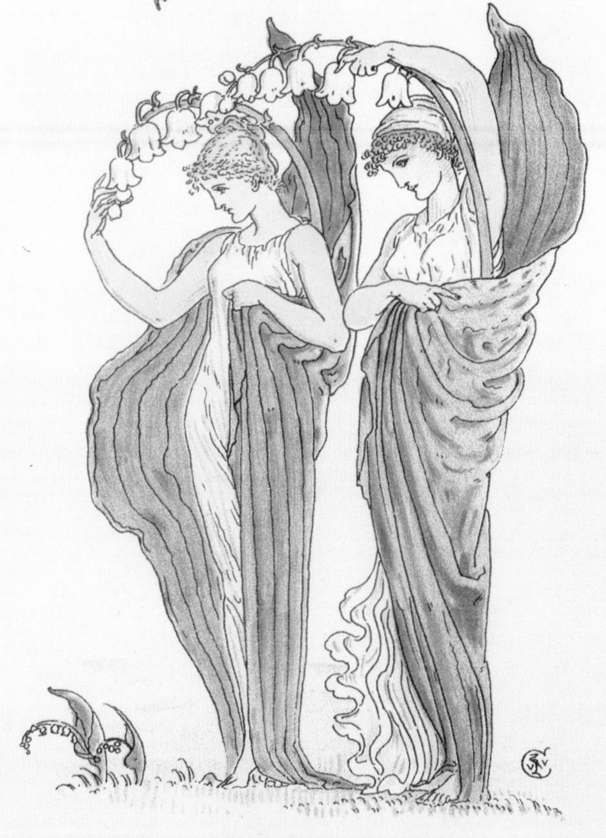

Reprinted by permission from "Flora's Feast."

Burne-Jones, Edward Coley

The Briar Rose Series 4: *The Sleeping Beauty*, 1870–90

Edward Coley Burne-Jones was a contemporary of William Morris and Dante Gabriel Rossetti and was greatly influenced by both men. Burne-Jones left Oxford University without graduating, having sensed that his future career lay not in the church, for which he had been preparing, but in the arts. After travelling in France and Italy Burne-Jones applied himself to painting, a medium in which he was largely self-taught. His work, influenced by Rossetti, Michelangelo and Botticelli, combined mystical and mythical figures with Romanticism. Like other Pre-Raphaelite artists, Burne-Jones found inspiration in medieval stories of chivalry, romance and ethereal heroes and heroines. Many of his paintings are subtle in their eroticism and inspired later Symbolists. His delicately sensuous lines inspired the work of Aubrey Beardsley (1872–98).

Burne-Jones collaborated with William Morris when they, with others, established Morris, Marshall, Faulkner and Co. in 1861 to promote the Arts and Crafts movement. The members of the fraternity experimented with different media and Burne-Jones designed stained-glass windows for the Church.

MEDIUM

Oil on canvas

MOVEMENT

Pre-Raphaelite

RELATED WORK

Flight Into Egypt, stained-glass window designed for St Michael's Church, Brighton by Edward Burne-Jones

Edward Coley Burne-Jones *Born* 1833 Birmingham, England

Died 1898

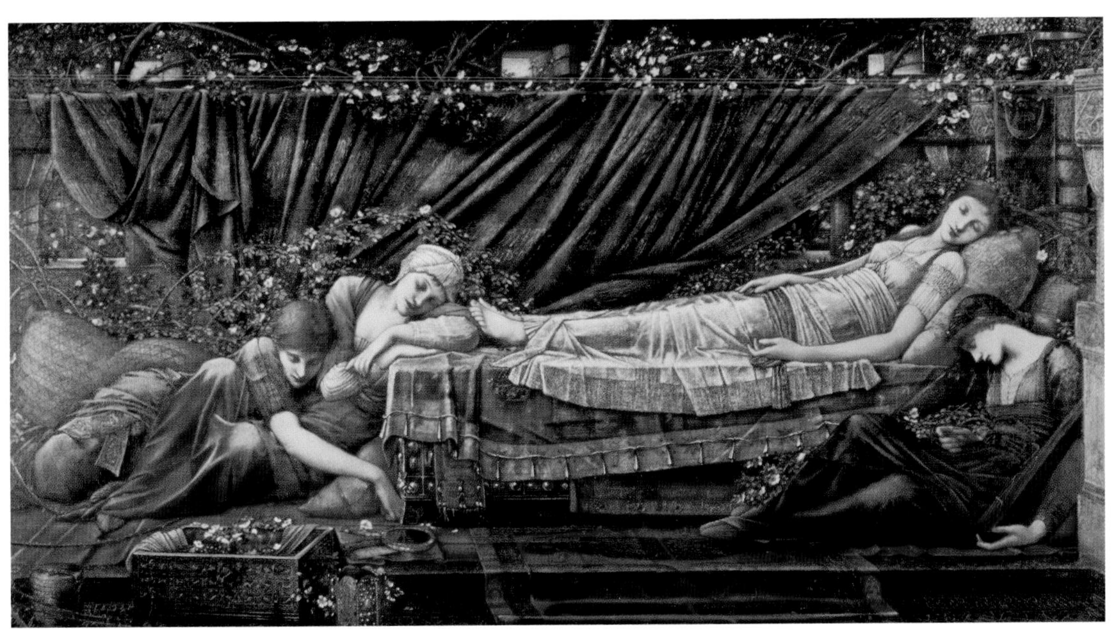

Burne-Jones, Edward Coley

The Baleful Head, c. 1876

Edward Coley Burne-Jones was perceived as a great artist even during his lifetime, but it is for his work in promoting the field of decorative arts in the twentieth century that he is often remembered today. Burne-Jones was a close friend and colleague of William Morris and helped him establish the Arts and Crafts movement. Like many people who worked with Morris, Burne-Jones was able to apply his talent to more than one field.

Edward Burne-Jones produced the illustrations for a number of Morris's books, including more than 80 designs for the *Kelmscott Chaucer* in 1896. This book is now regarded as one of the finest printed books in existence. The scene shown here was also recreated by Burne-Jones in oil on canvas. It is number eight in a series that depicts the legend of Perseus. Andromeda and Perseus stand over a well, in which they can safely see the reflection of the Gorgon, Medusa. The series appeared in William Morris's *The Doom of King Acrisius*, from *The Earthly Paradise*.

MEDIUM

Gouache on paper

MOVEMENT

Pre-Raphaelite

RELATED WORK

Sidonia von Bork painted by Edward Burne-Jones, 1860

Edward Coley Burne-Jones *Born* 1833 Birmingham, England

Died 1898

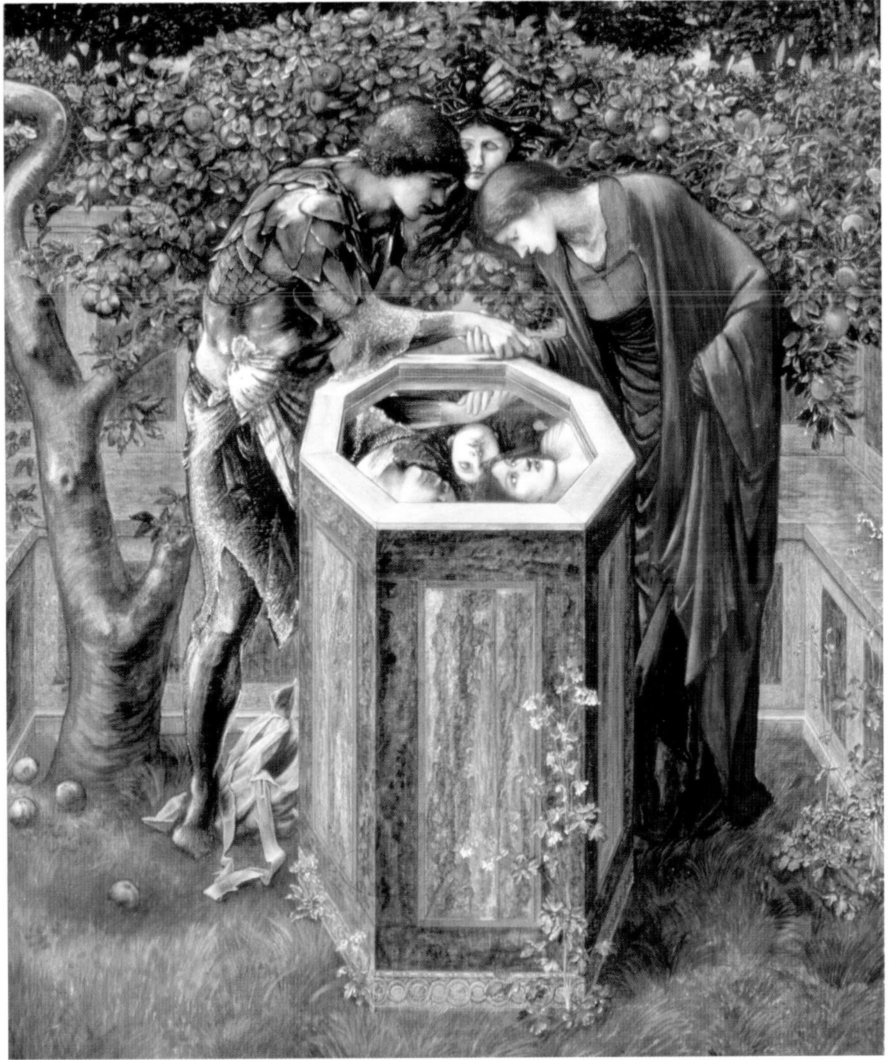

Whistler, James Abbott McNeill

Sketch for *Rose and Silver: La Princesse du Pays de la Porcelaine*, 1863–64

In 1862 the International Exhibition in London marked an important moment in the development of Art Nouveau and other influential art movements. It was here that William Morris showed the furniture, ceramics and stained glass of his newly formed firm. There was, however, an equally important range of decorative arts that was exhibited; this was the first major exhibition of Japanese art in Europe. Although many artefacts had made their way into western markets from the fourteenth century it was not until the 1850s, when Japanese ports were finally opened to foreign powers, that a flood of arts and crafts hit European shores.

Japanese art had a profound effect on the artists and designers of the late nineteenth century and the influence continued into the new century and the Art Deco movement. Liberty and Co., was a major retailer of Oriental art and its owner, Arthur Liberty, was a significant supporter of Art Nouveau. American by birth, James Whistler (1834–1903) had settled in London in 1859 and he was one of many Art Nouveau artists who were inspired by Japanese art.

MEDIUM

Oil on fibreboard

MOVEMENT

Aestheticism

RELATED WORK

Nocturne in Blood and Gold: the Old Battersea Bridge by James Whistler, *c.* 1872–75

James Abbott McNeill Whistler *Born* 1834 Massachusetts, USA

Died 1903

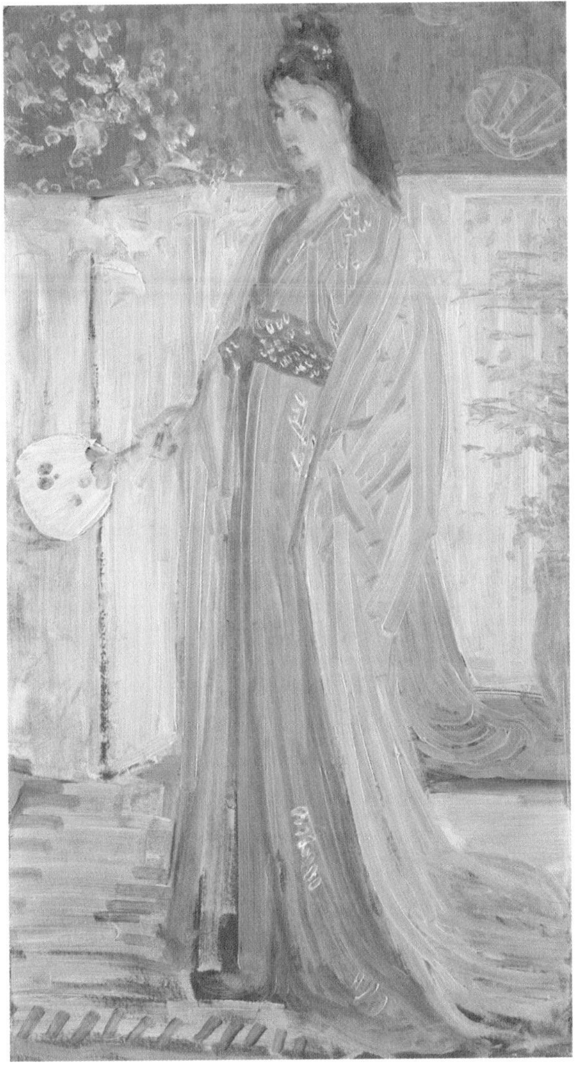

Whistler, James Abbott McNeill

Sketch for *The Balcony*

James Whistler was born in the USA, but studied painting in France. In 1859 he moved to London where he discovered Oriental art and the cult of Aestheticism. Aesthetes of the day, including Oscar Wilde, believed that the value of art owed nothing to politics or philosophy, and was purely based in the notion of beauty.

Whistler's early paintings often showed figures in Japanese attire, but his style developed and eventually his art enveloped the principles of composition and juxtaposition that are a feature of Japanese art (Japonism). Among his most important works were the Nocturne paintings, which demonstrated the Aesthetic quality of achieving maximum impact through total economy of line and colour. These paintings were produced from the 1870s and were the culmination of numerous influences, but in effect were entirely new and challenging. Like many artists of the day, Whistler did not confine himself to a single medium. He also designed interiors, including the famous Peacock Room for his patron Frederick Leyland. Whistler envisaged the entire room as a single design concept or work or art and contributed to the modern theory of interior design.

MEDIUM

Oil on panel

MOVEMENT

Aestheticism

RELATED WORK

Variations in Green and Blue by James Whistler, *c.* 1868

James Abbott McNeill Whistler *Born* 1834 Massachusetts, USA

Died 1903

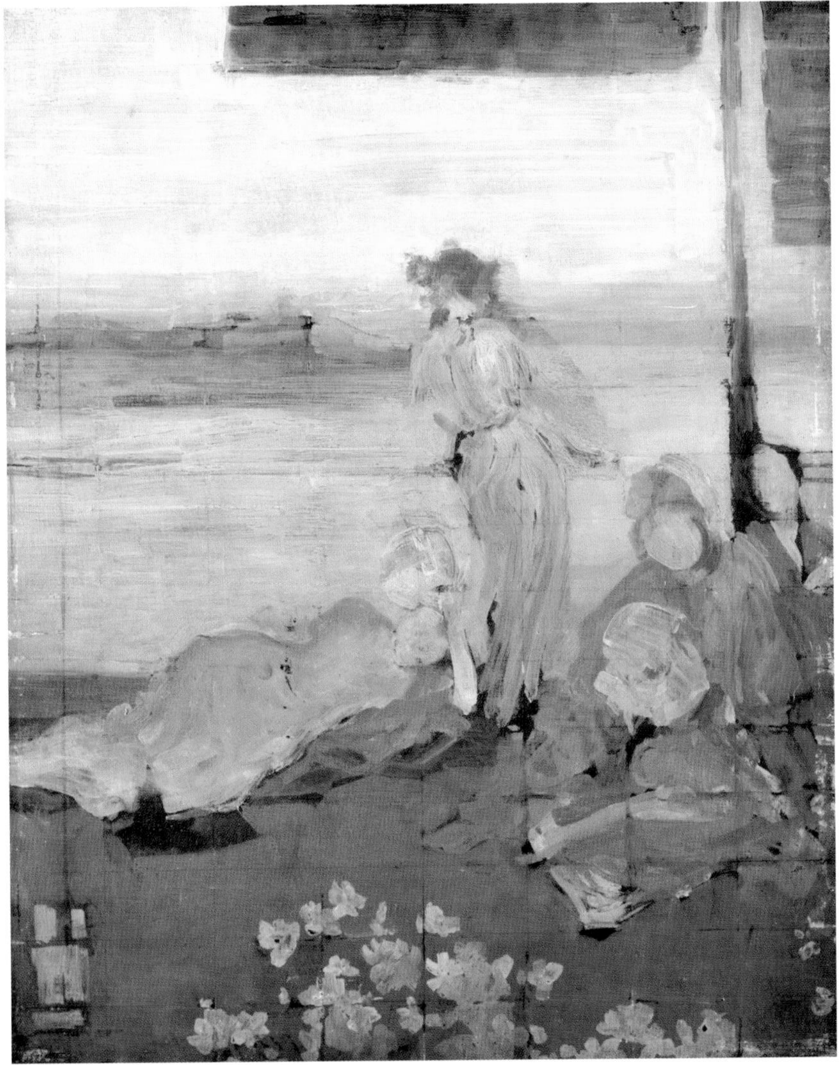

Beardsley, Aubrey

The Peacock Skirt, illustration for the English edition of Oscar Wilde's play *Salomé*, 1893–94

The Irish playwright, poet and wit Oscar Wilde was no stranger to controversy: rehearsals for his play *Salomé* were terminated by the censor because of its passionate theme and its use of Biblical characters. In 1893 the play, which was written in French, was first published. In 1894 an English translation followed, illustrated with Aubrey Beardsley's now-famous pictures.

The publication of this illustration by Beardsley is now regarded as one of the defining moments in the development of the Art Nouveau aesthetic. It first appeared in March 1893 titled *J'ai baisé ta bouche Iokanaan*, ('I have kissed thy mouth, Iokanaan') in a new magazine called *The Studio* and immediately attracted the attention of the European avant-garde. The picture contains many archetypal Art Nouveau elements: it is asymmetrical in structure and its sinuous lines create the arabesque (ornamentation constructed from an intricate line) that suggests flowing movement. There is strong sexual tension in the picture (and the play), which is revealed in the subtle, erotic images.

MEDIUM

Indian ink on paper

MOVEMENT

Aestheticism/Art Nouveau

RELATED WORK

Design for *The Climax* from *Salomé* by Aubrey Beardsley, 1893

Aubrey Beardsley *Born* 1872 Brighton, England

Died 1898

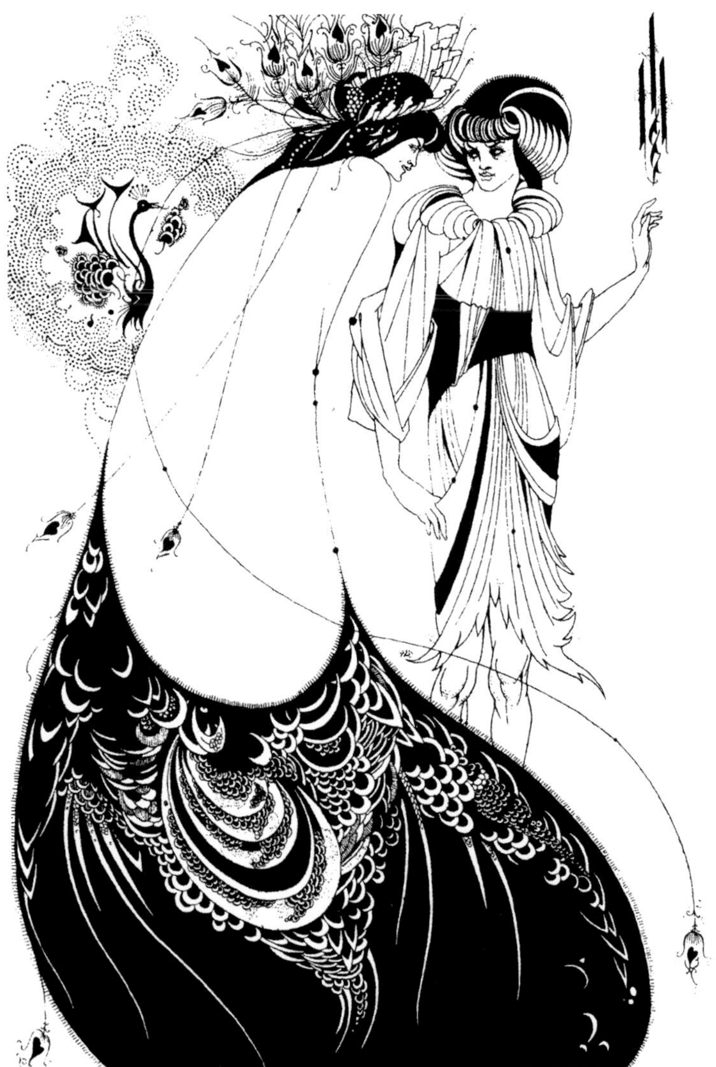

Beardsley, Aubrey

Isolde, illustration from *The Studio*, 1895

Aubrey Beardsley had shown a talent for drawing from an early age. As an adult his short-lived career was meteoric; he was catapulted to fame by his illustrations for magazines such as *The Studio* and *The Yellow Book*. The young man gained notoriety and adulation in equal measure before his premature death at the age of 26.

The work of this illustrator and artist pulls together many themes, styles and techniques of his era and earlier. Of all of the influences, Japanese woodcuts, which Beardsley collected, are possibly the most important. The overall effect, however, was to produce a highly innovative body of work. His stark use of black and white, his evocative lines and his tendency towards the erotic were considered outrageous and decadent by many. The effect and influence of his work is now regarded as being enormous, and unfulfilled predictions by fellow artists, such as Edward Burne-Jones, that he would 'most assuredly paint very good and beautiful pictures' are poignant. Aware that he was dying, Beardsley converted to Catholicism and begged that his obscene pictures be destroyed; fortunately for us, they were not.

MEDIUM

Colour lithograph

MOVEMENT

Aestheticism/Art Nouveau

RELATED WORK

The Dreamer, illustration by Aubrey Beardsley

Aubrey Beardsley *Born* 1872 Brighton, England

Died 1898

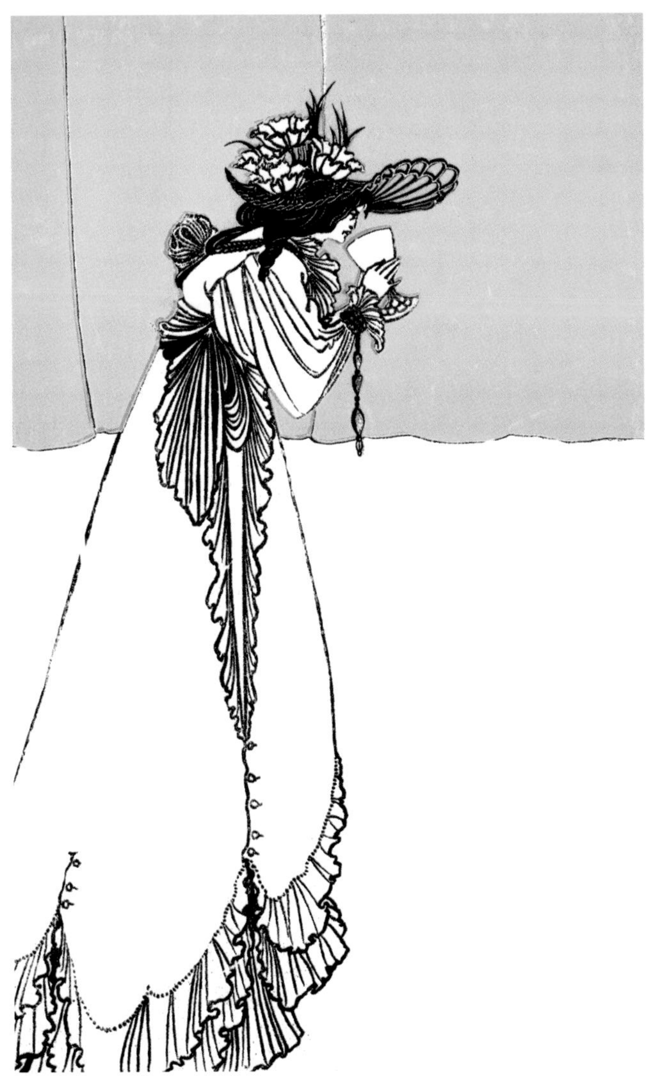

Beardsley, Aubrey

Cover for *Le Morte d'Arthur* by Sir Thomas Malory, 1893

The late nineteenth century saw a resurgence in interest in medieval legends and the story of King Arthur and his knights. The Pre-Raphaelites often sought inspiration from medieval stories and this became a defining influence of the Art Nouveau movement.

In 1892 publisher J. M. Dent asked Aubrey Beardsley to illustrate Sir Thomas Malory's fifteenth-century text of the legend of King Arthur. Unlike other elite publishers of the day, such as the Kelmscott Press, Dent wanted to deliver literature for the masses and combined cheaper materials with modern mechanical production to print a series of affordable books. Beardsley's black and white illustrations suited this concept well. The series of 12 books featured over 350 Beardsley designs, including letters, full-page illustrations and ornaments and was first published from 1893 to 1894. The success of the series, although originally sold only by subscription, enabled Beardsley to give up his office job and pursue art full time. The artist always worked by candlelight rather than gaslight, even during the day, when his curtains would be drawn. Sketches were completed in pencil first and then redrawn using a gold-nibbed pen and Chinese ink.

MOVEMENT

Aestheticism/Art Nouveau

RELATED WORK

Merlin, illustration from *Le Morte d'Arthur* by Aubrey Beardsley, 1893

Aubrey Beardsley *Born* 1872 Brighton, England

Died 1898

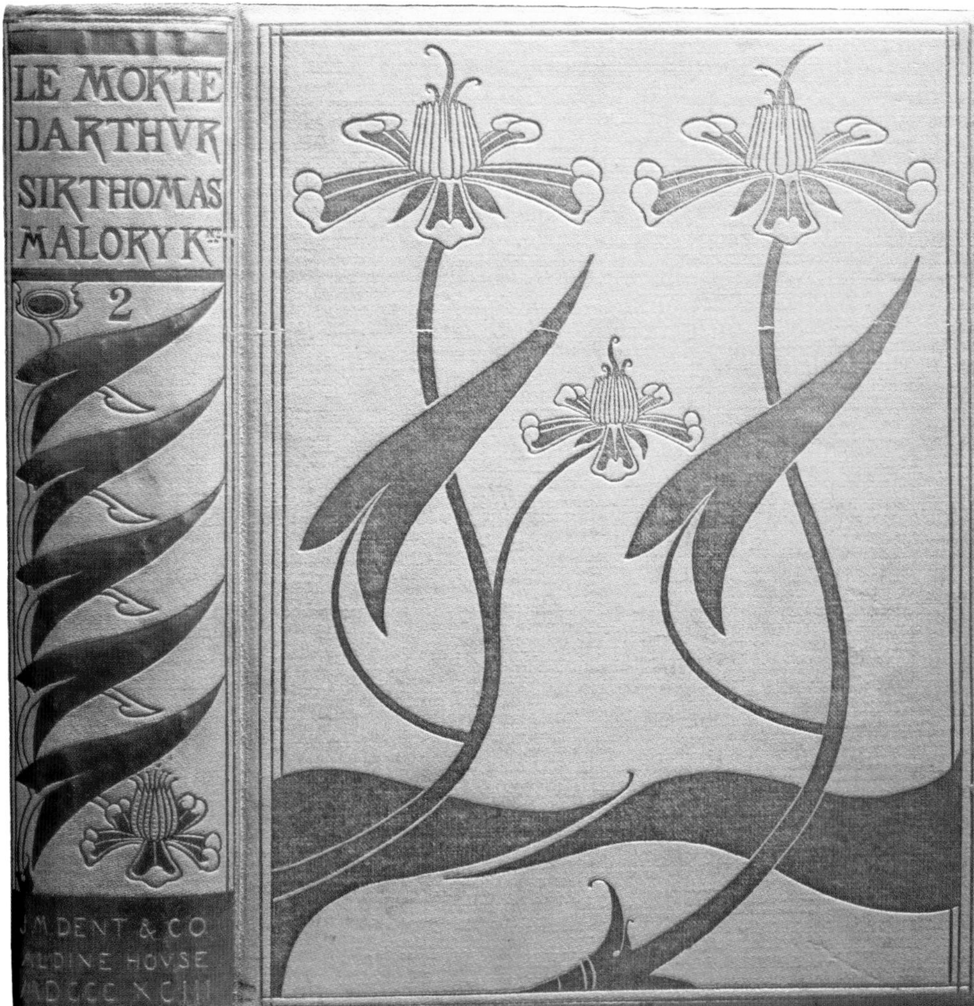

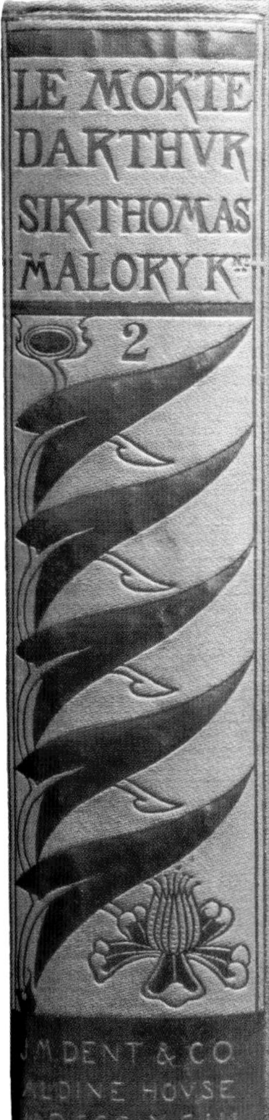
LE MORTE
DARTHVR
SIR THOMAS
MALORY KNT
2
J.M.DENT & CO
ALDINE HOVSE
MDCCCXCIII

Beardsley, Aubrey

Publicity poster for *The Yellow Book*, 1894–97

The idea for *The Yellow Book* was conceived by a group of writers and artists, including Aubrey Beardsley and expatriate American writer Henry Harland, in 1894. Tired of endless refusals from leading publications of the day, this cosmopolitan group decided to set up their own quarterly magazine, with the aim of providing a forum for the 'new movement' in art and literature. Contributors to *The Yellow Book* included Walter Crane, Sir Frederic Leighton (1830–96) and Henry James (1843–1916), although the magazine notably and purposefully excluded Oscar Wilde from its pages. The name was chosen to reflect the 'Yellow Nineties': a time during which staid Victorianism was rejected in favour of bright Regency and French influences. Yellow was not only the colour of the decade it was also the chosen colour for many French novels, which were perceived as decadent.

Although highly influential and successful, the magazine was roundly criticized and Beardsley's illustrations in particular were often regarded as 'freakish'. It continued in publication until 1897, but during its short lifespan opened the door to many new writers, including women.

MOVEMENT

Aestheticism/Art Nouveau

RELATED WORK

Poster for *The Studio* by Aubrey Beardsley, 1894

Aubrey Beardsley *Born* 1872 Brighton, England

Died 1898

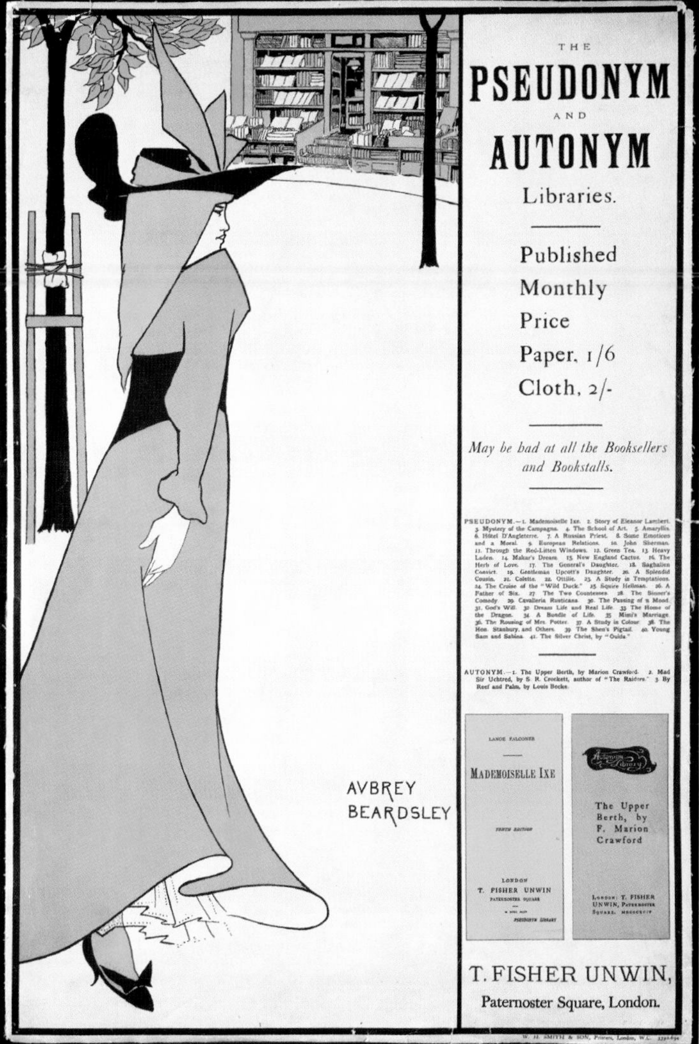
THE
PSEUDONYM
AND
AUTONYM
Libraries.
Published Monthly
Price
Paper, 1/6
Cloth, 2/-
May be had at all the Booksellers and Bookstalls.
PSEUDONYM.—1. Mademoiselle Ixe. 2. Story of Eleanor Lambert. 3. Mystery of the Campagna. 4. The School of Art. 5. Amaryllis. 6. Hôtel D'Angleterre. 7. A Russian Priest. 8. Some Emotions and a Moral. 9. European Relations. 10. John Sherman. 11. Through the Red-Litten Windows. 12. Green Tea. 13. Heavy Laden. 14. Makar's Dream. 15. New England Cactus. 16. The Herb of Love. 17. The General's Daughter. 18. Saghalien Convict. 19. Gentleman Upcott's Daughter. 20. A Splendid Cousin. 21. Colette. 22. Ottilie. 23. A Study in Temptations. 24. The Cruise of the "Wild Duck." 25. Squire Hellman. 26. A Father of Six. 27. The Two Countesses. 28. The Sinner's Comedy. 29. Cavalleria Rusticana. 30. The Passing of a Mood. 31. God's Will. 32. Dream Life and Real Life. 33. The Home of the Dragon. 34. A Bundle of Life. 35. Mimi's Marriage. 36. The Rousing of Mrs. Potter. 37. A Study in Colour. 38. The Hon. Stanbury, and Others. 39. The Shen's Pigtail. 40. Young Sam and Sabina. 41. The Silver Christ, by "Ouida."
AUTONYM.—1. The Upper Berth, by Marion Crawford. 2. Mad Sir Uchtred, by S. R. Crockett, author of "The Raiders." 3. By Reef and Palm, by Louis Becke.
LANOE FALCONER
MADEMOISELLE IXE
TENTH EDITION
LONDON
T. FISHER UNWIN
PATERNOSTER SQUARE
PSEUDONYM LIBRARY
The Upper Berth, by F. Marion Crawford
London: T. FISHER UNWIN, Paternoster Square.
AVBREY BEARDSLEY
T. FISHER UNWIN,
Paternoster Square, London.
W. H. SMITH & SON, Printers, London, W.C.

Toulouse-Lautrec, Henri de

Divan Japonais from *Les Maitres de L'Affiche*, 1892

Henri de Toulouse-Lautrec (1864–1901) was born into a wealthy and aristocratic French family. He showed early talent for drawing, as did his father and uncle. Although a cheerful and lively young boy, Toulouse-Lautrec was never very healthy and his mother tutored him at home for a number of years. The frail boy fell twice, breaking each leg, one in 1878 and the other in 1879. Despite the best medical care, his bones never set and Toulouse-Lautrec was left crippled. His legs never grew to full length; they were also weak and unnaturally thin. When an adult and living in the Montmartre district of Paris, Toulouse-Lautrec became a familiar figure; recognizable by his aristocratic manner, awkward walk and damaged legs.

This poster shows Jane Avril, a favourite model of the artist's, with the critic Edouard Dujardin. They are listening to the singer Yvette Guilbert. Notice how it is only her torso that appears and long sheath-like gloves. This chopping of figures and the powerful image of Avril, in a block of black superimposed upon the orchestra, demonstrates the influence of Japanese art in Toulouse-Lautrec's work.

MEDIUM

Crayon, brush, spatter and transferred screen lithograph in five colours

MOVEMENT

Post Impressionism

RELATED WORK

At the Moulin Rouge, oil on canvas by Henri de Toulouse-Lautrec, 1892

Henri de Toulouse-Lautrec *Born* 1864 Albi, France

Died 1901

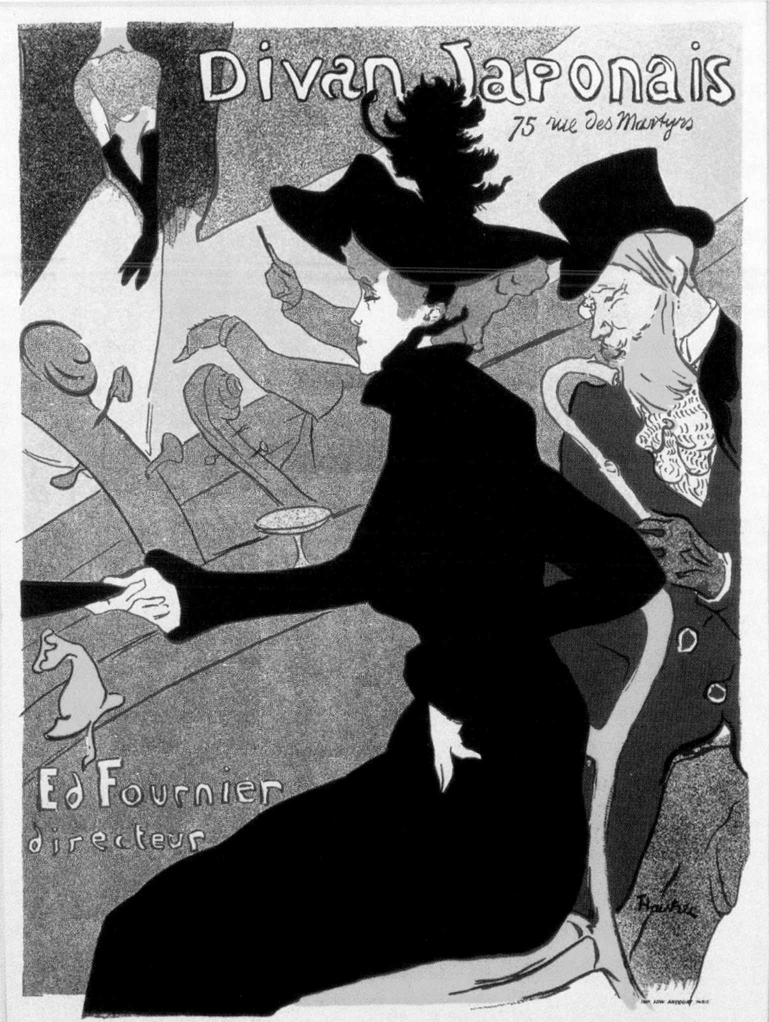
Divan Japonais
75 rue des Martyrs
Ed Fournier
directeur
Lautrec

Toulouse-Lautrec, Henri de

Confetti, 1893

At the age of 17 the young Toulouse-Lautrec embarked on his training in art. He had gained some academic success, but books held little interest for Toulouse-Lautrec: it was art that pulled him. Until 1893 he trained with different artists, learning the Classical skills of the day, but was unimpressed by the staid and static creations that tradition demanded. In 1886 he met Vincent van Gogh (1853–90) and the two men became friends. It was Van Gogh who persuaded Toulouse-Lautrec to head south, to find light, air and space for his work. The climate suited the younger man's poor health but he eventually made his way to the Parisian district of Montmartre and, supported by his parents, rented a studio. By the mid 1880s Toulouse-Lautrec was settled among the cafes, cabarets and nightclubs that were to inspire him to find new ways of catching life and energy.

This poster shows how Toulouse-Lautrec's style matured to the point where he could, through a series of well-placed lines and blocks of colour, create the impression of movement and joy.

CREATED

Paris

MEDIUM

Colour lithograph

RELATED WORK

Miss Loïe Fuller, brush and splatter lithograph by Henri de Toulouse-Lautrec, 1893

Henri de Toulouse-Lautrec *Born* 1864 Albi, France

Died 1901

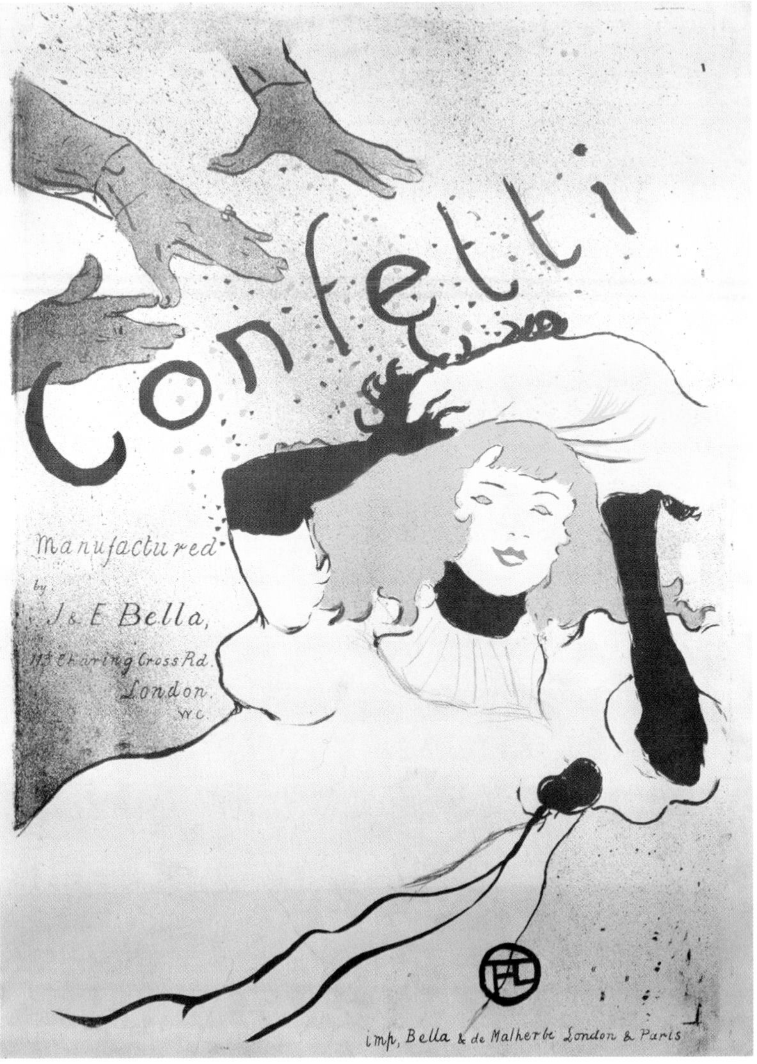
Confetti
Manufactured
by
J & E Bella,
113 Charing Cross Rd.
London.
W.C.
imp, Bella & de Malherbe London & Paris

Toulouse-Lautrec, Henri de

Ambassadeurs: Aristide Bruant, 1892

The subject of this lithograph was Aristide Bruant (1851–1925) a singer and entertainer who embodied the spirit of the Montmartre nightlife that Toulouse-Lautrec found so inspiring. Bruant published illustrated papers to which the French artist contributed and also commissioned Toulouse-Lautrec to design posters, such as this one, to promote his cabaret act. The posters decorated the walls of the cabaret and were placed around Paris, bringing the artist to the attention of many ordinary people in the city. Bruant was a captivating and imposing man, who wore a trademark wide-brimmed hat and red scarf, perfectly captured in this print. This powerful, strident image is dramatic in its composition and the restrained use of colour.

The two men were friends for a number of years and Bruant introduced Toulouse-Lautrec to many of the entertainers whom he painted and sketched. The artist became a familiar sight at clubs and bars as he intently observed then sketched the men and women who populated them. He drank heavily in the evenings while sketching and during the day he revised and improved his drawings in the studio.

CREATED

Paris

MEDIUM

Colour lithograph

RELATED WORK

Aristide Bruant in his cabaret, poster by Henri de Toulouse-Lautrec, 1893

Henri de Toulouse-Lautrec *Born* 1864 Albi, France

Died 1901

AMBASSADEURS
aristide
BRUANT
dans
son cabaret
H Lautrec

Toulouse-Lautrec, Henri de

Promenade on Yacht, c. 1896

This poster was designed to advertise the Exposition Internationale d'Affiches in Paris. Toulouse-Lautrec is best remembered for his images of nightlife in the pleasure halls of Montmartre, but his work was not confined to this area. In 1890 he had achieved some success and acclaim after being exhibited at the Belgian annual exhibition of Les Vingt (Les XX), an avante-garde art group and at the Paris Salon des Indepéndents. He received numerous commissions for book illustrations, covers and theatre programmes.

In 1891 Toulouse-Lautrec produced his first poster and by 1892 he was working on developing his lithographic techniques. In total he produced about 30 posters and had completed over 300 lithographs in ten years. In 1893 he produced an album of 11 prints, entitled *Le Café Concert* and in 1896 his lithographic series *Elles* was printed. These pictures portrayed the everyday lives of Parisian prostitutes and became one of his finest bodies of work. Toulouse-Lautrec was fascinated by his models and it could take as many as 70 sittings before he would be content with the finished picture.

CREATED

Paris

RELATED WORK

At the Nouveau Cirque, watercolour by Henri de Toulouse-Lautrec, 1891

Henri de Toulouse-Lautrec *Born* 1864 Albi, France

Died 1901

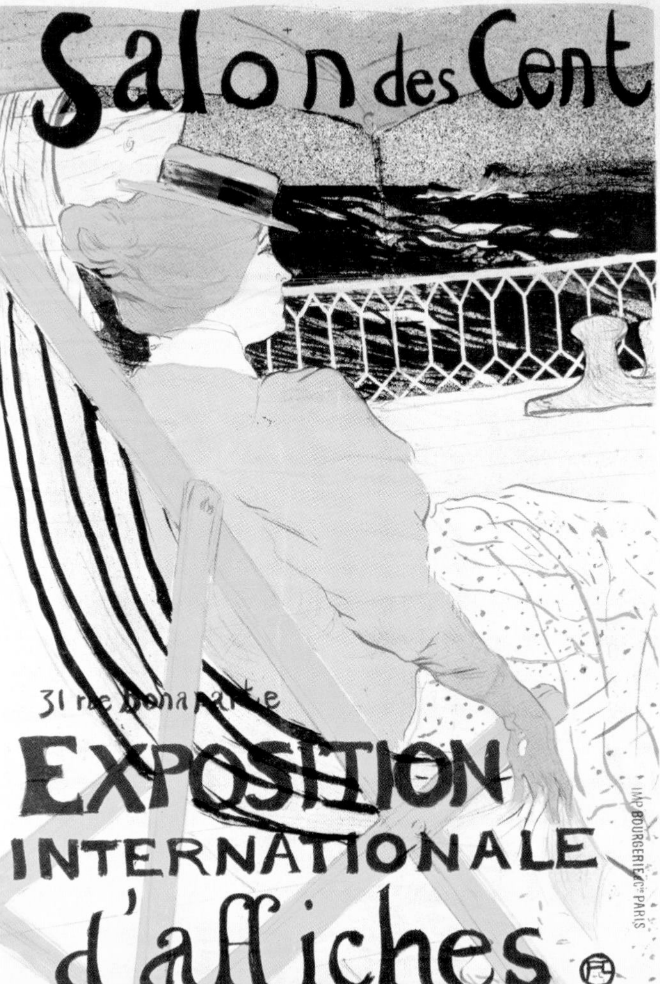
Salon des Cent
31 rue Bonaparte
EXPOSITION
INTERNATIONALE
d'affiches
IMP BOURGERIE & Cie PARIS

Toulouse-Lautrec, Henri de

Jane Avril, 1899

By 1898 Toulouse-Lautrec's health was in ruins; he had contracted syphilis and was a heavy drinker. Eventually his aggressive outbursts and alcoholism led him to being committed to a sanatorium. When released he set his affairs in order and worked whenever the opportunity and his health permitted. He suffered a stroke and died in September 1901 aged 36.

After his death, many critics reveled: some accused him of painting 'ugliness everywhere' and called his talent 'evil'. Like many artists who strike out at tradition and challenge conformity, Toulouse-Lautrec was misunderstood by a public who were challenged by images of real life. Unlike many contemporary artists, he captured the spirits of genuine, unstylized men and women; his work takes the eye beyond superficial appearances and digs deep into the essence of the subject's being. He said that he wanted to 'depict the true and not the ideal'. Just as photographs that have meaning do not capture a mere likeness, but evoke a feeling or a memory, his paintings caught moments, movement and emotions. The life and energy he encapsulated inspired the Fauvists and Cubists who followed him.

CREATED

Paris

MEDIUM

Colour lithograph

RELATED WORK

Jane Avril in the Entrance of the Moulin Rouge, oil on cardboard by Henri de Toulouse-Lautrec, 1892

Henri de Toulouse-Lautrec *Born* 1864 Albi, France

Died 1901

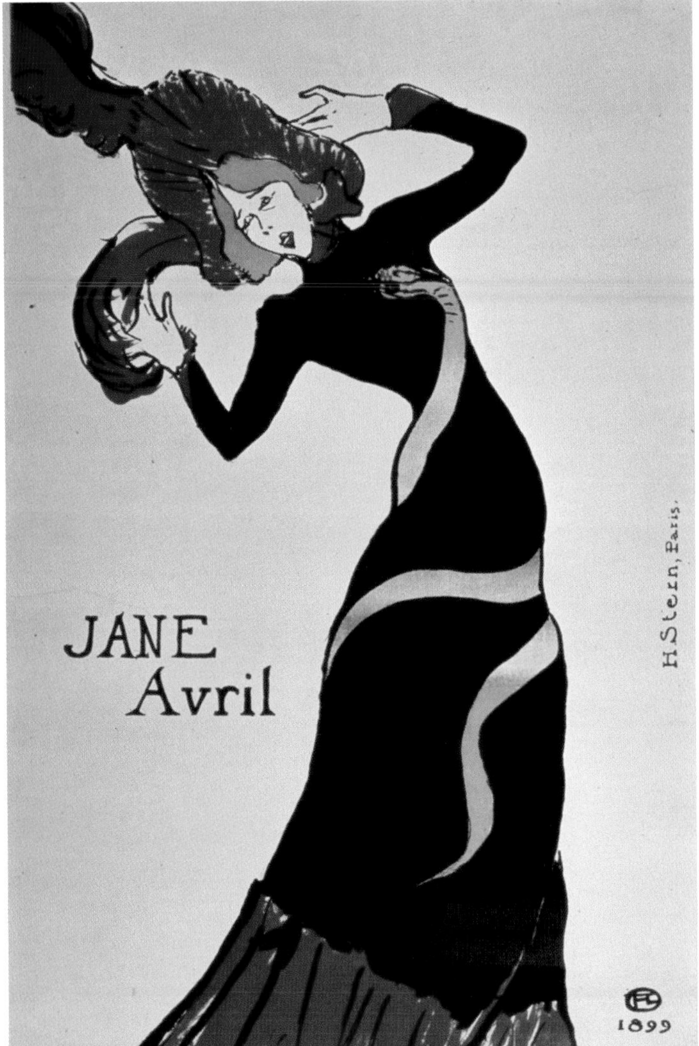
JANE
Avril
H. Stern, Paris.
1899

Daum Frères

Selection of Daum vases

In the middle of the nineteenth century glass-making in France concentrated on cut crystal and coloured glass. Among the most popular decorated glassware were the opaline varieties; these had a semi-opaque base colour that was decorated in gilt or painted in elaborate detail. As the end of the century drew near artists in France began to experiment and produce more interesting and varied glass.

There were three prominent French artists working in glass who influenced the development of glassware during the Art Nouveau period: Emile Gallé (1846–1904), Eugène Rousseau (1827–91), who used streaks of colour and interior crackling, and Joseph Brocard (died 1896). Brocard copied Islamic techniques of enamelling glass and developed a cloisonné method to outline designs in cells of gold or enamel. He taught these techniques to Gallé, who was also inspired to use Islamic motifs and designs. Although artists were able to design decorative effects, they were rarely able to execute the designs themselves since glass production and colouring are crafts that require a high level of skill and many years of training and experience. This is where the role of the Daum Frères (Daum Brothers), Auguste (1853–1909) and Antonin (1864–1930), contributed to the development of glass design during this period.

CREATED

Nancy

MEDIUM

Glass and enamel

RELATED WORK

Acid-etched vase with dragonfly motif by Daum Frères, 1904

Auguste Daum *Born* 1853 Bitche, France

Died 1909

Antonin Daum *Born* 1864 Bitche, France

Died 1930

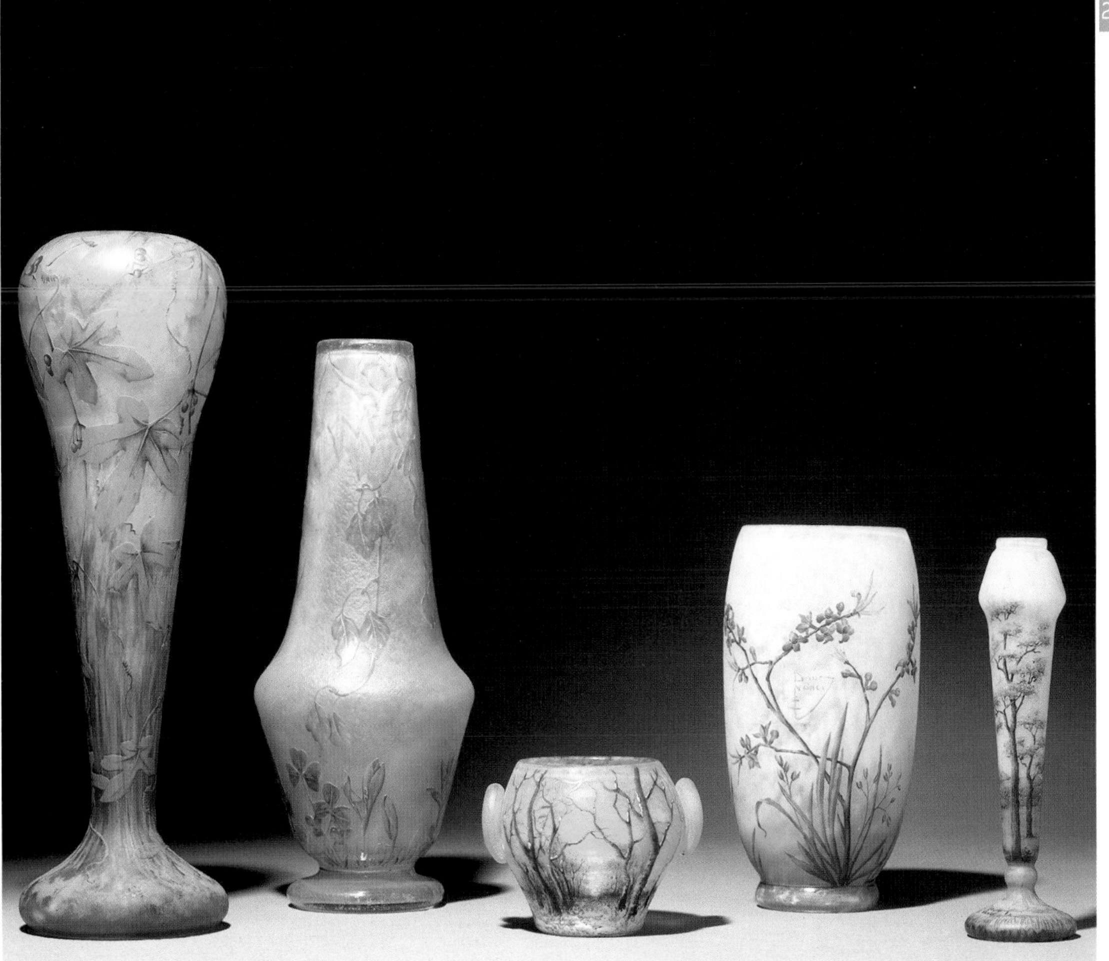

Daum Frères and Brandt, Edgar

Table lamp

The city of Nancy proved to be an influential and important place in Art Nouveau France. In the 1850s the town grew as the extraction of coal, salt and iron led to a rapid industrialization. In 1871 Nancy became annexed to France after the Franco-Prussian war and it attracted large numbers of immigrants who wanted to escape from the neighbouring German territory. The town's industrial wealth grew as its population expanded and a period of commercial and public building was ordered. It was this building programme that encouraged the Ecole de Nancy (School of Nancy), an artistic expression that was applied to contemporary building projects and decorative arts. Emile Gallé, Louis Majorelle and the Daum Frères were all able to exploit the mood in the town and its key industries to create products in the Art Nouveau style. These four entrepreneurs owed much of their success to their foresight: they were all willing, to a smaller or greater extent, to use industrial processes to produce quality goods thus making them affordable to a bigger market.

This lamp features a base cast from a model by French artist-blacksmith Edgar Brandt (1880–1960). Brandt combined traditional forging methods with new technologies such as torch-welding and power hammers.

CREATED

Nancy

MEDIUM

Bronze and glass

RELATED WORK

Wrought and cast iron table lamp by Daum Frères, *c.*1890

Edgar Brandt *Born* 1880 Paris, France

Died 1960

Auguste Daum *Born* 1853 Bitche, France

Died 1909

Antonin Daum *Born* 1864 Bitche, France

Died 1930

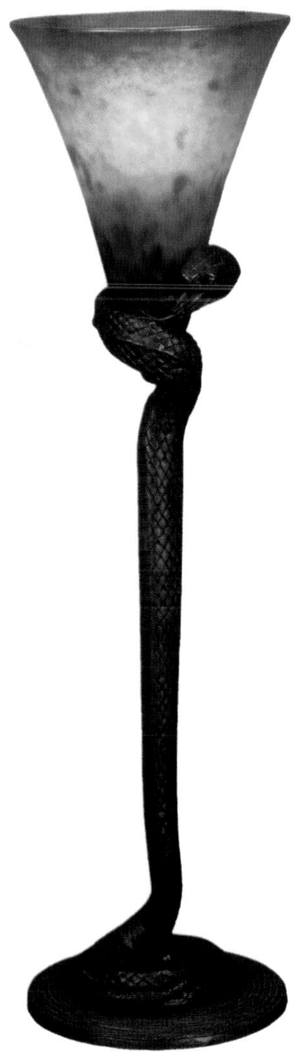

Daum Frères

Lamp with oak-tree decoration, *c.* 1900

Much of the work produced by the Daum factory was organic in style. As in Gallé's work, floral, organic and symbolic motifs predominated in the decoration of the glassware. This vase-shaped lamp is typical: the oak-tree decoration is absorbed into the glass, so the two meld into one. Contrasting media are employed: fragile, feminine and opalescent glass forms a background against which the strong, more masculine ironwork is wound. At the base of the lamp the ornamentation extends beyond the boundaries of its form, blurring the edges between the lamp and its surroundings, thus helping to unite them.

Electric lights and lamp fittings became increasingly popular at the *fin-de-siècle*, so the work of glass manufacturers was in particular demand for these products. The light bulbs at the time were very weak, however, and when combined with coloured opalescent glass the effect must have been more decorative than illuminating. The bodies of the lamps were often designed in such a way as to hide or disguise the electrical flexes that ran through them.

CREATED

Nancy

MEDIUM

Double-layered glass and wrought iron

RELATED WORK

Vase in green glass and metal by Johann Loetz Witwe, 1898

Auguste Daum *Born* 1853 Bitche, France

Died 1909

Antonin Daum *Born* 1864 Bitche, France

Died 1930

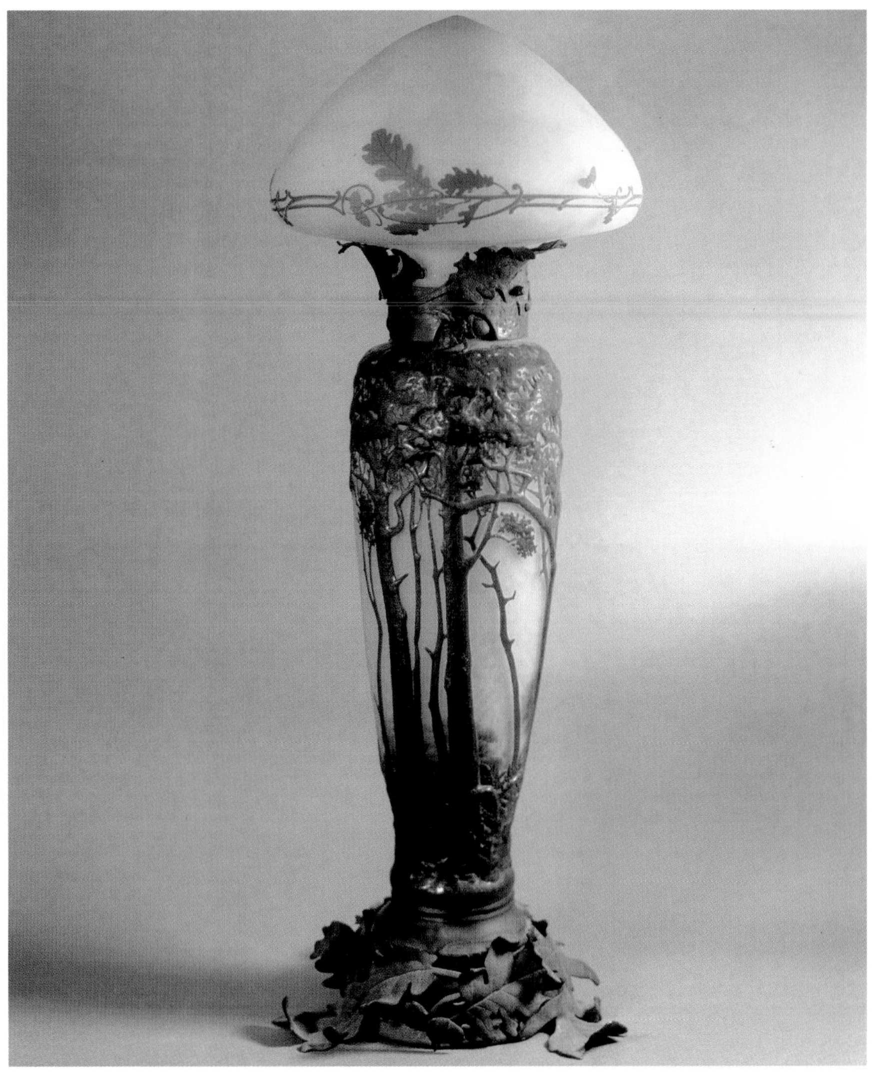

Daum Frères

Vase, 1901–02

The Daum brothers followed in the wake of Emile Gallé and were willing to experiment with their techniques in order to achieve startling and innovative effects. They were able to take advantage of the presence of many fine craftsmen in the town of Nancy and employed great designers, such as Jacques Gruber (1870–1936) who also designed many windows for the commercial and domestic buildings springing up in Nancy at this time.

Pâte de verre was one of the techniques used at the Daum factory: this involves the decorative use of powdered glass, which melts when fired. Cameo glass was also particularly popular. This method calls for the careful incising of a top layer of coloured glass, revealing a different colour below. Antonin Daum was the primary artistic director, and he controlled the aesthetic output of the factory and supervised the close-knit team of chemists, engravers, painters and designers. His brother Auguste looked after the commercial and financial side of the business. Auguste's son Paul Daum took over the factory and ran it from the 1920s.

CREATED

Nancy

MEDIUM

Glass, dyes and enamels

RELATED WORK

Windows of the Majorelle Villa in Nancy by Gruber, 1901–02

Auguste Daum *Born* 1853 Bitche, France

Died 1909

Antonin Daum *Born* 1864 Bitche, France

Died 1930

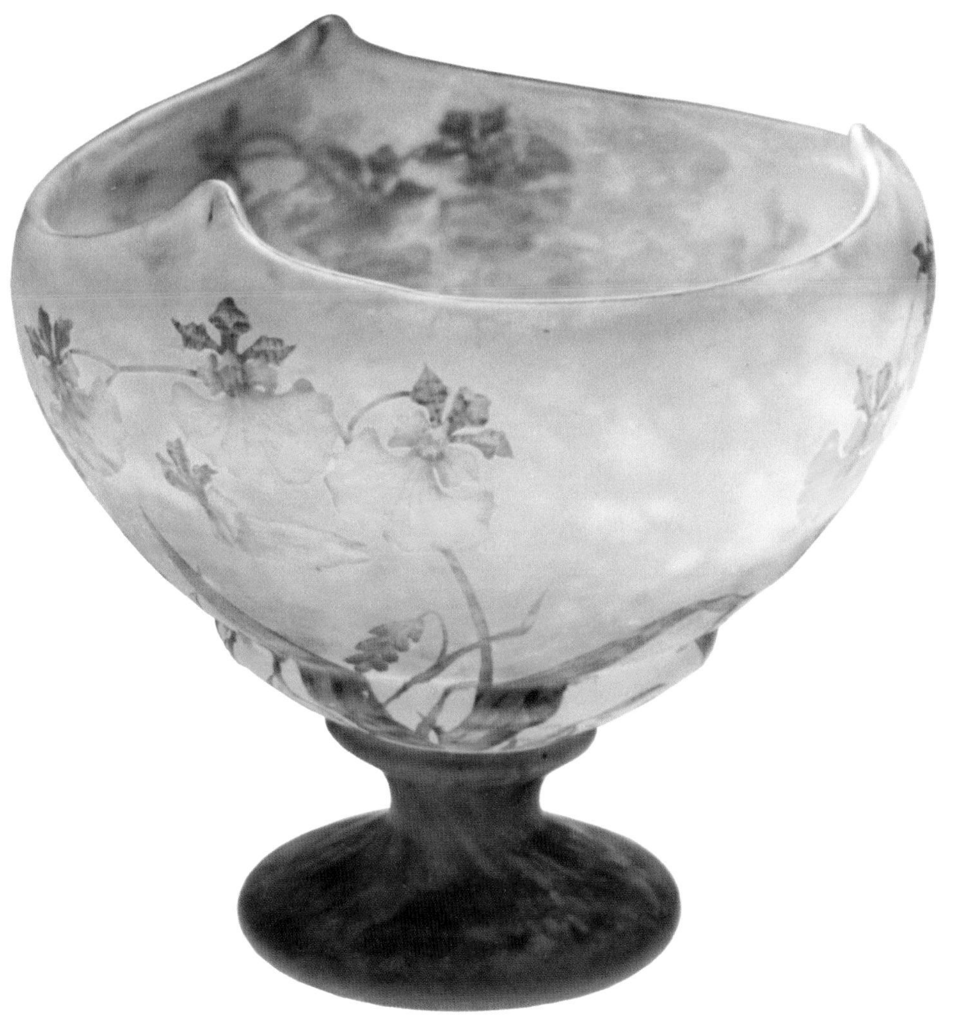

Daum, Auguste

Trumpet vase

The Daum brothers proved themselves to be sound businessmen; they kept their options open and provided a wide range of goods that were affordable at both ends of the market. They continued to produce art glass as one-offs or commissions; these were sometimes exhibited across Europe and brought wide acclaim for the artistry and technical skill associated with the Daum name. However, they also introduced some industrial production into the factory and were able to produce cheaper goods to supply the ordinary retail market. By the 1890s the Daum factory provided work for more than 300 people.

The brothers created a successful environment, which in many ways succeeded where the Arts and Crafts movement ultimately failed. Their model demonstrated how a business could keep both profitability and artistic integrity by complementing the skills of a handicraft with modern production methods and good marketing. The Daum brothers set in motion a business that was able to adapt as styles changed: when Art Nouveau faded during the First World War, the Daum designers changed their style to bold, geometric and stylish. Daum glassware is still produced today.

CREATED

Nancy

MEDIUM

Incised glass – internally decorated and acid-cut

RELATED WORK

The Glassmaker, vase by Daum Frères, 1908

Auguste Daum *Born* 1853 Bitche, France

Died 1909

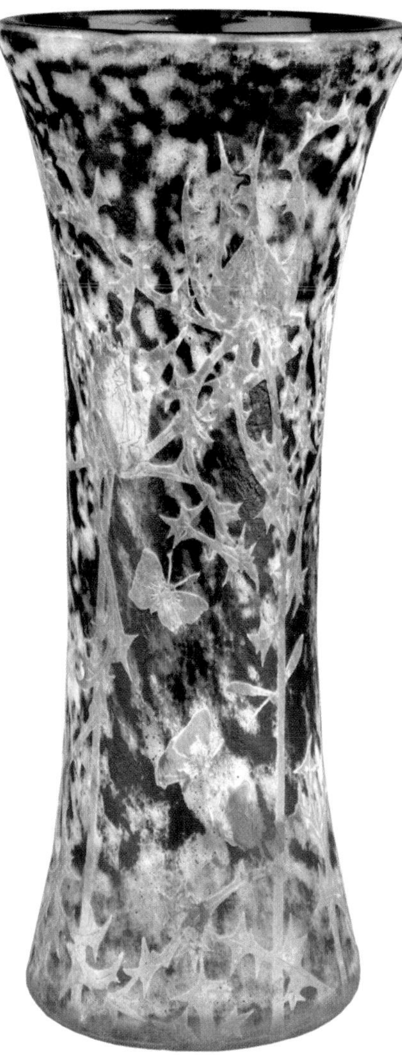

Hoffmann, Josef

Palais Stoclet, 1905–11

The crowing glory of Viennese Art Nouveau architecture was the Palais Stoclet, designed by Josef Hoffmann (1870–1956) for a wealthy young industrialist, Adolphe Stoclet. Although built in Brussels, the mansion demonstrates the move of the Viennese Secession and *Wiener Werkstätte* towards geometrical and linear designs in the early years of the twentieth century.

Despite its severe lines and cubic shape, the Palais Stoclet was not austere; built from sumptuous materials and with luxurious interiors it became an icon of the essential Art Nouveau objective of combining all elements of a building into a harmonious whole. The exterior is created from a series of white façades, each one enclosed and defined by black borders. The severity of this construction was complemented by an extravagant use of white marble, which sheathed the walls. Copper pipes accentuated the lines of the structure. The interior of the building was designed with no concern for cost and as a result Hoffmann was able to give full rein to his imagination and ideals. Gustav Klimt (1862–1918) designed a frieze for the building, drawing on a range of non-European art for his inspiration.

CREATED

Brussels

MEDIUM

Architecture

RELATED WORK

Pürkersdorf Sanatorium by Josef Hoffmann, 1904–06

Josef Hoffmann *Born* 1870 Pirnitz, Moravia

Died 1956

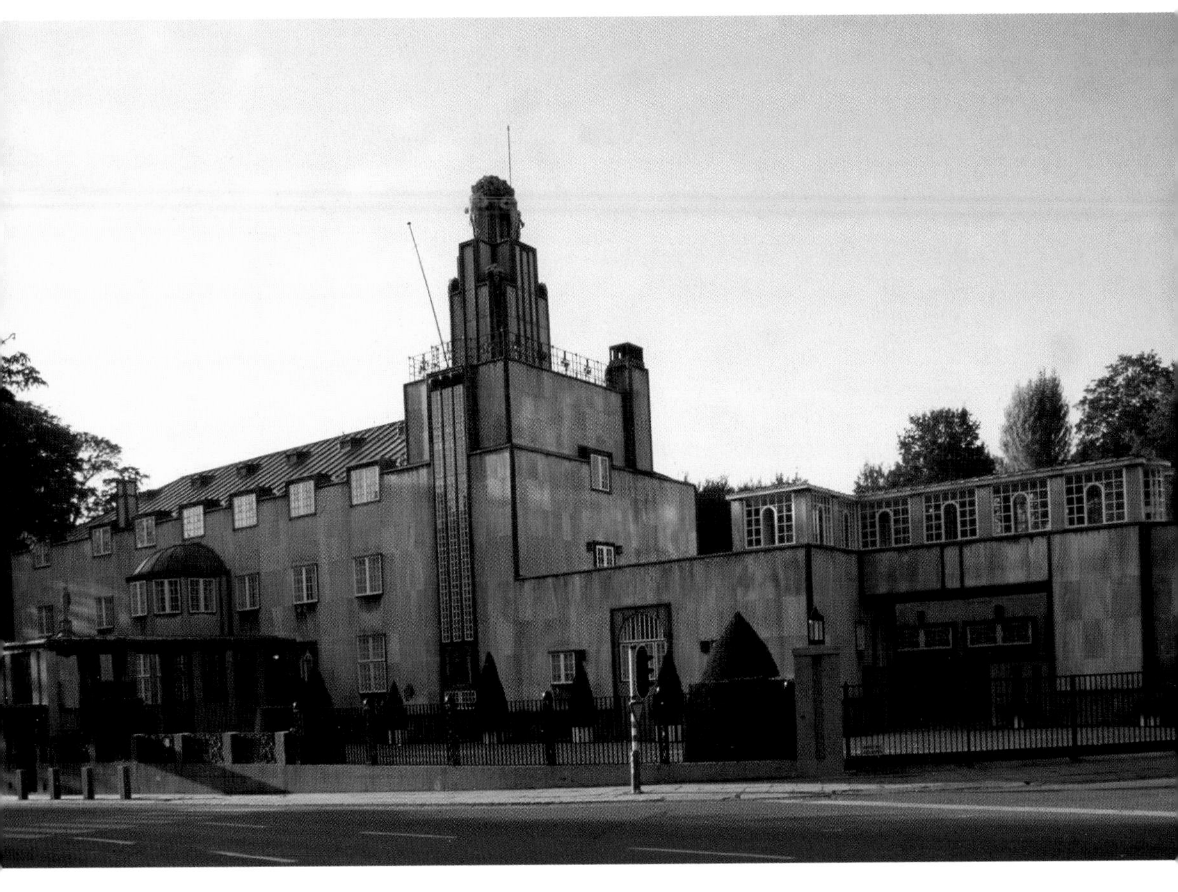

Hoffmann, Josef

Seven-ball side chair, *c.* 1906

The work of Josef Hoffmann encompassed many areas of design and his influence is still felt today. His Cubist forms and simple geometrical ornamentation are considered Classical elements of modern architecture and design. It was intrinsic to the Art Nouveau aesthetic that an artist should design for an entire interior. Thus architects such as Hoffmann also studied other art and craft forms, such as furniture, ceramics and silverware. As the artists searched for the meaning of modernity they questioned all the influences that were brought to bear on the design of their antecedents and broke away from historical styles.

Wooden furniture was criticized for being too static, heavy and solid: to bring nature into the craft of cabinet-making, designers sought ways to make wood come alive again, giving it fluidity through pliancy. To achieve the elongation necessary to suit the sinuous lines and organic feel associated with Art Nouveau, cabinet-makers steamed and bent the wood. Eventually this led to entirely new shapes being formed, many of which were criticized for being too radical or abstract.

MEDIUM

Bentwood

RELATED WORK

Adjustable armchair in steam-bent beech and plywood by Josef Hoffmann, *c.* 1908

Josef Hoffmann *Born* 1870 Pirnitz, Moravia

Died 1956

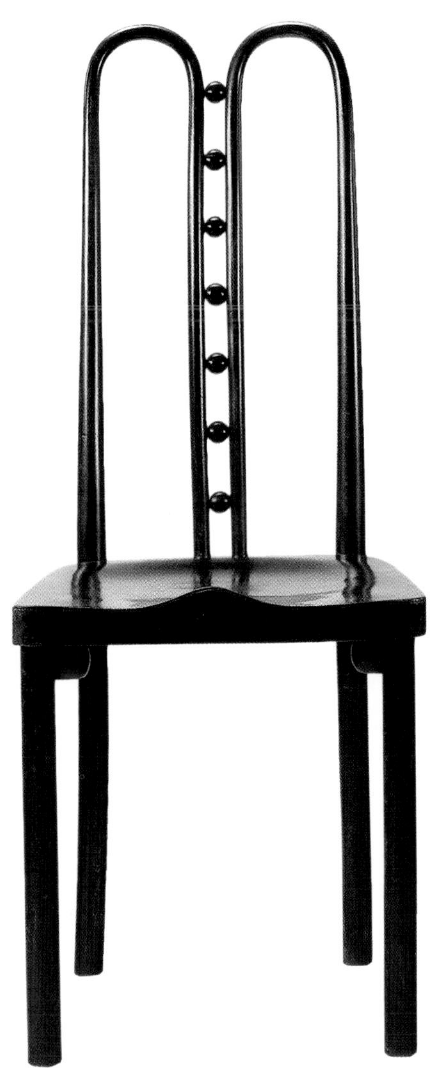

Hoffmann, Josef

Christmas tree design

The output of the *Wiener Werkstätte*, or Viennese Workshops, transcends the Art Nouveau aesthetic and links it with modernism: the community was founded by Josef Hoffmann and Koloman Moser (1868–1918) to produce high-quality goods that had strong design elements. Artists and craftsmen and women were involved in every aspect of production and oversaw their projects from inception to completion. This was a continuation of the Viennese Secession that was led by Gustav Klimt in a move to break away from traditional concepts of design.

The early work of the *Wiener Werkstätte* tended towards simple forms with geometric patterns, but motifs from folk art were later introduced and more decorative elements were included. The organization produced a considerable volume of interior furnishings for the luxury-goods market and textiles were produced both by hand and by industrial processes. More than 80 people worked in textile production and over 1,800 designs were created. The textile work of the *Wiener Werkstätte* was influential in clothing design and became an intrinsic part of the development of the Art Deco style, which dominated European and American culture until the Second World War.

MEDIUM

Colour lithograph

MOVEMENT

Secession/Art Deco

RELATED WORK

Manhattan furnishing fabric by Ruth Reeves, *c.* 1930

Josef Hoffmann *Born* 1870 Pirnitz, Moravia

Died 1956

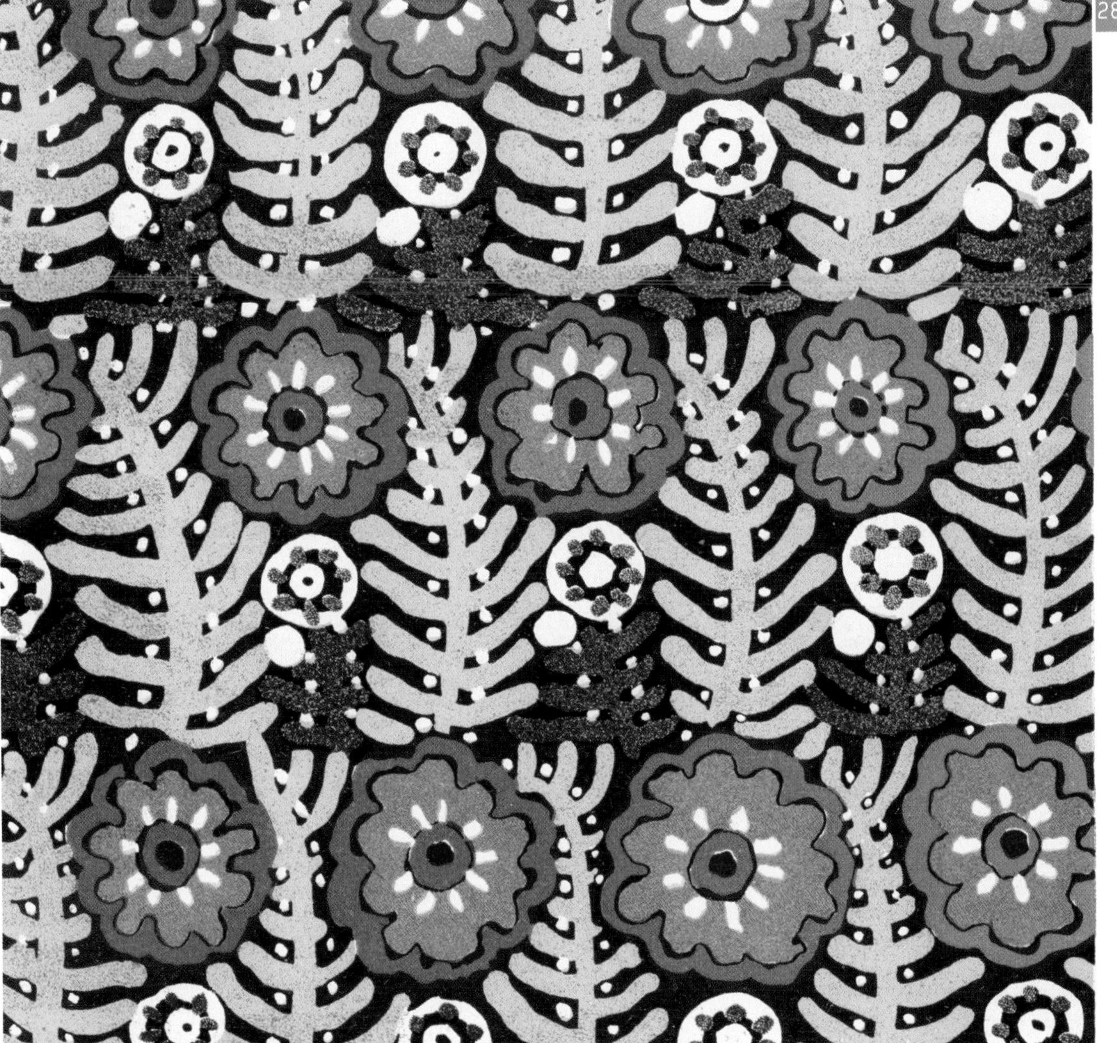

Hoffmann, Josef

Vase, 1910

Josef Hoffmann was greatly influenced by the architect Otto Wagner (1841–1918), who taught him at the Academy of Fine Arts in Vienna. Wagner was inspired to create buildings that were functional, modern and attractive; an aesthetic he taught to his students. After completing his studies, Hoffmann travelled to Italy where he discovered buildings designed as simple cubes with whitewashed walls and windows that appeared to be cut out of the masonry. The simplicity of this architecture impressed Hoffmann, who translated aspects of Italian design to his own architectural projects.

In 1903 he formed the *Wiener Werkstätte* with his colleagues Joseph Olbrich (1867–1908) and Koloman Moser. Their aim was to bring aspects of the Arts and Crafts Revival to the creation of luxurious artefacts in Vienna. Through skilled artisanship and the use of quality materials, workers at the *Wiener Werkstätte* endeavoured to bring beauty to everyday objects by combining functionality with refined decoration and simple geometric patterns. Hoffmann stated his belief that 'a house should be in one piece and that its exterior should disclose the interior'.

CREATED

Austria

MEDIUM

White glass with black décor

RELATED WORK

Silver teapot with rectangular handle by Josef Hoffmann, 1903

Josef Hoffmann *Born* 1870 Pirnitz, Moravia

Died 1956

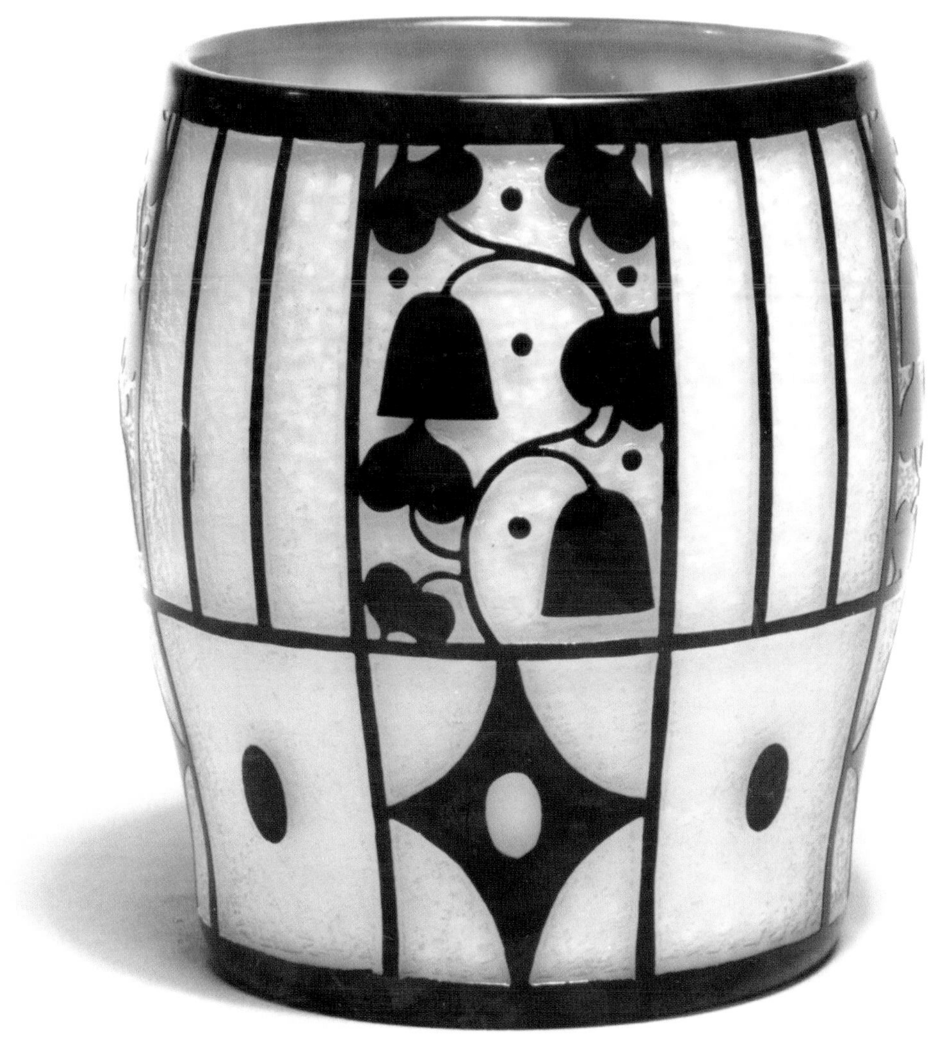

Hoffmann, Josef

Bureau and chairs from Hermine Gallia's boudoir, 1913

Hoffmann was interested in the work of the Glasgow School, especially Charles Rennie Mackintosh (1868–1928), whose simply elegant and decorated designs appealed to his own modern view. In 1897 he founded the Viennese Secession with Gustav Klimt and others, in an attempt to break away from the traditional idioms prevalent in architecture and design at the time. He later left the Secession to become a founding member of the *Wiener Werkstätte* and it was here that his mature style began truly to develop. His designs for metalwork, glass, ceramics, textiles and furniture lost the *Jugendstil* sweeping lines that he had once favoured. Instead they gained the elegant geometry of straight lines and repeated patterns that were eventually to become so popular in the Art Deco period.

Hoffmann's architectural projects proved that monumentality could be combined with elegance, and that beauty could be intrinsic to a building without the need for obvious ornamentation. His work in furnishings was a stepping stone between the Arts and Crafts aesthetic and the industrialization of good design, as exemplified by Bauhaus.

MEDIUM

White-enamelled wood, glass and silk

MOVEMENT

Art Nouveau/Deco

RELATED WORK

Koller Love Seat for Hans Koller House by Josef Hoffmann, 1911

Josef Hoffmann *Born* 1870 Pirnitz, Moravia

Died 1956

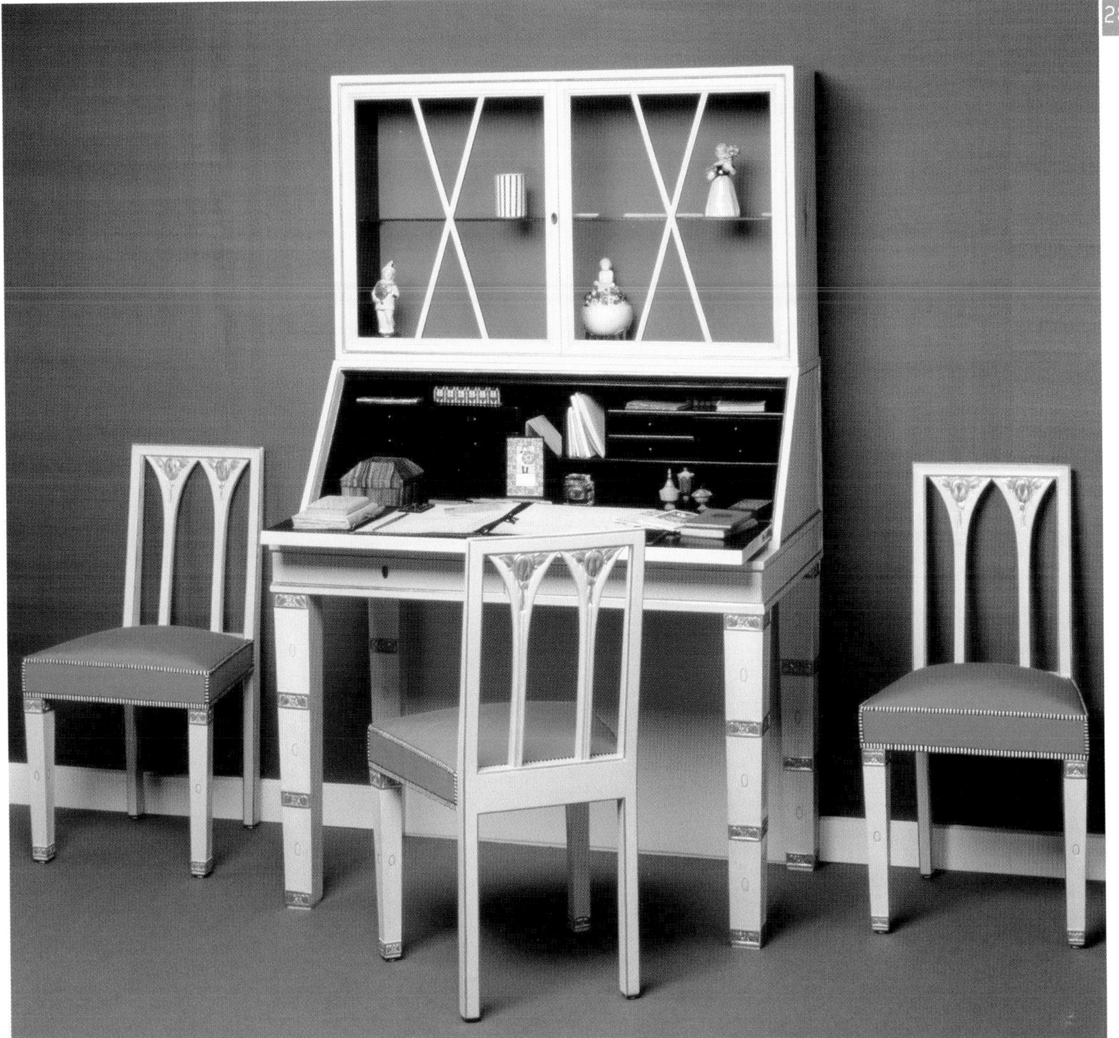

Mackintosh, Charles Rennie

Writing desk for The Hill House, Helensburgh, *c.* 1902

Charles Rennie Mackintosh designed The Hill House in Helensburgh, Scotland, for a wealthy publisher, Walter Blackie, around 1902. It is the largest and often regarded as the finest of the designer's domestic buildings. Affected by the Scottish Baronial style, Mackintosh explored the concept of rational modernity: he believed that local culture could be absorbed and incorporated into modern design and that it could last beyond the restrictions of time and fashion. The Hill House is imposing and austere in the Scottish Baronial style, having been made from local sandstone and rough-cast rendered. It has minimal decoration on the exterior, but the interior is instantly recognizable as Mackintosh's; white walls are simply and elegantly contrasted with oval motifs and dark geometric furniture.

This writing desk is made from mahogany, but has been ebonized to achieve the classic look of the hard, dark heartwood that comes from the ebony tree. It is reminiscent of lacquered Japanese work; since Japan had been forced to open its ports in 1853 the West had been influenced by Japanese art and this phenomenon is known as Japonism.

CREATED

Scotland

MEDIUM

Ebonized and inlaid wood

RELATED WORK

Toy chest in dark, stained wood for Windyhill by Charles Rennie Mackintosh, 1900

Charles Rennie Mackintosh *Born* 1868 Glasgow, Scotland

Died 1928

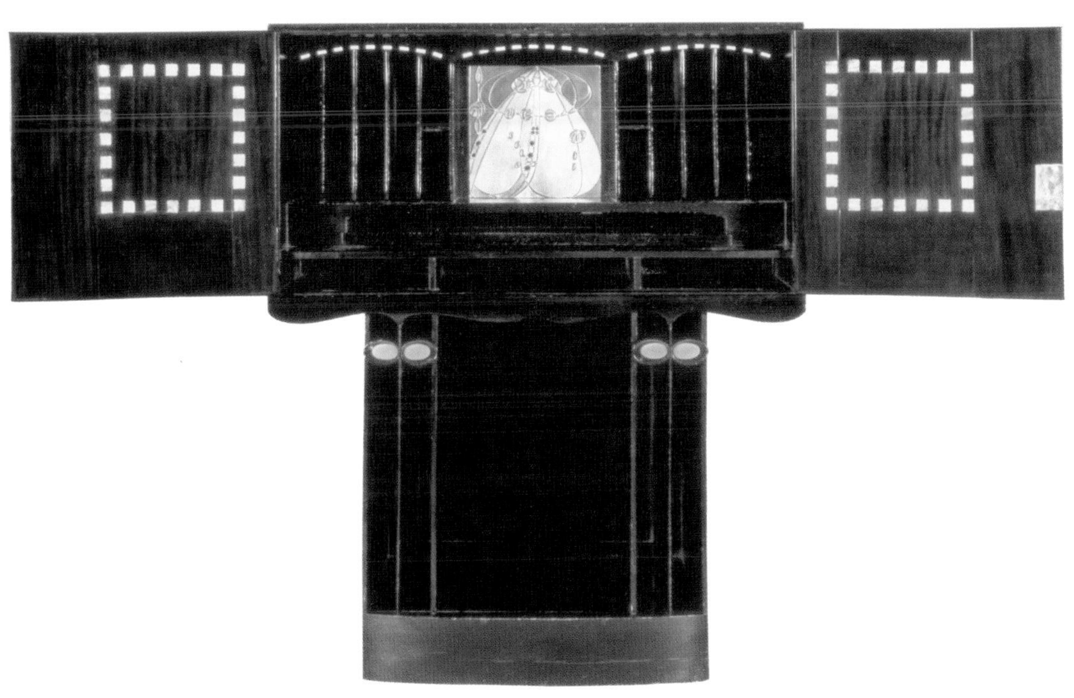

Mackintosh, Charles Rennie

Railing from the Willow Tea Rooms, 1901–04

The Willow Tea Rooms were designed for one of Mackintosh's most supportive clients: Catherine (Kate) Cranston. The daughter of a tea importer, Miss Cranston established a chain of tea rooms that offered genteel ladies and gentlemen an alternative meeting place to public houses or hotel lounges. The tea rooms designed by Mackintosh were carefully designed to suit their purpose. Light and elegant, they gave the impression of space yet were homelike, not austere. Ornamentation was everywhere, but it was subtle and never overwhelmed the surroundings. Mackintosh was influenced by the design tradition of Glasgow as well as Oriental art forms. His wife, Margaret Macdonald (1864–1933), was a talented artist and collaborated with Mackintosh on many projects, including the tea rooms.

During his career Mackintosh was to cite three factors that he considered crucial to good design in architecture: usefulness, strength and beauty. While influenced by the ambient culture of his day, Mackintosh had a unique vision that enabled him to create a truly new design initiative that incorporated simplicity, rhythm and inventiveness.

CREATED

Glasgow

MEDIUM

Wrought iron and leaded glass

RELATED WORK

Tall clock in dark-stained oak for the Willow Tea Rooms by Charles Rennie Mackintosh

Charles Rennie Mackintosh *Born* 1868 Glasgow, Scotland

Died 1928

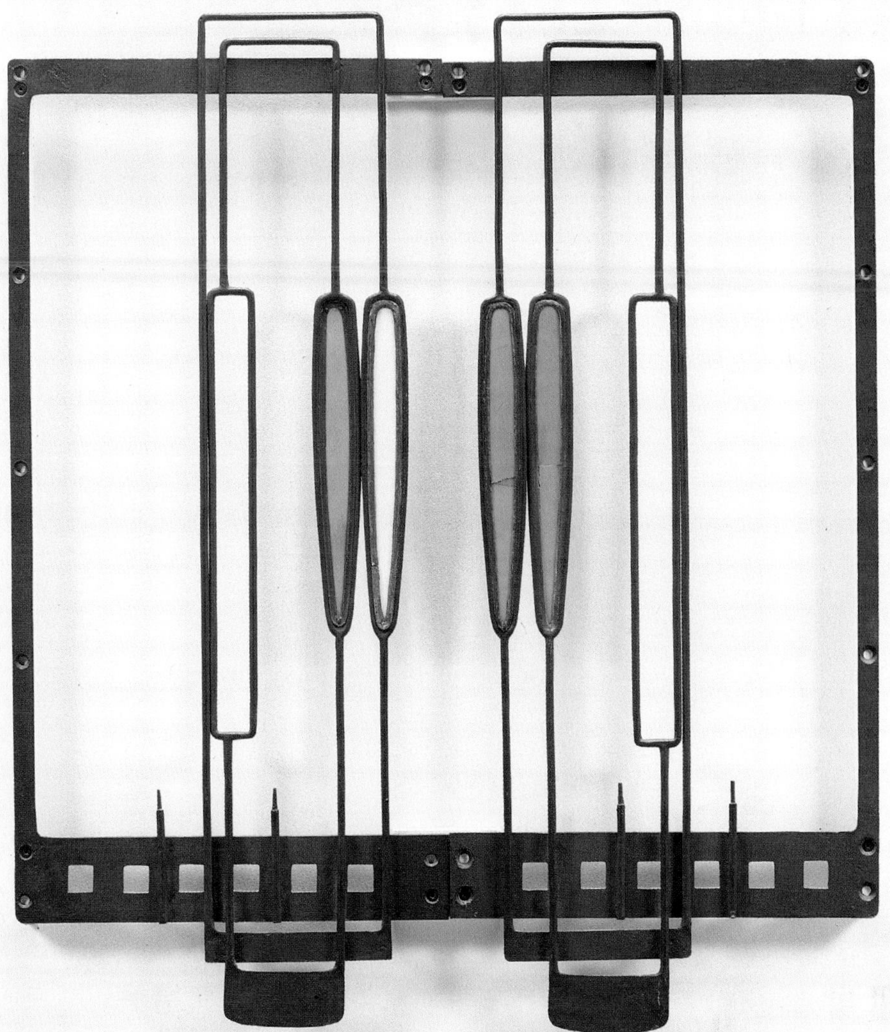

Mackintosh, Charles Rennie

Chair in the drawing room, Hous'Hill, Glasgow, *c.* 1904

Charles Rennie Mackintosh was an accomplished artist, architect and designer. He was apprenticed to a firm of architects when he was 16 and attended the Glasgow School of Art in the evenings. At the age of 21 he was appointed as a junior draughtsman at Honeyman and Keppie, a large and successful architectural firm. Here Mackintosh quickly established himself as a technically skilled architect with a distinctly modern eye. By the late 1880s Mackintosh had won many prizes for his architectural drawings and designs, and he began to develop a unique aesthetic.

Mackintosh was commissioned to design alterations and decorations to Hous'Hill in around 1903 by Major and Mrs John Cochrane. Mrs Cochrane, formerly known as Miss Cranston, was a patron and supporter of the Scottish architect. Although the house was demolished in 1933 after a fire, some drawings, photographs and a few items of furniture remain to testify to Mackintosh's maturing style. Inspired to create harmony in an interior, Mackintosh often used repeated motifs, such as decorative panels with simple vertical lines and open-plan spaces.

CREATED

Glasgow

MEDIUM

Wood stained dark and inlaid with coloured glass

RELATED WORK

High-backed chair by Charles Rennie Mackintosh, 1902

Charles Rennie Mackintosh *Born* 1868 Glasgow, Scotland

Died 1928

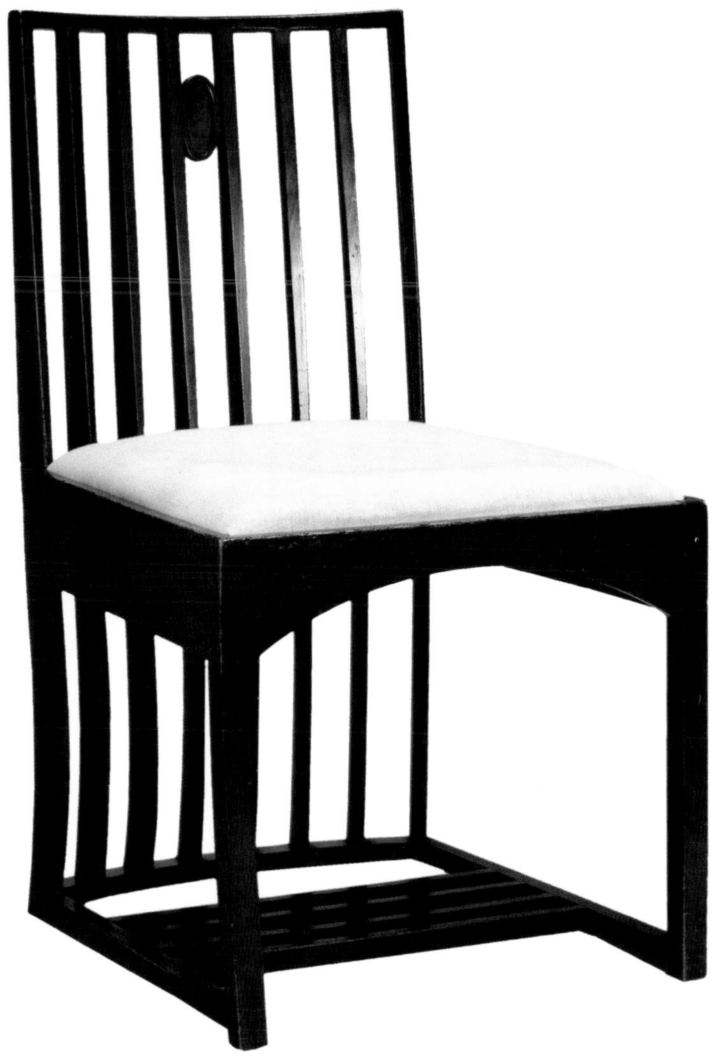

Mackintosh, Charles Rennie

Pen box for the White Bedroom, Hous'Hill, Glasgow, *c.* 1904

Charles Rennie Mackintosh was one of a number of artists who studied in Glasgow and came under the influence of the Glasgow School of Art. Under the direction of Francis Newbery (1855–1946) the school was a place where artists were encouraged to experiment and ignore the traditional boundary that lay between art and design. Artists who developed under this regime formed what has come to be known as the Glasgow School or style.

Deeply affected by the strong design tradition that Glasgow nurtured, artists and architects of the city were free to explore new styles. Their work is not as dependent upon the sinuous, willowy and two-dimensional idiom often associated with Art Nouveau; instead soft curves often interplay with straight lines and geometrical forms. This aesthetic was later adopted during the Art Deco period, when rhythmical geometry and repeated motifs became fashionable in both the decorative arts and architecture. This pen box, created by Mackintosh for Hous'Hill, demonstrates the simplicity of form that he extolled. He took a simple object and incorporated its decoration into its very form, creating a composition that is elegant, beautiful and functional.

MEDIUM

Ebonized wood inlaid with mother-of-pearl and walnut

RELATED WORK

Silver casket with chalcedony and lapis lazuli by Charles Rennie Mackintosh, 1909

Charles Rennie Mackintosh *Born* 1868 Glasgow, Scotland

Died 1928

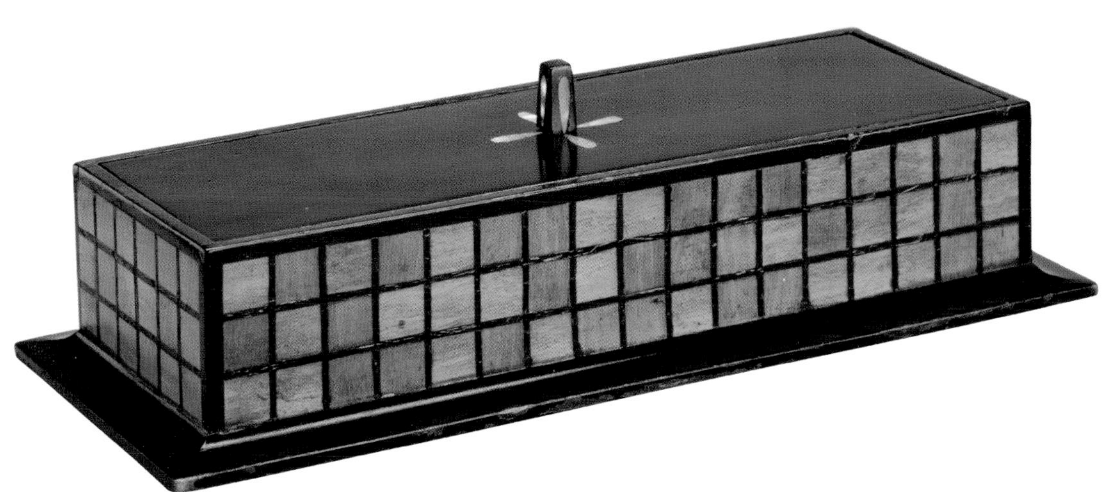

Mackintosh, Charles Rennie

Fireplace for the Willow Tea Rooms, Glasgow, *c.* 1904

When Charles Rennie Mackintosh was invited to design an interior he aimed to create an entire and balanced effect. His influences were varied, but the Glasgow School of Art doubtless made a considerable impact on his design ethos and that of the other students. Symbolism was an important influence at the time and the School of Art employed foreign lecturers, such as the Belgian Jean Delville, who helped to disseminate the language of Symbolism in Glasgow. Technical skills such as metalwork were also taught at the school and this offered artists a range of media in which to work.

Francis Newbery of the Glasgow School of Art was a crucial influence in the development of the Glasgow style as exemplified by Mackintosh. Under his regime students were encourage to diversify, experiment and innovate. Thus the local art evolved in a unique way. Sinuous, whiplash motifs, for example, were modified with severe rectilinear patterns that became characteristic of the Glasgow style. This fireplace displays the symmetry, repeated patterns, attenuated vertical lines and simple geometry that was so characteristic of the Glasgow style, especially Mackintosh's.

MEDIUM

Iron with ceramic-tile surround

RELATED WORK

Bracket lamp in metal by Charles Rennie Mackintosh, 1900–02

Charles Rennie Mackintosh *Born* 1868 Glasgow, Scotland

Died 1928

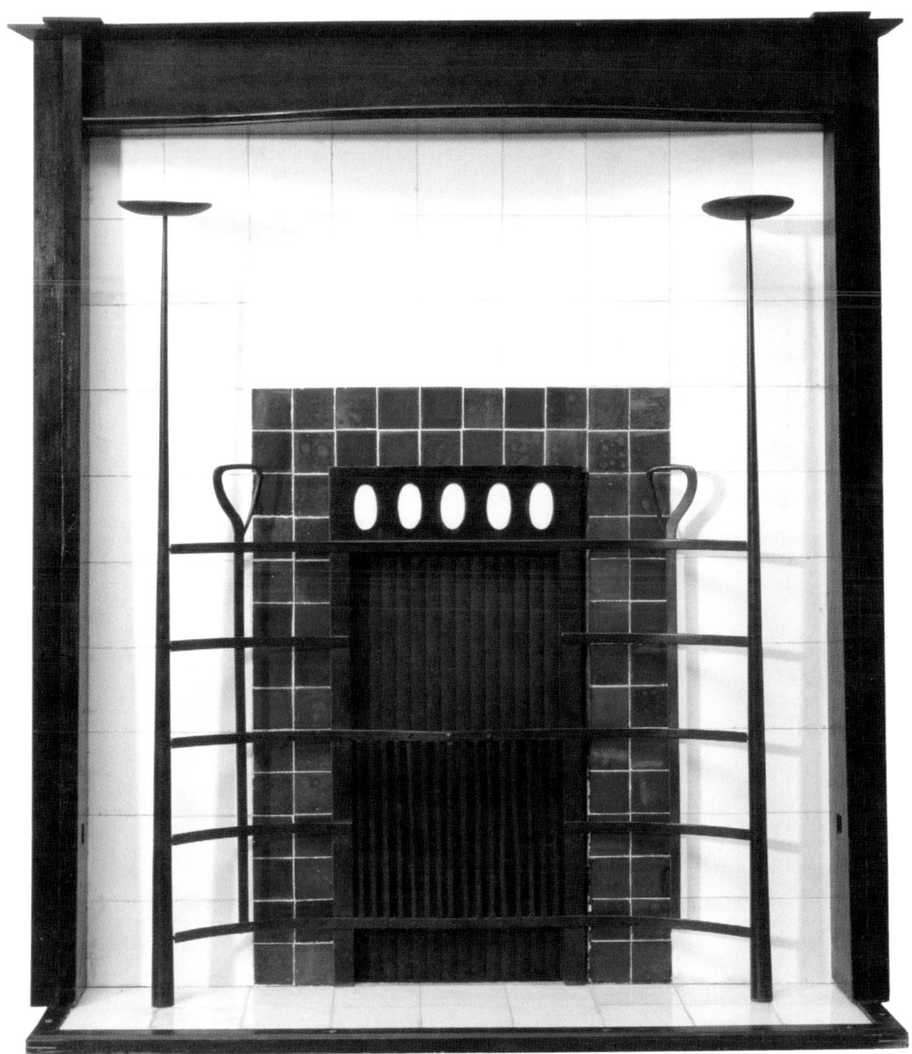

Art Nouveau

Styles & Techniques

Klimt, Gustav

Here's a Kiss to the Whole World! (detail from the *Beethoven Frieze*), 1902

When first performed in Dresden in 1846, Richard Wagner's interpretations of Beethoven's Ninth Symphony caused uproar. It was an appropriate theme for the exhibition staged by the Association of Austrian Artists of the Fine Arts Secession, for which the *Beethoven Frieze* was designed. This mural created by Gustav Klimt (1862–1918) is widely regarded as one of the most important contributions to the Art Nouveau/Secessionist movement.

The 1902 exhibition, organized by Josef Hoffmann (1870–1956), took place in the Secession building in Vienna, and aimed to create an entire artistic concept in tribute to the works of Beethoven. A large statue of the composer formed a centrepiece and the work of 21 Secession artists created a harmonized display. Klimt's frieze covered three walls. By an expressive use of line, monumental isolation of human figures and complex, dominating ornament and Symbolism, Klimt told a story of despair, evil and eventual happiness. The final scene shows how only art can bring true joy and peace, leading to paradise, where a man and woman embrace as a heavenly choir sings.

MEDIUM

Mixed media (including gold leaf, semi-precious stones and mother-of-pearl) on stucco

MOVEMENT

Secession

RELATED WORK

Judith I by Gustav Klimt, 1901

Gustav Klimt *Born* 1862 Vienna, Austria

Died 1918

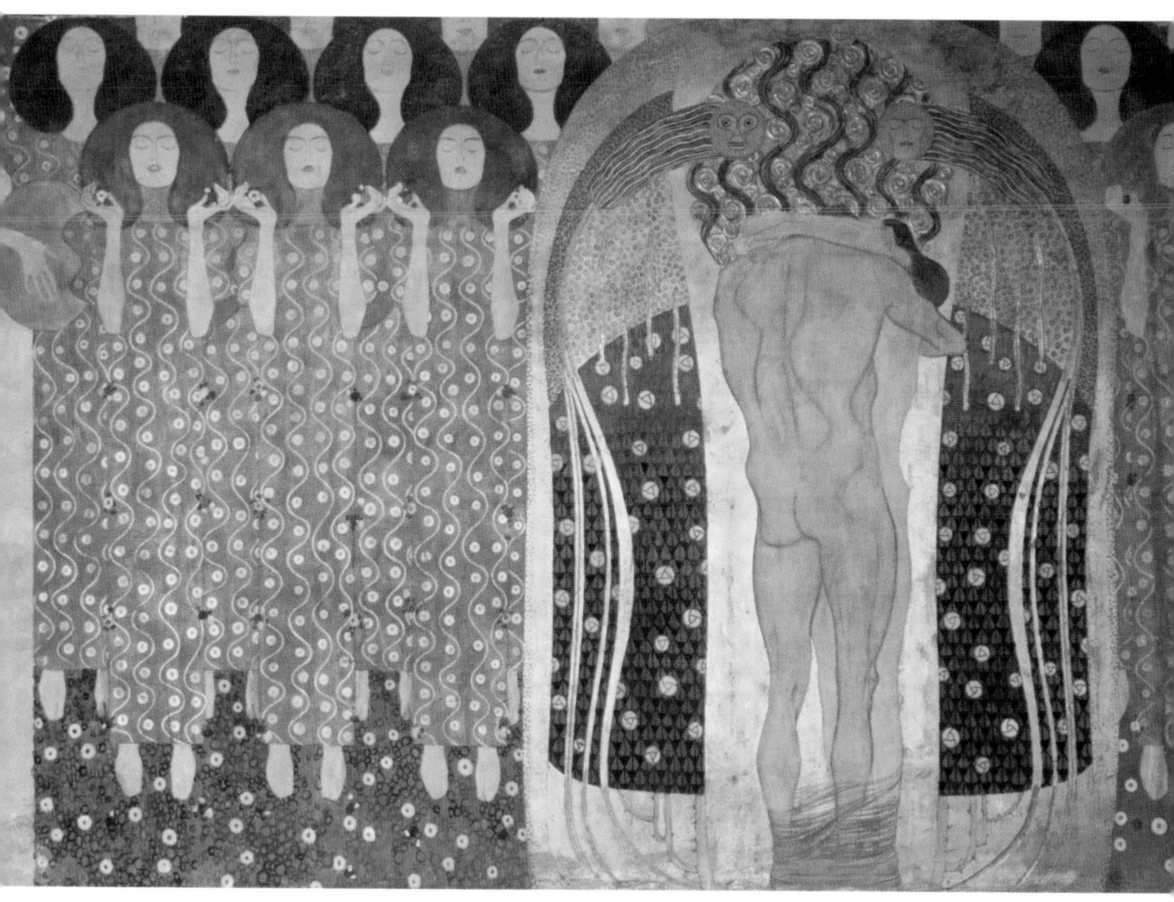

Klimt, Gustav

Tree of Life from the *Stoclet Frieze*, *c.* 1905–09

The building of Palais Stoclet was commissioned by Adolphe Stoclet, a Belgian millionaire, without any financial constraints. The result, designed by Josef Hoffmann and built in Brussels, was an extraordinarily successful collaboration between patron, architect and a team of artists and decorators from the *Wiener Werkstätte* (an Austrian alliance of artists and designers that evolved from the Viennese Secession in 1903).

The house was an unsurpassed example of the integration of the applied arts: decoration, architecture and furniture were designed to create a unified beauty, using skilled craftsmen and quality materials. Gustav Klimt was asked to decorate the dining room, which he created in mosaic. The designs were amongst his greatest; by 1902 Klimt's work was displaying complete maturity. He had left contemporary idiom behind and was exploring how Symbolism and decoration could combine to create a new and universal language. He combined the abstract with curvaceous Art Nouveau lines, which he interplayed with repeating geometric patterns that were to become so popular in the Art Deco movement.

CREATED

Vienna/Brussels

MEDIUM

Tempera and watercolour (mural completed in mosaic)

MOVEMENT

Secession

RELATED WORK

The Waiting by Gustav Klimt, 1905–09

Gustav Klimt *Born* 1862 Vienna, Austria

Died 1918

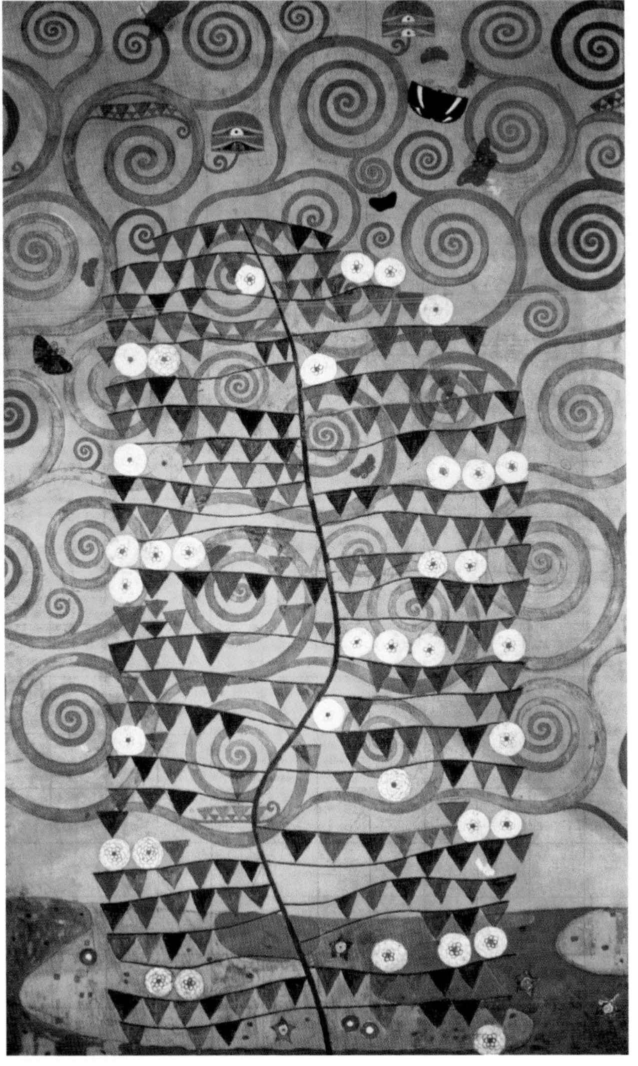

Klimt, Gustav

Emilie Floege

Gustav Klimt's father was a gold and silver engraver, a labour that doubtless had some effect on Klimt who later decorated his work with these precious metals. The family lived in a Viennese suburb and Klimt received a formal education in art at the Vienna School of Decorative Arts, specializing in murals. Gustav Klimt's talents were immediately spotted and he received commissions while still at college. He decorated two public buildings in Vienna: the Burgtheater and the Kunsthistorisches Museum, working in collaboration with his brother and a friend. By the age of 30 Klimt was a renowned and successful artist.

In 1893 Klimt received a commission to paint murals for a new university building. The ceiling paintings received some criticism from the rationalist, traditional quarters, for Klimt was beginning his experimental phase of art with intensive, creative energy. Three more commissions from the university caused uproar when they were unveiled (they were later destroyed by the Nazis). Packed with sensuality, Symbolist and Aesthetic ideology, Klimt's art could only find favour with those who understood his profound and challenging vision.

MEDIUM

Oil on canvas

MOVEMENT

Secession

RELATED WORK

Portrait of the Baroness Elizabeth Bachofen-Echt by Gustav Klimt, *c.*1914

Gustav Klimt *Born* 1862 Vienna, Austria

Died 1918

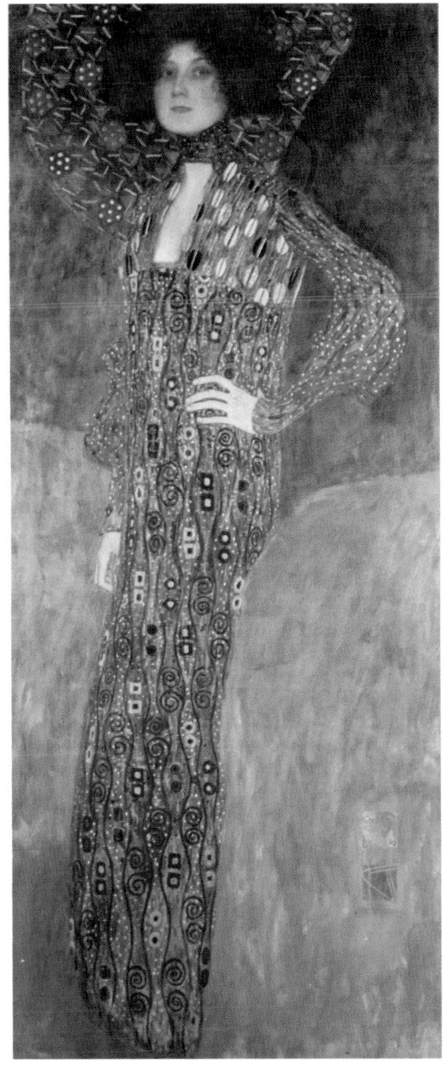

Klimt, Gustav

The Kiss, 1907–08

Possibly his most famous work, *The Kiss* achieves a balance between emotion and ornamentation. The lovers are encased in an embrace of golden fabric. The man is decorated in the cold colours and geometrical angular patterns that symbolize masculinity; the kneeling female is represented in warm colours by swirls and circles, the symbols of femininity. Together they create a harmonious whole.

When Klimt and his colleagues formed the Austrian Secession in 1897 they were announcing a formal separation from the traditional, academic art in favour of highly decorative styles. This aesthetic conformed to the European-wide Art Nouveau movement, which sought unity in the applied arts. The development of Secessionism reflected a profound historical and ideological revolution that characterized the *fin-de-siècle*. In Vienna Sigmund Freud's (1856–1939) analytical methods of exploring the subconscious were topical and Klimt's intensely experimental, controversial work explored the subconscious and emotional impulses and desires. Klimt's extraordinary creative energy, expressive use of line and dominant use of ornament captured the avant-garde spirit that helped develop the abstract aesthetic that followed.

CREATED

Vienna

MOVEMENT

Secession

RELATED WORK

The Virgin by Gustav Klimt, 1912–13

Gustav Klimt *Born* 1862 Vienna, Austria

Died 1918

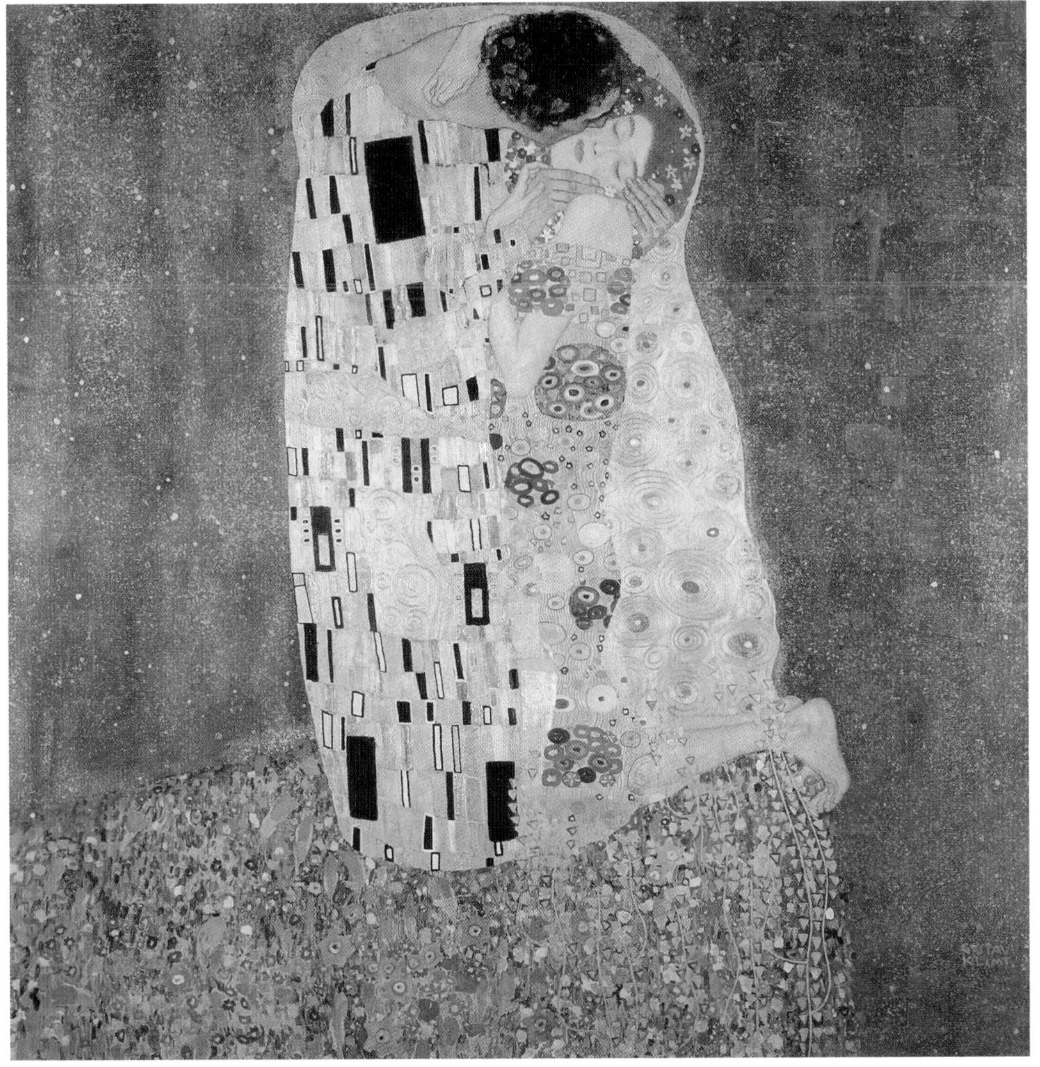

Mucha, Alphonse

La Danse

Alphonse Mucha's (1860–1939) patron for a number of years was the brilliant French actress, Sarah Bernhardt (1874–1934). She was also an astute businesswoman who recognized Mucha's unique talent. His posters were instantly eye-catching, captivating and beautiful; all qualities that could be attributed to Bernhardt. It is interesting to note that while many Art Nouveau images of women were almost ethereal and at least stylized, there were very occasionally real women, the *femmes nouvelles* of the era, behind the fakes.

Sarah Bernhardt was one of two entertainers who came to embody the Art Nouveau woman for many people: Loïe Fuller (1862–1928) was the other. Fuller was an American dancer who came to Paris's Folies Bergère in 1892 and became the darling of the Parisian avant-garde. She had choreographed a divine dance using layers of Chinese silk that billowed and undulated as she moved. Fuller danced on a glass floor that was lit from below, causing the veils of fabric to change colour as they flowed evocatively. Fuller was adored by Symbolist artists and writers and they tried to capture the effect that her visual display had had on them.

MEDIUM

Poster

RELATED WORK

Poster of *Les Saisons* by Alphonse Mucha, 1900

Alphonse Mucha *Born* 1860 Ivancice, Moravia

Died 1939

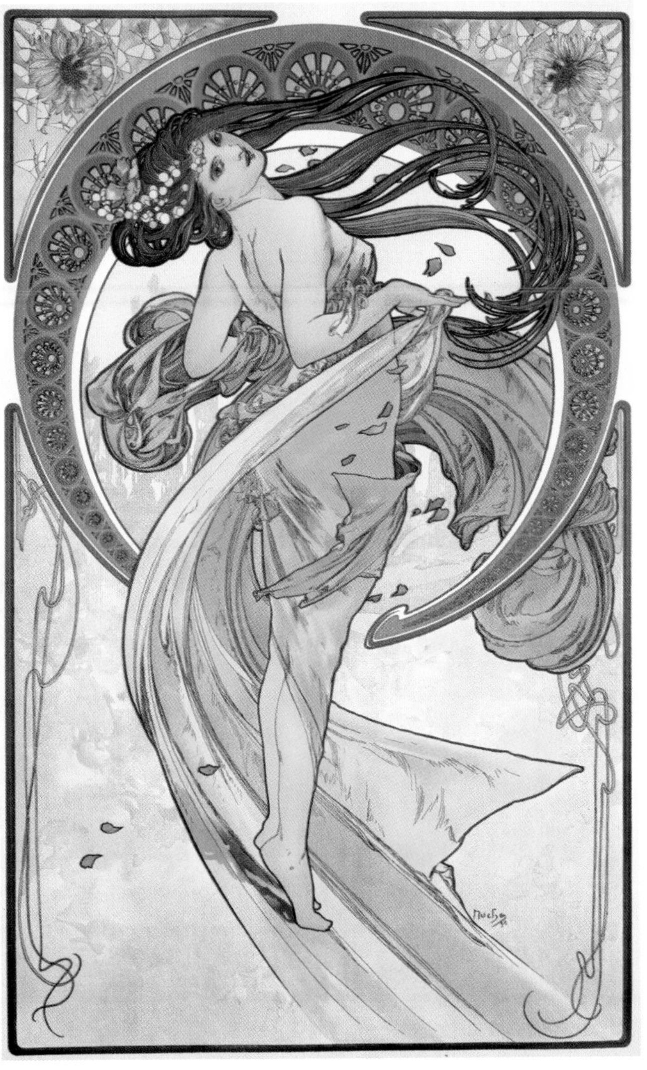

Mucha, Alphonse

The Seasons: Spring, 1897

Alphonse Mucha is one of the most famous names associated with the Art Nouveau period, particularly in the field of poster art. He was born in the Eastern European region of Moravia, which is now in the Czech Republic, and realized as a young man that his vocation lay in art. Mucha was fortunate to attract the attention of a patron who funded his mural paintings in Munich and then paid for him to attend the Academie Julian in Paris, 1887–88. After two years the patronage came to an end, and Mucha found himself struggling to live on the meagre sums he earned for his illustrations for low-quality magazines.

In 1894 fortunes improved for Mucha when Sarah Bernhardt, the greatest French actress of the nineteenth century, asked him to design a poster for her upcoming show. The result was *Gismonda*, Mucha's first poster, which Bernhardt adored and – against the advice of her printer – insisted on using. The poster was an immediate success and Mucha was propelled into the public eye. His future was assured when Bernhardt asked him to agree to a six-year contract.

MEDIUM

Colour lithograph

RELATED WORK

Documents Décoratifs by Alphonse Mucha, 1902

Alphonse Mucha *Born* 1860 Ivancice, Moravia

Died 1939

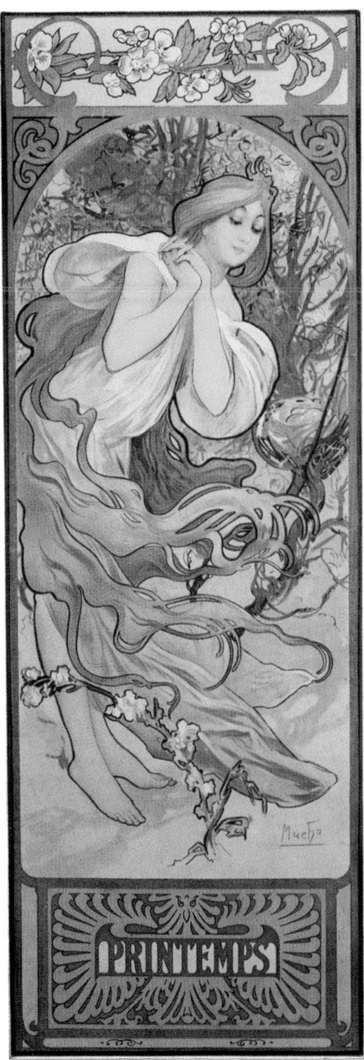
Mucha
PRINTEMPS

Mucha, Alphonse

Poster advertising *Cycles Perfecta*, 1902

Although Alphonse Mucha has been described as the quintessential Art Nouveau artist he himself rejected the notion. He believed that he produced art in his own way, without being part of a trend or fashion. His images are, nevertheless, iconic and readily associated with the New Art at the *fin-de-siècle*. Mucha's influences were drawn from a wide pool: Japanese woodcuts with blocks of bright colour were particularly common at the time and were an inspiration for many contemporary graphic artists. Being from Eastern Europe, it is not surprising that Mucha had been exposed to a wide variety of symbolic and decorative art, such as Byzantine and Moorish art, nor that he used these in his illustrations. As his work matured Mucha combined geometric images, particularly circles, with his more fluid and sinuous arabesques. His designs were always stunning with high-visual impact, displaying control, rhythm and freedom of form.

Many of Mucha's illustrations for posters featured strong central figures of young women. They are usually highly stylized, with perfect skin, nymph-like bodies and extraordinarily long tresses that more closely resemble the tendrils of a plant than real hair.

MEDIUM

Colour lithograph

RELATED WORK

Poster of Monaco by Alphonse Mucha, 1897

Alphonse Mucha *Born* 1860 Ivancice, Moravia

Died 1939

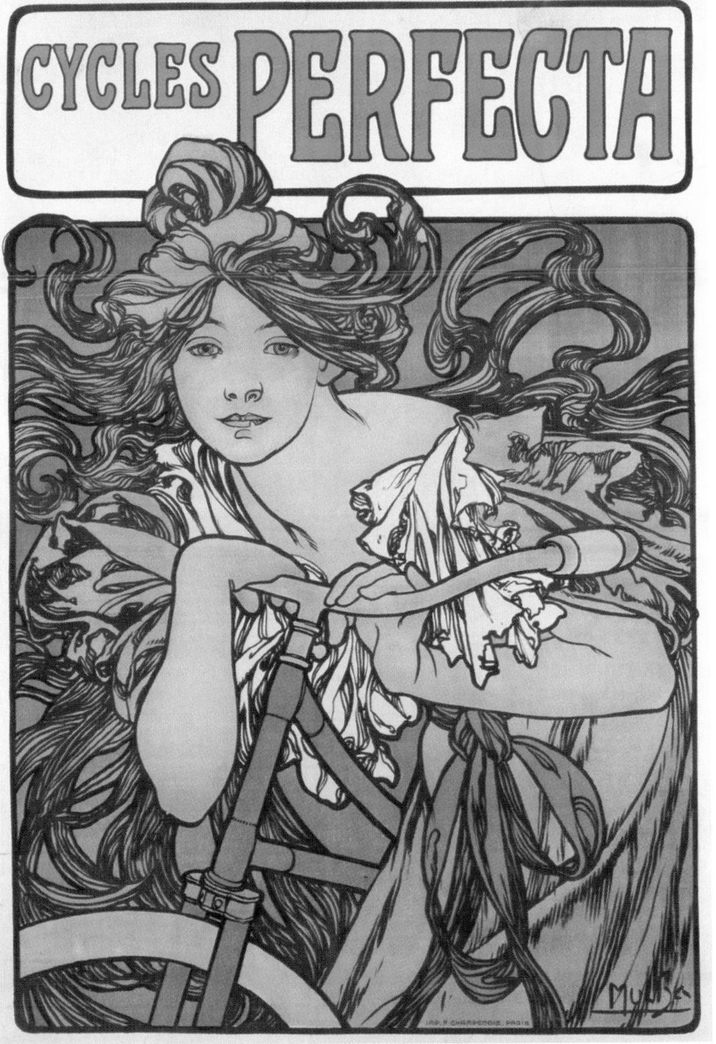
CYCLES PERFECTA
Mucha
IMP. F. CHAMPENOIS, PARIS

Mucha, Alphonse

La Nature, 1899

Alphonse Mucha's work displays a number of concurrent themes that were common in French Art Nouveau at the end of the nineteenth century. His work displayed an elegant skill in composition and he combined free, organic curves with the constraining perimeters of geometric shapes, using contrasts to create unity and harmony within a design.

Nature was a common theme in Mucha's work. While some artists, mostly rationalists, used nature to suggest science and progression, others, the anti-rationalists, employed natural themes to evoke mysticism and the unknown. This reflected a dichotomy in society at the turn of the century. Through the previous hundred years science had played an enormous role in industrial societies, changing them forever. Science was not, however, seen as the cut-and-dried answer for all the world's woes. Many understood its limitations, but wondered whether it could be used to explore the unexplainable, such as spiritualism and the occult. Mucha allowed séances to take place in his studio during the 1890s and he was profoundly interested in the Symbolism of mysticism.

MEDIUM

Bronze and amethyst

RELATED WORK

Cover of *Le Pater* by Alphonse Mucha, 1899

Alphonse Mucha *Born* 1860 Ivancice, Moravia

Died 1939

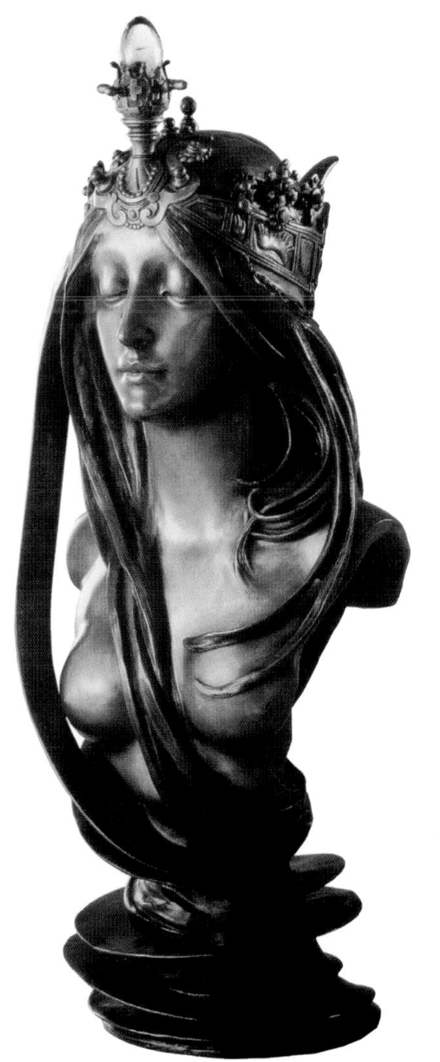

Mucha, Alphonse

Pectoral jewel made for Sarah Bernhardt, *c.* 1900

Although Mucha is best known for his highly individual style of illustration, he also designed jewellery, interiors and textiles. One of Mucha's most important interior designs was for the jeweller Georges Fouquet (1862–1957) in 1901. The finished shop was an extravagance of style that paid homage to almost every theme of Art Nouveau. Peacocks adorned the wall and counter, a nymph emerged from a spring and images of trees, water lilies and bamboo abounded. The message was one of romanticized idealism and pure aesthetic bliss; the art held no great meaning, but existed for the sake of its own beauty.

This jewel was designed for Sarah Bernhardt by Mucha and executed by Fouquet. Bernhardt had first commissioned Mucha to design jewellery for her after his great success with posters for her appearance in *Gismonda* at the Théâtre de la Renaissance in 1894. The first piece he designed, which was also made by Fouquet, was a combined bracelet and ring that encircled Bernhardt's hand in the form of a coiling snake. The bracelet and ring were attached by gold chains and the whole piece was decorated with enamel in red and turquoise.

CREATED

Paris

MEDIUM

Gold, ivory, precious stones and enamel

RELATED WORK

Woman with a Daisy by Alphonse Mucha, c. 1897

Alphonse Mucha *Born* 1860 Ivancice, Moravia

Died 1939

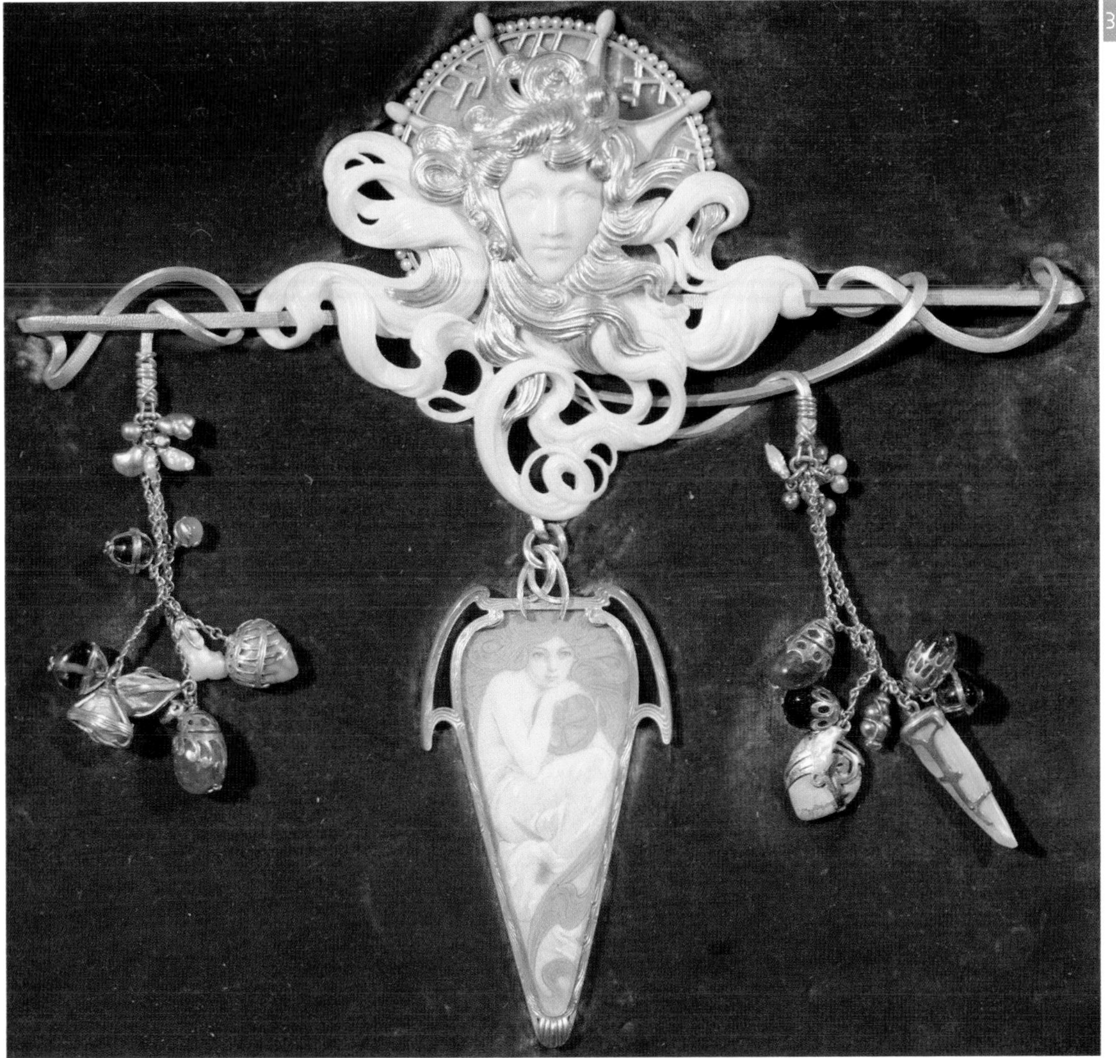

Gallé, Emile

Cabinet, *c.* 1900

Although the name of Emile Gallé (1846–1904) is most commonly associated with glassware, this is not the only area in which the master designer excelled; his factory in Nancy also produced ceramics and fine furniture in an Art Nouveau style.

In 1901 Emile Gallé began the Ecole de Nancy and became its first director. The school brought together some of the most influential French practitioners of the Art Nouveau movement and Gallé is widely hailed as the greatest of them. Furniture production of the period was varied and often innovative. Many French pieces, however, remained steeped in tradition or drew inspiration from the East, particularly Japan. Gallé, like many of his contemporaries, had a historicist approach to furniture design. He took inspiration from previous eras and his furniture in particular shows a strong debt to the Rococo style. Rococo developed in eighteenth-century France and it is characterized by fanciful, elegant and sometimes excessive ornamentation. Although influenced by Eastern and Islamic art, Gallé remained strongly affected by Rococo, although this was not an attempt to recreate history, but rather to absorb the luxury and opulence of the period for a new generation.

CREATED

France

MEDIUM

Marquetry inlaid and carved wood

RELATED WORK

Fire screen of ash with applied decoration and marquetry by Emile Gallé

Emile Gallé *Born* 1846 Nancy, France

Died 1904

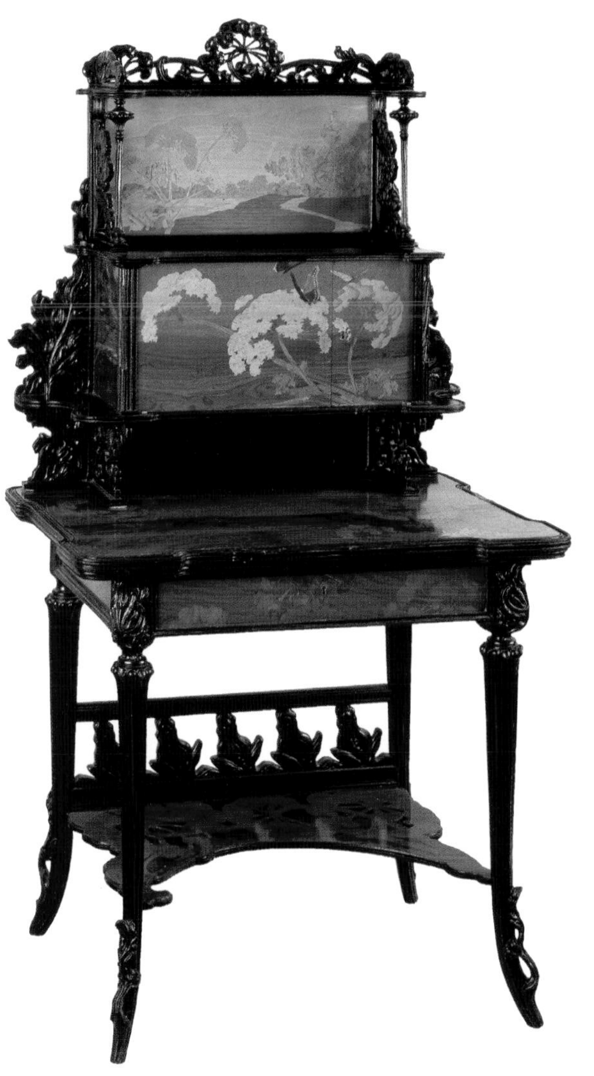

Gallé, Emile

Cameo glass vase, *c.* 1900

The furniture of Emile Gallé's factories often drew inspiration from the Rococo period, but his glassware, for which he is more famous, mostly demonstrates his interest in nature. Less formal than his furniture, Gallé's designs for glass were often highly detailed, sinuous, freely drawn and symbolic. The natural world was a common inspiration for the Art Nouveau movement: by combining his knowledge of plant and animal life with superb draughtsmanship and the technical skills of his craftsmen and women, Gallé was able to produce extraordinary pieces of decorative art in his preferred medium.

Emile Gallé was the leading producer of cameo glassware during this period, which was made by creating a vessel in layers of differently coloured glass. A design was cut or carved in the outer layers, revealing the hidden layer below in a contrasting colour. This is a method that dates back to Roman times, but Gallé took the technique to greater and more complex heights. Although glass-making is a labour-intensive process, Gallé brought modern production methods to his creative endeavours.

CREATED

France

MEDIUM

Mould-blown cameo glass

RELATED WORK

Large glass vase, etched with a design of hydrangea blossoms by Emile Gallé, *c.* 1900

Emile Gallé *Born* 1846 Nancy, France

Died 1904

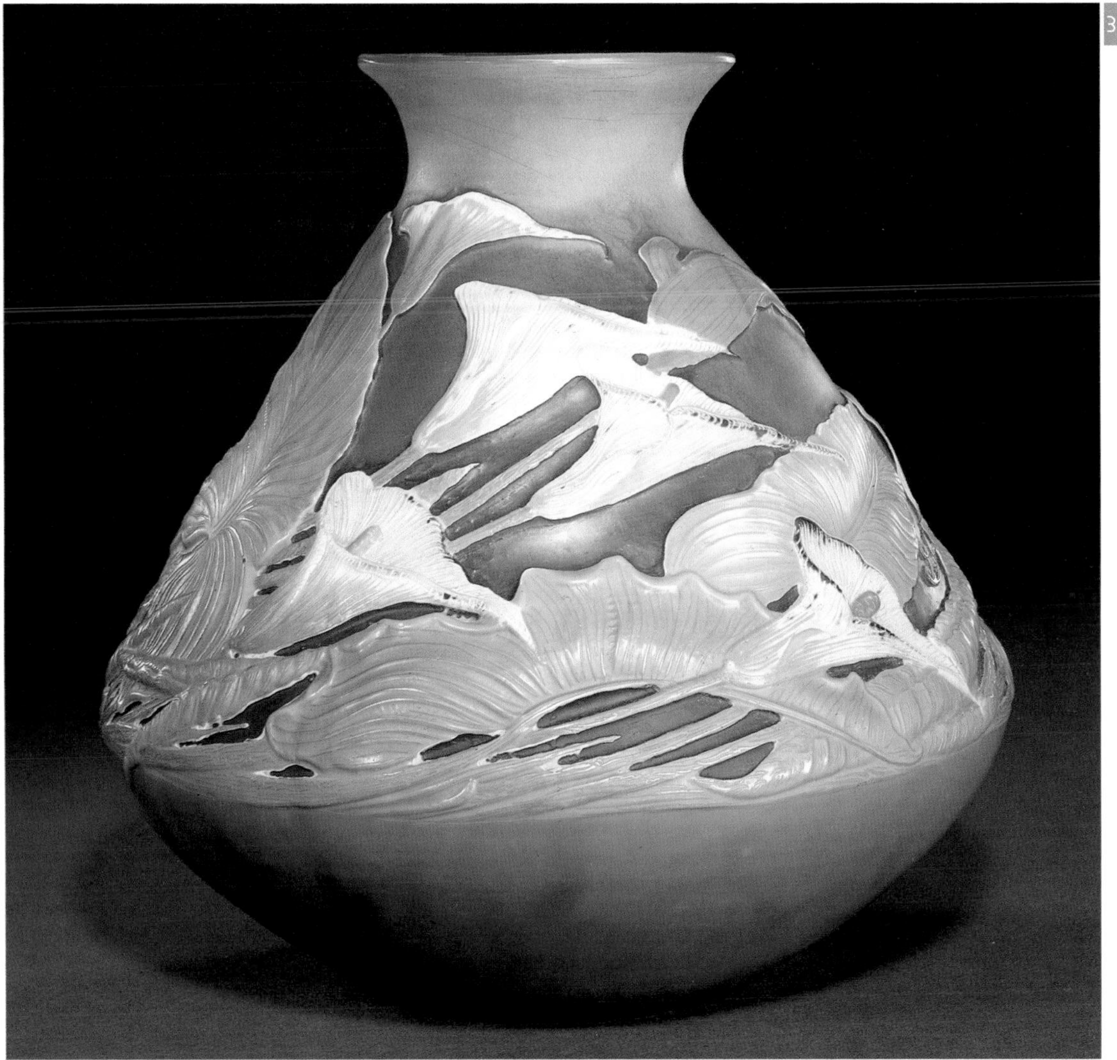

Gallé, Emile

Glass bowl

As the industrial age developed artists discovered new ways and rediscovered ancient methods of creating glassware. Artists and craftsmen experimented with decorative techniques and developed the processes by which glassware was produced, both individually and en masse. The Art Nouveau movement celebrated the diversity of the medium and the styles of glassware that emerged during this time not only paid homage to tradition, but also challenged it. Throughout this period artists such as Gallé and Louis Comfort Tiffany (1848–1933) experimented with glass-making and decorating techniques.

Although trained in a glassworks, Gallé, like Tiffany, was unlikely to have been involved in the hands-on production of items. These artists understood their chosen medium well, but probably left the actual creation of artefacts in the skilled hands of master craftsmen and women. It takes many years of experience to become an expert glass-blower, and the extra skills required by the designers challenged even the greatest of artisans. This field of creativity called on the skills of designers, glass-blowers and chemists who experimented with the many additives and colours that could react with molten glass to produce a range of shades, patterns and textural effects.

CREATED

Nancy, France

MEDIUM

Marqueterie intercalaire engraved, applied and overlay coupe

RELATED WORK

Canthare Prouvé, glass vase by Emile Gallé, 1896

Emile Gallé *Born* 1846 Nancy, France

Died 1904

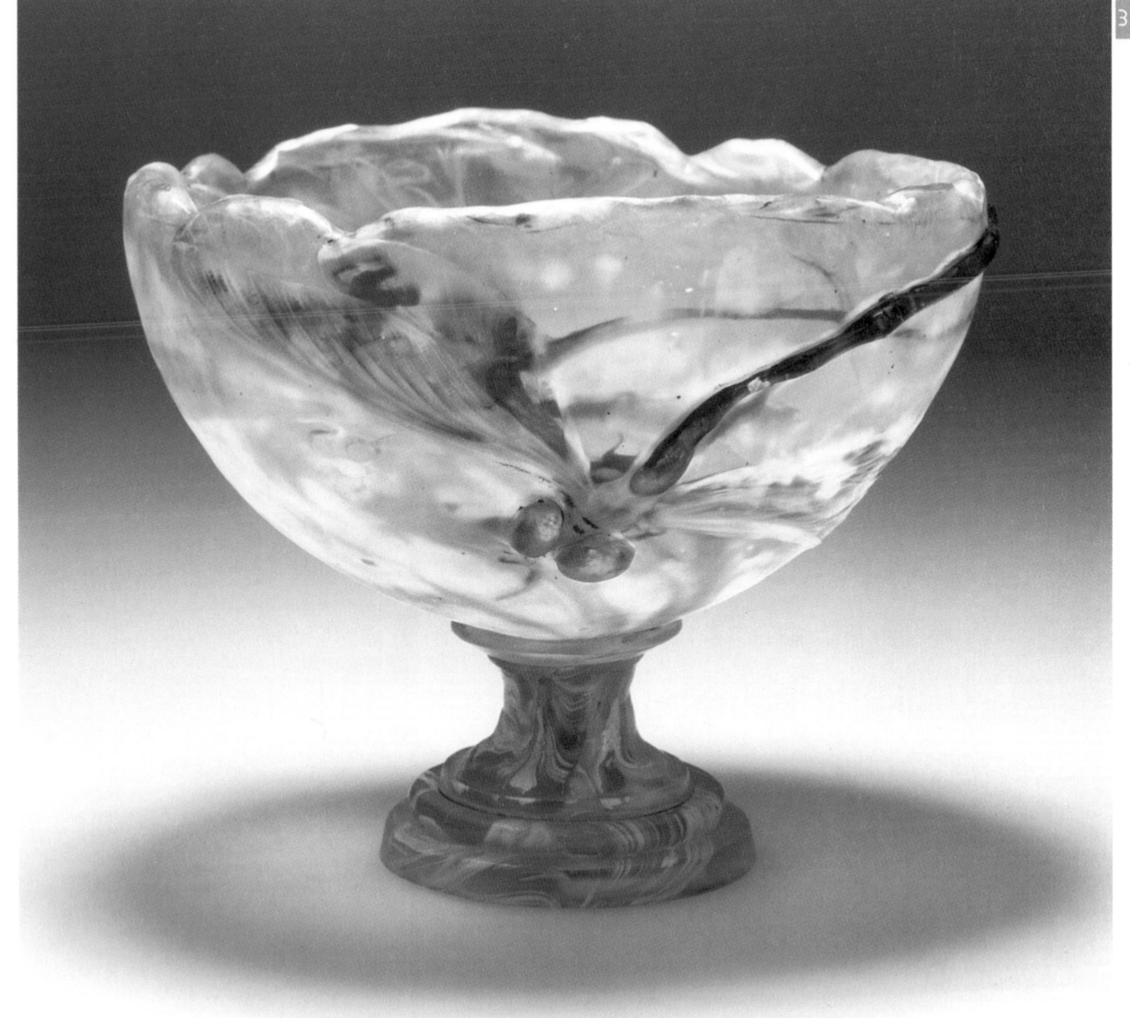

Gallé, Emile

Pair of wall lights

At the end of the nineteenth century examples of applied art were in considerable demand in France. Items of quality in terms of workmanship and design were desirable objects that represented a luxurious display of wealth and success. When designer Emile Gallé established his factories in Nancy he recognized that to be commercially successful he would need to be able to create quality goods en masse. Both his furniture and glassware were produced in large workshops that were organized with a division of labour according to the stages of production.

Some critics felt that mass production in the field of decorative art was vulgar; commercialism and industrialization were not always judged to be valuable objectives. Gallé, however, understood that the romantic notion of a single artisan creating unique pieces was not practical in the modern world. His large factories, which turned out furniture, ceramics and glassware, allowed for machine production, as well as hand-finishing and decoration. These methods enabled the master designer to offer his Art Nouveau pieces widely and often at relatively low prices.

CREATED

France

MEDIUM

Carved and acid-etched double-overlay glass

RELATED WORK

Tranquillity in Solitude, glass vase in carved glass and bronze cast by Emile Gallé, 1900

Emile Gallé *Born* 1846 Nancy, France

Died 1904

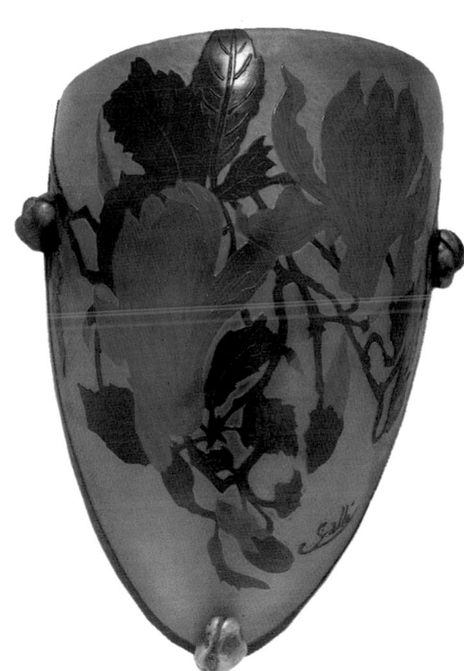
Gallé

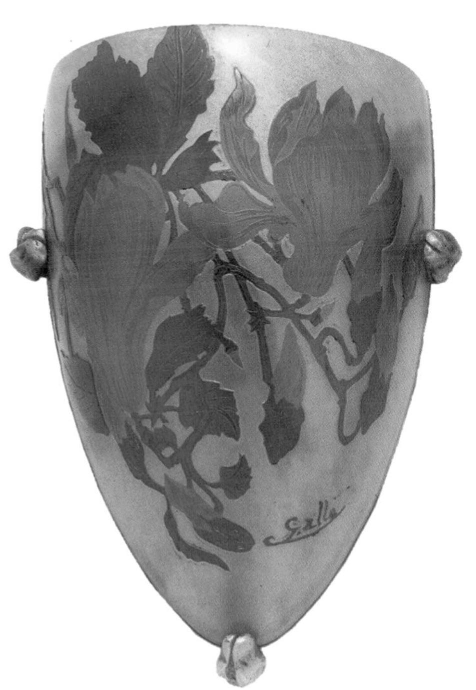
Gallé

Tiffany Studios

Sunset with Mountains leaded-glass window, *c.* 1900

All glass-makers are inspired by the quality of light that dances through their medium and the way that the colour and texture of glass interplays with that light. Louis Comfort Tiffany was no exception, and his stained-glass and leaded windows demonstrate how great his understanding was of the unique relationship between glass and light.

Tiffany was driven by a love of colour and his glass windows celebrate every nuance of shade, a feat only possible thanks to his enormous technical skill and that of his employees. In the 1870s Tiffany studied medieval glass windows, minutely examining every aspect of their construction, colour and design. There followed numerous experiments to discover which combination of metal oxides would produce the exact shades of glass Tiffany sought when added to molten glass. Throughout his career Tiffany designed and produced many stained-glass windows, most of which are now considered to be masterpieces of the medium. Some of his windows were religious, others such as this fine scene of a sunset were inspired by nature.

CREATED

Corona, Long Island, USA

MEDIUM

Leaded stained glass

RELATED WORK

Tiffany's *Four Seasons* window, 1897

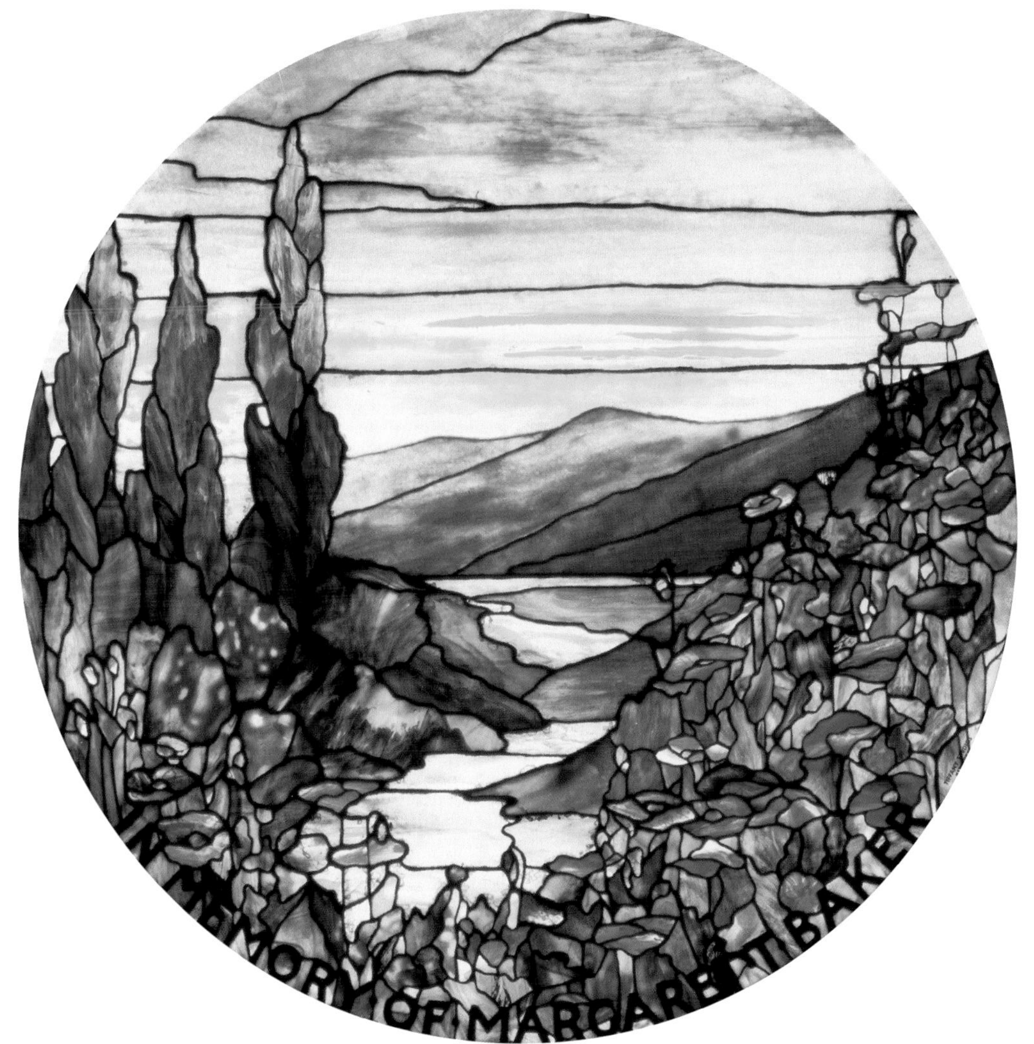
IN MEMORY OF MARGARET T BAKER

Tiffany Studios

Favrile vase

Louis Comfort Tiffany was producing Favrile glass at the Corona Factory in Long Island by 1894, although he had exhibited a number of pieces to great acclaim at the Columbian Exhibition of 1893 in Chicago. He began to sell it internationally two years later, after sending samples to the art dealer Siegfried Bing, as well as art galleries and museums in Europe, the Far East and America. When he first displayed the 'art glass' for which he was to become so famous, Louis Tiffany called it 'fabrile', from the old English term for craftsmanship, later changing it to Favrile. The glassware is unique in its fluidity of form and colour. Tiffany and his superb technicians and craftsman (including Arthur Nash and Fredolin Kreischmann) developed new methods of glass-blowing, while incorporating colours and patterns with skills that have rarely been surpassed.

It had long been customary to set decorative glassware in metal mounts and accordingly Siegfried Bing asked a Belgian artist and colleague to design suitable mounts for Tiffany's Favrile vases. Ormolu, used here, is an alloy that looks like gold and is often used to decorate furniture.

CREATED

Corona, Long Island, USA

MEDIUM

Favrile glass with ormolu base

RELATED WORK

Favrile Goldfish vase by Tiffany Studios

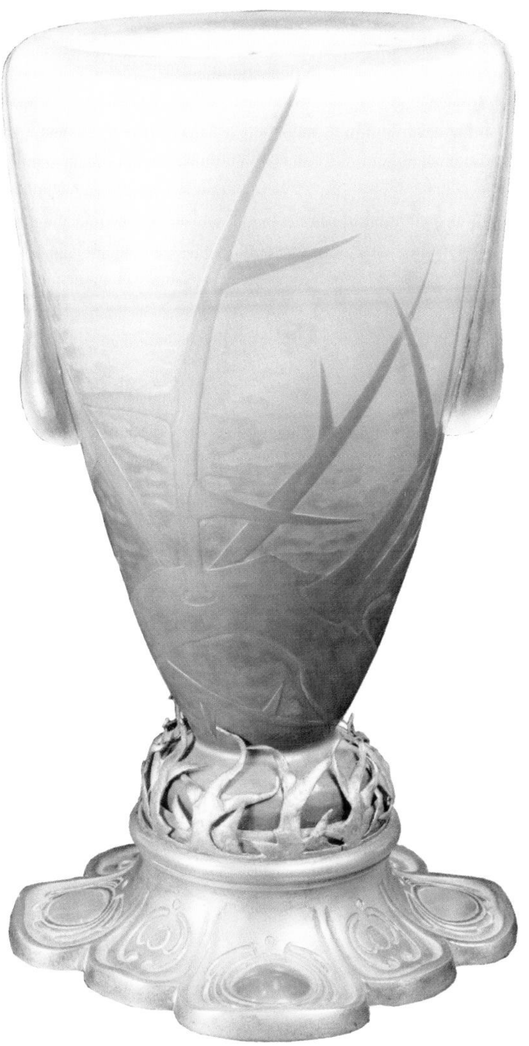

Tiffany Studios

Selection of paperweight vases

Creating stunning paperweight, millefiori blown glassware was one of the greatest achievements of the Tiffany craftsmen. Paperweight glass is so technically complex to produce that it defies many modern glass-makers. The Favrile method of repeatedly heating and cooling glass, while introducing and developing new forms and colours, is at the root of the technique.

These delicate, elegant vases were created from blown glass using the millefiori method, which originated in Venice in the second century BC. The balls of glass were heated and tiny petals, flowers or stems in different coloured glass were added at an early stage. By repeatedly cooling, heating and moving the glass the craftsman creates a pattern that grows as the vase is blown. The iridescent lustre of these vases is typical of the Tiffany Studios. Louis Tiffany had filed a patent for lustreware in the 1880s. He particularly enjoyed the reflective qualities of lustreware and the way it appeared to change colour depending on the strength and direction of light that passed through it. The lustreware effect was achieved by adding salts of metals into molten glass.

CREATED

Corona, Long Island, USA

MEDIUM

Iridescent millefiori glass

RELATED WORK

Jack-in-the-Pulpit lustreware vase in iridescent blue and green by Tiffany Studios

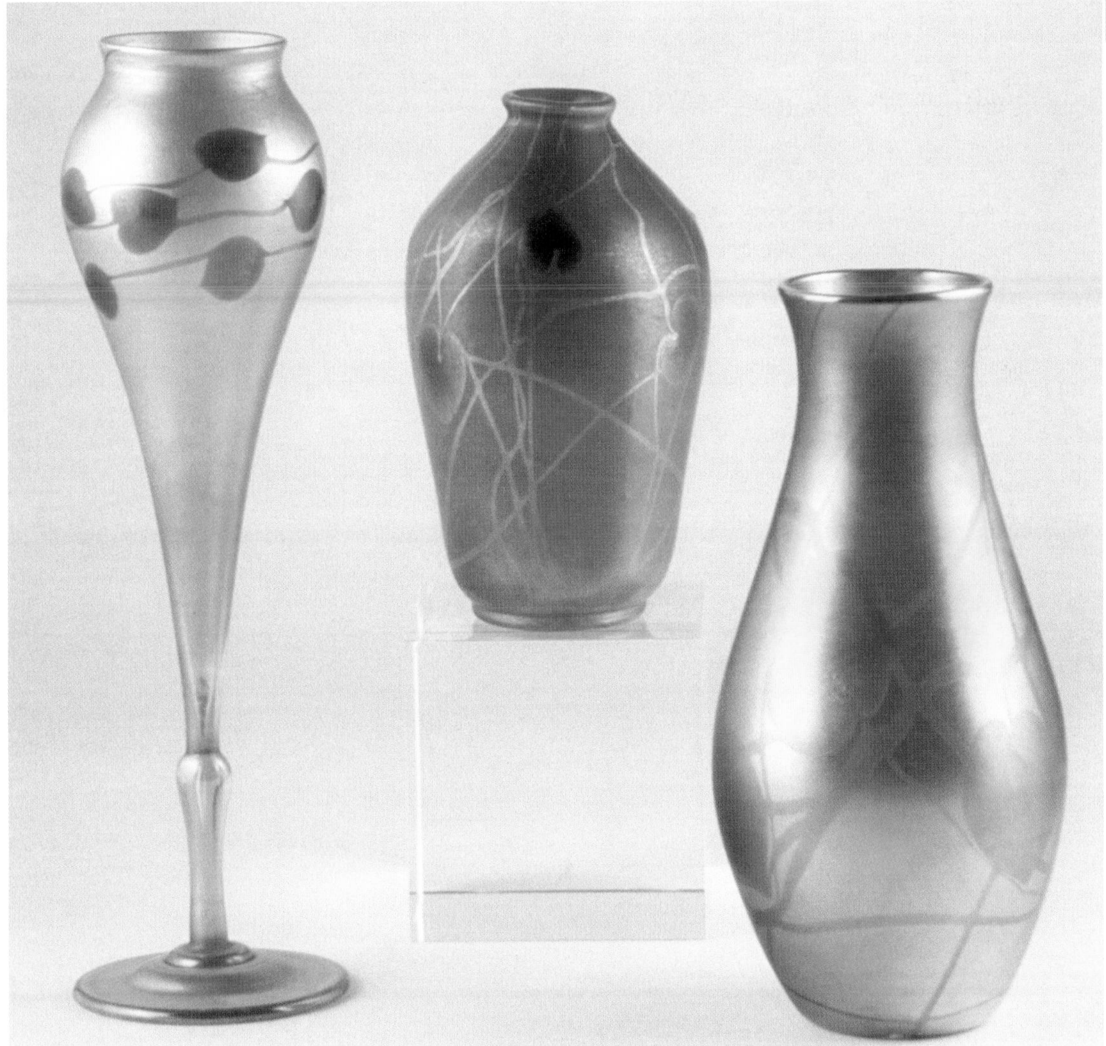

Tiffany Studios

Lava glass vase

The Tiffany studios have become particularly well known for the finely decorated, coloured or mosaic glassware they produced. The craftsmen who worked at the Corona Factory followed Louis Tiffany's direction and endlessly experimented with glass, seeking new techniques, styles and innovations of design and form.

Lava glass produces a rough, almost archaic form that lends itself to unpredictable patterns, shapes and textures. This effect was achieved by adding basalt (a dark and dense volcanic rock) or talc (a soft and soapy mineral) to the molten glass. The trickling glass mimics the flow of basaltic lava down the 'volcanic cone' of the vase. The surfaces of lava vases were often lustred with gold, to achieve a stark contrast between the dull, rough blackness of the glass and the smooth sheen of the metal. Having the finest of lustres, gold was also used to achieve a stunning red finish that adorns some of the most sought-after Tiffany pieces. Louis Tiffany achieved many other innovative effects: his Cypriote glass, for example, evoked ancient glassware that was pitted and eroded by time to create irregular patterns.

CREATED

Corona, Long Island, USA

MEDIUM

Lava glass

RELATED WORK

Iridescent gold Egyptian vases with decoration by Tiffany Studios, *c.* 1910

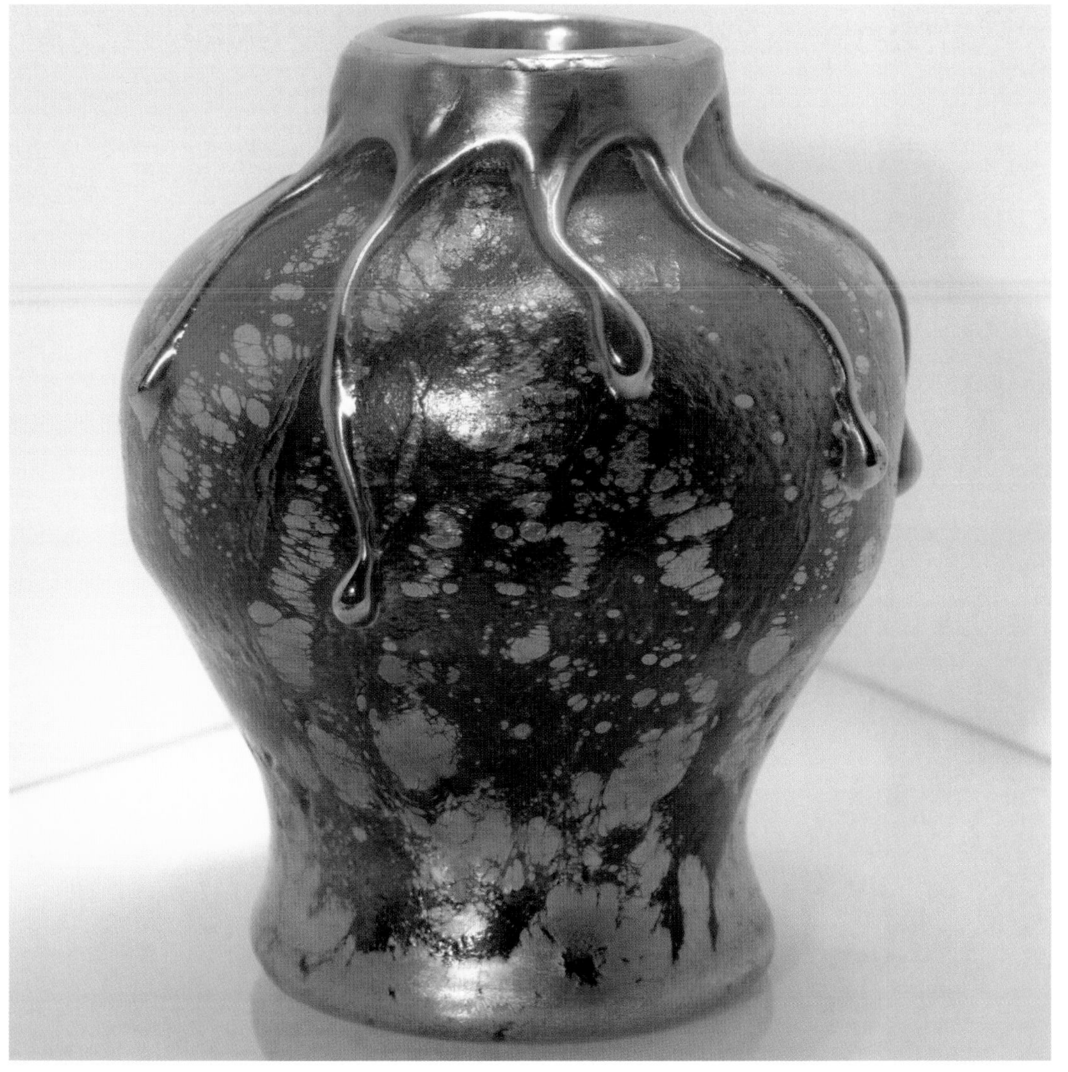

Johann Loetz Witwe Glasshouse

Lamp, *c.* 1900

The Johann Loetz Witwe Glasshouse was originally founded by Johann Baptist Eisner in 1836 before passing into the hands of the Loetz family. It was located in Klostermuhle, Bohemia, which was part of the Austro-Hungarian Empire at the time. Johann Loetz died in 1848 and the business passed to his wife, who ran it under the name Glasfabrik Johann Loetz Witwe, which means 'The Widow of Johann Loetz Glasshouse'. This name remained until the factory closed down during the Second World War.

The running of the business passed to Johann Loetz's grandson, Max Ritter von Spaun, and under his guardianship the factory gained an international reputation for producing fine glass in an extensive and diverse range. It became the most productive glassworks in Bohemia during the late nineteenth century and early twentieth century. It owed its success to intensive contact with the Viennese art scene and technical advances that enabled the production of speciality glassware. The glassworks won first prize at the 1889 Paris exhibition, contributing to the firm's commercial success.

CREATED

Bohemia

MEDIUM

Double-layered glass and bronze

RELATED WORK

Iridescent glassware by Richard Bakalowits, *c.*1902

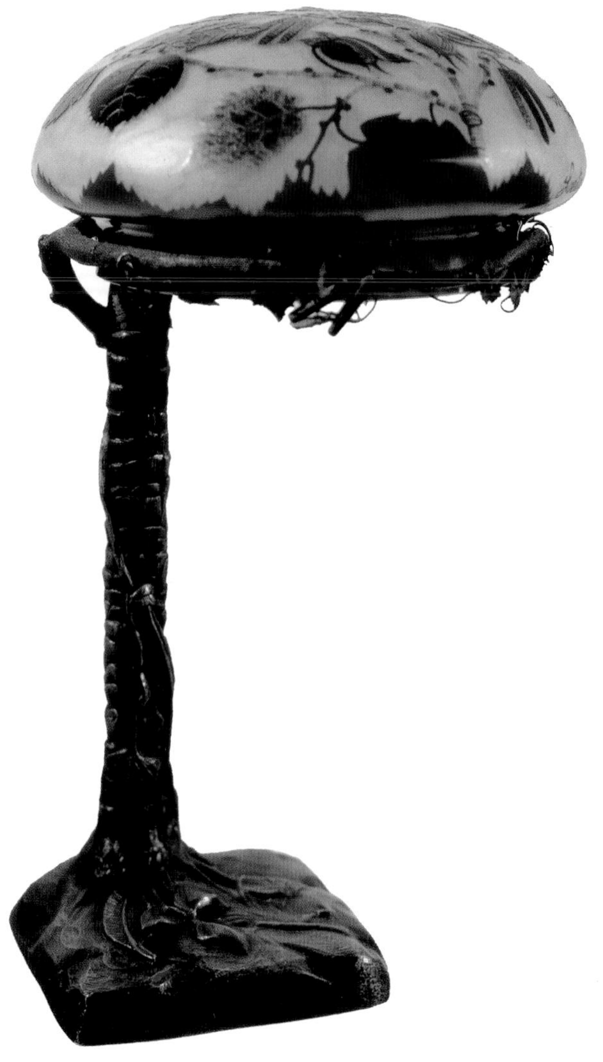

Johann Loetz Witwe Glasshouse

Iridescent vase, *c.* 1900

Bohemia, home to the Johann Loetz Witwe Glasshouse, had a long history of glass production, particularly cut and engraved glass. During the 1880s new techniques were introduced into the Johann Loetz Witwe Glasshouse, enabling this workshop to rise above the others operating in the region. Marbled glass was produced in different colourways: the Onyx range was reddish brown, the Karneol range was reddish pink and the Malachit range was green. Decorative effects from this period include the famous 'Octopus' in which the decoration spans the glassware like tentacles. Iridescent glassware became particularly popular in the 1890s and the olive-green variety was introduced in 1896.

Ancient Roman glass provided inspiration for many product lines of the Johann Loetz Witwe Glasshouse. Motifs from nature also appeared as decoration on vases and more abstract forms and patterns emerged. The range was widely marketed in Europe where it was well received. Few designers in glass had the knowledge and skill to execute their designs themselves and so they collaborated with glass-makers and technicians to achieve the effects they desired.

CREATED

Bohemia

MEDIUM

Iridescent glass

RELATED WORK

Glass vessel with 'Octopus' design by Johann Loetz Witwe Glasshouse, 1885–90

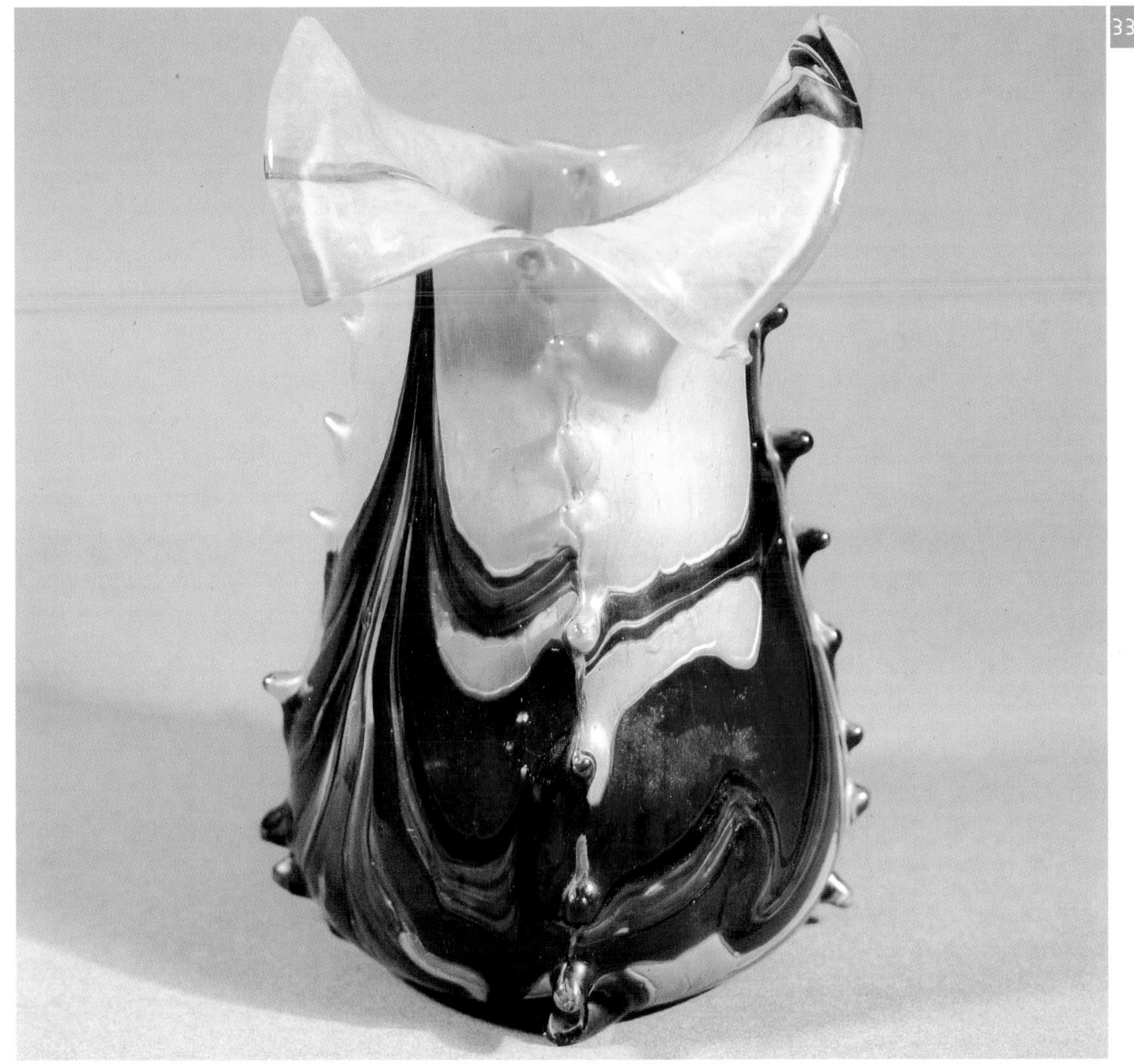

Johann Loetz Witwe Glasshouse

Selection of Loetz vases

During the 1880s and 1890s glass-makers reviewed the techniques available to them and sourced new methods of generating their wares. Influences from Japan and the Middle East were brought to bear and enamelling on glass enjoyed a revival. The rise of archaeology had resulted in large numbers of excavated items of Roman glassware being shown in Europe: with age this glass gained an iridescent hue that the glass-makers sought to recreate using new techniques. Huge advances in industrial processes had also meant that the art of glass-making became a less ad hoc affair than it had been previously. Metal foil and other materials could be added to the molten glass to produce entirely new colours and effects. Furthermore, firing methods could also be standardized, with better control exerted over temperature.

With a new palette and methods, artists found new freedom. At the Johann Loetz Witwe Glasshouse technicians developed the Chiné décor, in which thin glass threads were spun around the vessel's body, creating irregular patterns. The Loetz Chiné ware was characteristically opal, green, pink or clear.

CREATED

Bohemia

MEDIUM

Iridescent glass

RELATED WORK

Wheel-cut glassware by the Imperial Glassworks in St Petersburg, 1904

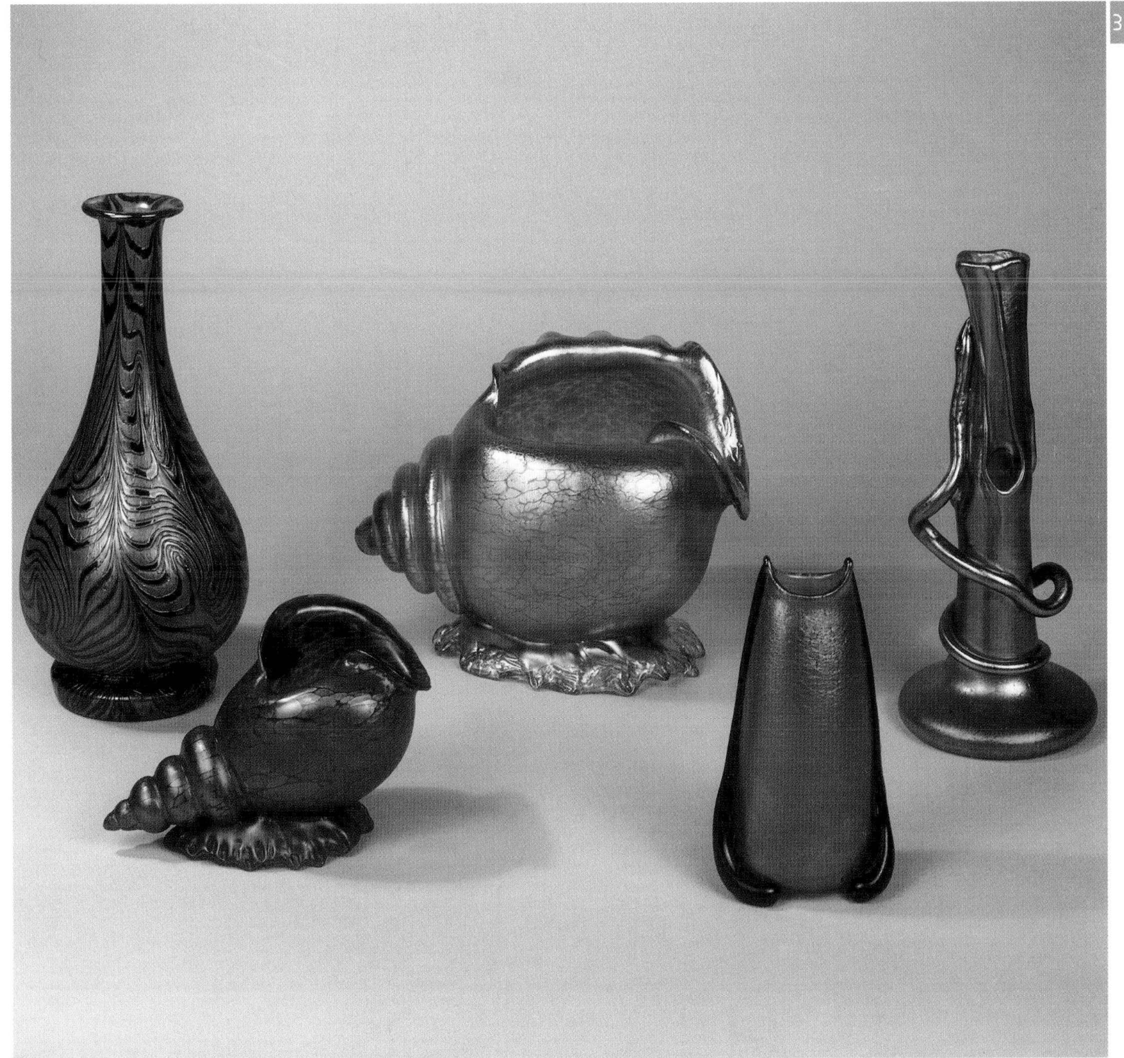

Johann Loetz Witwe Glasshouse

Pair of Loetz vases, *c.* 1900

One of the most popular effects produced by the Johann Loetz Witwe Glasshouse was named *Papillon* (butterfly). The iridescent base colour ranged from green, cobalt blue, amber, orange to a rich ruby red. Beautiful silver dots were added to some of the products, particularly on vases that were created in the form of seashells. This effect remained in demand through the Art Deco period and is probably the most ubiquitous of all effects in Loetz glassware. The success of the Johann Loetz Witwe Glasshouse and its international renown led to a number of collaborations with artists and designers. Avant-garde designer Josef Hoffmann, for example, worked with the factory from 1899 to produce a range of glassware for a firm of Viennese retailers. Hoffmann eventually progressed to lead crystal, which he designed with minimal decoration and clear, concise lines.

By the end of the Art Nouveau period, glassware had proved itself to be a medium worthy of the versatility and range of influences of styles that made up the international movement. The skill of glass-making had truly been elevated to an art form and has remained so ever since.

CREATED

Bohemia

MEDIUM

Iridescent glass

RELATED WORK

Lamp-worked goblets by Karl Koepping, 1895–96

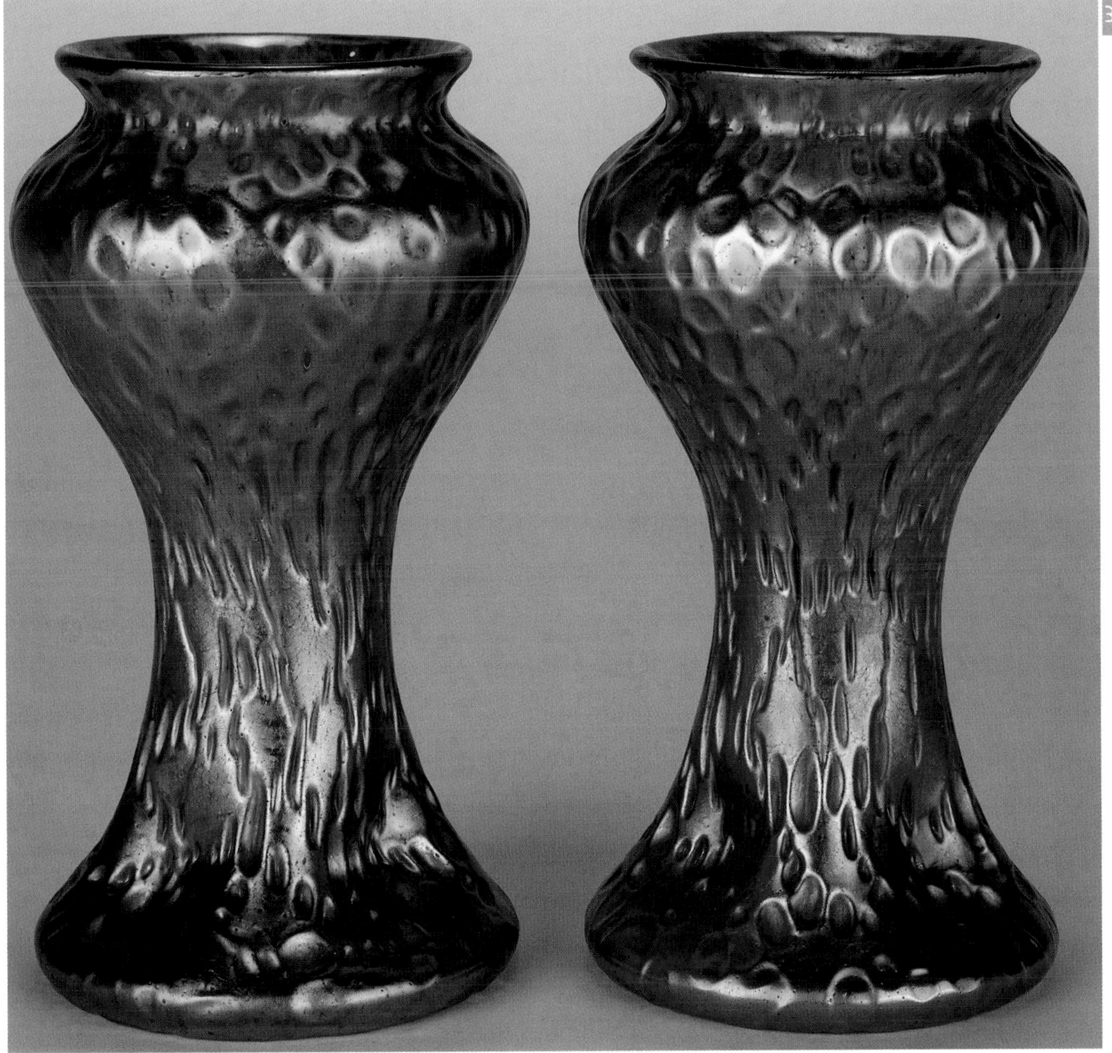

Lalique, René

Coiled snake pendant with chain, 1898–99

Although René Lalique (1860–1945) was trained and skilled in the use of the finest materials, gold, silver, diamonds, he did not restrict himself to them. For this great artist, the integrity and vision of a piece demanded that his materials, techniques and design worked in harmony to create an original piece of art.

This snake pendant was created using enamel. This method was often used in Japanese metalwork: like many artists of his day, Lalique was greatly influenced by Japanese art and culture, which was displayed in various exhibitions in Paris and covered in great detail in numerous publications. Japanese arts and artefacts played an important part in the development of Lalique's style and the techniques he employed. Detailed designs were difficult to achieve in *champlevé* and they are often simpler than those carried out in cloisonné work. The base was cast in bronze and the design was then carved out of the metal before enamel was laid into the depressions. Because bronze is hard to carve the designs were unlikely to be detailed: despite using a difficult technique Lalique still managed to achieve great delicacy in this pendant.

MEDIUM

Gold, pearls and *champlevé* enamel

RELATED WORK

Princesse Lointaine pendant by René Lalique, 1898–99

René Lalique *Born* 1860 Marne, France

Died 1945

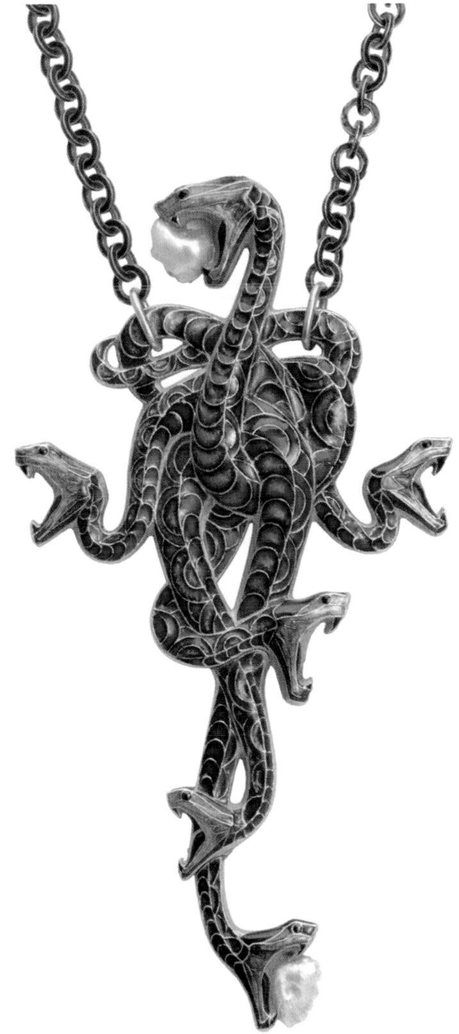

Lalique, René

Pendant brooch designed as two dragonflies

Entomology, the study of insects, was a popular hobby during the Victorian and Edwardian eras. Enormous numbers of insects were captured, impaled and put in display cabinets, where amateur and professional scientists could ruminate about their phylogeny (evolution of a specific group of organisms) and taxonomy (naming and classifying of organisms).

As early as the 1850s, insects had been identified as an inspirational source of material for the Gothic designer and jewellers in particular. It required an advance in technology, however, before that vision could become reality. By the 1890s technology had advanced to a stage where the tiny and delicate structures of an insect's wing, or the iridescent colours of a beetle's carapace, could be captured in enamel, metals and stones. Dragonflies, in particular, were a favourite of Art Nouveau jewellers. Graceful to watch, elegant and delicate in form, they suited the aesthetic of the time: the beauty of their metallic-sheen bodies, resplendent in greens and blues, can be matched only by Lalique's masterly simulations in enamel and semi-precious stones.

MEDIUM

Diamond, tourmaline and *plique-à-jour* enamel

RELATED WORK

Damselfly necklace by René Lalique, *c.* 1900–02

René Lalique *Born* 1860 Marne, France

Died 1945

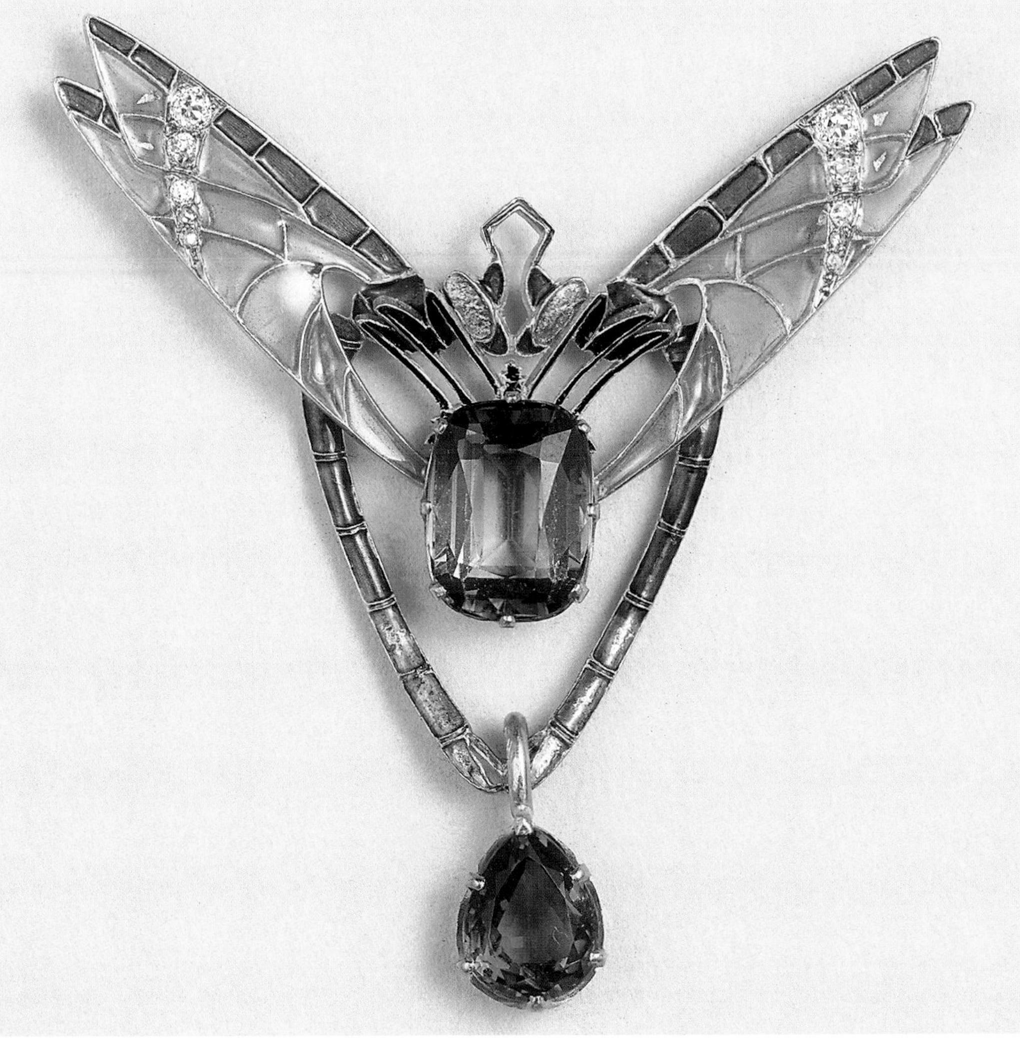

Lalique, René

Horn comb, 1900 –02

Hair combs were popular accessories towards the end of the century. Fashions of the day demanded that women were tightly corseted to create unnatural hourglass figures, and that their hair was thick and piled luxuriously on their heads to support large hats with feathers and similar adornments. Needless to say, achieving this look took many hours and numerous hairpins.

Lalique's workshops produced combs and hair accessories, from pins that were decorated with exquisitely created scenes of insects and plants to simple combs carved from horn. By heating the horn, Lalique discovered that he could make this organic material more malleable and therefore mould it into new shapes. When the horn was carved thinly light could pass through it, creating an amber tone. In 1892 Lalique was commissioned by the actress Sarah Bernhardt to design jewellery for a new role. Bernhardt was interested in the Art Nouveau style and she was an accomplished sculptor. Many women of the day enjoyed experimenting with the most outrageous styles of jewellery or dress that they could find.

MEDIUM

Horn

RELATED WORK

Orchid hair comb by René Lalique, *c.* 1902

René Lalique *Born* 1860 Marne, France

Died 1945

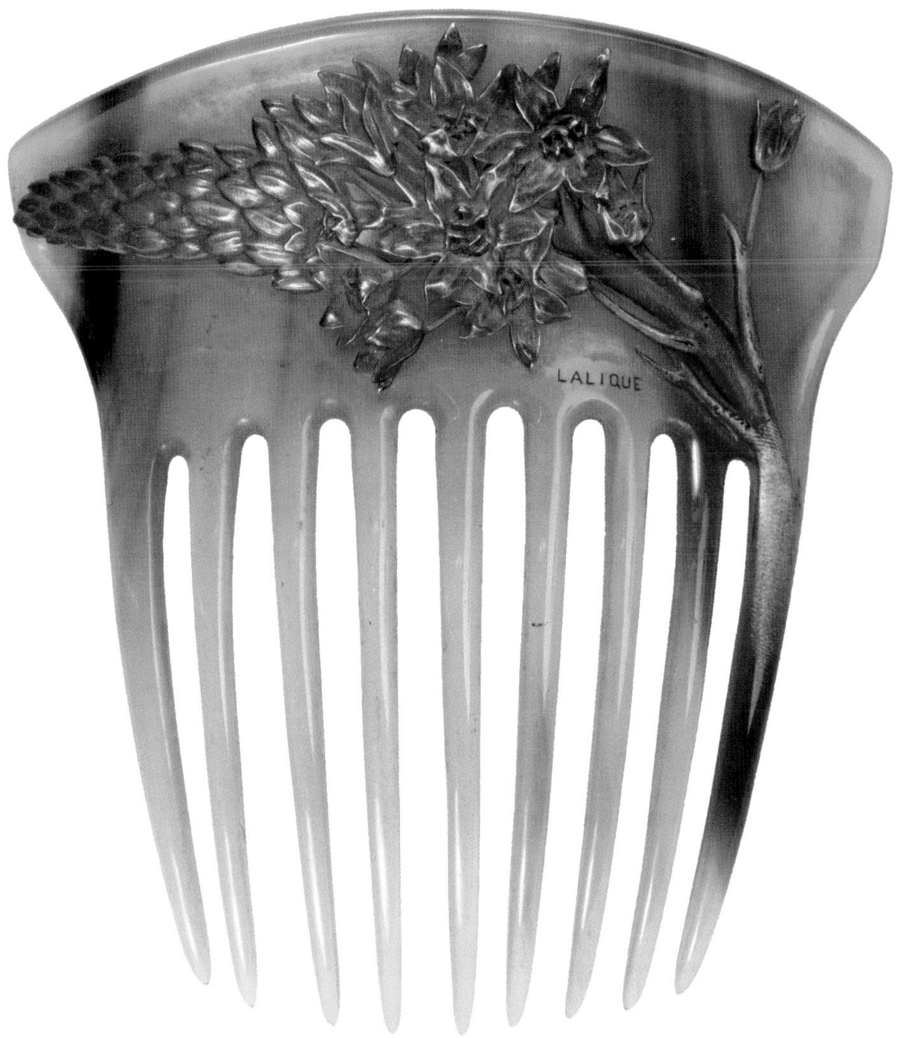
LALIQUE

Lalique, René

Plate decorated with violets, *c.* 1900

Lalique was one of a few artist-designers working at the turn of the century who was able to contribute to both the Art Nouveau and the Art Deco styles. His versatility and originality meant that he was at the vanguard of both movements, setting a path for others to follow. Always experimental in his approach, Lalique began to replace the sinuous, sensual idioms of his jewellery for more geometric and abstract ones. He tried some of the 'new materials' too, steel and aluminium, and began to make more decorative artefacts for the home, such as this plate of enamelled silver.

But it was for his move to glass that Lalique was to become a truly household name. This was not only thanks to his innovative style, but also because of his Modernist approach towards production. While some of his glassware was created as one-off pieces, or hand-blown and crafted, Lalique also invested heavily in glass manufacturing. His mass-produced perfume bottles graced the dressing tables of women across Europe, making beautifully designed objects available to more women than ever before.

MEDIUM

Enamelled silver

RELATED WORK

Platter decorated with enamel and semi-precious stones by René Lalique, *c.* 1900

René Lalique *Born* 1860 Marne, France

Died 1945

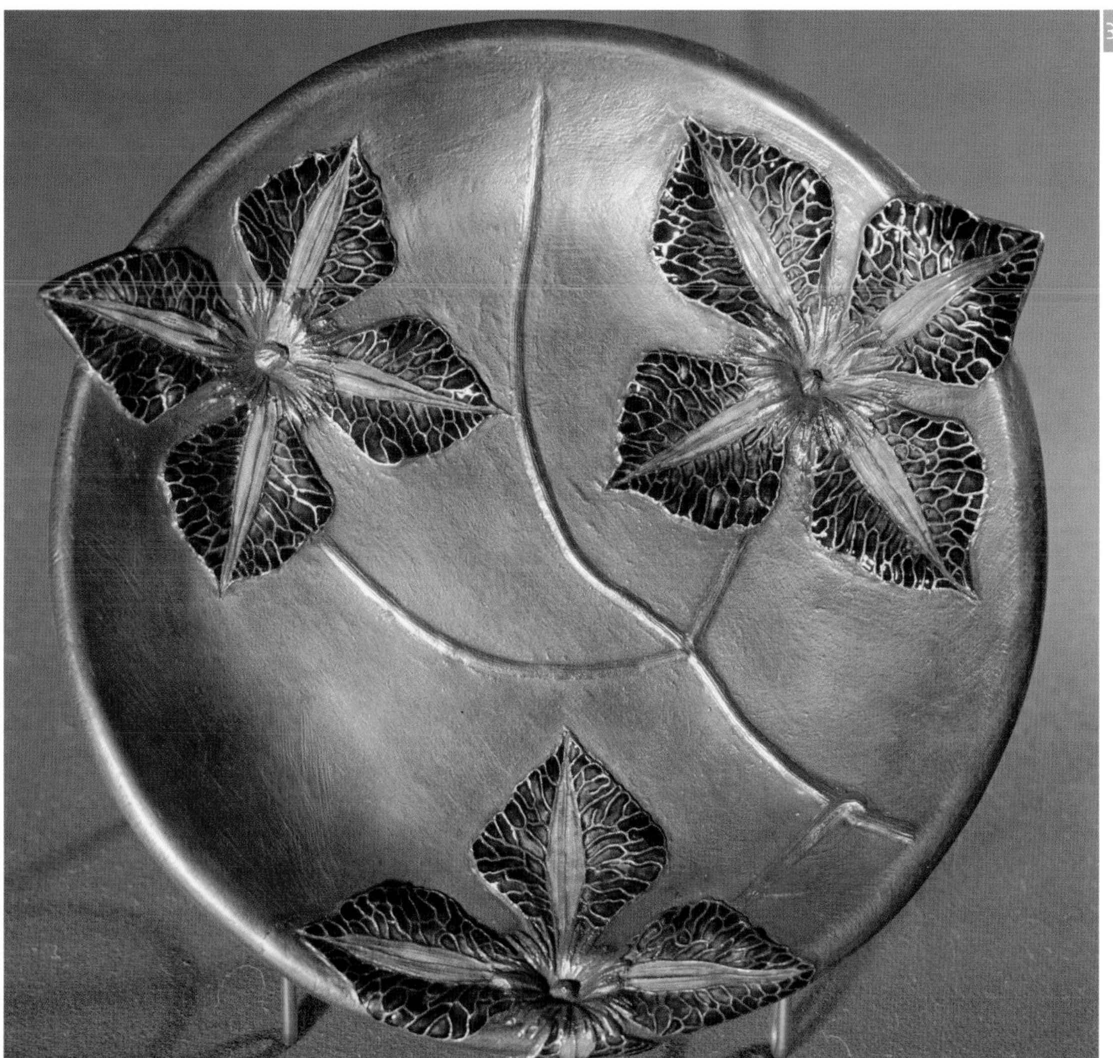

Larche, Raoul-François

Loïe Fuller sculpture, *c.* 1900

Decorative French sculptures of the late nineteenth century and early twentieth century were ornamental objects, designed to adorn a sideboard or table. They were often functional too: electric lamps, letter holders and vases were often transformed from functional objects into elaborate centrepieces.

The subject of this lamp by Raoul-François Larche (1860–1912) is the American dancer Loïe Fuller whose expressive dancing style captured the spirit of the *fin-de-siècle*. Fuller's dancing evoked billowing, swirling clouds, or the movement of water and air. She had worked as actress, but gained fame through performing dance at a Parisian nightspot, the Folies Bergère, in 1892. Using layers of diaphanous veils and under-floor lighting, Fuller astonished her audiences, which often included artists and designers who had flocked to Paris, with her ability to metamorphose into different forms as she moved to the music of Chopin, Debussy and Schubert. At the time Parisian decorative sculpture did not aim to reproduce a true likeness of the female form: women were usually portrayed as ideal, stylized figures that displayed grace and unity with nature.

CREATED

Paris

MEDIUM

Gilded bronze

RELATED WORK

The Veil Dancer, sculpture by Raoul-François Larche, 1900

Raoul-François Larche *Born* 1860 Gironde, France

Died 1912

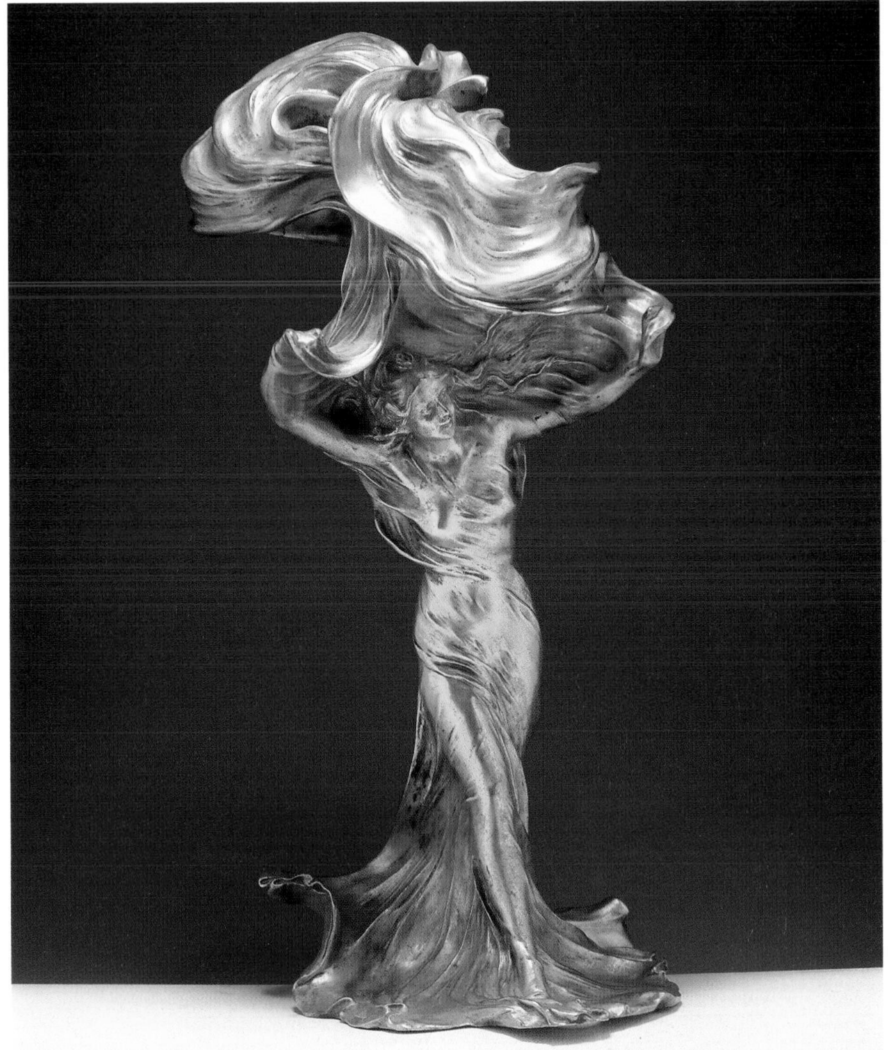

Larche, Raoul-François

Tempête et Ses Nuées bronze sculpture, *c.* 1900

French sculptor Raoul-François Larche was born in Saint-Andre-de-Cubzac, Gironde. He was the son of an ornamental sculptor and in 1878 began his professional studies at the Ecole des Beaux Arts in Paris. Here he was trained by famous sculptors François Jouffrey (1806–82) and Alexandre Falguière (1831–1900). Larche first exhibited his work in 1881 at the Salon of the Société des Artistes Français and was awarded the Grand Prix de Rome in 1886. At the 1900 Exposition Universelle in Paris he won the gold medal for his sculpture. Larche's fame grew after his sculpture of the dancer Loïe Fuller was shown in 1900, but he also created monumental sculptures for public spaces. These included a statue of Joan of Arc for La Madeleine and one of St Anthony for St Antoine. He died in a traffic accident aged 52.

This statue was first exhibited by Larche at the 1899 Salon of the Société des Artistes Français and again at the 1900 Paris exhibition. Further editions were manufactured at the Siot-Decauville foundry after 1900, using a model in four parts. The sculpture exemplifies nature: a common theme for sculptural work of the era.

CREATED

Paris

MEDIUM

Patinated bronze

RELATED WORK

Nautilus lamp by Gustav Gurschner, 1899

Raoul-François Larche *Born* 1860 Gironde, France

Died 1912

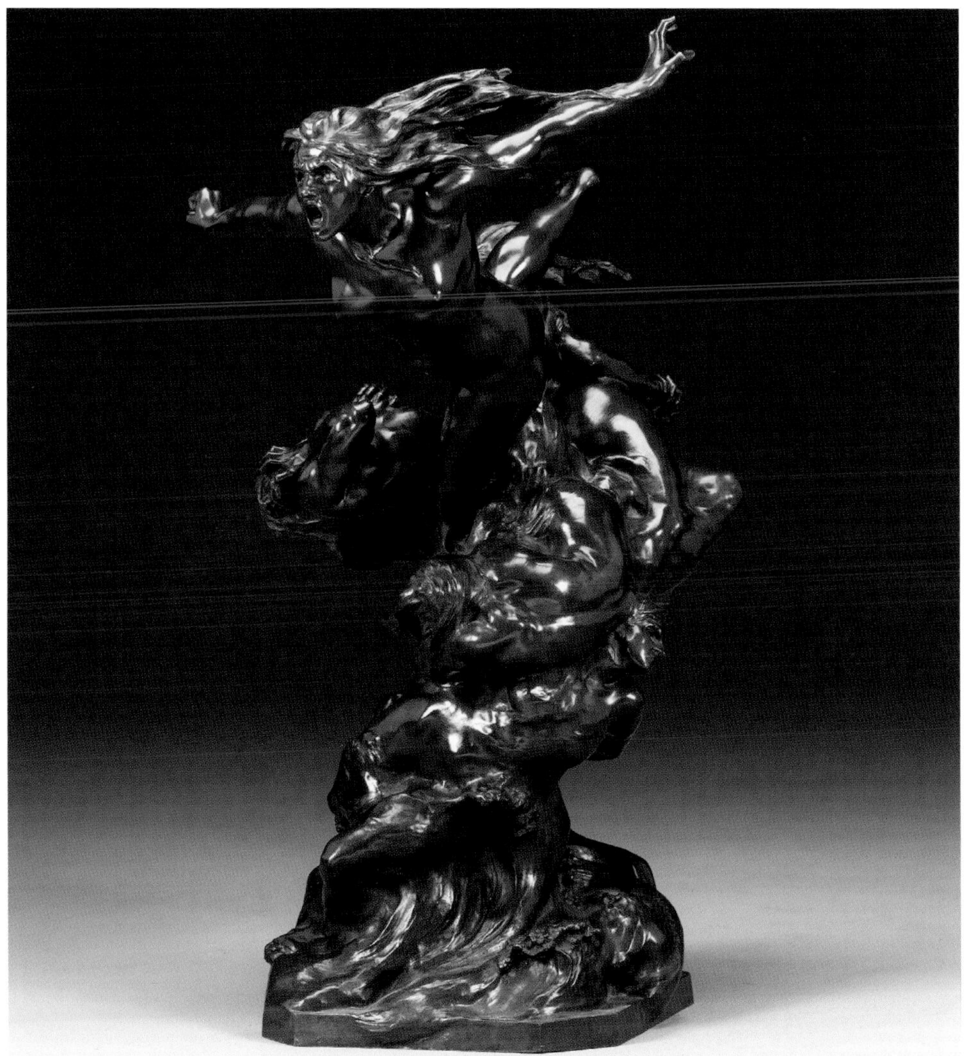

Larche, Raoul-François

La Mer figural inkwell

Metalwork and sculpture enjoyed something of a revival in the Art Nouveau period. This was due partly to recent developments in the Arts and Crafts movement and the creation of artists' guilds and workshops that advocated handcrafted items of quality. This was compounded by a new set of decorative motifs that became fashionable at the time. A member of the bourgeoisie may not have been able to afford a new house built by Victor Horta (1861–1947) or Charles Rennie Mackintosh (1868–1928), but they could exhibit their cognizance of the style with small decorative objects placed strategically in their homes.

As with other media, metalwork and bronze or gilt sculptures show the range of styles that made their mark during the Art Nouveau period. The Oriental influence was evident in the sublimely simple and clean lines of metalwork by Christopher Dresser (1834–1904). Geometry and stylized ornaments characterized the metalwork of Mackintosh and his wife Margaret Macdonald (1864–1933). Themes of nature and mythology were used as inspirations for many decorative bronzes. This sculpture by Larche depicts the sea as a stylized fantasy figure.

MEDIUM

Gilt bronze

RELATED WORK

Head of a Girl by Alphonse Mucha, 1900

Raoul-François Larche *Born* 1860 Gironde, France

Died 1912

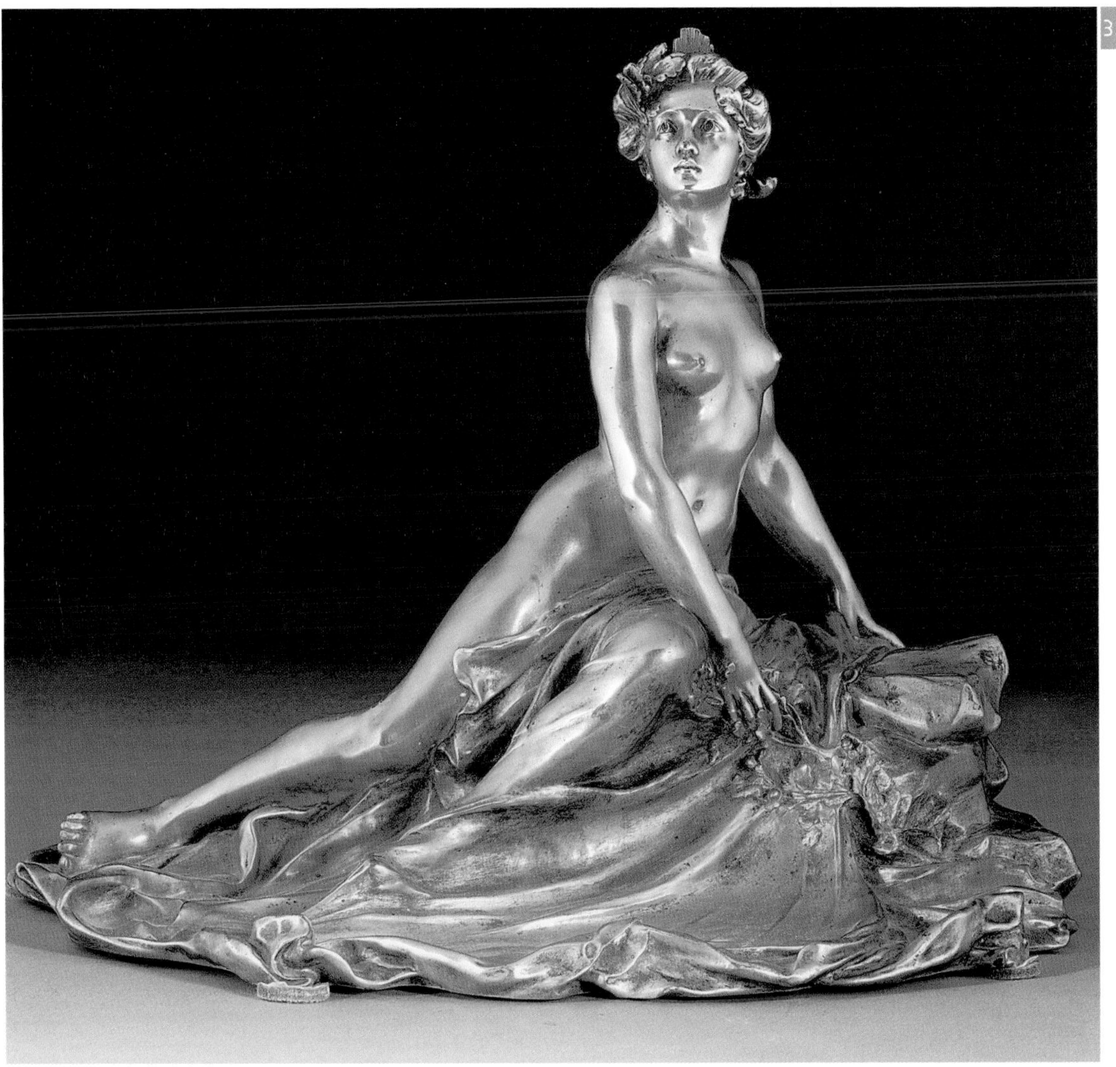

Gurschner, Gustav

Vide Poche

Sculpture at the turn of the twentieth century was entering a new phase in its development. Some of this was owed to the influence of Japanese art, which had flooded into Europe from the 1860s onwards. Experimentation with new materials and the challenge set by incorporating the Art Nouveau line, which is two-dimensional, into three-dimensions, contributed to a revolution in sculpture. While some sculptures were made in traditional materials such as bronze, others used contrasting materials such as ivory and dark metals to great effect. Figures of women were often used to create the three-dimensional form of a line; the sensuous curves of a young woman's body or flowing strands of hair were used to personify the sinuous line that, in other forms, existed purely as an abstract idiom. In German *Jugendstil* sculptures the female shape is often idealized to incorporate the political and social ideas of the nation.

A *vide poche* is a 'wall pocket', such as this one by Gustav Gurschner (1873–1970). Often ceramic or made from glass, bronze or metal these artefacts could be used temporarily to store keys, small change, letters or trinkets.

MEDIUM

Bronze

RELATED WORK

Sphynx Mystérieux, ivory and silver gilt sculpture by Charles van der Strappen, 1897

Gustav Gurschner *Born* 1873 Bavaria

Died 1970

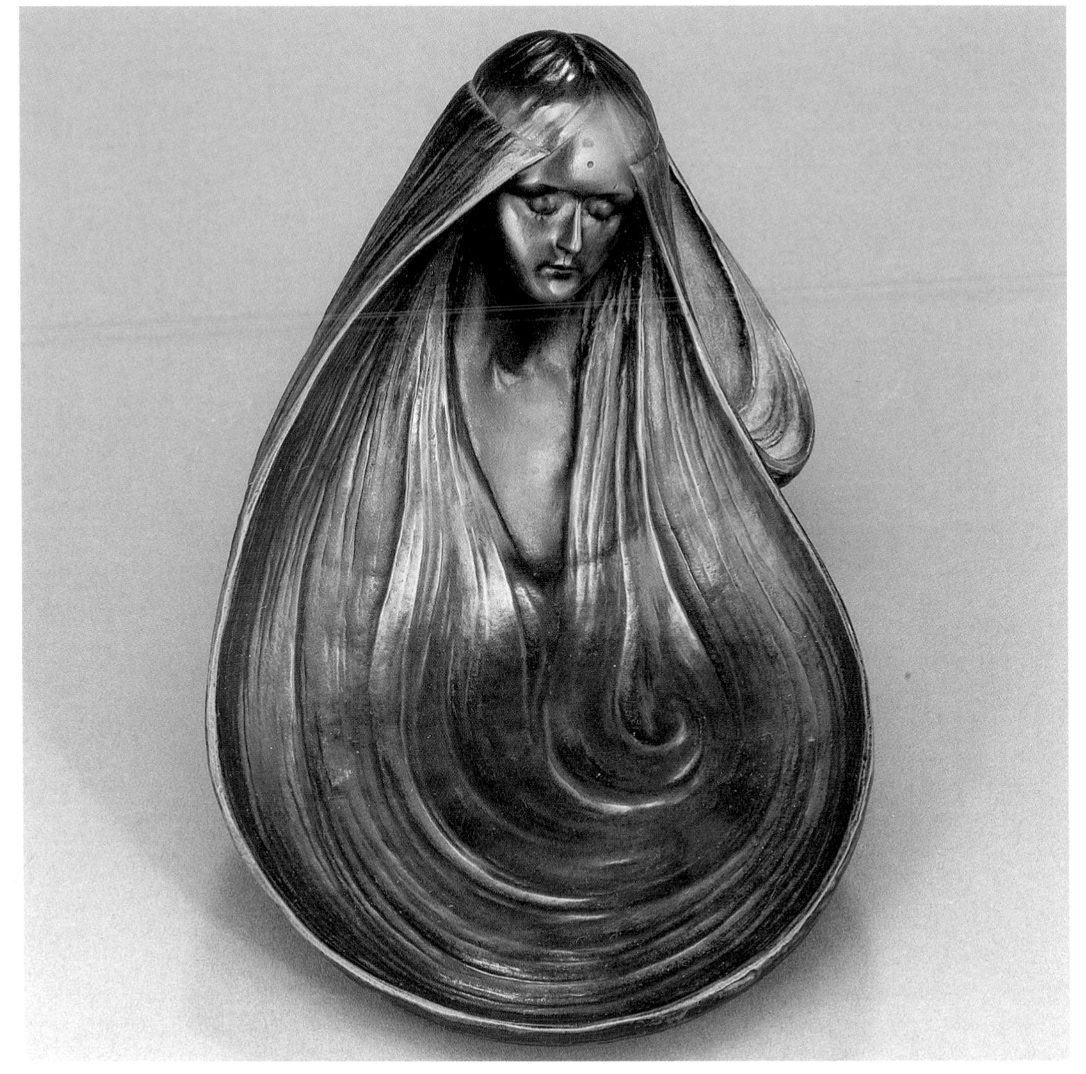

Gurschner, Gustav

Nautilus lamp, 1899

The role of women in society at the end of the nineteenth century went through an enormous change as women became more vocal in their demands for enfranchisement, protection, education and health services. Meanwhile many of their male counterparts sought to maintain the status quo. A new breed of woman was recognized and named: the *femme nouvelle*, or 'new woman'.

Artists rarely chose to portray women of the era in their roles as 'new women'. Instead they continued to use women in their art to sell products, in advertising posters, or to adorn objets d'art. Often women were depicted as being almost entwined with nature with leafy tendrils weaving their way through their hair, or wrapped around an abstract shape so the two forms become one. The proliferation of these feminine fantasy images, which were known as *femmes-fleurs* ('flower-women'), illustrates how the Pre-Raphaelite depiction of women and nature had become enveloped by Art Nouveau. Despite the efforts of Impressionist painters, who had portrayed real women in their everyday lives, many Art Nouveau artists preferred to depict women in a stereotypical fashion, perhaps in a subconscious attempt to deny female emancipation. Indeed, following the Romantic and Decadent movements, some Art Nouveau artists depicted women as sinister, dangerous *femmes fatales*.

MEDIUM

Bronze

RELATED WORK

Candelbra in silver and ivory with female form by Hoosemans and Rombeaux, 1899

Gustav Gurschner *Born* 1873 Bavaria

Died 1970

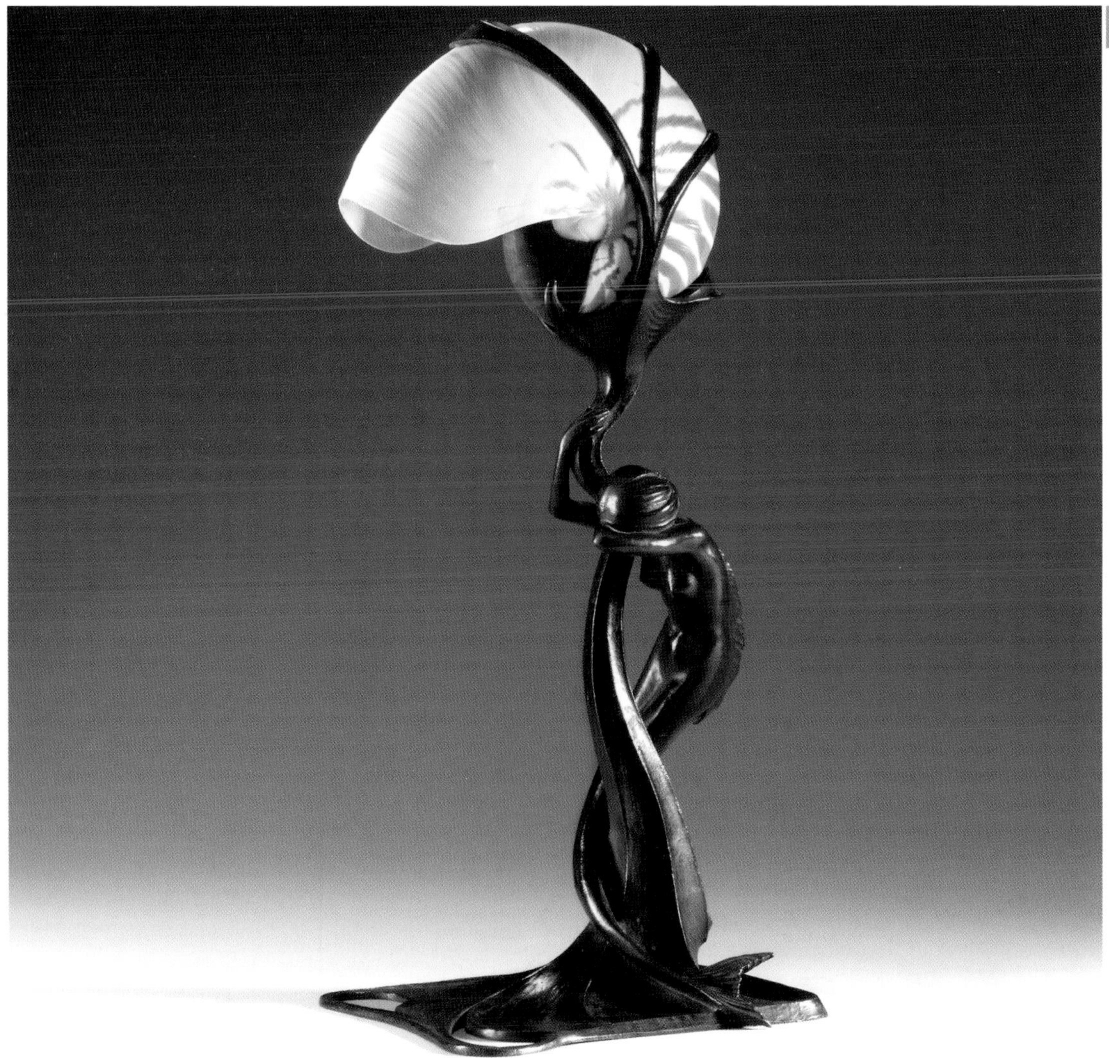

Gurschner, Gustav

Sculpture of a Maiden, c. 1900

Sculptors use a variety of methods. The lost-wax method is an ancient skill that is still followed today. At the end of the nineteenth century a group of artists who trained at the Parisian Ecole des Beaux Arts developed the French Bronze method, which enabled the artist to retain his mould after each casting and achieve a consistently high degree of integrity. It was common that each component of a sculpture was recreated in parts, to ensure that every detail was retained, and then carefully soldered together afterwards. Laborious metal-finishing techniques, similar to those used in the jewellery industry, such as grinding, chasing and polishing were required to produce a final sculpture of high quality. Many Art Nouveau sculptures used more than one material: in this instance the bronze is mounted on marble.

By the end of the nineteenth century traditional sculptures based on Greek or Roman themes and techniques were falling from favour. The work of Auguste Rodin (1840–1917) demonstrated superb and sumptuous portraiture in stone. He removed sentimentality from sculpture and inserted undisguised sexuality into his work.

MEDIUM

Bronze on marble base

RELATED WORK

The Walking Man, sculpture by Auguste Rodin, 1905

Gustav Gurschner *Born* 1873 Bavaria

Died 1970

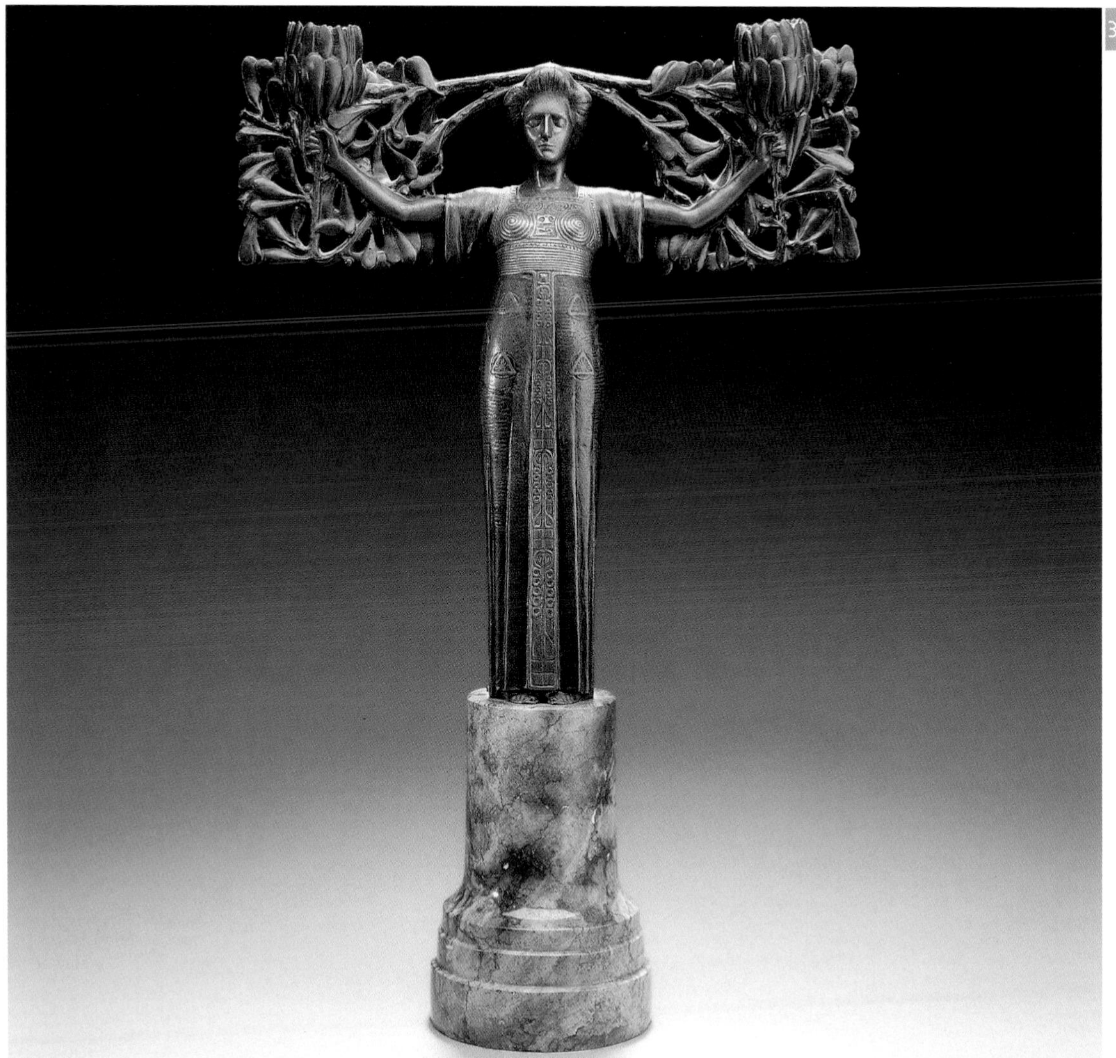

Sèvres Manufactory

Yellow-ground bottle vase

The Sèvres factory was established under the name of Vincennes in 1738 at the Château de Vincennes. In 1753 Louis XV took over ownership of the ceramics factory and was persuaded by his mistress, Madame de Pompadour, to move the business to Sèvres in 1756. From its early days the Sèvres factory employed the best designers to compete in the international marketplace and a distinctive Sèvres style was soon identified. Technical skills were developed in gilding, which was superlative, and the characteristic Sèvres colours of turquoise and pink became very popular.

During the 1890s the factory maintained its position as a leading innovator in technical proficiency. Designers were invited to contribute to the Sèvres policy of aggressive aesthetic competition, and this enabled the business to evolve and stay continually ahead of trends. At this time there was considerable international competition to discover new glazes and decorative techniques, which encouraged ceramicists to experiment. Special glazes using zinc and quartz oxides were developed at this time and mounts in precious metals were often added as luxurious adornments to ceramics.

CREATED

Sèvres, France

MEDIUM

Ceramic decorated with transparent blue, edged in gilt

RELATED WORK

Fennia earthenware vase by the Arabia Factory, Finland, *c.*1902

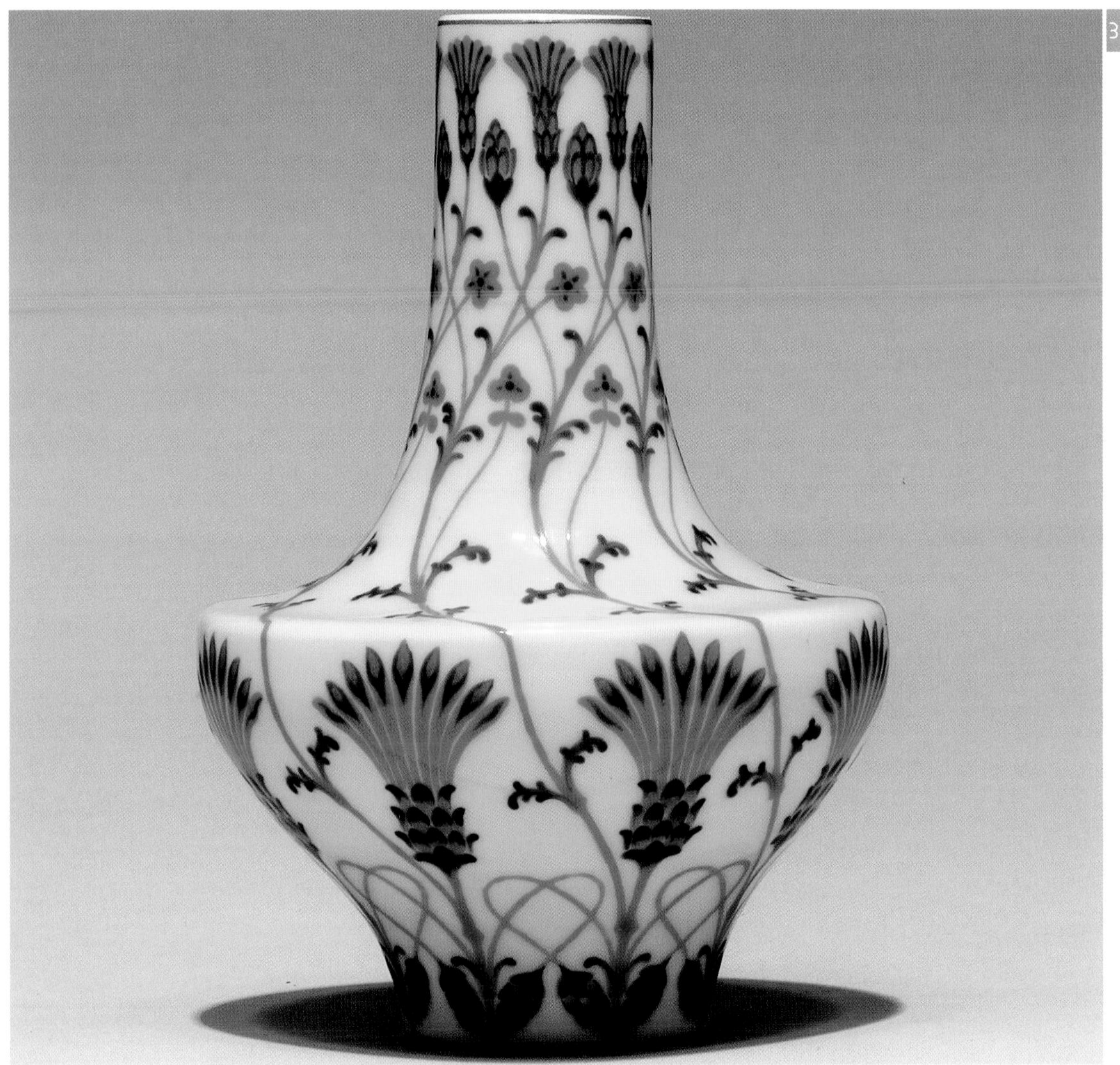

Doat, Taxile for Sèvres Manufactory

Paperweight, 1900

Born in Britain, French ceramicist Taxile Doat (1851–1939) made his name working at the Sèvres factory and through his work as an independent designer and technician. Doat often used *pâte-sur-pâte* as a decorative technique: this involves laying medallions of clay upon a vessel, giving the appearance of a cameo. The medallion is then incised to introduce further decoration and definition.

In 1909 Doat travelled to University City in Missouri, USA, and was invited to establish a ceramics school as part of the Art Academy. He collected a team of skilled technicians and ceramics painters from France and Britain to set up the school. Financial problems in the university meant that the project never developed as originally planned; although Doat was able to teach, he also had to produce pottery commercially to pay for administrative and teaching costs. He specialized in Asian porcelains, bronzes and enamels and was particularly interested in creating ceramics that were shaped like gourds or other pieces of fruit. His palette of crystalline glazes included both glossy and matte finishes and a wide range of colours.

CREATED

Sèvres, France

MEDIUM

Ceramic with incised and applied relief decoration

RELATED WORK

Corn vase by Taxile Doat, *c.*1900

Taxile Doat *Born* 1851 England

Died 1939

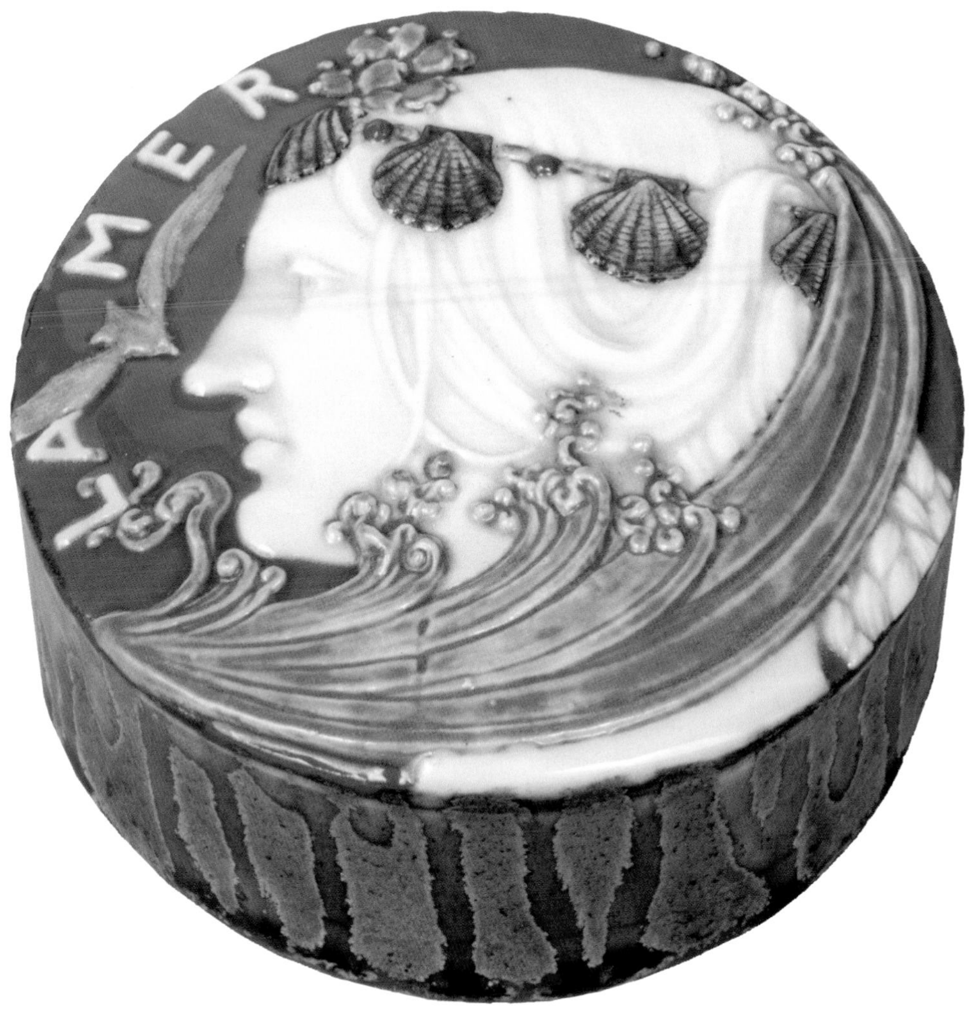
LA MER

Sèvres Manufactory

Silver-mounted porcelain vase, *c.* 1895

Unlike metalwork and glassware, pottery is a craft that has traditionally been accessible to many people. While many areas of decorative arts require years of training and experience, the ceramicist can learn relatively quickly how to produce interesting and original pieces. The technicians and chemists who create glazes require particular skills and knowledge, but the application of a glaze by a ceramicist is not a difficult task. The raw materials can also be inexpensive, although some glazes do contain expensive minerals, and are widely sourced. For these technical reasons, ceramics were a particularly good medium for Art Nouveau designers who wanted to cross the divide between designer and artisan.

Ceramics also proved to be an extremely successful medium for the Art Nouveau idiom. As stoneware it could be rough, textural and earthy; very much part of the vernacular and ideal for creating the natural motifs of plants, creeping vines and organic movement associated with the style. As porcelain it could be simple, elegant and refined; perfect for works influenced by the Orient, or those that required the arabesque and gentle curves of Art Nouveau.

CREATED

Sèvres

MEDIUM

Porcelain ceramic and silver

RELATED WORK

Coffee service by Maurice Dufrêne, *c.* 1900

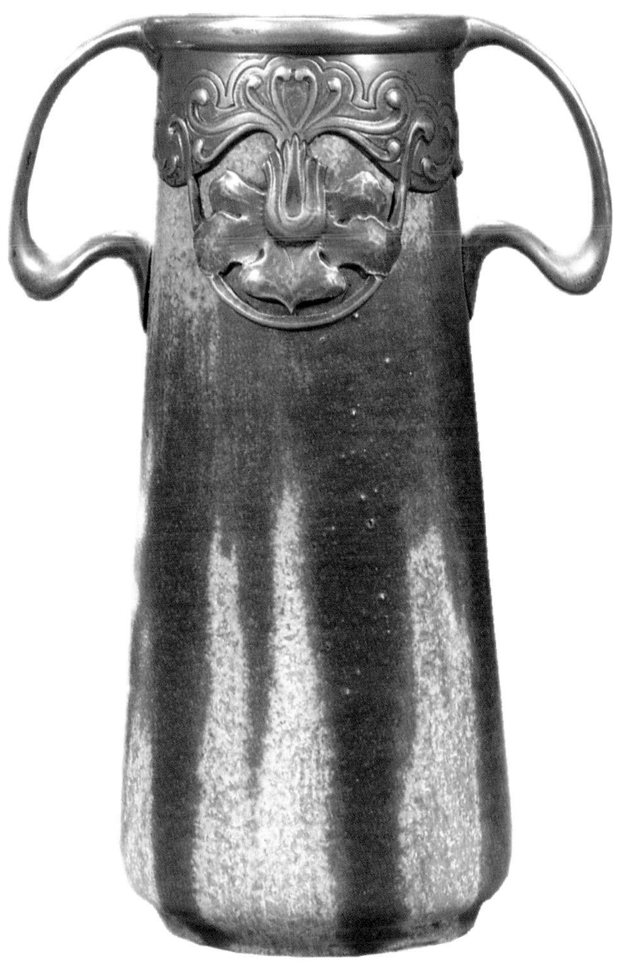

Léonard, Agathon for Sèvres Manufactory

Dancing figures from a table centrepiece, 1900

Figurative ceramics appeared during the Art Nouveau period, although they are not the most characteristic ceramic style of the time. Maidens were popular subjects for artists; often portrayed dancing or entwined with plant stems and leaves, or adorned with lilies, orchids and ivy. The idealism and Symbolism inherent in this style continued into the Art Deco period. The women depicted became ever more stylized; long, lean and elegant, and made their way into sculptures as well as ceramics (often in bronze and ivory). The plant motifs disappeared, to be replaced by animals; particularly deer, greyhounds and gazelles. Dance was a continued theme and Classicism also provided inspiration.

These statues of dancing women in French porcelain are part of a 15-piece table setting designed by Agathon Léonard (1841–1923) in 1898 and exhibited in Paris in 1900. The set was called *Jeu de l'Echarpe*, or Dance of the Scarves. It was loosely based on the performances of Loïe Fuller who excited Parisian crowds with her exotic dance of veils at the Folies Bergère from 1892.

CREATED

Sèvres, France

MEDIUM

Gilded bronze

RELATED WORK

Starfish vase by Alf Wallander, 1897

Agathon Léonard *Born* 1841 France

Died 1923

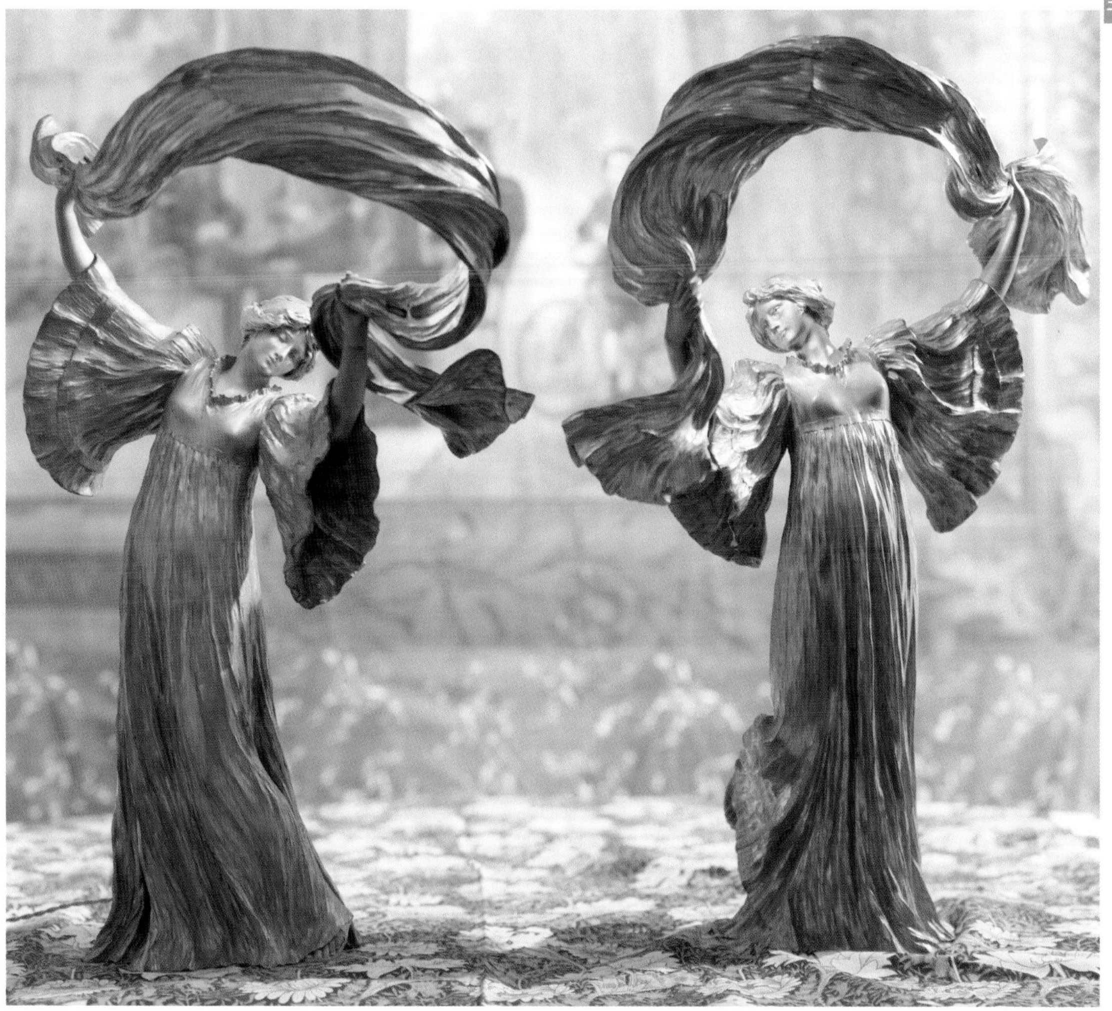

Dalpayrat, Pierre-Adrien

Two-handled vase

At the age of 15 French ceramicist Pierre-Adrien Dalpayrat (1844–1910) began his training at a school of drawing and then went to a municipal college to study the art of painting ceramics. He was then apprenticed to the renowned pottery firm of J. Vieillard and Co. in Bordeaux. Dalpayrat developed an interest in stoneware and exhibited his work at the Chicago Columbian Exhibition in 1893; he won a gold medal for his exhibits at the Exposition Universelle in Paris in 1900. He worked with his sons in a small family firm, often in collaboration with other workshops.

The Dalpayrat family aimed to produce affordable items of stoneware for a commercial market, but the artists also created more luxurious, handcrafted items and sculptures. Their work was often glazed in a unique red and green speckled colour, called Rouge Dalpayrat. By the 1920s ceramics of this type had become largely unfashionable as the Art Deco wave swept in with a new concept of modernity. It became popular again in the 1960s and 1970s, when interest in Art Nouveau was rekindled.

CREATED

France

MEDIUM

Glazed pottery

RELATED WORK

Tulip pottery vase by Pierre-Adrien Dalpayrat, *c.*1900

Pierre-Adrien Dalpayrat *Born* 1844 Limoges, France

Died 1910

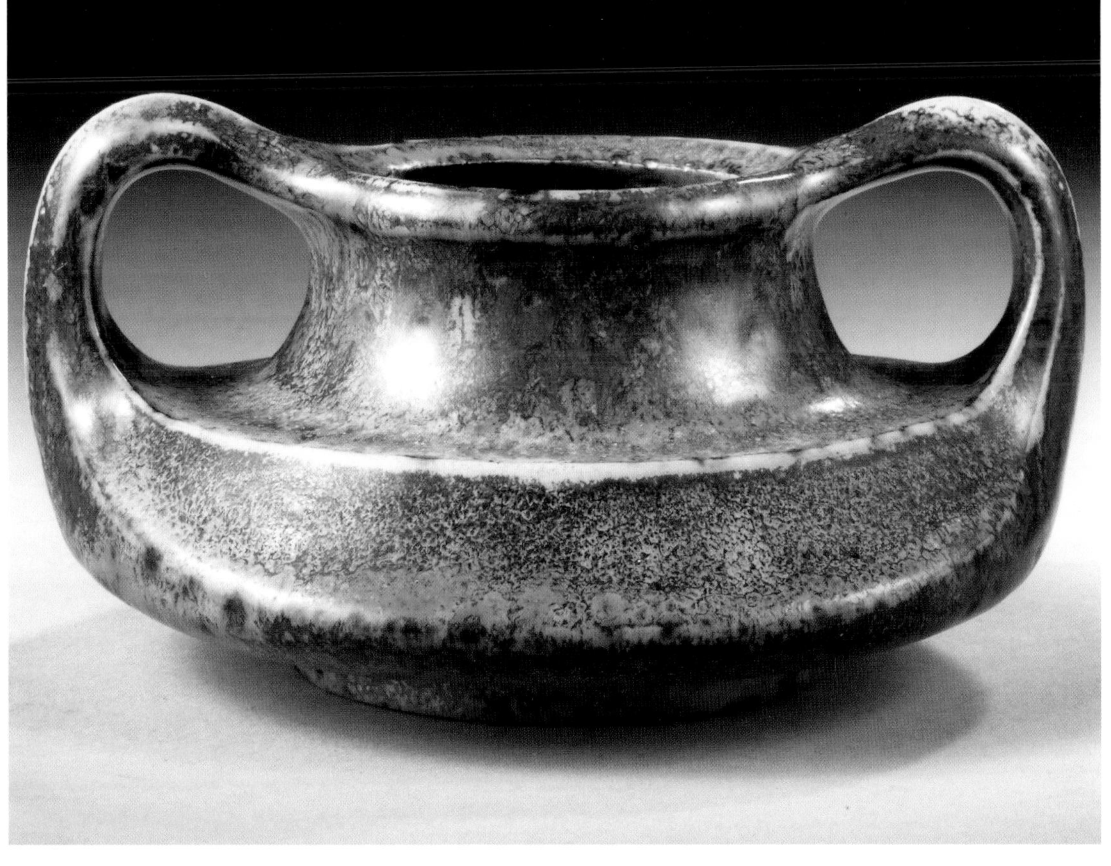

Dalpayrat, Pierre-Adrien

Earthenware vase

The Art Nouveau movement was built largely on the revival and elevation of handicrafts. For this reason it was inevitable that ceramics, like glassware, would enjoy the attention of designers. Porcelain had been the medium of choice for many potters for decades, but the new generation of artists and designers sought to separate themselves from the mainstream styles and media. Instead they turned particularly to the traditional stoneware that was seen as pottery for everyday and for ordinary people. So, just as supporters of the Arts and Crafts movement rejected fine mahogany and ebony for the more prosaic and accessible oak, ceramicists often chose stoneware in preference to porcelain, which was perceived as a luxurious ceramic.

Inspired by the influx of Oriental ceramics from the mid-nineteenth century onwards, ceramicists experimented with achieving different effects from their glazes. Some artists experimented with creating abstract patterns and textures by mixing glazes, others added materials, such as metal, to create contrasts between media. The natural world also provided inspiration for decorative effects, particularly in tiles, which became a popular way of introducing Art Nouveau and Arts and Crafts motifs to an interior.

MEDIUM

Earthenware ceramic with parcel gilt and silver mount

RELATED WORK

Metal-mounted stoneware vase by Pierre-Adrien Dalpayrat, *c.* 1900

Pierre-Adrien Dalpayrat *Born* 1844 Limoges, France

Died 1910

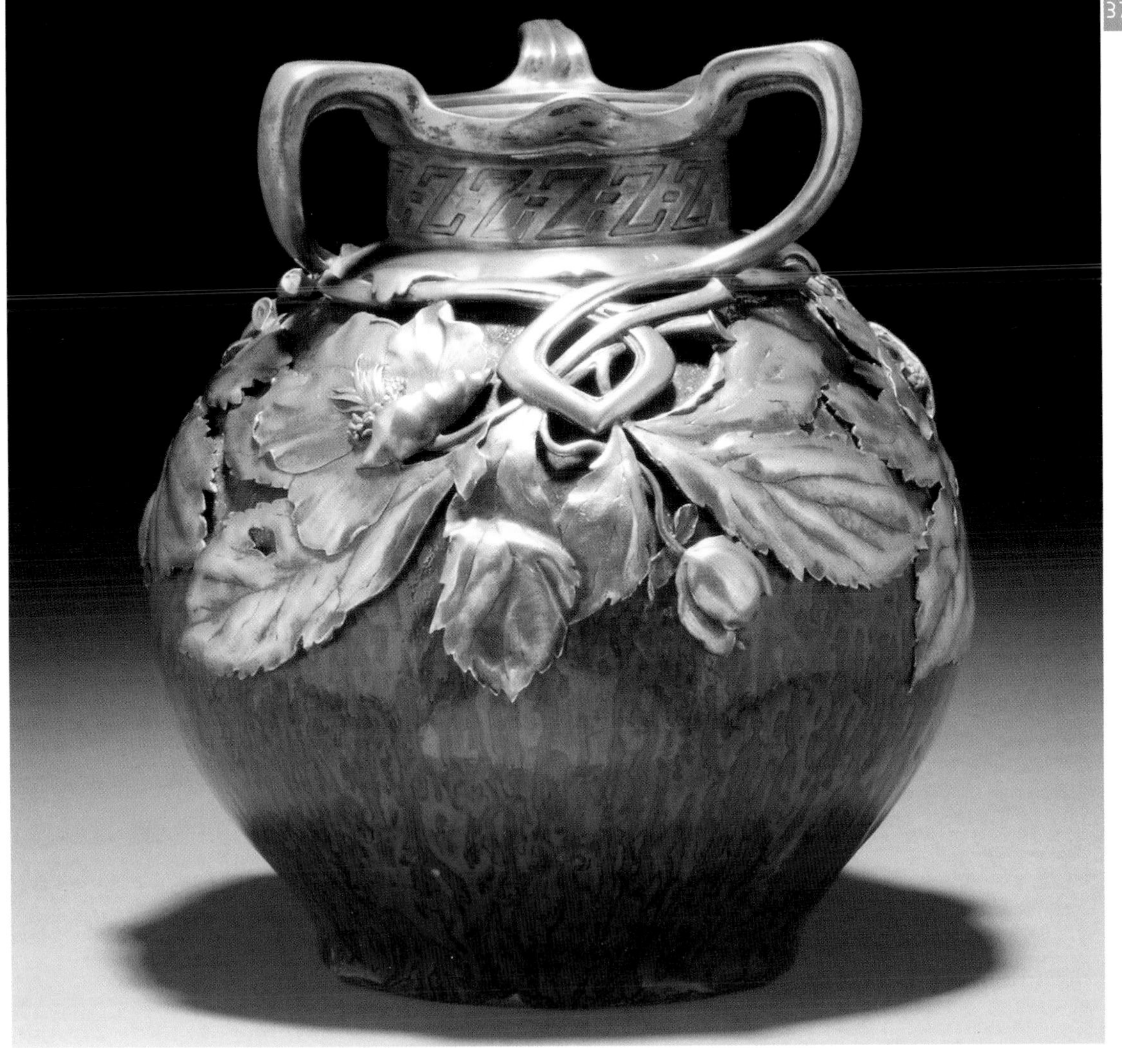

Dalpayrat, Pierre-Adrien

Pottery inkwell

Pierre-Adrien Dalpayrat was one of many ceramicists who helped bring Modernism into the art of pottery. Driven by a desire for experimentation and innovation, ceramicists became chemists: through processes of trial and error, and thanks to the development of industrial chemistry; they learnt new techniques for firing and decorating their work. Dalpayrat became particularly famous for a rich red and green glaze that bore his name. This was similar to the prized Chinese-inspired glaze *sang-de-boeuf* (ox-blood) that was used by Ernest Chaplet (1835–1909).

Ernest Chaplet was born in Sèvres, the home of the state-owned pottery factories where he trained. Although he originally worked in the production of porcelain, after travelling and encountering stoneware factories in Beauvais, Chaplet became interested in developing this medium further. Inspired by Oriental glazes, Chaplet experimented to create an entirely new range of glazes and finishes. He became one of the most influential ceramicists of the Art Nouveau period and even collaborated with Paul Gauguin (1848–1903), whose work in clay has rarely been matched for its originality.

CREATED

France

MEDIUM

Ceramic

RELATED WORK

Stoneware jug in abstract form by Paul Gauguin, 1886–87

Pierre-Adrien Dalpayrat *Born* 1844 Limoges, France

Died 1910

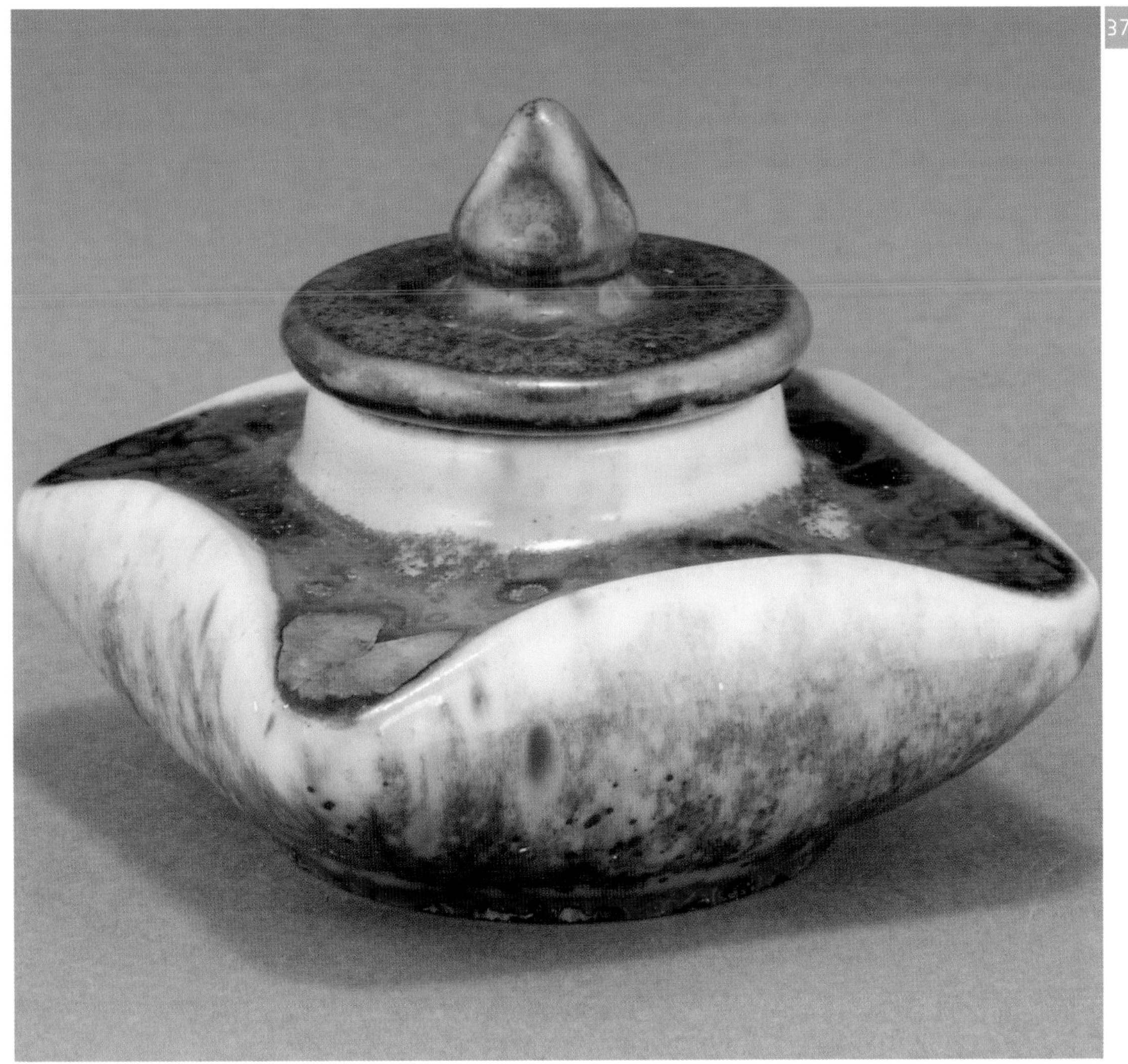

Author Biographies

Camilla de la Bedoyere (author)

Camilla de la Bedoyere is a graduate of Bristol University. She is an experienced researcher, writer and journalist who has a special interest in modern art and design, particularly the Art Nouveau era. She is a regular contributor to magazines and newspapers and has written numerous educational books for children, non-fiction titles for adults and learning materials for visitors to the Natural History Museum, London. She is also the author of *World's Greatest Art: Art Deco*. Camilla lives in London, where she combines writing and research with raising a family.

Alice Jurow (Foreword)

Alice Jurow has degrees in Aesthetic Studies and Architecture from the University of California. The editor of *The Sophisticate: Journal of the Art Deco Society of California* since 1996, she is a longtime aficionado of the aesthetic movements of the late nineteenth and early twentieth centuries. She is currently working on a book based on her popular lecture, 'The Androgynous Dandy: An Art Deco Icon', and lives in Berkeley, California, with her husband and two sons.

Picture Credits: Prelims and Introductory Matter

Pages 1 & 3: Gustav Klimt, *Fulfilment* from the *Stoclet Frieze* © Osterreichische Galerie Belvedere, Vienna, Austria/www.bridgeman.co.uk

Page 4: William H. Bradley, Reproduction of a poster advertising 'When Hearts are Trumps' by Tom Hall (detail) © Estate of William H. Bradley/Private Collection, The Stapleton Collection/www.bridgeman.co.uk

Page 5 (l to r top): Tiffany Studios, Peacock leaded-glass window © Christie's Images Ltd, 2005; Johann Loetz Witwe Glasshouse, Selection of Loetz vases © Johann Loetz Witwe Glasshouse/Christie's Images Ltd, 2005; Alphonse Mucha, Zodiac, Grand Bazar and Nouvelles Galeries (detail) © Mucha Trust/www.bridgeman.co.uk

Page 5 (l to r bottom): Emile Gallé, Lamp © The Art Archive/Private Collection/Dagli Orti; Charles Rennie Mackintosh, Glass panel (detail) Photo © Hunterian Museum & Art Gallery, University of Glasgow, Mackintosh Collection; René Lalique, Pendant Brooch, Courtesy of Christie's Images Ltd, 2005/© ADAGP, Paris and DACS, London 2005

Page 6 (l to r top): Gustave Serrurier-Bovy, Mantel wall clock © Christie's Images Ltd, 2005; Antonio Gaudí, Exterior of the Casa Batlló apartments © akg-images/Joseph Martin; Archibald Knox, Biscuit box © Delaware Art Museum, Wilmington, USA, Gift of Mrs H. W. Janson/www.bridgeman.co.uk

Page 6 (l to r bottom): Charles Rennie Mackintosh, Fireplace for the Willow Tea Rooms, Glasgow © Victoria & Albert Museum, 2005; Josef Hoffmann, Christmas Tree Design © Estate of Josef Hoffmann/Calmann & King, London, UK/www.bridgeman.co.uk; Joseff Hoffmann, Vase © Estate of Josef Hoffmann/Private Collection/www.bridgeman.co.uk

Page 7: René Lalique, Pendant brooch designed as two dragonflies, Courtesy of Christie's Images Ltd, 2005/© ADAGP, Paris and DACS, London 2005; Tiffany Studios, *Sunset with Mountains* leaded-glass window (detail) © Christie's Images Ltd, 2005; Gustav Kimt, *Tree of Life* from the *Stoclet Frieze* (detail) © Osterreichische Galerie Belvedere, Vienna, Austria/www.bridgeman.co.uk

Further Reading

Arwas, V. & Newell S., *The Art of Glass: Art Nouveau to Art Deco*, Rizzoli International Publications, 1997

Bayer, P., & Waller M., *The Art of René Lalique*, Bloomsbury, 1998

Boyer, P. E. (ed.), *The Nabis and the Parisian Avant-Garde*, Rutgers University Press, 1988

Cooney Frelinghuysen, A., *Louis Comfort Tiffany at the Metropolitan Museum of Art*, Metropolitan Museum of Art, 2000

Escritt, S., *Art Nouveau*, Phaidon Press Ltd, 2000

Greenhalgh, P. (ed.), *Art Nouveau 1890–1914* , V & A Publications, 2000

Greenidge, D. (ed.), *Josef Hoffman: Furniture, Design and Objects*, Delano Greenidge Editions, 2002

Hiesinger, K. B. (ed.), *Art Nouveau in Munich: Masters of the* Jugendstil, Prestel Verlag, 1988

Kaplan, W. (ed.), *Charles Rennie Mackintosh*, Abbeville Press, 1996

Krekel-Aalberse, A., *Art Nouveau and Art Deco Silver*, Harry N. Abrams Inc., 1989

Livingstone, K. & Parry, L. (eds.), *International Arts and Crafts*, V & A Publications, 2005

Mascheroni, M. (ed.), *Klimt*, Park Lane, 1993

Mortimer, T. L., *Lalique Jewellery and Glassware*, Pyramid Books, 1989

Mucha, S., *Alphonse Mucha*, Frances Lincoln Ltd, 2005

Naylor, G. (ed.), *William Morris by Himself*, Time Warner Books Ltd, 2004

Newark, T., *The Art of Emile Gallé*, Grange Books, 1995

Ogata, A. F., *Art Nouveau and the Social Vision of Modern Living: Belgian Artists in a European Context*, Cambridge University Press, 2001

Thiebaut, P., *Gaudí: Builder of Visions*, Thames & Hudson Ltd, 2002

Thomson, R., Cate, P. D. & Weaver Chapin, M., *Toulouse-Lautrec and Montmartre*, Princeton University Press, 2005

Tilbrook, A. J., *The Designs of Archibald Knox for Liberty & Co*, Richard Dennis Publications, 1995

Wilde, O. & Beardsley, A., *Salomé*, Dover Publications, 1968

Index by Work

General Index